The Transatlantic Constitution

① Note that the developing constitution has little or nothing to do with the Indians. In a way, by defining the colony as a plantation, the English assume that the settlement will consist only of English + Scots + Protestant families.

② The Eng. clearly developed their imperial policy on a case-by-case basis and not ~~as the~~ from a theoretical basis ~~or~~ by legislation.

The Transatlantic Constitution

Colonial Legal Culture and the Empire

Mary Sarah Bilder

HARVARD UNIVERSITY PRESS

Cambridge, Massachusetts

London, England

2004

Library of Congress Cataloging-in-Publication Data

Bilder, Mary Sarah.
    The transatlantic constitution : colonial legal culture and the empire /
Mary Sarah Bilder.
        p.   cm.
    Includes bibliographical references and index.
    ISBN 0-674-01512-6 (alk. paper)
    1. Constitutional history—United States. 2. Constitutional history—Rhode
Island. 3. Constitutional history—Great Britain—Colonies. I. Title.

KF4541.B55 2004
342.7302′9—dc22   2004052615

Contents

Acknowledgments

In writing this book, I have benefited from advisors, colleagues, friends, and family. I am grateful to the three readers of my dissertation, on which the book is based: Bernard Bailyn, David Hall, and Morton Horwitz. I am equally appreciative to Alfred Brophy, Kathryn Preyer, and Aviam Soifer for much encouragement and advice. Within the legal history profession, I would like to thank, for particular assistance with this project, Barbara Black, the late Elizabeth Clark, Charles Donahue, Robert Ferguson, David Konig, Maeva Marcus, Bruce Mann, David Seipp, Chris Tomlins, Bill Treanor, Michael Vorenberg, and Carol Weisbrod, as well as Harvard University Press's outside readers. I appreciate the support of many colleagues, and for specific encouragement for this endeavor I thank Sharon Beckman, Daniel Coquillette, Anthony Farley, Phyllis Goldfarb, Frank Herrmann, Ruth-Arlene Howe, Sanford Katz, Ray Madoff, Sharon O'Connor, James Rogers, and Fred Yen of Boston College Law School; John O'Keefe and the late Alan Heimert of Harvard University; Kevin Van Anglen of Boston University; Standish Henning of the University of Wisconsin; and the late Francis Murnaghan of the United States Court of Appeals for the Fourth Circuit. Lastly, I am grateful to my editor, Kathleen McDermott, for her insightful comments and excellent suggestions throughout the publication process, and to Wendy Nelson for her careful copyediting.

This project started after I began teaching at Boston College Law School, and I thank Boston College and the Law School under Deans Aviam Soifer, James Rogers, and John Garvey. I am grateful to the alumni for generous financial support through the Boston College Law School Summer Research Grants from the Law School Fund, the Libby Fund, and the Wekstein Fund, and to the University for support through a Boston College Distinguished Research Award, a Research Incentive Grant, and a Boston College Travel Grant. I am particularly appreciative of Director Joyce M. Botelho and the John Nicholas Brown Center for the Study of American Civilization at Brown University for providing support during the fall of 1998, which made the Rhode Island archival research far easier. Presentations at the annual meeting of the American Society of Legal History, University of Alabama Law School, Arizona State University School of Law, Boston College, the University of Chicago and the American Bar Foundation, Columbia Law School, Fordham Law School, the John Nicholas Brown Center, the University of Illinois Law School, the University of Kansas Law School, the University of Virginia Law School, and the University of Limerick College of Law provided helpful comments, and I thank all of the individuals who extended invitations and offered comments.

Many librarians and archivists provided valuable research assistance. Archivist Stephen Grimes at the Rhode Island Supreme Court Judicial Records Center provided invaluable assistance, and I appreciate his endless efforts and those of Andrew Smith in tracking missing case files. I am grateful to Jonathan Thomas, Stephen Salhany, and Jonathan Koffel at Boston College Law School for their efficient acquisition of books through interlibrary loan. I also appreciate the assistance of David Warrington at Harvard Law School's Special Collections Department and the archivists and librarians at the National Archives Public Record Office in Kew, the British Library, Lambeth Palace Library, the John Carter Brown Library, the Rhode Island State Archives, the Newport Historical Society, the Rhode Island Historical Society, the Rhode Island Supreme Court Judicial Records Center, the Boston Public Library, the Massachusetts Historical Society, and the Law Library of Congress. I thank these collections and the United Society for the Propagation of the Gospel for permission to use and quote their materials. I am grateful for typographical and other assistance from Virginia Grogan, Alice Lyons, Ann McDonald, Liza Miller, and the Word Processing and ATR staff at Boston College Law School. I also thank Kimberly Dean, Elizabeth Costello, Michael Goldman, and Allison Schwartzman, who helped me recheck footnote sources.

My husband, David Mackey, has been optimistic throughout that the book would see the light of day, and I am endlessly grateful for his good humor and love. Eleanor Mackey patiently kept me company through many revisions. Dana and Elisabeth Mackey were always enthusiastic. Anne, David, and Deborah Bilder, Lawrence and Veronica Bilder, Bill

Mackey, and my grandfather, the late Harry Robbins, were encouraging throughout. Above all, I am grateful to my parents, Sally and Richard Bilder. Without their example and love, I would not have been steadfast until the end.

Chapter 1 draws on my earlier article "The Lost Lawyers: Early American Legal Literates and Transatlantic Legal Culture," 11 *Yale Journal of Law & the Humanities* 47–117 (1999). Some material in chapter 2 draws on my "The Origin of the Appeal in America," 48 *Hastings Law Journal* 913–968 (1997), and my "Salamanders and Sons of God" in *The Many Legalities of Early America,* ed. Christopher L. Tomlins and Bruce H. Mann (Chapel Hill: University of North Carolina Press, 2001). An earlier version of portions of the book appears in my Ph.D. dissertation, "Salamanders and Sons of God: Transatlantic Legal Culture and Colonial Rhode Island" (Harvard University, 2000). Readers interested in knowing more details of many of the cases might consult that version.

A Note on Legal Terms

This book has been written for those interested in American history and legal history. Portions of the discussion necessarily delve more deeply than others into legal issues. I have attempted to briefly explain legal terms within each section. Nevertheless, the following brief overview of some basic legal terms and concepts may be a helpful reference for readers, though it necessarily omits many details.

A colonial lawsuit involved a plaintiff (the person who was bringing the suit) and a defendant (the person who was being sued). The plaintiff filed a complaint to start the suit in the courts. The defendant could file an answer to this complaint. The court (the judges and jury) would hear the case. The judges usually decided any questions about the law before the jury made the decision. The losing party could ask for a rehearing of the case in the same court or appeal the case to a higher court. The party bringing the appeal was called the appellant. The party defending the appeal was called the appellee. The reasons of appeal were the appellant's explanation of why the initial decision was wrong. A brief was a more formal legal document summarizing the facts and legal issues in an appeal.

A person could sue as long as there was a recognized legal action that gave a right to sue. Civil suits—suits for property or personal damages—could not be brought forever; they were limited to a certain period of time set by a statute of limitations. Once the statute of limitations had run out the person had no legal recourse even if the person remained wronged. A person suing had to fit the dispute into preset categories, such as trespass or slander. In England, lawsuits were heard in two different sets of courts: the common law courts and the chancery courts. The division was complicated, but chancery courts basically heard the subset of laws involving equity—for example, cases involving wills and inheritances, many commercial law cases, cases alleging fraud, and cases requesting waivers of traditional legal rules such as the timely repayment of mortgages. In the colonies, this division between law and equity was a contested issue.

A number of the cases discussed in this book involved property law—cases about land (real estate) or money and goods (personal estate). The law treated land not only in terms of physical boundaries but also conceptually as an "estate." An estate described the manner in which the possessor of the land held the land—in essence, the rights the person had with respect to the land. There were many rights over land, but the crucial ones were the right to possess and use the land (often referred to as the right to "enjoy" the land), to sell or give the land, and to devise the land (leave it in a will).

Three basic kinds of estates appear in this book: fee simple, fee tail, and life estate. A person passing land in a will or a grant would specify which estate the recipient would hold. Fee simple carried with it all land rights recognized by law. A person who held land in fee simple could use, sell, give, or devise the land. The other two estates gave only limited rights in the land. Fee tail (often also referred to as "entail") allowed the person who possessed the land to use it; however, that person could not sell or give the land away forever, nor could he or she devise the land. The person who possessed the fee tail was called a "tenant in tail." Land held in fee tail automatically descended at the possessor's death to a predesignated person (usually the next living male relative, but it depended on the entail). This person was usually referred to as holding a remainder or a reversionary interest. After receiving the land, he or she became a new tenant in tail; a new person held the remainder, and so forth over time until the bloodline ended. The third kind of estate, the life estate, was the right to possess and use the land during one's life. The possessor of a life estate was called the "life tenant." Because the estate evaporated at the life tenant's death, the life tenant could not leave the land in a will. The land passed automatically to a predesignated person (a remainder) or the heirs of the grantor (a reversion).

Many of these cases involved inheritances. A person could devise property by will or could die without a will. A person who left property by will was a testator (if male) or testatrix (if female). A person appointed to handle the estate after the death was an executor or executrix (if named in the will), or administrator or administratrix (if named by a judge). A person who did not leave a will died intestate. Intestate property descended to the people recognized by law as the heirs—such as the eldest son, the male children, all the children, brothers, sisters, or a parent. In England, intestate property usually passed according to primogeniture. Under primogeniture, the eldest son received all the land. If there was no eldest son, then the eldest male relative took the land. There were complicated rules for determining who the eldest male relative was. In some areas of England, intestate practices passed the land to all the children equally (this was often referred to as "gavelkind" or "partible inheritance"). Other variations on intestate laws included the land passing to sons only or a scheme in which the eldest brother received a double share.

Wives and husbands did not inherit land as an heir from a spouse. Women lost rights over property when they married. The law referred to them as "feme coverts." The husband and wife were seen as one—with the husband being the one. The husband had the right to manage the property; people sued the wife in her husband's name; and she sued in her husband's name. Under intestate law, a wife received a dower estate in her husband's property: usually one-third of the real estate for life and one-third of the personal property. If a wife had property in her own name, her husband acquired an estate of jure uxoris—in essence, a life estate in her land while they were both alive. If they had children, he acquired an estate by curtesy (another type of life estate), with the land passing automatically to the children at his death.

The law recognized that land could be co-owned. There were two basic forms of co-ownership: tenancy in common and joint tenancy. Tenants in common simply held land in common, each with the right to use the entirety. When they tired of the shared relationship, they could ask a court to divide the land into shares (partition). When they died, the shares would descend to each co-owner's heirs or under the co-owners' wills. Joint tenants also held the land in common, but joint tenancy property was treated differently at death. When one joint tenant died, the land automatically went to the surviving joint tenant. Nothing passed to an heir under a will or intestate law. The surviving joint tenant ended up with the entire property free of restrictions and could leave it in a will or allow it to pass under intestate law.

The Transatlantic Constitution

Introduction: The Transatlantic Constitution and the Colonial World

In December 1772, Chief Justice Stephen Hopkins, who soon would be a revolutionary and would sign the Declaration of Independence, wrote to the English Privy Council that he and his fellow Rhode Islanders were "judges, under a peculiar constitution." Explaining what he meant, Hopkins said that the "local situation"—that is, circumstances in Rhode Island—created a "necessary and unavoidable difference in our modes of practice, laws & customs." He assured the Council, however, that these differences were "not in any essential point whatever repugnant to the laws of Great Britain."[1] The central principle—that a colony's laws could not be repugnant to the laws of England but could differ according to the people and place—bound all the American colonies. This repugnancy principle became the basis of what I call the *transatlantic constitution*. For a century and a half, this constitution developed as a continuous conversation among litigants, lawyers, legislators, and other legal participants over how and when the laws of England should apply in the colonies. While the empire that created the transatlantic constitution faded with the American Revolution, its legal culture survived to construct the skeleton of federalism and mold early national constitutionalism in the United States. This book is about the development of the transatlantic constitution in terms of one particular colony, Rhode Island, and, of no less importance, the legal culture that grew up around it.

Contemporaries did not call it the "transatlantic constitution." As

Thomas Paine wrote in *Common Sense* (1776), the American colonies had "a constitution without a name." In choosing the phrase, I use the term *constitution* in a sense unfamiliar to some readers. Through most of the seventeenth and eighteenth centuries, that term did not refer to a specific document or even a specific, known set of laws. In certain situations, *constitution* meant "that which is constituted," an idea of the constitution as representing an almost anthropomorphic, organic body politic, with its history, geography, social and cultural composition, and well-being. At other times, *constitution* related to more specific laws, principles, customs, and institutions, but here again, not to a discrete group of laws. The transatlantic constitution encompassed the political structure of the English empire in North America (the dual authorities of England and the colony); the central legal arguments legitimated by this structure (the principles of repugnancy and divergence); the determinative underlying policy (the effective functioning of the English empire); and the accompanying practices (such as the Privy Council's review of colonial acts and hearing of colonial appeals).[2]

This transatlantic constitution existed as both an unwritten and a written constitution. As an overarching arrangement of authority, it was unwritten, located in the history and purpose of the English empire in America. Nevertheless, specific boundaries were written into the colonial charters. The 1663 Rhode Island charter articulated the two central principles—repugnancy and divergence:

> [T]he laws, ordinances and constitutions [of Rhode Island], so made, be not contrary and repugnant unto, but as near as may be, agreeable to the laws of this our realm of England, considering the nature and constitution of the place and people there.

First, the colony was an extension of the realm of England. Colonial laws, therefore, could not be contrary or repugnant to the laws of England. As the Board of Trade wrote in the 1730s: "All these colonies . . . by their several constitutions, have the power of making laws for their better government and support, provided they be not repugnant to the laws of Great Britain, nor detrimental to the Mother-Country." *Repugnant* carried a broad set of cultural meanings including being contrary, contradictory, inconsistent, incompatible, and oppositional, as well as eventually also connoting strong dislike or aversion. Second, however, law and government should relate to the people and the place. Colonial laws thus only needed to be "agreeable" or, in the words of the Rhode Island charter, "as near" to English laws as "may be" "considering the nature and constitution of the place and people there." In short, colonial laws could diverge for colonial circumstance so long as they were not repugnant to the laws of England. The repugnancy and divergence principles of the transatlantic constitution linked the organic and legal notions of constitution.[3]

This structure related to the basic English understanding of law and the empire. As England had grown into a nation largely defined by law, it had aspired to have a universal set of "laws of England" to apply to all of its various regions. At the same time, English legal thinkers recognized that law needed to be diverse to respond to local circumstance. The developing idea of the common law attempted to resolve the problem by hypothesizing "common" laws growing out of the condition of being English in England. Imperial colonization expanded the problem. As an *English* colony, Rhode Island's laws and governmental structures were to reflect those of England. As a far-off English *colony*, however, these laws and structures were expected to be in some way divergent. Too much divergence and the colony would not be English; too little and law would not be responsive to local conditions. Balancing the two depended on conceptions of the English empire. Uniformities in law and custom demarcated Englishness; divergences designated the advantages and diversities of empire. Colonial law was diverse because the local conditions—of people, economics, and authority—meant that the conversation between English law and local concerns played out differently in different places. Colonial law had commonalities, however, because the Privy Council used transatlantic legal culture to maintain consistency over aspects of policy that were crucial to the functioning of the empire at an imperial and a local level.

Because of the physical and temporal space presented by the Atlantic Ocean, the ambiguities inherent in transatlantic legal culture tended to remain unresolved. The continuation of a vision of England expressed in certain cherished English laws reassured colonists that they remained English far away from England. At the same time, an ocean away, colonial divergences were also less threatening and less likely to affect the uniformity of law in England. Temporal space similarly smoothed divergences and supported the unresolved ambiguities. The time involved in transporting laws and letters across the Atlantic allowed assemblies to alter laws and for possibly troublesome cases to settle. Indeed, time even provided a perfect excuse for divergence. In 1681 the English attorney general argued that general parliamentary laws could not be binding on the colonies because the colonists could not know about such laws until they were already technically bound. Temporal space, however, also increased the appearance of colonial repugnancy. When English law changed through statutes or cases, hitherto conforming colonial laws suddenly appeared contrary. Although dual legal authorities would come to be seen as theoretically incoherent—the classic *imperium in imperio* problem—for most of the colonial period the Atlantic permitted, and indeed necessitated and mediated, their coexistence.[4]

The conversation between colonists and London officials created the distinctiveness of transatlantic legal culture. English law and Rhode Island law *each* had plausible claims to determine particular issues. English officials *and* Rhode Island officials had legitimate reasons for believing that certain cases were more appropriately dealt with by their respective authority. Colonial and English officials thus often avoided placing the dual authorities in irreconcilable conflict. The Privy Council tried to promote its ultimate authority, while acknowledging the reality of colonial governance. The colonial government tried to self-govern, while acknowledging the Council's theoretical hierarchical authority. This book portrays a Privy Council that, until the 1760s, dealt with numerous aspects of colonial regulation not with "salutary neglect" but instead under a certain set of rules. Through a transatlantic legal conversation of statutes, appeals, replies, reversals, affirmances, and dismissals, the representatives of these dual authorities negotiated the boundaries and dimensions of the transatlantic constitution. In certain legal situations, one side chose an English side and the other a colonial side. Yet in as many cases, Rhode Islanders argued both English and colonial law, Rhode Island courts disagreed among themselves over whether English or colonial law was authoritative, and the Privy Council alternated between upholding English law and deferring to colonial practices. In the end, for a century and a half, the transatlantic constitution worked because it was a constitution of nuanced context, not strict textual construction. Its legitimacy depended on its being a constitution not of answers but of arguments.

Rhode Island is admittedly off many historians' beaten path. Although it was the first colony to join in revolution against the British, it was left with a bad reputation for its refusal to participate in the writing of the federal constitution. Moreover, its reluctance to abandon its colonial charter, until forced to by internal rebellion in the 1840s, makes it a somewhat atypical American state. Yet Rhode Island was a theoretically perfect American colony and an ideal location for exploring the repugnancy principle and the transatlantic constitution. Unlike most other colonies, Rhode Island retained its early corporate charter giving legislative and judicial power directly to the elected colonial government. The charter included no legal obligation to send colony laws to England, and the colony successfully fought off such a requirement. In other colonies, royal charters, crown-appointed governors, and a requirement that laws be sent to England for review ensured that transatlantic constitutional arguments arose as internal debates between a royal-appointed governor or judge and a colonial-elected legislature or in the private review proceedings of colonial statutes in England. In Rhode Island, however, transatlantic constitutional arguments arose in cases between private litigants that were appealed to the Privy Council. This development and the colony's small bar made appealing to England more popular than in other colonies. As a consequence, Rhode Island sent more appeals to the Privy Council than any other mainland colony—approximately 30 percent of the total cases appealed. Through these cases, the transatlantic constitution becomes visible.[5]

Because transatlantic legal culture took local conditions into account, a brief background on Rhode Island may be useful. The colony was small. Land was not an inexhaustible resource, and the colony litigated boundary disputes with both Massachusetts and Connecticut. With around 10 percent of New England's population, Rhode Island grew from approximately 5,200 people in 1675 to 60,000 by 1775. Refugees from the religious and governmental practices of Puritan Massachusetts settled there. Consequently, Rhode Island's governing structure and a significant portion of its population retained an agnostic, at times hostile, attitude toward religious establishment and neighboring colonies. For years its white residents, particularly those in positions of governance, were largely of British descent. Intermarriages among the older families in the colony meant that by the early eighteenth century many families could trace their roots back to the original English settlers. The colony's extensive coastline and seaports ensured that many Rhode Islanders participated in the mercantile trade. Merchants participated in the African slave trade, and in the exportation of Indian slaves and indentured servants. In the Narragansett region there arose a plantation economy dependent on slavery. The Narragansett tribe, which had controlled the area prior to English settlement, remained in possession of some of its land, and the tribe and the colony struggled over increasing English domination.[6]

These local circumstances influenced the types of issues that arose under the transatlantic constitution. In Rhode Island, Privy Council appeals were initially tied to boundary fights and large land claims. Disputed areas shifted toward land and family inheritance and then toward trade and currency. Cases involving Indian slave exportation and the Narragansett tribe also briefly appeared. Throughout the colonies, the transatlantic constitution and the repugnancy principle structured disputes. Were colonial laws repugnant to the laws of England and thus also violations of colonial charters? Were the laws, alternately, simply responding to local conditions? Did the colonies have to follow the traditional English common-law practice of primogeniture, or could they have intestate laws that left property to all sons or all children? Could the colonies have equity courts, or was the crown-appointed governor alone permitted to exercise such power? Were the colonies required to account for depreciation of their paper currency in the laws governing commercial transactions? Colonies with different histories, local economies, and social structures had different shifts in substantive transatlantic jurisprudence. For example, a study of appeals from the Virginian and Caribbean plantation economies might reveal a larger number of cases relating to slavery and inheritance. In these colonies, the repugnancy principle raised questions, such as whether colonies could consider persons held as slaves to be real property instead of personal property in intestate proceedings. Yet everywhere, legal disputes were repeatedly framed by consideration of the transatlantic constitution and the arguments of repugnancy and divergence.[7]

This book revisits two subjects of prior scholarship: the "imperial constitution" (the traditional term for the constitutional relationship between England and the American colonies) and the Privy Council appeals. In returning to these subjects I have drawn on recent work that views law as a legal culture composed of people and practices and sees the colonial world as part of a greater "Atlantic world." Although, like scholars of the imperial constitution, I address issues of authority,

constitutionalism, and judicial review, I have been less interested in constructing a conceptual demarcation of the legal structure of the empire
than in engaging in a practical analysis about how the legal empire
worked and, more importantly, how litigants worked within it. Implicit in this book is a belief that colonial legal practices shaped certain
fundamental aspects of early national legal culture as much as English
political or legal theory. Similarly, I address the appeals to the Privy
Council, which were the subject of Joseph Smith's impressive *Appeals
to the Privy Council from the American Plantations* (1950). Smith went far
in discussing administrative and procedural aspects of the Privy Council, carefully explicating many of the transatlantic arguments relating
to prerogative, parliamentary, and charter authority; for the interested
reader, these sections will reward a careful reading. But Smith's work
left many aspects of the transatlantic relationship unclear. As Smith acknowledged, his sources had "much less to yield in respect of substantive law." Emphasizing lawyers, litigation, lawyering, and legal culture, I
have embedded the appeals in the context of the people of Rhode Island
and their legal life.[8]

In approaching the subject of the application of English law to the
colonies, I have diverged from certain earlier approaches. What troubled
Smith and has continued to bedevil scholars is that there seems to be
no clear answer about when English law applied. I do not see this absence of clarity as a product of modern misunderstanding or a failure of
logic on the part of the eighteenth-century world; instead, I believe it
was essential to the functioning of the empire. Although the standard of
Privy Council review in most cases—no repugnancies to English law—
was simple on its face, legal participants understood that any particular
case involved unresolved arguments over what constituted English law
and whether something was repugnant or was a permissible departure
for local circumstances. If modern American law has longed for theoretical, logical, and conceptual consistency over doctrines and institutions,
transatlantic legal culture valued a certain pragmatism and flexibility.

I also have tried to avoid the tendency to write about colonial law as if
it were trapped between opposites: either derivative and "English" or
"colonial" and "American," the frontier thesis in action. In truth, English law was not frozen in time but constantly changing. As I show, colonial observers followed English legal developments with great interest,
the result being that old and new "English" law often coexisted in the

colonies. In a similar vein, I attempt to establish the importance of statutes in the colonial period and the interplay of statute and case law both within the colony and between the colony and England. Lastly, I seek to illuminate the colonists' pre-Revolutionary mindset, in which disagreement over the content, extent, and application of English law was a legitimate expression of English men and women on both sides of the Atlantic. Nonetheless, it has been difficult to completely abandon earlier conventions. At times, I contrast an "English" practice (one that had become the contemporary norm in England) with a "Rhode Island" practice (one that resonated in the colony, despite its origins in English practice or theory). In that vein, the brief last chapter traces the transformation of transatlantic legal culture into the constitutionalism and federalism of our modern American legal culture.[9]

The sources for this type of early colonial legal history are annoyingly sparse. There were no law schools or bar associations back then. The colonial Rhode Island courts and the Privy Council did not issue reasons for their decisions. Nor did anyone write treatises on colonial law or procedural guides to Privy Council practice. Moreover, there are interpretive problems with the sources that do exist. The dates and wording in statutory compilations are less than reliable. Seemingly familiar entities often have unfamiliar dimensions, and standard legal practices appear in strange locations: assemblies operate as courts; legal matters are raised in legislative petitions; courts rehear cases without regard to error; colony lawyers plead for English rules; crown law officers argue cases for colonists. Furthermore, familiar modern substantive law takes on a different historical shape. Areas of law such as equity that in our day have faded from view were in colonial days extensive, meaningful bodies of law, covering everything from inheritance to commercial law. Technical details of inheritance and property law—now ignored or forgotten—mattered. Seemingly simple exchanges of commercial paper, mortgages, and debt were actually leveraged transactions in a world of rapidly changing currency valuations. Lastly, factors that were blatantly obvious to contemporaries are almost impossible to rediscover. Aspects of everyday life such as extended family relationships, political friendships, and trading alliances likely influenced decisions more than can be discovered by resurrecting genealogies and commercial partnerships.

To recover the most from the documents and case files, I borrow methodological approaches ranging from prosopography to microhistory. These files are not representative of the "average" fact-based dispute. Although some of the litigants in the following pages appear to have commanded few economic resources, in Rhode Island it was overwhelmingly white litigants with economic means and political resources who participated in this transatlantic legal culture. The sole significant exception is the participation of the Narragansett tribe in a long appeal to the Privy Council. None of the Rhode Island cases I have examined involved an African or African-American litigant. Given the religious diversity in Rhode Island and the shifting areas of substantive law, however, the litigants included descendants of the Puritan settlers of Massachusetts, sons of the Jewish merchant families of Newport, members of the Anglican society of southern Rhode Island, daughters of prominent Quakers, and others. Most of the cases discussed were brought by affluent (and somewhat obsessed) litigants and appear today as "thick" files. A typical file for the Superior Court usually includes: a copy of the case in the inferior court (the warrant, the declaration, the answer, any pleas and answers, any evidence, the judgment); the reasons for an appeal to the Superior Court; the Superior Court case (testimonial evidence given, usually in the form of affidavits, documentary evidence, maps, objections, Court rulings on objections, any special verdict, the judgment); request for rehearing and judgment in rehearing; and notice of appeal to the Assembly or Privy Council. To this material, I have added any proceedings in the Assembly (reasons of appeal to the Assembly, response, evidence, judgment), at the Privy Council (petition of appeal, briefs, Committee report, order), and at any other local courts. In addition, where possible I have looked for relevant probate proceedings in town council and Governor's Council, admiralty proceedings, related petitions to the Assembly, and parallel and ancillary cases.[10]

Judicial reasoning is rarely recorded for these cases. Explicit evidence of the rationales behind decisions survives only in written dissents and in occasional handwritten comments. My descriptions of arguments and reasoning are therefore usually based on reconstructing the case against the background of English and colonial law. In constructing the relevant English law, I have faced the same ambiguity that confounded colonists. The phrase *laws of this our realm of England* was used as the baseline against which to judge the possibly repugnant laws and practices of the colony. But did it mean *all* the various laws of England or a national conception of *the* laws of England? Were they embodied in a single text (such as Magna Carta), composed of a set of principal statutes and ancient property laws, or comprehended in the continually developing body of English law? Were they specific statutes and common-law doctrines, or did the above phrase signify the unwritten constitution of England itself? A variety of English legal sources, from treatises to statutes and case reports, might all be relevant—or not. I have attempted to construct the relevant law from texts and treatises that were available to Rhode Islanders and appear in their libraries. I am more confident of my reconstructions in the property and inheritance area, where my background as a teacher of property law has made it far easier for me to identify specific property law issues. The coverage of commercial cases after 1755 is therefore less detailed, and I hope that a commercial law expert will someday write a detailed treatment of transatlantic commercial law. Similarly, although repugnancy and divergence were fundamental principles in transatlantic legal culture, they were not the only available bases for argument. Many appeals also involved disputes over such matters as the scope of authority granted in charters or the breadth of parliamentary and crown prerogative. I focus on the repugnancy-divergence strand because it consistently structured the legal debates during these years.[11]

The first three chapters explore the beginnings of the transatlantic constitution and its transatlantic legal culture. Seventeenth-century Rhode Island attorneys and legal practitioners debate which laws of England apply and struggle to construct local authority through enacting and eventually publishing the laws of Rhode Island. The next three chapters investigate the early eighteenth century. Lawyers and litigants develop the appeal to the Privy Council as a powerful litigation tool to decide land disputes and issues contested on both sides of the Atlantic—in particular, what patterns of female inheritance are appropriate for the colonies. The final three chapters explore how substantive aspects of the transatlantic constitution changed on such matters as religious establishment, commercial law, and the regulation of paper currency.

The transatlantic constitution cast a shadow across this country's constitutional founding and early national period. Its existence helps explain the rapid acceptance of federalism and judicial review of state legislation and the profound theoretical problems with judicial review of congressional action. The transatlantic constitution, with its principles of repugnancy and divergence, remains deeply embedded in American legal culture. We see it in our commitment to federalism as a conversation between dual authorities and our desire to have clear constitutional prohibitions and fuzzy areas of divergence. We hear it in our endless debate over whether the written constitution can be read as a living constitution that should change with a changing vision of the nation. We speak it when we maintain our commitment to dialogue in which the laws of the states are reviewed for conformity with the laws of the United States. The transatlantic constitution was our first constitution; it shaped the new country and in surprising respects continues to define the nation we share today.

I

The Transatlantic Legal World

1

Legal Practitioners and Legal Literates

In September 1699, Richard Coote, the Earl of Bellomont, arrived in Rhode Island to investigate the colony for possible violations of English law. He found little to praise, in particular condemning the men who practiced law. He disparaged the general attorney, John Pocock, as "a poor illiterate mechanic, very ignorant, on whom they rely for his opinion and knowledge of the law" and the former general attorney, John Greene, as "very corrupt" and "brutish," with "no principles in religion." For good measure, Bellomont added that the governor and assistants also knew "very little law." These practitioners had not learned law at an educational institution (such as the Inns of Court); they were not members of an official regulated lawyer community (for instance, admitted as a solicitor or barrister); and they did not have the social background and status of elite English counselors-at-law. Therefore, in Bellomont's eyes, they could not be lawyers. This myth of the seventeenth-century colonies as being a world of "law without lawyers" has maintained a powerful hold. Local residents, however, perceived their world differently. A lens of "legal literacy"—the practices that relate to lawyering and the conduct of litigation—reveals that attorneys and legal practitioners were an accepted, even ubiquitous, part of Rhode Island legal culture. In striving to win cases and in working to shape the law to their advantage, these practitioners helped create the transatlantic legal culture.[1]

Admittedly they were dissimilar to the elite lawyers of late seventeenth-century England, but the early seventeenth-century Rhode Island practitioners were the colonial cousins of the branch of the early English legal profession known as "attorneys." In early modern England, *attorney* referred to a specific legal job. Although the position emerged only gradually out of the confused history of the early English legal profession, attorneys rose to prominence in late sixteenth-century England, and by the turn of the century the number of attorneys had dramatically increased. Attorneys tended to be minor gentlemen farmers, scriveners, clothiers and drapers, as well as sons of attorneys and practitioners. A 1614 order barring attorneys from the Inns of Court stated that "the purpose of the inns was the education of the nobility and gentry" and that "there ought always to be observed a difference between a Counselor at law which is the principal person next to Sergeants and Judges in the administration of Justice and attorneys and solicitors w[hi]ch are but ministerial persons and of an inferior nature." Attorneys "acted for defendants and plaintiffs involved in lawsuits and were responsible for helping to further the cause by keeping abreast of procedural developments and by framing pleadings so that cases could be considered by the judges." They served as "advocates" in routine procedural decisions in Common Pleas and King's Bench, as well as in cases in Chancery, quarter sessions, and municipal courts. Attorneys played a particularly important role in the chancery courts and could join an Inn of Chancery.[2]

The focus of an attorney's learning was practical rather than theoretical. Because a large part of the attorneys' work involved writing and strategizing, attorney training in England remained diverse and "even by 1650, no single method of training was officially specified." Young men, after learning to read and write, might enter into a clerkship with another attorney or in the courts. Attorneys also served as clerks of the courts. Clerks wrote writs and interrogatories and also "dealt with individual clients, gave advice, organized litigation." In Chancery, for example, "the right to act as an attorney was one aspect of the six clerks' monopoly." In 1633 the first specific rule for qualifications for practicing in King's Bench and Common Pleas codified the long-standing overlap between attorneys and clerks. An attorney had to have "served a Clerk or Attorney" of the court for six years or have sufficient "education and study in the law."[3]

When the English came to the colonies in the early to mid-seventeenth century, they understandably thought that being an attorney was a plausible vocation. Many of the legal practitioners who initially arose

in the colonies resembled in education and in socioeconomic background the English attorneys. When they referred to themselves in laws
and ordinary speech, they chose the word *attorney* and, eventually, *practitioner.* In Rhode Island, the "1647 Code," as it was eventually called,
provided that "any man may plead his own case in any court or before
any jury" or "may make his attorney to plead for him" or "may use the
attorney that belongs to the court." A 1666 law noted that the parties
"or Attorneys who are to plead their cases" could put in lawful exceptions. The general colony legal procedures referred throughout to the
party "or Attorney." The town of Providence's legal procedures permitted both parties to have an attorney open and debate the case until "the
Bench shall say it is enough." The town of Warwick appointed John
Wickes as an attorney to "manage" a suit against the town. The town
of Portsmouth appointed William Hall to join Philip Sherman as the
"town's Agent and Attorney" "to prosecute and finish" a suit about lay-
ing a highway, and John Sanford was "added unto them to Assist in
the Matter." Attorneys were at the foundation of Rhode Island's legal
culture.[4]

Attorneys appeared regularly in the General Court of Trials, which
met several times a year throughout the colony to hear cases. On the
Court of Trials, the governor, deputy governor, and elected assistants sat
as a bench, joined by a jury. Attorneys appeared in almost half of the
eighty-four cases heard by the Court between 1655 and 1670. Thirty-six
cases (approximately 43 percent) involved an attorney on one or both
sides. Twenty-five of these cases (30 percent) listed attorneys on both
sides. More attorneys may have been present, for the recorder noted an
attorney only when he acted by joining issue, protesting some aspect of
the case, or having a power of attorney disputed. Unfortunately, the recorder did not often note the attorneys' names. Usually he merely wrote
such notes as "attorneys joined issue" or "Mr. Brenton's attorney . . ." By
combining identified attorneys with references in the town courts, the
General Assembly, and town records and deeds, a list of twenty-eight
men who served as attorneys in 1650–1670 can be compiled. The list
includes such well-known Rhode Islanders as Benedict Arnold, John
Greene, William Harris, John Sanford, Peleg Sanford, and Joseph Torrey.
Even when attorneys do not officially appear in the records, they may
have provided assistance. The lawsuit by the illiterate Francis Uselton
against Thomas Stanton, a prominent Connecticut legal literate and

eventual judge, was more feasible if Uselton's landlord, John Greene Jr., was helping him. Although the designations of a shipmaster, a mariner, and a son as "attorney" indicate that the term occasionally continued also to refer to a person who was merely representing an absent party (the "attorney in fact"), it appears that the majority of attorneys were managing cases.[5]

These attorneys shared similar backgrounds. Through either formal or informal education, almost all had gained basic literacy skills of reading and writing. Moreover, most had held a position that provided access to courts, legal records, and legal arguments. For example, John Greene had served as recorder, general attorney, secretary to the Governor's Council, Warwick clerk, and the colony's English agent. Greene was not unusual. Eight attorneys had served as general solicitor or general attorney for the colony. Ten had served as clerks for towns or the recorder for the colony court and Assembly. Others had been either the governor or an assistant; both positions involved sitting on the colony's Court of Trials. Still others had been town treasurer, the person who represented the town in litigation. Of course, not every "attorney" had such strong legal abilities. At least one "attorney" apparently served only within his own town: Elizur Collins, a lieutenant and a minor town official, limited his appearances to Warwick town court.

Beyond representing others, attorneys often represented themselves in legal matters. Recorders and general attorneys like John Sanford Jr. and John Greene Jr. consistently sued in their own names. The acceptance of attorney self-representation appears in early Rhode Island laws. A 1659 statute stated that the general sergeant could not be an attorney "in any person's case" but could be an attorney in "his own." This practice of self-representation left the civil legal system dominated by attorneys and legal practitioners. When men who served as attorneys are included when they appeared as parties, fifty-eight (69 percent) of the cases between 1655 and 1670 involved, at least on one side, an attorney representing either himself or another person. Thirty-seven (44 percent) of the cases involved attorneys on both sides representing themselves or others. In fact, if one counts those litigants who held an office that facilitated or required legal literacy—such as governor, assistant, recorder, judges, general sergeant, or colony agent—seventy-five cases (89 percent) involved at least one legally literate party and fifty-four cases (64 percent) involved attorneys or legal literates on both sides. Regardless of

what the legal system looked like to English outsiders, to Rhode Islanders the civil legal system seemed the province of attorneys, practitioners,
and other legal literates.[6]

Attorney Culture

These legal practitioners participated in an attorney culture that maintained its connections to both sides of the Atlantic. Some of the original
settlers had been trained in England as law clerks or attorneys. Warwick
town clerk Edmund Calverly had acted as an attorney when he was
"keeper of the Ely house in London." Another town clerk, John Porter,
had been given a letter of attorney to supervise a Hingham estate as early
as 1640, suggesting that he brought legal skills with him. Others, like
William Harris and Philip Sherman, had enough attorney or clerk training to write with the careful handwriting to which English clerks and attorneys aspired. They had departed England when acting as an attorney
was a respectable activity and, not surprisingly, in Rhode Island they
continued to find the job of attorney useful and important.[7]

Legal practitioners who grew up in the colony learned their skills
from others. As William Harris noted, that was about the only way a lawyer in the colonies could learn. At the only college in Cambridge, "many
Preachers, Physicians, & Indians (but no Lawyers) are bred." Some
learned from their English fathers. John Sanford's father, John Sanford
Sr., had been recorder in the early days of the colony and eventually became the young colony's president. At twenty-three, Sanford Jr. followed
in his father's footsteps by becoming recorder, a position he held for
most of 1656–1670. Sanford's legal abilities were apparent to Rhode Islanders, who elected him assistant, commissioner, general attorney, and
treasurer. John Greene Jr. similarly learned from his father. John Greene
Sr., a surgeon in England, had been another colony recorder. His son
also became recorder and general attorney.[8]

Men without such strong family connections acquired their legal skills
through observation and participation. The personal legal travails of Edward Richmond provided him entry into the legal world. In the 1650s,
Richmond was a young man with plans to marry Abigail Davis. Pres-
sured by her family, Davis instead married Richard Ussell. In his complicated efforts to marry Davis, Richmond learned Rhode Island legal practice. In June 1656, Richmond's attorneys first unsuccessfully sued Ussell

in trespass, based on Richmond's perception of himself as the injured party. Later they more successfully argued trespass on the case for breach of covenant against Ussell and Davis's father, John Cowdall, "for forcing Abigail Davis the spoused wife of Edward Richmond and for taking, keeping and withholding her from Edward Richmond." Richmond received six pounds in damages, but Davis remained married. After a petition in Davis's name was presented to the General Assembly, the Ussell-Davis marriage was declared "an unlawful marriage." The following spring Richmond and Davis each paid a forty-shilling fine for living together and conceiving a child. In June 1658, "for preventing of the like Temptation," the Court of Trials married the couple. Richmond benefited personally and professionally from his endeavor. By the late 1660s, he was serving as general solicitor and general attorney.[9]

Attorneys learned the substance of Rhode Island law and legal procedure not through books but by obtaining access to the colony's legal records and legal proceedings. In the seventeenth century, there were no printed records of Rhode Island law. Even the colony's statutes remained in manuscript until 1718. Access to colony manuscript records therefore provided power. When one town dissolved into two separate factions, William Harris, "having got the table," "denied the books" to the opposing faction and "dared the Company to touch the books." Certain positions—recorder, governor, town clerk, town treasurer—provided easy and repeated access to these manuscripts. Consequently, many of the attorneys were men holding these jobs.[10]

Ten attorneys and five of the six men who served as the general attorney had also served as recorder or clerk. The general recorder kept "a copy of all the Records or Acts of the General Assembly, General and particular Courts of Judicature, Rolls of the Freemen of the Colony, Records, Evidences, Sales and Bargains of Land, Wills and Testaments of the Testators, and orders of the Townsmen touching the Intestate, Records of the Limits and Bounds of Towns, their Highways, Driftways, Commons and Fencing, Privileges and Liberties." The recorder also kept the key to the chest containing the charter. Not only did the recorder have physical custody of most documents, but he also had oral knowledge of the court proceedings. The recorder handled the filing of court actions, wrote writs, made copies of declarations and answers, and provided summons. Furthermore, because the recorder often was the clerk to the Assembly, he knew most of the official business of the colony. Indeed, the recorder rewrote each Assembly session to send a record to the towns.[11]

The governor had similar access. Five attorneys served as governor of the colony. The governor not only attended all important legal meetings, but also held many of the records of the colony. (At the death of a governor in 1666, one of the first things the Assembly did was appoint several people to obtain "the Charter, with his Majesty's letters, and such other writings as concern the colony" from the deceased governor's house.) It was easier to perform the duties of these positions if one had legal knowledge, and in turn these positions provided access to written records that strengthened such knowledge.[12]

Other attorneys learned the colony's law through access to town records. At least four attorneys held positions as town clerks. The town clerks copied and composed documents for their towns and received and copied the copies of the General Assembly's acts and orders. In theory, the towns were supposed to hold copies of the colony's statutes. Town clerks also wrote and copied deeds, wills, and other legal documents for individuals. Towns also appointed a treasurer, who represented the town in litigation. Three attorneys—two Portsmouth innkeepers, William Baulston and Ralph Earl, and Zachariah Rhodes—served as town treasurers.[13]

For Rhode Island attorneys, copied legal documents transmitted knowledge of local laws and legal culture. Indeed, one of the chief functions of the attorney was to copy documents. In 1677 each of attorney William Harris's bills against defendants included a charge for "obtaining writings." The recorder received statutorily set remuneration for copying documents: a shilling for simple documents under twenty lines; up to three shillings for more complicated writs and longer pieces; up to ten shillings for copies of the Court's orders. Copies permitted permanent, individual access to colony laws. Harris, for example, carefully made himself a small bound copy of the Rhode Island Charter, the central legal document in the colony. Other records from town and colony books were copied for lawsuits. Copies also transmitted knowledge of legal forms. Attorneys learned how to write deeds when they copied them as evidence of land transactions. They learned about wills when they copied them for purposes of inventories and probate. In addition, copies were a way for individual attorneys to share legal interpretations and strategies. A long paper in Harris's file bore the explanatory endorsement:

> A copy of a paper sent to William Arnold & the Rest, opening the true intent of the agreement of the arbitrators . . . about Patuxet. Showing & reasoning a difference with W. Carpenter, Z. Rhoads, & Will. Arnold about an arbitration or the award which they will not truly but fraudulently understand.

When Harris was kidnapped by Barbary pirates, he wrote to obtain copies of his legal documents. He sought copies from friends among the colony's legal literates. The Providence clerk, John Whipple, was to find "all the affidavits, and protests against the only pretended Executions." Another attorney, Francis Brinley, was to "endeavor a recruit of all other papers for all lost." In an August letter, Harris added a postscript: "I forgot, but get me Thomas Wards and others protests against their pretense of unlawful execution, or as they call it." When Whipple and Brinley found the documents and copied them, they added to their repertoire the types of legal claims brought by Harris and others.[14]

Learning the laws of England was more difficult for Rhode Island attorneys. Attorneys trained in England undoubtedly shared their knowledge in private conversations, although unfortunately little evidence remains of such exchanges. Rhode Island attorneys, however, worked to obtain unmediated knowledge of the laws of England. Six attorneys served as the colony's agent to England, an appointment that gave them physical access to English law and legal culture. Trips to England also enabled attorneys to bring English law books back to Rhode Island. William Harris took advantage of this access and during several trips to England in 1664 and 1676 acquired an important law library.

Harris had settled in Pawtuxet in 1638, after traveling first to Massachusetts and then Rhode Island. He likely received at least some attorney training in England, for his careful handwriting demonstrates knowledge of the specialized scripts used by attorneys and clerks. He used his legal abilities in a decades-long lawsuit to retain lands for a group of landholders known as the Pawtuxet Proprietors. Harris signed as an "attorney"; indeed, he closed one 1678 document on his lengthy lawsuit: "A long & great sufferer therefore complainant and demandant And Attorney &c." Harris's legal endeavors irritated Roger Williams,

who used an occasional epithet for lawyers to refer to Harris as "the sala-
mander always delighting to live in the fire of contention as witnesses
his several suits in law." Williams more pointedly wrote of Harris in
1668 that "he hath tacked about, licked up his vomit, adored (like Saul
as some have told him), the Witch at Endor, the Laws and Courts and
Charters which before he damned; and turned his former traitorous
practices into 10 years vexatious plaguing and tormenting both Town
and Colony and the whole Country with Law, Law Suits and Restless
Fires and Flames of Law Contentions." Harris's practice as an attorney
also may have been what led Edmund Calverly, his frequent adversary, to
write: "We much marvel how he escaped being indicted for a common
barrator." Yet Harris retained friendships with and respect from a number of prominent Rhode Islanders, and throughout Rhode Island his
knowledge of the law was widely recognized. He served as an assistant
for several years in the 1660s, was asked to look over the law revision in
1666, and was named general solicitor in 1671.[15]

Harris's lasting contribution to Rhode Island legal culture was his
library of English law books. Harris died in 1681, shortly after being
ransomed out of captivity in Algiers. His wife and daughter, Susan and
Howlong Harris, inventoried his library for probate. The inventory revealed a collection useful to any colonial Rhode Islander: two Bibles and
several other religious books; a farrier's handbook; books on artillery
and trigonometry; and Nathaniel Morton's *New England's Memorial,*
locally printed in Cambridge, Massachusetts. The more than thirteen
printed law books, however, were particularly important to attorneys. In
addition, the library included related books: a dictionary, an introductory Latin grammar, a text by legal writer Matthew Hale, and a volume
on war. A few books were large and rather expensive. Harris's copies of
Coke's *Commentary upon Littleton* and Pulton's *Sundry Statutes* each cost
more than one pound, nearly the value of a young cow in the inventory.
Most of the books, however, were smaller and more portable, and valued
at one to five shillings. Harris had bought editions with an eye to value
rather than ostentation.[16]

Harris's books demonstrated Rhode Island attorneys' interest in the
general laws of England. The books were not esoteric or ancient but
fairly contemporary works aimed at practitioners such as attorneys or
clerks. *Tryals per Pais* was intended for "the Practicers of Law (especially
Attorneys, Solicitors, Clerks, etc.)." *Declarations and Pleadings* was "use-

ful for all practicers and students of the law, of what degree soever." The books offered substantive knowledge of the basic laws of England. Pulton's *Sundry Statutes* provided the text of crucial English statutes, beginning with Magna Carta. Coke's *Commentary upon Littleton* was a classic text, explaining in detail the history and current state of English property law. Two other books—*Office and Duty of Executors* and *Touchstone of Wills*—explained English inheritance practices. The *Lawes Resolution of Women's Rights* concerned "points of learning in the law, as do properly concern women." The *Lay-man's Lawyer* and *Justice Restored* described English criminal law. *Tryals per Pais* elaborated the structure and procedure of the English jury system, as well as challenges available, types of evidence, and the differences between special and general verdicts. Other volumes offered overviews of English legal procedures. Dalton's *Countrey Justice* provided background knowledge and forms. *The Compleat Clerk* alphabetically offered "exact draughts of all manner of Assurances, and Instruments, now in use," and *Declarations and Pleadings* offered models of pleadings. To explain confusing legal words, Harris had Rastell's *Termes de la Ley* and, for Latin, *A Short Introduction of the Grammar.*[17]

Coke's *Commentary upon Littleton* and Dalton's *Countrey Justice* were among the few law books in Harris's library that were first published before the English Civil War. The texts were popular in the seventeenth-century colonies, and the Massachusetts government ordered copies in 1647. Most of the remaining books were published in the 1650s and 1660s. Many of these could be found in other early seventeenth-century colonial libraries. Arthur Spicer of Virginia, who died in 1699, had fifty-three law books, including Brownlow's *Declarations and Pleadings,* a *Compleat Clerk,* a *Lay-Mans Lawyer,* Rastell's *Les Termes de la Ley,* and Wentworth's *Office and Duty of Executors.* Books like these offered an accessible, general knowledge of the laws of England.[18]

Other Rhode Island attorneys shared the knowledge of English law available from Harris's library. At Harris's death, over half his books had been borrowed by Thomas Olney Jr., Nathaniel Waterman, John Whipple Jr., Francis Brinley, and John Pocock. Olney, Waterman, and Whipple were learning the law through serving as town clerks. Perhaps befitting the stage of their legal careers, Olney and Whipple borrowed books on basic legal knowledge. Olney had Coke's *Commentary upon Littleton* and *Compleat Clerk* and Meriton's *Touchstone of Wills.* Whipple took *Office and Duty of Executors,* Pulton's *Sundry Statutes,* and *The Lawes Resolution of Women's Rights,* among others. Brinley and Pocock had been active as attorneys; Pocock would eventually become the general attorney and Brinley would serve as a judge. Brinley was refining his legal knowledge by borrowing Lambarde's *Perambulation of Kent,* a book on the history and law of Kent, a part of England that diverged from the laws of England. Through their jobs, Harris's library, and each other, the Rhode Island attorneys sought to learn the laws of both England and Rhode Island.[19]

Attorneys and the Legal System

With this legal knowledge, attorneys were an integral part of Rhode Island's legal system because ordinary people found themselves, as Hannah Taylor put it, "very unskillful in law matters." In managing and prosecuting a suit, the attorney engaged in various activities. Attorney fee statutes indicate that the job was divided into two parts: preparing the case and filing initial papers, and pleading at trial. In preparing the case, attorneys possessed the important skill of written literacy. The residents of seventeenth-century England and its colonies had a spectrum of reading and writing skills: some could neither read nor write; a few could read Latin and write in the formal scripts of the law courts; many could sign only their names, read only printed type, or write only in a simple hand. When compared to England and Europe, the New England colonists were surprisingly literate, but colonial literacy rates, particularly with respect to the ability to write, were still low. Rhode Island fell within the classic statistics for New England literacy: "60% of men could read fluently, less than 60% could write, 20% were semi-literate, and 20% were illiterate." Nevertheless, to bring a legal action the plaintiff had to "declare his case in writing": compose a description of the parties, the form of action, and the damages. The written literacy requirement meant that bringing a civil action in the colony's Court of Trials was limited to those who could write or were willing to hire someone to write for them.[20]

For much of the seventeenth century, town courts explicitly assisted illiterate defendants. In Providence, the declaration was to be "read them twice" and the defendant had the "Liberty whether he will answer in Writing or no." The more formal procedures of the General

Court of Trials were similarly protective of defendants who chose to answer orally. If the defendant showed up at Court, even after failing to file a written answer, the Court would hear the defendant. In 1657 the colony passed a law declaring that if a *nihil dicit* (a motion literally translated as "he says nothing") was filed in the recorder's office, "yet if the defendant appear in Court and give his answer, the matter shall proceed to trial." Eventually, this protection disappeared. In 1698 the Court noted that although defendant Thomas Durfee "could put his answer in court," the action "shall not be a precedent for the future." By the beginning of the eighteenth century, written literacy was a requirement for both civil plaintiffs and defendants. An attorney offered this power of the written word.[21]

Beyond written literacy, an attorney offered legal knowledge. This advantage of the attorney was sufficiently well recognized in Rhode Island that it affected criminal procedures. In 1669 the colony gave defendants the right to bring an attorney in a criminal case. The statute explained that a person "may on good grounds, or through malice and envy be indicted and accused for matters criminal, wherein the person that is so [accused] may be innocent." That person, however, "may not be accomplished with so much wisdom and knowledge of the law as to plead his own innocency, &c." Therefore, the statute declared that it will be the "lawful privilege of any person that is indicted, to procure an attorney to plead any point of law that may make for the clearing of his innocency." Attorneys had such wisdom and knowledge of the law.[22]

Attorneys used their knowledge in pleading the case. In Providence, an attorney received statutory fees for every court in which "he appears, or Pleads in a case." A significant component of the attorney's job took place in drafting the pleadings. If the case were continued before the jurors were impaneled, the attorney still received half the fee. When the declaration was drafted, parties and damages had to be noted with care. In a world where extended family members shared identical names, correct identification was essential and parties had to be identified by name, place of residence, and sometimes profession. Inaccuracy left the declaration open to challenge. In one case, the attorney for William Coddington objected to a declaration because it had the word *plaintiff* instead of *defendant*. The attorney for William Brenton, however, knew how to respond to technical arguments: argue that the error had made no substantive difference. The Court concluded that the error was merely a "verbal oversight" because the defendant's answer showed that he had "clearly understood and answers according to the scope of it." Answering the declaration required care. In one case, an attorney denied a claim that a fence had been destroyed so that it did not give rise to an inadvertent admission that the fence was actually on the plaintiff's property.[23]

Pleading the proper form of action also involved legal knowledge. As in England, most cases involved debt, trespass, actions on the case, and ejectment (a way to recover land). Some actions did not require much legal understanding. Slander required only a claim of a statement by the defendant, often a prior accusation in a criminal proceeding. In such cases, parties sometimes chose to venture into court unrepresented. Two plaintiffs who did not seem to have legal literacy and were unrepresented won slander cases against legally literate defendants. Debt suits were similarly easy to bring. The only evidence necessary in a debt case was the paper with the debt written on it, and the burden lay on the debtor to provide proof that the debt had been paid. Yet debt cases reveal that even in such easy cases, attorneys might have an advantage. Robert Westcott briefly served as general sergeant and had represented himself apparently somewhat successfully in a few debt cases. When Westcott was sued by attorney Francis Brinley (a borrower of Harris's books), Westcott lost. Legal knowledge—and the social standing that often accompanied it—mattered in court.[24]

Attorneys also used their legal skills to avoid trial. One popular tactic was the demurrer, a procedural move used to delay the case. Indeed, the demurrer was so frequently invoked that the colony passed laws reducing the number of demurrers permitted. Nicholas Easton successfully used the demurrer and other techniques to delay the colony's effort to obtain an accounting of prize money acquired in the early 1650s from a boat seizure. When the Court finally received the case five years later, it concluded that "it is not convenient to prosecute the said action" because there were "very great alterations &c. since the former order was made." Another technique was to challenge the other attorney's authority. In Warwick town court, John Greene Jr. sued Mathias Harvey. When William Carpenter appeared "making answer as Attorney" for Harvey, Greene asked Carpenter to show "his warrant of Attorney." The court concluded that the warrant "gave him no Authority at all as Attorney to this suit." When Carpenter offered to bring in witnesses to testify as to "the intent of the Letter of Attorney," Greene successfully argued that "the Letter of Attorney could not be enlarged by verbal witnesses." The case went to the jury with no defense. Lastly, attorneys sometimes sought to remove certain assistants from the bench, apparently because they may have served as attorneys for the opposing side. In Providence town court, attorney Hugh Bewitt objected to Robert Williams by noting that his client "question[ed] whether he shall have a fair trial or due progress in the said Cause, whilst the said Robert Williams is one upon the bench deputed."[25]

Attorneys were particularly useful when a case was initially lost. They often refused to accept execution of the judgment. Appeals from town courts offered one avenue for disagreeing with the outcome. An appeal to the General Court of Trials allowed a second chance to argue the case. A defendant had ten days before execution of a judgment "to remove his Case if he judge himself wronged" by obtaining a writ from an assistant. Appeals offered the prospect of a jury composed of a larger segment of the population. Attorneys did not always accept even the procedural limits on appeals. In the 1650s, William Cotton of Boston retained Benedict Arnold as an attorney to see if anything could be done about a judgment against Cotton in a case brought by William Field. Arnold had gone to "Mr. Dexter (who was Attorney in the case for Mr. Cotton) and asked his advice about an appeal." Dexter had stated that "according to the Town order it was too late to Appeal." Arnold, however, believed that the appeal should not be barred. He wrote to the assistant with "power to grant Appeals"—who also happened to have been the plaintiff in the case. To Field, Arnold argued that there had been "no certain court, place, nor time to appeal unto" because of disruptions in the colony. Implicitly threatening Field, Arnold noted that if the appeal were refused, Arnold would show the request at the town meeting "for upon the sight hereof I doubt not but the Townsmen will so far agitate the thing that it shall be so ordered." The attorney's legal and political persuasion proved successful.[26]

Attorneys also aided litigants who wanted to dispute decisions decided by the General Court of Trials. Initially, the colony permitted only discretionary rehearings. Attorney efforts to obtain these rehearings, however, proved overly disruptive of the colony's politics. In 1656, two of the wealthiest and most powerful men in the colony, William Brenton and William Coddington, clashed over arrangements to export horses to

Barbados. Disliking the initial judgments, their attorneys attacked the composition of the bench and petitioned the Assembly. The dispute led the Assembly to develop "a method and Rule to be given touching a re-hearing of causes." The new law gave plaintiff and defendant the "liberty of one rehearing." As William Harris later noted, a rehearing was ob-tained by law in Rhode Island "without showing any reason, error, or attaint."[27]

Attorneys loved this new rehearing as of right. Between 1655 and 1670, twenty-two rehearings were filed in the Court of Trials, of which seventeen were eventually heard. Of the twenty-two rehearings filed, most were brought by attorneys: sixteen by attorneys; six by other legal literates. The challenge communicated to the new jury the strength of a party's belief in his or her argument. Defendant attorneys were quite suc-cessful at reversing the sentence or having the damages reduced. Of course, not all plaintiffs accepted a defendant's success on rehearing and requested another rehearing. Joseph Torrey, for example, won at trial, lost on the first rehearing, but won on the second. Court costs meant that not every rehearing was worth bringing. Three cases were dropped before rehearing, probably because the damages awarded against the de-fendants were less than what a rehearing would cost. For those willing to bear the costs, rehearings were a matter of course in Rhode Island. By 1698 practically every court session began by rehearing cases. Attorneys had successfully developed a procedure that advantaged them even fur-ther in the courts.[28]

Rehearings offered a second chance at evidence, argument, and jury. A 1701 description of the rehearing emphasized if a party was "grieved" with the judgment, a rehearing with "new evidences" and a new jury could be obtained. In some cases, a change in the case's presentation led to a different result. For example, when Jan Gereardy sued the estate of Virginian Colonel Scarbrough for a tobacco debt, the jury found for Gereardy in the amount of 72 pounds, 11 shillings, and a penny. At the rehearing, the attorneys no longer agreed on the issues and the Court redefined them for the jury. This redefinition of the issues was decisive; the jury now found for Scarbrough. In other rehearings, the hope was simply to get a new jury more favorable to one's argument. A Warwick town court jury had awarded Gereardy 150 pounds, although on rehear-ing the sum was reduced to 81. At a hearing and a rehearing at the Gen-eral Court of Trials, juries with fewer Warwickers found no debt owed.

Through procedural maneuvering, Gereardy managed to have the case heard a third time with a fifth jury, which contained Richard Burton, a Warwick man who had sat on the case in Warwick town court. At some point in the deliberations—likely, when the jury verdict was going against Gereardy—Burton and a fellow Warwick juror rebelled. The other jurors explained that the two had been asked to "agitate" with the others; however, the two had responded that "it was time for Travelers to go to Dinner" and left without dissenting or agreeing. Gereardy consequently did not recover the debt. Rehearings changed outcomes.[29]

Over time, attorneys and litigants wanted to challenge even decisions that had been reheard in the General Court of Trials. Two audiences seemed available: the Rhode Island General Assembly and the English crown. Although parties had occasionally petitioned the General Assembly, as had occurred with discretionary rehearings, people came to desire a standard mechanism. In 1680, in response to a suit over the administration of an estate, a new law provided for appeals to the Assembly. In "all actional cases," the aggrieved party could appeal to the General Assembly. The Assembly provided a decisionmaker even further removed from the litigants. In October 1680 the Assembly resolved its first official appeal involving an estate "according to the equity of the said case." The availability of rehearings and the late seventeenth-century political disruption over the establishment and collapse of the Dominion of New England meant that the Assembly appeal was seldom used until after 1700. During these same years a few Rhode Islanders, like William Harris, began to petition the crown and council to review decisions of the Rhode Island courts. The petition and appeal to England, however, would prove far more controversial.[30]

Into the late seventeenth century, attorneys flourished in Rhode Island. The transatlantic character of the colony's legal culture continued to deepen. To learn Rhode Island law, attorneys and practitioners served in official positions that gave them access to the colony's repositories of statutes. To learn the laws of England, English law books—bought and borrowed—remained an essential resource. Throughout, attorneys spoke with each other and observed each other in court. The civil legal system fostered attorneys and practitioners who used their legal and political knowledge to advance their clients' cases and sought new ways to challenge court decisions.

2

The Laws of England

The precise role of English law in colonial attorneys' legal practice was unclear. Did colonial law have to conform to English law? Could colonial law ignore English law altogether? As England had expanded as a nation and an empire, English law had developed a conceptual structure that embraced both a universal idea of the laws of England and an awareness of the need for regional diversity. Rather than resolve this tension, early seventeenth-century transatlantic law perpetuated it. In 1608, *Calvin's Case,* the first English case to address the question, merely created more arguments about the application of the laws of England to English colonies. The colonial charters subsequently adopted language that permitted both uniformity and divergence. Colonial attorneys thus legitimately could draw selectively on English law to resolve their legal problems. By the mid-seventeenth century, the crown began to consolidate authority over the application of the laws of England in the colonies by authorizing appeals from the colonies to the crown.

The problem of applying English law to new areas of the empire had a long history prior to North American settlement. England and the empire had arisen through the conquest of different realms with varied legal rules and practices. The tension between the aspiration to a uniform body of law and the need for legal divergence due to local circumstance had been politically recognized. The ubiquitous phrase *the laws of England*—or, more properly, *the laws of this realm of England*—reflected these entangled desires. On the one hand, *the* laws of England reflected the aspiration of an empire linked by uniform laws. On the other hand, the *laws* of England continued to attest to the legitimate diversity within England and the empire. Law provided a realm for a vision of the English empire. Throughout the sixteenth and the early seventeenth century, in legislation and legal literature addressing the laws of England, *the laws of England* offered a path to define legal Englishness.[1]

The act incorporating Wales under Henry VIII in 1535 embraced an aspirational imperial vision. Although Wales had been confiscated and annexed centuries earlier, the act "concerning the laws to be used in Wales" used "the laws, ordinances and statutes of this realm of England" to finally "reduce" the Welsh with their "divers" and "discrepant" laws and customs to "perfect order." The Welsh could keep "necessary" diverse laws. English law, however, displaced a broad swath of Welsh legal authority: "any act, statute, usage, custom, precedent, liberty, privilege, or other thing had, made, used, granted or suffered to the contrary in any wise notwithstanding." A defining aspect of the crown's imagined empire of uniformity involved primogeniture, the requirement that the eldest son alone inherit land. Of course, England was not completely uniform on primogeniture; various areas such as Kent had other inheritance practices. Indeed, in 1540 the Statute of Wills would allow testators the ability to devise land in ways other than primogeniture. Nonetheless, in 1535 and in centuries to come, to be "English" was to follow primogeniture. Measured by this standard, Wales was decidedly un-English. It practiced gavelkind, the equal division of inherited land among all sons. The 1535 act thus replaced Welsh gavelkind with English primogeniture. The Welsh were to become English by following "the laws of England," such as primogeniture, that defined an imagined legal Englishness.[2]

Nearly a century later, Francis Bacon imagined a different vision of legal Englishness, independent of property law. In studying the union of Scotland and England arising out of the succession of James I, Bacon recognized that nations had similar and divergent laws due to different histories and geographies. He proposed that English and Scottish lawyers create "a digest, under titles, of their several laws and customs, as well as common laws as statutes." In synthesizing any such digest, Bacon described a different account of imperial uniformity and diversity. Bacon agreed that a nation or empire needed "uniformity in the principal and fundamental laws." For him, principal laws included criminal laws, religious laws, and laws relating to legal procedures. These areas directly affected and defined the state. Bacon did not believe uniformity was required in property laws. He explained, "For we see in any one kingdom, which is most at unity in itself, there is diversity of customs for the guiding of property and private rights." In Bacon's imagination, legal Englishness was not tied to a feudal dependence on land but to an almost proto-modern construction of individuals' connection to the mechanisms of the state.[3]

The abandonment of property law as a defining legal characteristic of the English empire was not to be. In 1628 Edward Coke codified aspects of the traditional vision of legal Englishness embodied in the Welsh act of union and the newer vision described by Bacon's study of Scottish union in the most famous early seventeenth-century legal text: *The Institutes of the Laws of England*. Coke declared that the *Institutes* were designed to teach "the national Laws of England": property and inheritance in the first volume; certain statutes and Magna Carta—"for the most part declaratory of the principal grounds of the fundamental laws of England"—in the second; criminal law in the third; and, in the fourth, "all the high, honorable, venerable, and necessary tribunals, and courts of justice within his majesties realms and dominions" drawn into "one map, or table (which hitherto was never yet done)." Coke's *Institutes* transformed a geographically defined nation into a legally defined one and assured readers of the ability to abandon geographical boundaries without losing national legal identity.[4]

Despite Coke's aspirations, the *Institutes* betrayed the lack of uniformity in the laws of England. In attempting to describe a set of national laws (*the* laws of England) Coke actually reflected that, as he acknowledged, "there be diverse laws within the realm of England." To accurately describe English law, Coke had to include the notable variety of sources: the common law of England; statute law; "customs reasonable"; canon law; civil law; forest law; law of marque; law merchant; the laws and customs of Jersey, Guernsey and Man; the "law and privileges" of the Stanneries; and the laws of the East, West, and Middle Marches. Moreover, he noted that there was an "admirable benefit, beauty, and delectable variety" with respect to courts. Beneath the description lay a normative problem of identity. Could laws based on the peculiar history of English feudalism become a set of national laws capable of expanding beyond English shores? Could *Commentary upon Littleton,* as the title to the first volume claimed, be "[not] *the name of a Lawyer onely, but of the Law it selfe*"? The wide popularity of the volume, with its nickname *Coke on Littleton,* testified to a growing belief in a set of national laws founded on English feudal property practices.[5]

By the late seventeenth century, the commitment to definable, national *laws of England* became entwined with idea of an English common law. The wave of English law publishing in the first half of the seventeenth century advanced the project by circumscribing certain customs and selectively turning others into "common law." Ultimately, as in Matthew Hale's *History of the Common Law of England,* the history of England became a legal history bound by a national common law. According to Hale, in the fourteenth century Edward III had extracted "one law to be observed throughout the whole kingdom" from diverse customary provincial laws like the Mercian laws, Danish laws, and West-Saxon laws. This law was the common law: "that law, which is common to the generality of all persons, things, and causes, and has a superintendency over those particular laws that are admitted in relation to particular places or matters." This law not only was "a very just and excellent law in itself," but was "singularly accommodated to the frame of the English government, and to the disposition of the English nation." It had become "the complexion and constitution of the English commonwealth." The "settling of the common law of England" in Ireland, Wales, and the isles of Man, Jersey, and Guernsey had marked the spread of England beyond its initial boundaries. In Ireland, Irish customs, particularly those related to inheritance and property, "contrary to the laws of England are disallowed." English law, national law, and common law were to be one.[6]

The history and theory of English law, however, continued to defy simplistic efforts to emphasize only uniformity. The logic of the argument that the common law deserved superintendency because it was well suited to the experience, use, government, and disposition of England implied that, where it was not well suited, it should not apply. Indeed, the common law did not apply universally throughout the English kingdom. As Hale acknowledged, there existed "particular customary laws." Within England itself, "descents at common law, dower at common law, are in contradistinction to such dower and descents as are directed by particular customs." Moreover, areas like Berwick in Scotland and the islands of Jersey and Guernsey were permitted to follow the customary laws of Scotland and Normandy. Even in Ireland, the crown had only "done as much to introduce the English laws there, as the nature of the inhabitants, or the circumstances of the times, would permit." The rationale for the national supremacy of the common law and the laws of England led to the corollary that particular localities with different circumstances should be allowed to follow particular customs. The legitimacy of national and imperial law thus inherently included the exception for local custom and law. English legal thinkers continued to embrace potentially conflicting arguments: first, that in order to be part of the English empire, certain laws of England had to be followed; second, that the laws of England did not need to supplant the particular customs of certain people and places within the empire.[7]

Calvin's Case

England's settlement of new North American colonies put pressure on this tension between these two perspectives on the laws of England— as signifying national uniformity and as reflecting that law should be suited for local circumstances. Although the colonial relationship evolved along with the English political state, at the outset the broad outlines were relatively clear. The colonies themselves were seen in the first instance, as L. Kinvin Wroth writes, as "personal holdings of the King and were thus ruled by the King directly through the prerogative as though he were their medieval feudal lord." Initially, however, the crown did not directly rule the colonies. Instead, the early seventeenth-century colonies were understood to be "franchises," "exercises of the king's rights by private persons." In short, the crown delegated various aspects of its power to individuals or corporations. Patents or charters eventually established the rights, powers, obligations, and duties of those delegated authorities. Supervision of the charter obligations was placed with the crown and important councilors, an entity referred to by contemporaries as "the King or Queen in Council" or, as it would come to be known, the Privy Council. Over time, alterations in the balance of power between crown and Parliament, as Parliament moved into a position of supremacy, transformed certain aspects of this structure.[8]

The structure left unclear a series of questions about when English common law and statute law applied in any new colonies and what were the respective roles of Parliament, the crown, and the colony. Did the common law necessarily extend to the colonies? Did it extend only by some statement of the crown? Could the colonies through their legislatures extend it—or receive it—to themselves? Once extended or received, could it insulate the colonial government from alterations by either crown or Parliament? Did parliamentary statutes passed before colonial settlement apply in the colonies? Did parliamentary statutes passed after settlement apply? Did the colonies have to be specifically mentioned for the statutes to apply? Could Parliament even legislate directly over the colonies?[9]

In 1608, in *Calvin's Case*, Edward Coke described an approach to address some of these questions. Although the case is usually understood as providing an incipient theory of the legal relationship of colonial law to English law, it is more accurately seen as structuring the theoretical confusion that would continue to surround the colonial legal relationship. The factual controversy had little to do with the situation in which it came to be applied: the developing possibility of North American colonies. Moreover, despite being decided in 1608, the printed opinion did not circulate in English until the 1650s. *Calvin's Case* decided the legal claims to English property available to a Scot born after the accession of James I to the thrones of both Scotland and England (the so-called *postnati*). Under English law, aliens could not claim English land. Consequently, if Scots remained aliens despite the unification of crowns, they could not bring any land claims. Coke decide in favor of the *postnati* after a long discussion about theories of allegiance, the status of aliens versus that of subjects, and the particular problems presented by the accession of Scotland. He implicitly rejected the claims of another group of Scots born before the accession—the *antenati*—who he said remained aliens. A Scot's claim to English land thus depended on his or her date of birth.[10]

In the lengthy opinion, only one now much scrutinized paragraph on Ireland could be read to bear directly on the future colonial relationship. Moreover, nothing in the paragraph explicitly addressed future colonies. It did, however, create a set of classifications about the application of law in new realms. Coke classified acquired lands as (1) Christian kingdoms conquered, (2) infidel kingdoms conquered, and (3) inherited kingdoms. Coke then distinguished three kinds of situations: (1) those in which the king could grant and change laws; (2) those in which the king could grant laws but was then unable to alter them without the consent of Parliament; and (3) those in which the king could never alter laws without the consent of Parliament. Coke concluded that in conquered infidel kingdoms, the king could grant and change laws; in conquered Christian kingdoms, the king could give laws but was then unable to alter them without consent of Parliament; and in inherited kingdoms, the king could never alter laws without consent of Parliament.[11]

Although these classifications seemed to articulate a careful theory, they are perhaps better understood as necessary to distinguish the Scottish *postnati* from the *antenati*. According to Coke, it was the king's relationship to the *postnati* that made them subjects capable of inheriting, despite the fact that England and Scotland remained governed by different laws. Under this reasoning, the *antenati* also should be subjects. Coke kept the *antenati* classified as aliens by arguing that the king's power was limited and that the king could not extend the laws of England and turn aliens into subjects capable of inheriting in England. The major problem for Coke's argument was the precedent of Ireland. As Coke noted, although England and Ireland had remained governed by two different systems of law, "any that was born in Ireland were no alien to the realm of England." The Irish were subjects. Two different theories could have been advanced to justify the subject status of the Irish: first, Henry II had conquered the Irish in the mid-twelfth century; second, King John had extended the laws of England to the Irish in the early thirteenth century. Coke chose the conquered interpretation. The Irish had been conquered; the Scots had not been. This conclusion, however, did not exclude the possibility that a king could nonetheless extend English laws to aliens. Coke barred the application of this rule to the Scots and emphasized that when a king had benefited by the laws of the kingdom by inheriting its throne (as James did in inheriting Scotland), he could not "change those laws by himself, without consent of Parliament."[12]

Although the case tantalizingly hinted at a theory of the legal relationship between England and future colonies involving conquered status and the extension of laws, Coke's opinion merely opened a space for argument. Coke's rigid list of kingdoms and his focus on conquered kingdoms did not really fit the nascent colonies. Therefore, in 1693 in *Blankard v. Galdy*, the chief justice of King's Bench, John Holt, added an alternative classification for colonies: uninhabited countries found out by English subjects. In these discovered colonies, Holt said, settlers brought English laws with them. With the 1717 publication of *Blankard* in a printed volume of case reports, English law largely seemed to abandon the classifications of *Calvin's Case* in the colonial context. A 1720 opinion on an admiralty issue by Richard West, counsel of the Board of Trade, adopted the *Blankard* approach and stated that English settlers always carried the common law and "statutes in affirmance" of the common law with them. Two years later, a Privy Council memorandum on the application of the Statute of Frauds to Barbados again applied the *Blankard* category of "found out" colonies. Because Barbados was an uninhabited country, the laws of England had been brought with the English settlers; however, the statute did not bind the colony because it postdated settlement and did not mention Barbados. Some colonists even rejected the necessity of choosing a single classification. A 1728 set of instructions from Connecticut to agent Jonathan Belcher referred to *Blankard* and concluded that the colony had been part uninhabited and part conquered and therefore could determine its own laws. "Found out" or conquered, neither or both, remained legitimate competing arguments throughout much of the colonial period.[13]

Similar ambiguity continued on the significance of the extension of the laws of England. Coke's discussion of the extension of the laws of England provided little guidance with respect to any colonial settlement. Coke did not resolve whether extension of the laws of England required the preemption of local laws; indeed, he supported the opposite conclusion. He approvingly reported that, although "the laws of England became the proper laws of Ireland," the Irish had "made divers particular laws" and were governed by "laws and customs, separate and diverse from the laws of England." Coke's lengthy examples of areas of the empire governed by local laws reinforced the idea that the extension of the laws of England and English authority did not end local diversity. In 1681 the attorney general, Sir William Jones, embraced this diversity vision of the empire by concluding that the plantations were bound by parliamentary statute only when they were expressly named in the statute. Jones reasoned that the colonies were not represented in Parliament and therefore Parliament could not know whether the laws were suited to the colonies. According to Jones, the colonies themselves could choose to be bound by parliamentary statutes through explicit acceptance by an official legislative act. In the late 1720s, evidence of colonial intent outside of the legislature was held to be valid for acceptance. While accepting that general parliamentary acts did not necessarily bind the colony, Attorney General Yorke concluded that a colony could receive an English act by "long uninterrupted usage or practice." The 1729 opinion increased the likelihood that general parliamentary acts passed after colonization would be found to have been adopted by long practice. By acting English, the colonists in essence could extend the laws of England to themselves.[14]

William Blackstone's *Commentaries on the Laws of England* (1765) reveals that, even among English legal commentators, uncertainty over the application of the laws of England in the colonies remained up to the eve of the Revolution. In his chapter entitled "Of the Countries subject to the Laws of England," Blackstone accurately wrote that the "distant plantations" were "in some respects subject to the English laws." Blackstone distinguished conquered countries (covered by *Calvin's Case*) from discovered countries (covered by *Blankard*). He then, however, claimed that the American plantations were "principally" considered conquered and "therefore the common law of England" initially had no authority there. As Elizabeth Brown aptly points out, Blackstone must have been not entirely persuaded that this conclusion explained English and colonial legal practice. In the 1775 edition of his *Commentaries*, he added a more extensive discussion of which laws of England settlers brought with them to discovered countries. He argued that settlers brought only "so much of the English law, as is applicable to their own situation and the condition of an infant colony." While they likely would have brought general rules of inheritance, they would not have brought more "artificial refinements" about property or rules regarding the maintenance of ministers of the established church. In this description, Blackstone more accurately described transatlantic practice. In both editions Blackstone noted that, although colonial legislatures could adopt laws, they were subject to a repugnancy standard judged on appeal to the King in Council (the Privy Council).[15]

For colonial attorneys and crown officers, the relationship between English law and the colonies was an evolving set of arguments, not a simple rule. In 1608, *Calvin's Case* created one argument: if the colony was conquered, prior laws of England had no effect. After 1680 an additional argument arose: if Parliament had named the colony in an act or the colony had officially adopted the law, the English law applied. In the 1690s it became possible to argue that a colony was discovered and therefore the laws of England in force at the time of settlement applied.

After the 1720s one could allege that even if there had been no official action, the colony had adopted English statutes by usage and practice. Over a century and a half, even though *Calvin's Case* was never abandoned, it became easier to claim that the laws of England applied in the colony.

Repugnancy and Divergence

The ambiguity in interpretation reinforced ambiguity in the language traditionally used in patents and charters about the relationship of the laws of England to a colony's law. These were extraordinarily important, powerful documents, literally kept under lock and key, that granted the colony the power to make laws within certain bounds. Reflecting the belief that law should relate to the people, these documents did not require the colony's laws to be identical to the laws of England. Some colonial documents stated the relationship affirmatively: the colonial government should make laws, statutes, ordinances, and proceedings as "near as conveniently may be made agreeable" to the laws, statutes, customs, and rights of the "realm of England." Typical language appeared early in the letters patent to Sir Humphrey Gilbert in 1578 and to Sir Walter Raleigh in 1584: they were to hold the land "according to the order of the laws of England, as near as the same conveniently may be." Others described it negatively: the government could make laws so long as they were not "contrary" or "repugnant" to the laws and statutes of England. Beginning in the 1620s, certain charters began to describe the legal relationship using both affirmative and negative phrases. These phrases affirmed the desire for uniformity with the laws of England and acknowledged the reality of diversity. The language melded easily with the vision in *Calvin's Case* of an empire in which English subjects could be born beyond England, governed by divergent laws, and retain the rights and privileges of Englishmen.[16]

Rhode Island's initial charter and subsequent one followed these models by explicating the relationship between the colony and the laws of England, but with a crucial addition. As colony agent, Roger Williams obtained a charter from Parliament in 1644. The charter affirmatively gave the colony broad authority: "the laws, constitutions and punishments, for the civil government of the said plantation, are conformable to the laws of England, so far as the nature and constitution of that place will admit." Although laws were to be "conformable," the "nature and constitution" of the place innovatively authorized divergence. When the charter was replaced in 1663 after the Restoration of Charles II, a similar theory appeared. The new charter was well received in Rhode Island, with Roger Williams referring to its "inestimable Jewels." It declared affirmatively that the laws were to be agreeable to the laws of England and negatively that the laws were not to be contrary or repugnant. It provided that "the laws, ordinances and constitutions [of Rhode Island], so made, be not contrary and repugnant unto, but as near as may be, agreeable to the laws of this our realm of England, considering the nature and constitution of the place and people there." Like the earlier one, the charter provided for legitimate divergences. The repetition of "constitution" at the beginning and end of the sentence emphasized that the legal structures should bear a relationship to the physical, social, and cultural ones. The Rhode Island laws were only to be "as near" to English laws as "may be," "considering the nature and constitution of the place and people there." Williams praised this aspect: the charter had a "liberty (which other Charters have not) to wit of attending to the Laws of England with a favorable mitigation via: not absolutely but respecting our wilderness, estate, and condition." The divergence argument seems to have begun with the colony—perhaps arranged by the colony's attorneys and agents—and would spread to other charters. If the constitution of the colony and its people required, the colony's laws could diverge. Divergence or uniformity depended on the characteristics of Rhode Islanders in Rhode Island.[17]

Under the charter, any colonial law or practice could be attacked or defended. To attack a colonial law, one argued that it was repugnant to the laws of England. To retain it, one argued that it was an acceptable divergence, considering the people and place. The repugnancy argument embodied the vision that the laws of England should create a uniform nation and empire. Although what constituted "repugnancy" was a matter of interpretation in particular cases, the principle of repugnancy recognized that some laws were against the idea of what it meant to be English. The divergence argument embodied the diversity vision of the empire, recognizing that law should reflect the experience of specific peoples and places. Although what constituted "the nature and constitution of the people and place there" was also a matter of interpretation, divergence recognized that a distant colony required different laws. The divergence and repugnancy language would continue to appear in later seventeenth-century charters and the act regulating the trade with the colonies. This language came to embody the transatlantic constitution.[18]

The language of repugnancy and divergence was used by attorneys like William Harris in litigating cases. The transatlantic legal culture arising out of the charter and the colony's relationship to the laws of England is apparent in Harris's library, letters, and legal copies. Harris's library contained the materials for arguing within the boundaries of this transatlantic constitution. He carefully created a six-inch copy of the charter, including the crucial phrase on repugnancy and divergence quoted earlier. To search for repugnancies, Harris had books to guide him, such as Pulton's *Sundry Statutes* and Coke's *Commentary upon Littleton*. To justify divergence, he held the first domestically printed history of New England—Morton's *New England's Memorial* (1669). Finally, Harris had Lambarde's *Perambulation on Kent*, which described the legitimacy of local custom in English law and linked Kent's divergence on inheritance to the history of the county's people, land, and legal institutions. Such books reminded Harris that this conversation about repugnancy and divergence was intertwined with English law and history itself.[19]

Harris outlined his arguments about the transatlantic constitution in letters, legal copies, and scribbled notations in Pulton's *Sundry Statutes*. He assumed that the laws of England expressed in his books could apply to his cases. Often he referred generally to the "law of England" on particular issues to support his conclusions. On occasion he made more specific references. Basic English common law in Coke's *Commentary upon Littleton* and the *Lawes Resolution* appeared in his 1678 will, where he promised that if his female descendants were to marry and have children, "by the law of the Curtesy of England," their husbands could still use the land. Other examples of English wills may have provided the form for his personal preface to the will: he was sixty-eight years old and "must die ere long"; smallpox and fevers lay "not far off"; and his impending voyage raised "the danger of the sea by storms, leaks, and enemies." He likely used his English texts on executors and women's property in his attempt to acquire the administration of his sister's estate. English statutes that had no parallel in the colony laws were particularly useful. Harris was fond of the English statute of limitations for land actions (21 James 16). In a grouping of statute excerpts entitled "the court to be held at Providence the 3d of October 1677," Harris cited the statute for the conclusion "that no demand by any suits, by any person hath been commenced against us this forty years . . . our title justified." He later referred again to the statute in his declaration against an entry made by John Towers, stating that the entry was against "the law of England that giveth title to the possessor if not demanded by action within twenty years" and included the legal citation. In Rhode Island's world of uncertain and continual land claims, the English law was an essential addition. In matter after matter, Harris revealed his assumption that the laws of Rhode Island should be agreeable to certain English laws.[20]

Many English statutes failed to address precisely Harris's situation. He was constantly combing Pulton for plausible statutes. He excerpted six statutes about the types of suits that executors could bring—perhaps for reference to his sister's estate. Another six statutes on the duties of the sheriff may have served as the basis for his suit against the general sergeant for failure to execute a judgment. He cited statutes relating to forcible entries, the action that he brought against one of the defendants in his land suit. Gathering material for his letter suggesting the convening of an intercolonial court, Harris noted statutes relating to the holding of sessions and special commissions. Other citations on juries and judgments related to the formation of an intercolonial jury and Harris's later desire to have it reconvened to explain its judgment. To resolve the problem, Harris promoted the English legal principle of equity of the statute, which legitimized his inability to precisely apply statutes to his situations. Equity of the statute suggested that statutes could be interpreted expansively to apply to additional circumstances. In the front of Pulton, Harris noted a number of such instances. For example, one statute (28 Henry 8, chap. 15) showed that "by the equity of the said statute" a special commission could be authorized to decide certain matters. Similarly, another (23 Henry 8, chap. 3) suggested that "by the equity of the said statute" if there were not enough competent jurors in one place, the case could be removed to another place and court. Equity of the statute provided Harris with some flexibility in reconfiguring the laws of England to serve his purposes.[21]

Harris accepted that Rhode Island laws and practices were not supposed to be repugnant to English law. He firmly believed that no law, colonial or English, could be repugnant to Magna Carta. Adopting the *Ch*-spelling, *Charta,* which emphasized its fundamental, charter-like nature,

Harris wrote that "all statutes contrary to magna charta are void" and that "all laws, statutes, or customs contrary to the great charter shall be void." Harris presumed that Magna Carta applied in the colonies, noting that the "great charter" could be pleaded in all courts. He applied this principle in a December 1669 letter to the Providence town meeting in which he referred to the "law of England," stating that "no Corporation may make any law in diminution or dishertion [sic] of the rights or prerogatives of any of the king's liege subjects and people" and "trespassers against Magna Charta shall by the law of England be inquired into." Arguing direct repugnancy was often difficult because most of the statutes applied to Harris's case only by analogy and extension. In an undated document objecting to a new tax to pay for an English agent to address the Connecticut claims, Harris cited ten English statutes. The lengthy quotations were designed to "lay down" "the law and clauses of the law of England supposed to be the rule of judgment (in such cases)."[22]

In other situations, Harris argued for legitimate divergence because of his circumstances. Like several other Rhode Islanders, Harris entailed his land in his will. In England, entail resulted in land passing among issue, usually firstborn sons and their male descendants, without any ability to sell or devise the land. Harris adapted English entail to the circumstances of his life in the colony. Although in England an entail lasted until the bloodline ended, Harris entailed his land only to his "fourth Generation," that is, to his great-grandchildren. Similarly, although in England entail kept land together, descending only to one person, Harris ordered his entailed land equally divided in each generation. He accomplished this division by adopting gavelkind. Unlike primogeniture, under which land passed to the eldest son, gavelkind allowed the land to descend to all sons equally and had been the custom in the county of Kent since perhaps before the Norman Conquest. Harris explained his choice of gavelkind. His heirs would enjoy their parts "according to the custom of gavelkind land, (as in the law expressed) and as by the Kings patent to this his Colony (saith according to the custom of his manor of East Greenwich in Kent) which by Lambath preambulations &c, are intended Custom of Gavelkind (that is to say) if male heirs, then the land to be equally divided among them."[23]

Harris justified gavelkind with the charter, which stated that the corporate founders of Rhode Island and their heirs and assigns held "as of the Manor of East Greenwich, in our county of Kent, in free and common socage." This passage had most likely been designed to ensure that the colonists did not pay rent for the land. Harris, however, reasoned that if the initial corporation held land as in Kent, then those subsequently holding land in the colony held as if they were in Kent, and therefore gavelkind applied. Lastly, although Harris seemed to create a particular English entail known as fee tail male that limited the entail to male descendants, he specifically stated that if his son had no male heirs then the land should descend to female heirs and their daughters.[24]

Other Rhode Islanders used Harris's books to follow the commands of the charter and the transatlantic constitution. The Pulton statute book was most useful because it stated the laws of England verbatim. In 1673 the Assembly noted that the "Statutes, or Book of Statutes" was not at the Assembly. It added that the book containing many statutes of England should always be in the Assembly and also in "every Court of Trials" so that "proceedings in the said Courts may be guided thereby, and in conformity thereto." In 1678 the Assembly kept Rhode Island law and practice agreeable to the laws of England by noting that it had mistakenly used *executor* in statutes where *administrator* was the correct word. This correction led the Assembly to conclude that there was a "great necessity for the more full and clear stating of the laws of this Colony, concerning the probate of wills and intestate." In another instance, in October 1673 the Assembly enacted a law adopting all the English statutes on forcible entry. Because "the laws of England concerning the same were enacted after hundreds of years' experience of the need of the said laws," the Rhode Island law provided a list of English statutes ("5 R ii 7, 15 R ii 2, 4 H iv 8, 13 H iv 7, 8 H vi 9, 19 H vii 13, 23 H viii 14, 31 El 11 & 21, Jac xv") that were to "stand in full force." Despite adopting the laws of England, the Assembly preserved the possibility of divergence. A parenthetical to the act noted that these laws were in full force under the charter "so far as the nature and constitution of this place and people can admit."[25]

The legal community outside of Rhode Island also thought about colonial law in terms of repugnancy and divergence. In 1667 Harris wrote to Colonel Nichols, then governor of New York, about the legality of fines placed upon Harris. In response, Nichols wrote to the Rhode Island governor: "you will not find in any one law book of England a precedent for so doing, but the contrary." The Assembly reversed itself, accepting the argument that its practice was repugnant. In 1678 Harris wrote to

Serjeant Steele, likely serjeant-at-law William Steele, in England for a "clear answer in writing" about gavelkind. Harris asked whether the land should "descend as gavelkind to all male heirs equally (if that be) &c or the eldest male heir or how else." Harris emphasized that there "is great need of a resolution in the said case for here is no certain knowledge of the full and certain meaning of the said words." In April 1678, Harris cited English statutes to persuade Thomas Hinckley of Massachusetts that he had the power to recall an intercolonial jury to determine the precise line of land division.[26]

As always, the statutes and Harris's description were not precise. Harris relied on the "equity of the 13 Edw. 1, ch. 25" to justify that "where there hath been a verdict and judgment yet if he that had judgment against him can produce record or rolls" in his favor, the court could require the juries to return. The statute actually related to the technical request for a writ of *venire facias de novo* (in essence, a writ for a new trial) and procedures involving assizes, one of which permitted a previously absent defendant to obtain a reconvening. Hinckley accepted Harris's interpretation and wrote to jurors in Connecticut asking that they reconvene to clarify "divers and dubious interpretations" about the division line. He based his actions on this same statute "whereby Justices in Cases shall send for the same Jury that hath before given verdict and after judgment granted." This interpretation also was cited by Rhode Islanders Peleg Sanford and John Coggeshall in a subsequent petition to the king.[27]

The Appeal

The ambiguity in the application of the laws of England in the colonies raised disagreements over which authority would decide repugnancy and divergence. For those seeking refuge in the laws of England, an English decisionmaker seemed vital. Harris, for example, traveled to England several times to seek redress in cases involving internal boundary disputes. Yet early patents and charters gave extensive authority to the colony and did not specify whether the English crown retained supremacy in this area. Concerns about the authority of colonial governments over laws took the form of a debate over whether there was an appeal from colonial governments to the crown.

For centuries, the availability or absence of an appeal signified the larger hierarchical relation of legal authority. Throughout the Roman Catholic world, cases had been appealed from local authorities to the pope. Civilian lawyer John Cowell's 1607 dictionary, *The Interpreter,* stated: the "appeal is used in our common law divers times, as it is taken in the civil law: which is a removing of a cause from an inferior judge to a superior as appeal to Rome." By the seventeenth century, legal writers insisted that the appeal was in essence an individual right. Edward Coke similarly stated that the "appeal is a natural defence" and cannot be taken away "by any prince or power." He added, if the appeal is "just and lawful, the superior judge ought of right and equity to receive and admit the same, as he ought to do justice to the subjects." Refusing appeals symbolized rejection of authority. In 1164, maintaining the pope's authority against Henry II's effort to end appeals had sent Archbishop Thomas à Becket to a violent death. In 1533, Henry VIII's act preventing appeals to the pope, "For the Restraint of Appeals," signaled new royal supremacy. Establishing an excuse for preventing appeals beyond the rejection of authority, Henry VIII blamed procedural problems. Appeals were often brought for "the delay of justice"; they created "great inquietation, vexation, trouble, cost and charges"; and the "great distance" to Rome meant that necessary proofs, witnesses, and "true knowledge of the cause" could not be known. Barring appeals relocated supreme authority.[28]

At the outset of settlement in Massachusetts, the absence of clarity about the availability of appeal proved controversial. The early colonial patents and charters contained no express statements about appeals to the king. Some colonists, unhappy with the local government, assumed that the grant included an implicit reservation for an appeal to the crown, as with other English franchises like the isles of Jersey and Guernsey. In 1636 Edward Winslow warned John Winthrop that if "new England will afford no Justice," he would "appeal further." In 1637 John Wheelwright appealed to the "king's court" after a judgment by the General Court banished him for religious beliefs. In late 1641 Thomas Lechford noted that, although there was "no appeal" from the General Court in Massachusetts to England, he "presume[d] their Patent doth reserve and provide for Appeals, in some cases, to the King's Majesty." In the 1640s, Robert Child appealed to England, arguing that the colony should follow the laws of England rather than "arbitrary government." Appealing seemed the only remedy to balance local authority.[29]

An appeal to the crown threatened those in authority in Massachusetts. John Winthrop argued that no appeal had been reserved by the
king and that the patent had delegated authority without an appeal. In
1637 Winthrop persuaded John Wheelwright that "an appeal did not lie;
for by the king's grant we had power to hear and determine without
any reservation." Later, in 1644 in A Short Story, his recounting of the
Wheelwright appeal, he explained in more detail:

> an appeal did not lie in this case, for the King having given us an au-
> thority by his grant under his great seal of England to hear and deter-
> mine all causes without any reservation, we were not to admit of any
> such appeals for any such subordinate state, either in Ireland, or Scot-
> land, or other places; and if an appeal should lie in one case, it might
> be challenged in all, and then there would be no use of government
> among us.[30]

Winthrop's theory drew on other corporation charters. Some of the
trading companies had complete authority over matters without appeal
to the crown and had charters that delegated to the governor and company the power to do justice and to pass laws not contrary or repugnant
to the laws of England. John Wheeler's famous Treatise on Commerce
(1601) described the Merchant Adventurers' power to "end and determine all Civil causes, questions, and controversies . . . without Appeal,
provocation, or declination." Similarly, the charter to the King's Merchants of the New Trade stated that there would be no "further appeal or
provocation whatever" from the power and authority of "the Company
and Fellowship." Winthrop similarly drew on English precedent to
claim that practical procedural problems supported the absence of an
appeal. In his 1646–1647 petition to English commissioners, Winthrop
based the colony's opposition to appeals on the inconvenience and the
absence of a fair hearing. Referring to Henry VIII's act restraining appeals, he noted the wisdom of "our ancestors" who "acknowledged a supremacy in the bishops of Rome in all causes ecclesiastical, yet would
not allow appeals to Rome." Winthrop claimed that appeals "would be
destructive of all government" because in England "the evidence and
circumstances of facts cannot be so clearly held forth as in their proper
place" and the expenses would be great. The commissioners' response
was ambiguous. They "intended not . . . to encourage any appeals from
your justice" nor to "restrain the bounds of your jurisdiction to a nar-

rower compass than is held forth by your letters patent." While preserving the ability to argue that Massachusetts's patent reserved appeals, the response suggested that some limit on appeals was permissible. In fact, Massachusetts limited appeals to England into the 1660s.[31]

In Rhode Island, the appeal to England in certain cases was seen as more attractive. For some individuals, the appeal seemed a much needed balance to Massachusetts authority. Religious dissenter Samuel Gorton had been banished to Rhode Island in 1639 for heretical lay preaching, and in 1643 Massachusetts sent an armed force to capture him. Gorton attempted to make an "appeal to the honourable State of England." When Massachusetts refused to permit the appeal, Gorton argued that it could try him only "by virtue" of the judicial power given them from the "State of old England." To deny his appeal was to "either presuppose a superiority in them that deny it, or an equality at the least, with the State appealed unto." For Rhode Island, an appeal to the crown seemed a remedy for boundary disputes with Massachusetts and Connecticut. The new Rhode Island charter thus contained an express provision permitting appeals to England in cases of public controversy between colonies. The colony took rapid advantage of the provision. In 1670 Roger Williams approvingly compared Rhode Island's decision to seek redress by appeal before the king in a boundary dispute to "the Case of Paul appealing to Caesar." Of course, appealing in matters of public controversy between colonies did not answer whether an individual right of appeal existed.[32]

Even as Rhode Island obtained its charter with its public appeal provision, the crown was exploring mechanisms to secure national and imperial legal uniformity and to remodel English local government. One year after the Rhode Island charter was granted, the 1664 Maine charter to the Duke of York authorized appeals. The grant of authority to the Duke of York was made "saving and reserving" to the crown the "receiving hearing and determining of the appeal and appeals of all or any person or persons." By 1674 the appeal and the requirements on repugnancy and divergence appeared in the same provision. The Maine charter gave the crown authority to determine the relationship between the laws of England and the colony through the appeal. With later charters beginning to include appeals provisions, the appeal began to seem the permissible path to challenge to laws contrary to the laws of England.[33]

Although by the end of the 1660s, appealing to the crown had become a method by which colonists might attempt to dispute the application of the laws of England to Rhode Island, for most of the seventeenth century it was not a particularly popular path. Most prospective litigants had little choice at first but to bring the appeal personally. As Harris's journeys showed, traveling back and forth to England was not easy, and once one arrived in England the procedural path was not entirely clear. In Rhode Island, for the next several decades, the private appeal to the Privy Council lay largely dormant. Disputes over the laws of England and colonial law occurred in a different arena.

3

The Laws of Rhode Island

For the latter half of the seventeenth century, Rhode Island statutes were the contested area of the transatlantic constitution. The printed statute collections disguise the degree of disagreement. In a 1725 case, the deliberateness of the disguise became clear. Two young Rhode Islanders—James Honeyman Jr. and George Dunbar—disagreed on the validity of a will signed by two witnesses between 1677 and 1718. According to the printed laws, *Acts and Laws of His Majesties Colony of Rhode Island, and Providence-Plantations in America* (1719), the will was void. Since 1664–1665, "An Act for the Probate of Wills" stated that all wills required "three or four Credible Witnesses, or else shall be Void and of none Effect." The marginalia emphasized: "All Wills devising Lands shall be in Writing, and shall have 3 Witnesses." Honeyman, however, argued that the three-witness rule was new to the 1719 statute book. A list of seventeen Newport wills written since 1676 with only two witnesses was introduced. Former governor Samuel Cranston stated that the act had a "mistaken date as it stands in our printed laws." He explained that it had been written in 1705 in "Major Coddington's Transcript," who "in the time of drawing out that transcript advised with me about putting three witnesses to a will." Lastly, a memorial to the Assembly declared that the three-witness requirement had been added to "accommodate that original law . . . unto the Law of England."[1]

Honeyman was right. The printed law had silently backdated the new witness requirement to accommodate the law to the laws of England. Until 1677 the colony's original law requiring two or three witnesses had conformed to the laws of England. Henry Swinburne's *A Brief Treatise of Testaments and Last Wills* (1590) stated that a will in England needed "but two witnesses." In 1677, as William Nelson's *Lex Testamentaria* (1714) explained, the Statute of Frauds had made "considerable Alteration . . . of the Law relating to Wills in Writing" by requiring that a will have "three or four witnesses." After the Statute of Frauds, a will had to have "three witnesses at least, or else to be utterly void." The list of two-witness post-1676 wills suggests that the Statute of Frauds initially had little or no effect in the colony. However, in 1704–1705 a Rhode Island committee reviewing the laws for publication concluded that the colony's law should conform. They not only altered the earlier act to state that "all wills put in writing shall have three witnesses thereto" but backdated the change to make it appear as if the colony had always been in conformity. The Assembly ultimately decided not to publish this version; indeed, the legal status of the 1705 manuscript was sufficiently in doubt that the memorialists could urge that the probate act be applicable only to post-1719. Only in 1719 did the colony publicly proclaim conformity with the forty-year-old English legal requirement by declaring that its 1664–1666 probate act required "three or four credible witnesses."[2]

The peculiar approach taken by the Assembly to wills, like other aspects of the colony's long effort to print its laws, was a product of the transatlantic constitution. Rhode Islanders needed to conform to the laws of the English empire to avoid losing the charter through procedures such as *quo warranto* (a procedure requiring that the corporation show "by what warrant" it exercised its powers). However, they also wanted to diverge to maintain the colony's self-governance over its own circumstances. By "accommodating," or acknowledging, the laws of England in a way that also reinforced or at least did not diminish the colony's own power, Rhode Islanders hoped to protect the colony's charter from antagonists in England and dampen disagreement within the colony. The form and timing of writing, publishing, and printing the laws of Rhode Island arose from this strategy of transatlantic accommodation.

Complying with the Charter

In 1664, Rhode Island officials began the first of many attempts to ensure that the colony statutes complied with the charter's command to be, as near as may be, agreeable to the laws of England, given Rhode Island circumstances. In the spring the Assembly had declared several laws "null and void" because they were "inconsistent with the present government." In the fall a committee was given instructions to look for laws that were "not agreeable to the Charter." It was also to put the laws "in a better form for finding of them when there is occasion to look for any law." It took two committees several years to finish the project. Although men like Roger Williams sat on the committees, the bulk of the work was done by attorneys. John Clarke, the man who had obtained the charter, was "to compose all the laws of the colony . . . leaving out what may be superfluous, and adding what may appear unto him necessary." The recorder, John Sanford, was to "help with the perusal of the Book of Records." After the composure, William Harris and John Greene, the general attorney, were to "have the view of them, and give their thoughts thereupon." The documents prove the attorneys' participation. The text, citations, and marginalia are in the hand of John Sanford. Other comments are likely in Harris's handwriting. The Assembly had taken care to appoint members with extensive knowledge of Rhode Island and English law.[3]

Although Rhode Island historians usually refer to these laws as the "1647 Code," they are more properly understood as a 1664–1666 composure to comply with the charter's command regarding repugnancy and divergence. A marginal notation in Sanford's hand states: "Laws as made according to the Laws of England or near as the constitution of the place will bear." Similar language appears in the provisions themselves. The text notes that under the charter the colony has the power to make laws and constitutions that "shall be conformable to the laws of England so far as the nature and constitution of our place will admit." The laws stated that "we do agree . . . to make such laws and constitutions so conformable, &c., or rather to make those laws, ours, and better known among us, that is to say, such of them and so far, as the nature and constitution of our place will admit."[4]

The substantive laws demonstrated this effort to conform to the charter. As other scholars have noted, certain provisions are borrowed from Magna Carta, Dalton's *Countrey Justice* (a book in Harris's library), and other English texts. The sections on women resemble sections in *Lawes Resolution* (another book owned by Harris). The definitions of crimes and applications often seem to rely on *Countrey Justice*. Other provisions end with citations to English statutes. Although the references to Eng-

lish statutes have been conventionally referred to as "no more than win-
dow dressing," they were integral to ensuring that the laws complied
with the transatlantic constitution. These provisions also demonstrated
the need for divergence. The section on archery began by noting the
circumstances of Rhode Island life: "as we are cast among the archers,"
referring to the presence of indigenous peoples. As William Staples
pointed out, a provision from Magna Carta regarding criminal laws was
amended to exclude implied and constructive felonies. The statutory citations themselves often appear as string cites, implying ideas abstracted
from various English statutes, not literal adoption of the statutes. The
composure reflected the Assembly's determination to be the English colony of Rhode Island and Providence Plantations in America. In this initial attempt, they were surprisingly successful. The composure remained
the only organization of Rhode Island law for the next thirty years.[5]

Scrutinizing Colonial Statutes

Compliance with the charter arose from concern over possible reaction
by English authorities to the colony's laws. In the mid-1660s, this concern was still somewhat hypothetical. English officials had been interested in reviewing colonial laws since the 1650s. As a legal matter, however, only the royal colonies (Jamaica, Barbados, the Leeward Islands,
and Virginia) were required to send their laws to England, and in 1665
several laws from Caribbean colonies were sent. Other colonies were under no such obligation. An alternative route for crown officials to learn
of enacted colonial law was by obtaining copies of such statutes. Yet access to the manuscript version required money and the assistance of colonial clerks in finding and copying the laws. In theory, obtaining a
printed compilation was easier. In practice, however, Massachusetts was
the sole colony to print its laws domestically before 1672. Versions of
laws from Virginia and New Haven colony were published in London,
but without any consistency or accuracy. Most early seventeenth-century laws were therefore unreviewable for compliance with the laws of
England and the charters.[6]

In the 1670s, English authorities began to contemplate the advantages of greater control over colonial laws. At first, they attempted to end
local legislative authority by writing the laws for royal colonies in England. In 1676 the new twenty-one-member Lords of the Committee for

Trade and Plantations considered the acts of Jamaica "all bound up in a particular book." The following year, the Committee ordered the attorney general to "frame a body of Laws" to send with the new governor of Jamaica and also considered preparing the laws for Virginia. Colony opposition doomed the effort. In a concession to the dual authorities of the transatlantic constitution, English officials concluded that a colony had self-governing authority to write laws. In 1680 the attorney general wrote that Jamaica would be "governed 'by such laws [only] as are made *there* and established by His Majesty's authority.'" Although colonial laws would be subject to London review, all colonies could draft, enact, and alter their own laws. Crown authority would be limited to post hoc review.[7]

During these years, Massachusetts faced similar scrutiny about its laws. Under its corporate charter, the colony had no obligation to send laws to the crown for review. In fact, some colonists took an aggressive position on whether the laws of England even applied to the colony. In 1678 the General Court argued that "the lawes of England are bounded within the four seas, and so not reach America." To declare self-governing authority, the colony made an early commitment to print its laws. The practice of printing laws, however, made the colony open to English scrutiny. John Winthrop had foreseen the dilemma: "the Puritan laws, if fixed in a printed book of statutes, would show up at once as repugnant to English law and hence violations of the charter." In the 1670s, English officials like Edward Randolph believed that the colony had diverged from the laws of England in matters of trade, coinage, oaths of allegiance, appeals, and religious toleration. At Randolph's urging, the printed laws were sent to the attorney general and solicitor general. The attorney general concluded that many of the acts were repugnant to the laws of England and the charter. Officials began to consider *quo warranto* proceedings in order to revoke the charter. In response, the General Court moderated its approach to compliance with the laws of England. Although the Court refused to "acknowledge Parliament's right to enact laws for New England," it agreed as a voluntary matter to use its own authority to enforce the English navigation laws.[8]

Although crown officials were unwilling to relinquish authority, they accepted the principle of divergence. In 1681 the crown's attorney general, Sir William Jones, concluded that Virginia did not have to follow the witness requirements in the Statute of Frauds. He reasoned that Par-

liament should not be presumed to have considered "the particular circumstances and conditions of the plantations" because "no Members
come from thence to the Parliament in England." Moreover, without
such a rule, colonists would be bound by statutes of which they "are, or
may be reasonably supposed, necessarily or invincibly ignorant." A parliamentary statute without naming the colonies could apply only if the
colonial assembly explicitly accepted it. Jones's opinion reinforced the
dual authorities. The colonial assemblies were to the colonies what Parliament was to England. Because laws should consider particular circumstances, the colonial laws might, on occasion, rightly diverge from
the laws of England.[9]

Recognition of the reality of dual legislative authorities did not lead
the crown to abandon completely its claim of superior authority and its
commitment to uniform laws of England. Edward Andros, the governor
of the short-lived reconstruction of the northern colonies known as the
Dominion of New England in the late 1680s, complained during his
subsequent imprisonment that the New England colonies esteemed "no
laws to be binding on them, but what are made by themselves, nor admit
English laws to be pleaded or appeals to his Majesty." By the 1690s, although crown officials accepted that the colonies could legislate for
themselves, they also moved to secure colonial compliance with the
laws of England. New royal charters brought New Hampshire, New
York, and Massachusetts under the requirement of submitting laws for
review to the King in Council. Proprietary colonies soon began to be
brought within the same scheme: Pennsylvania and Maryland became
subject to the review requirement. The review was not without substance; in 1695 the Committee began to disallow some of the colonial
laws.[10]

These developments left Rhode Island in stark relief as one of the
few remaining colonies without a review requirement. Since the late
1680s, Edward Randolph had blamed colonial difficulties on the authority given corporate chartered colonies such as Rhode Island. The Dominion of New England had attempted to end such independence by
confiscating the charters. Although the colonial government had submitted to Andros's authority, the legislature had not turned in the colony's 1663 charter. In 1692 the English attorney general concluded that
the corporation of Rhode Island had not lost "their right and title to the
said Colony and government . . . by virtue of the charter," and in 1694

the Queen and Council reconfirmed the charter. The colony stood alone with Connecticut at the end of a spectrum of possible relationships under the transatlantic constitution. The past decades had altered the relationship for most other colonies, but not for Rhode Island. For other colonies, the boundaries of the transatlantic constitution would be fought over through the review process. Without a review requirement, it was left unanswered how the crown could supervise Rhode Island's compliance with the laws of England and the charter.[11]

Strategies of Statutory Accommodation

At the end of the century, a new reorganization of crown advisors brought renewed pressure to convert the corporate colony charters to royal charters. In February 1697 the attorney general was asked to inspect the charters of Connecticut and Rhode Island. In addition, the new 1696 navigation act focused transatlantic disputes. The act merged questions about the laws of England and the charter with internal disagreements over which Rhode Islanders would wield power. Under the charter, the crown had been given no role in internal colony appointments. After the act's passage, the Board of Trade sent new commissions for an admiralty judge (Peleg Sanford) and register (Nathaniel Coddington); required oaths of support from colony officials; and threatened charter revocation if Rhode Island failed to comply with the act. The elected Rhode Island officials, including the Quaker governor, Walter Clarke, resisted taking oaths and appointing the men. The crown-appointed Rhode Islanders scurried to tell England of the defiance. Peleg Sanford, the appointed admiralty judge, relayed to the Board of Trade that the governor had called the provisions a "violation and infringement of their Charter right and privileges." Within the year, the dispute endangered the charter.[12]

Rhode Islanders like Peleg Sanford and Francis Brinley wanted a new royal charter and therefore needed evidence that the colony was failing to follow the laws of England. During the Dominion they had been among those given royal appointments, and they remained loyal to a crown-appointed administration—perhaps each hoping to be the new royal governor. Sanford acquired the appointment to the admiralty court. Brinley wanted London aid for land litigation that was going badly in the colony courts. To promote forfeiture of the colony's charter, they attempted to help acquire copies of the colony's laws. In May 1698, Edmund Randolph suggested that the Board ask for "an authentic copy" to be made of all laws "now kept in loose papers." Sanford and Brinley, two men of "great estates," could be trusted to examine and compare the laws to ensure that the Rhode Islanders sent accurate laws. The following spring, Lord Bellomont, who had been sent to Rhode Island, was assured that he could ask Brinley and Sanford to assist. The hope was that the laws would confirm Rhode Island's "lawless government" and show "their ignorance in making, and their arbitrary execution."[13]

For others, copies of the laws served local purposes. Jahleel Brenton, a socially prominent legal literate (referred to as "Esqr.") and a descendant of one of the colony's first English settlers, lobbied for a printed statutory collection. Brenton was not averse to crown interests: he was Sanford's brother-in-law, the former collector of customs for New England, the carrier of the royal commissions to Rhode Island, and a coauthor of the critical report. Yet Brenton's interests also lay with the colony. In 1699 he would be employed as the colony's agent to England "to answer to what shall be objected against us." Brenton wanted the Rhode Island government "to print all such laws, as have been there made, and are now in force." While a collection would "much conduce to his Majesty's service," Brenton emphasized that it also would work to "the good of his subjects in the colony of Rhode Island." The laws "are so meanly kept, and in such blotted and defaced books (having never yet, any of them been printed), that few of his Majesty's subjects there are at present able to know what they are." Brenton's suggestion would aid crown officials, but it would also display the colony's authority and facilitate local accessibility to the laws.[14]

The threat to the charter was sufficient that by late 1698 the Assembly decided to respond to the Board of Trade's request for copies of the laws. The Board continued to consider *quo warranto* proceedings against any colony that claimed a charter "intitling them to absolute government." In its response, the Rhode Island Assembly aimed for sufficient compliance to avoid revocation while preserving, even declaring, the colony's continued self-governance. Through three strategies—convening a committee, controlling the form in which the laws were sent to England, and keeping command of the conversation about the transatlantic relationship—the Assembly mitigated much of the potential danger to the charter from publishing the laws. For two decades, the Assembly would use these strategies to successfully organize and eventually print the laws.[15]

The first strategy was to use committees to delay in hopes that passing time would alter English politics in favor of the colony. Although the Board had asked for a copy in the spring of 1698, it was not until December 1699 that a final copy was prepared for London officials. The state of the records admittedly caused some difficulties. Governor Cranston pointed out, "our law and Acts [are] of many years standing, and in several books and schedules." Much of the delay, however, was deliberate. In May 1698 a committee was initially appointed "to inspect into our body of laws." In August the committee was reformed. By October, delay was blamed on the "remoteness of the persons so appointed, and the difficultness of their coming together." A third, smaller committee was appointed to "make what expedition they can for the perfecting what is needful in said laws." Yet by the following spring no copy had been prepared. Only in May 1699, when a crown representative appeared, did an even smaller committee (likely the recorder and governor) complete the task. Nevertheless, another committee had to be appointed in October to search the records, as some "laws omitted" might be added and other laws "might be proper to be repealed." At last, in December the transcript was confirmed and sent to London. Crown observers were not fooled. Bellomont remarked that "the world never saw such a parcel of fustian" and the government had taken "all this time" to "prune and polish 'em." Accommodation, however, had served its purpose. Committee delay had left authority in the colony and charter for two years.[16]

The second strategy of accommodation was to control the form in which the colony's laws were sent to England. Crown officials wanted an exact copy of all existing laws; Rhode Island officials instead prepared an abstract. English officials, as well as Sanford and Brinley, thought that the instructions were clear that the Assembly should prepare an authentic copy of the laws. Repeatedly, crown officials employed similar phrases: "authentic copies of all the acts or laws"; a "perfect copy of all your laws, in authentic form"; a "fair transcript of all the said laws." The Board expected a book of the colony's session laws, arranged by date, with no additions or subtractions. The Assembly, however, sent a "true abstract": a "stitched together" volume without an official seal. The Board complained that "whatever is meant by" "true abstract," it was "very different from a true copy." The production of such an inaccurate and unreliable composition could only be "negligence"—perhaps even, the Board seemed to imply, willful negligence.[17]

The abstract reflected the colony's statutory practices influenced by early seventeenth-century transatlantic legal culture. Each individual statute was an abstract rather than a carefully delineated set of precise words. As Sidney Rider notes, the Assembly acted "only upon measures in the forms of 'abstracts,' but seldom or never in the forms of statutes fully drawn." The act abstracts then were given to the Recorder "to be written out . . . at his convenience and in his own way." This practice meant that over time the specific language of the statutes could be silently revised without requiring repeal of the statute. Similarly, the entire body of laws was a coherent code—a "Body of Laws"—not a set of sequential acts, repeals, and amendments. Repeatedly in instructions there appears the word *compose,* which denoted rewriting into a certain form. Each revisal committee or reviser was to put the laws into a "better form." They were to mark any laws that were "defective, or any way jarring" (1654); address "inconsistent" laws (1664); compose the laws, "[leaving] out what may be superfluous, and [adding] what may appear unto him necessary" (1666); and engage in "extracting and composing" (1686). As the Assembly told the 1686 committee, it was to have the laws "composed, extracted, altered, amended, and drawn up into a better method and form."[18]

In preferring a code, the Assembly followed a practice of statutory arrangement popular in the colonies with attorneys and assemblies. Into the 1690s, manuscript and printed colonial editions arranged statutory materials in code form either by subject or alphabetically without regard to date. Like contemporary English publications, early Massachusetts statutory collections were the "Body of Liberties" (1641) and *An Abstract of Laws and Government* (1655). In fact, until the 1660s all early colonial manuscript and printed collections were arranged by alphabet or subject. The early printed Massachusetts laws appeared as a code "collected out of the records," and the 1665 New York manuscript transcription ("The Duke of York's Laws") similarly appeared with the laws "collected out of the several laws now in force" and "digested into one volume." Alphabetical or subject matter arrangement made it easy to find the laws. Moreover, the structure made it simple to alter laws without evidence of alteration. For example, Connecticut's 1673 code publication announced that the laws were "lately revised, and with some Emendations and Additions." The alphabetical arrangement and absence of dates made pinpointing any change impossible. Most importantly, the code made compliance with the requirements of the transatlantic constitution simpler. The Connecticut preface noted that, "although we may vary, or differ, yet it is not our Purpose to Repugn the Statute Laws of England, so far as we understand them, professing ourselves always ready and willing to receive Light for emendation or alteration as we may have opportunity." The code form preserved the legislative ability to make alterations if crown officials complained.[19]

Although Massachusetts began to print session laws in the 1660s, colonial statutory compilations shifted definitively toward chronological session law publications only as the requirements of the transatlantic constitution changed in the mid-1690s. English statutory publication itself shifted over the seventeenth century. Whereas the second part of Coke's *Institutes* had not listed all English statutes and had not bothered to arrange them in strict chronological order, by the end of the century the reign of William and Mary brought increased availability of session laws. Colonists knew well these publications. Rhode Islander Jahleel Brenton owned *An Abridgment of the Statutes,* but also Keble's *Statutes at Large* (a post-1676 publication arranged chronologically) and four bound volumes of session laws from the first year of William and Mary to 1696. The new review provisions encouraged, indeed required, sessional publications. If London officials were to review the laws as they were enacted, it made sense to arrange and send the laws in groups by session. In fact, review gave the colonial assemblies an incentive to disaggregate laws and to move away from an abstract approach to laws. If a law was likely to be disallowed, a slightly differently worded version could be enacted and remain technically valid. Similarly, if certain acts were invalid, the remaining bulk of the laws remained in force. A sessional approach served both London and colonial interests.[20]

Because Rhode Island was not bound by a review provision, the Assembly clung to the code to preserve flexibility and avoid crown scrutiny. The laws prepared in 1698 and 1699 for England retained code formats. The 1698 "body of laws" contained "abbreviate[d]" laws. The list of laws added in 1699 was referred to by the Assembly as a "true list" and "deemed . . . the whole body of laws to be observed." The result once again was a code. The Board complained bitterly: there were "blots," "blanks," "the want of sense in some expressions," the "want of titles to the different Acts," and an overall "disorderly placing" of some acts by putting later dates before the former. Brinley and Sanford wrote that the laws had not been transcribed "as they stand on record" and one-third had been deleted. On others, the committees had "put a wrong date to those Acts they have sent to his Majesty, to make them more authentic." Brinley even argued that a code had "no legal foundation." Only "law making Assemblys" could pass laws and Assembly "confirmation" could not make laws "according to a maxim in the law of England." The code approach, however, continued to protect the charter.[21]

As a final strategy, Rhode Island officials kept command of the conversation between the crown and the colony by emphasizing both repugnancy and divergence provisions of the charter and the transatlantic constitution. The Board of Trade initially took a broad approach to repugnancy in investigating both colony laws and practices. Bellomont was to "compare the methods and rules established by" the Rhode Islanders with "the laws of this our kingdom of England." Had they observed or breached any of "the acts of Parliament" which had "any relation to our Plantations in America"? Had they "deviated from and gone contrary to the rules" in the charter or had "usurped and exercised" its authority? The Board did not remind Bellomont of the legitimacy of divergence. The Rhode Island Assembly, however, insisted that the crown follow the charter and the transatlantic constitution. In May 1699 the governor sent the laws to England but reminded the Board that the colony was "wholly ruled and governed by the good and wholesome [laws] of our Mother, the kingdom of England, as far as the constitution of our place will bear." If the laws of England were not strictly followed, it was not an intended repugnancy but was because "in these remote parts, we cannot in every punctillo follow the niceties of the laws of England." Most importantly, the governor pointed out that a refusal to permit divergences "will be a great damage to his Majesty's interest in the settling and peopling of the country." Rhode Island's authority to diverge, he argued, ensured the empire's growth.[22]

Another example of controlling the conversation involved the Assembly's passage in 1700 of an introduction statute that shifted to England the burden to prove that the colony did not comply with the laws of England. The new law stated that "where the laws of this colony or custom shall not reach or comprehend any matter, cause or causes," it "shall be lawful to put execution the laws of England, &c." Although legal historians have called this a "reception statute," contemporaries referred to English statutes being "introduced" through the statute, and *introduction statute* is a more historically accurate term. The very existence of the statute reaffirmed the colony's authority. Although the statute permitted the laws of England, nothing required them. The decision to follow the laws of England now was with the Rhode Island Assembly's permission, not under the mandate of the crown. The statute broadly included local laws and customs as the practices that took precedence over the laws of England. Lastly, Rhode Island practices governed if they either reached or comprehended the matter. The statute merely introduced the possibility that an English law could apply. Rhode Islanders would decide in individual cases whether there was a colonial custom or law, whether it reached the matter, and whether a law of England should be put into execution instead.[23]

The introduction act remained in manuscript for almost two decades, leaving additional flexibility in the Rhode Islanders. A 1701 report of the Assembly to the crown offered an interpretation that implied far greater compliance with the laws of England than the statute required. The report explained that "in all cases where the laws of the colony do not speciall[y] provide for, they do allow the laws of England to take place and be the rule both in civil and criminal cases to all intents of the same." The report suggested that only official colony acts explicitly addressing a subject displaced applicable laws of England. The Rhode Island Assembly remained nervous about the language of the introduction statute. In the printed 1719 statutes, the text was altered to limit colonial authority. In the original version, if the colony's laws or customs reached or comprehended the matter, the laws of England did not apply. In the printed version, this default position was reversed and made more strict. Unless a "particular law" of Rhode Island "decide[d] and determine[d]" the issue, the laws of England applied. Similarly, the permissive manuscript phrase—"it shall be lawful to put into execution"—was replaced by a mandatory command that the laws of England shall be put in force. The 1719 version interpreted the transatlantic constitution's requirement in favor of the laws of England.[24]

Printing the Laws

After 1701 the Rhode Island Assembly grew more confident about its authority under the charter and the transatlantic constitution as legislation to revoke the remaining nonroyal charters had once again failed. With the threat to the charter seemingly fading, the Assembly turned to solve the problems caused by the absence of a printed statutory compilation. In 1701 the Assembly noted "the great confusion and disorder of the laws of this Colony, for want of a due record of the same in a book." It passed a new act for "fitting the Colony's laws for the press." The committee contained those whose loyalties had lain with the colony (the governor, Cranston, and the recorder, Clarke) and those who had favored the crown (Nathaniel Coddington). In the summer of 1705, the transcription of the laws was "completed for the most part." A final committee was to "view over and perfect" them and, in return for printing, was given the profit.[25]

The manuscript revealed the shifting expectations for statutory publication. It was referred to as "Major Coddington's Abstract" and "Major Coddington's Transcript," presumably because Nathaniel Coddington did much of the work. As Sidney Rider noted, "it really partakes of the nature of both [a digest and a collection]." It contains the 1664–1666 composure, but later acts appear in chronological order. Acts passed in 1666–1699 betray the spotty record keeping: sometimes there are titles; sometimes there are none. After 1699, all acts are titled and arranged by date. Nonetheless, the committee continued to feel free to alter the precise language of the earlier composure. The two-witness requirement was changed to three. The first law—"that no person, in this Colony, shall be taken or imprisoned, or be disseised of his lands"—was shortened to "imprisoned or disseised." High treason and petit treason were reordered and subsumed within the criminal lists. Explanations of laws were dropped. Some changes were superficial or nonsubstantive; others reflected efforts to accommodate the laws of England.[26]

Yet even as the abstract was nearing completion, new charges were being raised that the colony was ignoring the laws of England. In August 1705 the colony's officials repeated to the crown their understanding of the transatlantic constitution:

> [in Rhode Island] they do allow the laws of England to be pleaded in all cases, without partiality (as well for strangers as for serving their own turns) where their own laws do not extend to, and that the various circumstances of time and place and people do often make it necessary to enact and establish laws different (though not repugnant) to the laws of England, and say that their charter expressly empowers them so to do.

As late as May 1706 the Assembly continued to express hope that the laws would be printed, but events were making a printed publication too dangerous. Not only was there a new bill to vacate the Rhode Island and Connecticut charters, but the crown investigator, Lord Cornbury, was relying on Connecticut's printed statutes to prove misfeasance. Cornbury wrote that Connecticut would not "allow the laws of England to be pleaded in their courts otherwise than as it may serve a turn for themselves." He added, "To prove this, I must refer your Lordships to the first law in their book, page the first, marked in the margin (general privileges of the inhabitants)." Citing page after page, Cornbury used the statute book to criticize Connecticut's policy on militia, maritime affairs, religious discrimination, oaths, and divorce. Indeed, Cornbury pointed out that "the first law in their book, abrogates all the laws of England at once." Emphasizing the danger posed by a book, Cornbury added he could make other observations, but "since I send the book, I am satisfied you will make much better observations upon them than I am capable of doing." With the printed statutes in the Privy Council's hands, there was little colony officials could do. With such collections likely to jeopardize the charter, Rhode Island refrained from printing the 1705 abstract. For the next decade, Rhode Island retreated to a form of publication that controlled access and availability: to publish the acts in manuscript and by reading them in public, not by the printing press.[27]

At last, in 1714, crown officials began to signal a willingness to respect the remaining nonroyal charter governments. In an opinion on a Pennsylvania matter, Attorney General Edward Northey wrote that the proprietors "have a right vested in them of the power of making laws granted by their charter, and are not, nor can now, be put under any other restraint or regulation" except by act of Parliament. This recognition extended to corporation charter colonies. Northey added that "there is not any obligation by charter to return the laws made in the proprietary plantations of Connecticut and Rhode Island for Her Majesty's approbation." He concluded that an act of Parliament would be needed to "oblige them to transmit their laws, and to have them submitted to Her Majesty's approbation." Although Northey's opinion did not end the possibility of charter revocation or of parliamentary alteration, the broad language and acceptance of no review signaled a willingness to respect the existing dual authority structure.[28]

In 1715, freed from the threat of forced submission of the laws, the Assembly returned to the subject of printing its laws. The passage of time had made matters worse for residents. The "body of laws" as well as "those other laws, which have been made since the said body of laws, lie in a very disordered condition, and only in the hands of some few persons." The cost of paying a clerk to copy a law had become a concern as well. The Assembly pointed out that most of the inhabitants "cannot purchase them without great charge." Two years later, the Assembly explained that, because of the state of the laws, the majority were "not in a capacity to know the laws that are extant." In response, the Assembly appointed a new committee to "transcribe, fit and prepare for the press, all the laws contained in the aforesaid body of laws and also, all other laws now in force in this colony." This effort still remained somewhat close to a code revision. The committee could "improve," "revise, correct, transcribe" the laws, and the Assembly was to confirm them. The venture was slow, and subsequent committees were appointed in 1716 and 1717. By June 1718, either the committee system was abandoned or the revising effort was completed. The recorder, Richard Ward, who had his own collection of law books, became in charge of transcribing and fitting "the laws for the press, with marginal notes." The governor and the clerk, Thomas Frye, were to look them over and Frye was to have them printed.[29]

In printing the laws, Rhode Island officials continued to control the conversation about the transatlantic constitution. In May 1719 the eighty law books were returned from Boston printer John Allen with an important addition. By Assembly order, each volume began with a copy of the charter declaring the colony's lawmaking authority. The largest words on the title page of the charter were CHARTER and COLONY. Only in smaller typeface did the words *Granted by His Majesty King* CHARLES appear. Similarly, on the title page of the statutes, the only reference to the crown was *Of his Majesties* in extraordinarily small print. The remaining words—ACTS, LAWS, COLONY, AMERICA—boldly proclaimed Rhode Island's authority. The act of printing had become a path to display, not lose, authority. Although any copy sent to London would include the charter, the Assembly seems to have taken steps to reduce the likelihood of any copies reaching London. Every copy was explicitly distributed to either an Assembly member or the nine towns. A crown agent would have to obtain a copy from a colonist. Nearly eighty years after its founding, Rhode Island had a printed statute collection.[30]

Critics continued to complain in London about the colony's authority and laws. In September 1719, Caleb Heathcote, the surveyor general of customs, wrote the Commissioners for Trade and Plantations about "that unlimited power, the charter governments lay claim to, of making laws." According to Heathcote, this power had led Rhode Island to pass laws "repugnant" to the laws of Great Britain and the charter. Moreover, they "wholly neglected" sending "home their laws." Heathcote complained that the crown's inaction had strengthened the governments by confirming "that absurd notion of their laws being sufficient in themselves; and to have no need of the royal assent." Heathcote predicted that these governments "are daily growing very numerous and powerful, so a neglect therein, may with time, be attended with very ill consequences." The strategies that Rhode Island officials had employed for more than half a century in avoiding crown review of laws had resulted in a far stronger belief, both in Rhode Island and in England, in the colony's governing authority.[31]

Nevertheless, the Assembly remained wary and continued to protect the charter. Complaints about the 1719 *Acts and Laws* were taken seriously. Immediately after the publication, the Assembly appointed a new committee to "correct the errors of the press, committed in printing the laws of this colony, and to get them printed." By offering to alter "errors," the Assembly absorbed disagreements internally and thereby discouraged complaints to London. The primary complaint involved a significant divergence from the laws of England in intestate inheritance. The printed intestate act distributed the estate to all children equally, save a double share to the eldest son. Interestingly, although the entire approach diverged from English primogeniture, the criticism focused on the act's application to estates in fee tail. Under fee tail, the entire land went to the eldest child in each generation. Because entailed land in essence passed intestate, the equal distribution seemed repugnant to English fee tail law. The Assembly acted quickly to retain its divergent law of equal division and avoid the complaint of repugnancy. It printed an "act in explanation" of the laws. The explanatory act stated that the act was not to be "taken, deemed, or construed" to divide any estate tail where the tenant in tail died intestate but that the estate shall "enure according to the laws of England." In short, the act stated that entailed lands would not be divided under the intestate act. With the explicit complaint resolved through legislative explanation instead of repeal, the Assembly maintained the far more radical abandonment of primogeniture in all other intestate cases.[32]

The colony's preference for divergences such as equal division in intestate continued to cause problems. In February 1728, Connecticut's similar intestacy law was disallowed by the Privy Council. The disallowance triggered a request for Connecticut's entire body of statute laws. In June 1728, shortly after news of the repeal must have arrived in the colony, the Rhode Island Assembly convened a new committee to print a new version of the laws. The committee contained four of the most prominent legal practitioners in the colony: Richard Ward (transcriber of the 1719 edition and recorder), Daniel Updike (the general attorney), Henry Bull (speaker), and Nathanial Newdigate (attorney). In the resulting revisal, twenty-one acts were repealed and abrogated. Some of these acts (such as the criminal provisions) were replaced with new statutes; the intestate act and others disappeared altogether. Noting simply that the intestate act destroyed inheritances, it was repealed prospectively; previous estates would be distributed under the old intestate procedures. The Assembly was wary of replacing the act, and the 1730 edition of *Acts and Laws* included no new intestate law. Although a marginal note signaled the old act's deletion, the printed book gave no guidance as to whether the colony followed English primogeniture or Rhode Island's prior practice of equal division. Whatever the towns did in probating intestate estates, no overt evidence proved that the colony's intestate laws were repugnant to the laws of England.[33]

The Assembly's actions were well advised. In the summer of 1731 the Board of Trade sought copies of law books from Rhode Island and Connecticut. Connecticut sent its 1715 and 1731 printed law books; the Rhode Island governor did not send any volume. The Connecticut volume and subsequent session laws were forwarded to Francis Fane, the Board of Trade's legal advisor, to advise on which acts were "repugnant to the laws of this Kingdom." Fane reviewed the laws according to the boundaries of the transatlantic constitution, considering whether the laws were repugnant to the laws of England. A great number of the laws were found "reasonable" and "agreeable" or not "contrary to the law of England." With respect to other laws, particularly criminal laws, Fane found a number of acts to be too general, too uncertain of application, or too severe. With respect to certain laws that diverged, Fane considered local circumstances. Regarding a law that gave a town a right of first refusal in house sales, Fane noted that the act "would be very extraordinary in England but whether it may not be proper in a country where they are encompassed with enemies is humbly submitted to your Lordship's consideration." With respect to Connecticut's intestate act, Fane suggested that it should be repealed as the "rules [were] very different from the laws of England." Nevertheless, he did not exclude the possibility of divergence. A new intestacy law could be "either as is now done in England, or by such other methods as may best fit the province where this law is to take effect." Not only were his conclusions balanced, but his review suggested little desire for immediate revocation. In 1733 he submitted his first review on the 1702 laws; nine years later, in 1741, he had reviewed the laws only to 1721. According to the report's modern editor, Charles M. Andrews, the reports were never presented officially and had no overt legal impact. Once again, the corporate chartered colonies had survived review efforts.[34]

For more than a century, the charter's wording and approach to the transatlantic constitution bound and bolstered colonial lawmaking authority. The explicit absence of a review provision in the Rhode Island charter had not left the colony free to pass any and all laws, nor did the Assembly take the opportunity to pass whatever laws it wanted. The Assembly and attorneys worked to revise the laws to sufficiently accommodate the laws of England while also asserting the right to pass divergent laws for local conditions. The long refusal to print the laws had internal costs. As the witness requirements and intestate act revealed, Rhode Island's printed laws were misleading. Moreover, the Assembly remained concerned with crown review and for decades would revise its laws with one eye toward English objections.

Yet English interest in Rhode Island's statutes was quickly becoming informational rather than investigatory. In the 1730s, Ferdinando John Paris, an English solicitor with an extensive transatlantic practice, owned or had access to law books and laws for Connecticut, Massachusetts, New York, Pennsylvania, Rhode Island, New Hampshire, New York, New Jersey, Maryland, Virginia, and the Bermudas. By then, the major route for disputes over Rhode Island laws was becoming private litigants' appeals to the Privy Council. Embedded in the facts of particular cases, critiques of Rhode Island's laws became piecemeal and non-threatening. In the 1750s, while acknowledging that charter governments did not have to transmit laws, the Board of Trade suggested that copies should be sent to assist in appeals to the Privy Council. With the turn to the appeal, litigants, judges, attorneys, assemblies, and the Privy Council would share interpretations of the transatlantic constitution.[35]

II

Transatlantic Legal Practice

4

The Transatlantic Appeal

Rhode Island successfully avoided mandatory Privy Council review of its statutes, but it reluctantly accepted that private cases, particularly those involving large land claims, could be appealed to the Privy Council. These appeals became the sole method to debate repugnancies to and divergences from the laws of England. The appeal developed with the same tensions over dual authorities that affected the publication of statutes. The particular characteristics of the appeal, however, were the outcome of negotiations among the Assembly, the Privy Council, and private litigants. Early appeals to the Privy Council undermined the Rhode Island Assembly's practice of hearing appeals as an equity court, and the Assembly sought to accommodate both procedures. More than statute review, the Privy Council appeal came to serve the particular interests of private litigants and attorneys. Indeed, several Rhode Island attorneys bore individual responsibility for the appeal's institutionalization. By the late 1720s, the typical appeal involved the relationship of the laws of Rhode Island to the laws of England. Although during these years the Assembly began to permit appeals to the Privy Council, it never wholly embraced them and it persisted in its efforts to limit or burden the process to maintain local authority.

Rhode Island's 1663 charter contained no explicit mechanism for challenging laws and practices repugnant to English law. No provision required crown review of legislation, and the only reference to appeals involved "public controversy," such as boundary disputes between

Rhode Island and the other New England colonies. Nonetheless, initially some litigants attempted to seek redress from the crown through petitions, often referred to the attorney general. These early efforts involved disputes arising from the original division of the colony pursuant to royal patents, charters, or acquisitions from native tribes. The desire for crown oversight arose from the crown's original grant, the understandable bias of the colony's appointed judges, and the significant public nature of the disputes. In the late 1670s, William Harris and his associates complained to the crown about litigation related to the Providence–Pawtuxet boundary. Other petitions were brought regarding disputes over land on Hog Island and in the Narragansett region of the colony arising from grants to the Council of Plymouth. These early petitions, however, were dealt with in a case-by-case manner by the crown.[1]

By 1690 the crown began to formalize the appeal process as part of its larger effort to centralize and strengthen authority over the colonies' lawmaking activities. Under new charters or instructions, New Hampshire, Pennsylvania, Virginia, and New York were required to permit appeals. In 1691 the new Massachusetts charter created an appeal to the crown limited to personal actions. In England, the appeal procedure became formalized. In 1696 the Lords Commissioners for Trade and Plantations, or Board of Trade, was reorganized. A committee of at least three members of the Privy Council was designated to hear colonial appeals. This new Committee for Hearing Appeals from the Plantations was to report an opinion to the entire Council, which would vote to approve. The decision thus was technically issued as an order of the King or Queen in Council. The new structure initially had little impact on Rhode Island practice. In 1698 the Committee heard one appeal from a Rhode Island court verdict in a case regarding title on Prudence Island. It referred the case to the attorney general to "inspect the charter" and report what could be done "for the petitioner's relief." No record appears of any action. At the end of the century, the appeal remained largely a theoretical remedy.[2]

Among the first in Rhode Island to attempt to use the new procedures were attorneys and legal literates with crown connections. Jahleel Brenton learned of the appeals process while serving as the colony's agent in England. His father served as governor of the colony, and the family possessed large landholdings. As a young man, Brenton became interested in law, particularly in the debate over the application of the laws of England to the colony. In 1678 Brenton joined with several others, including the governor and Francis Brinley, to urge the appointment of bankruptcy commissioners for the estate of one George Brown, pursuant to a month-old colony law establishing new bankruptcy procedures according to the "statutes of Queen Elizabeth and King James." Even at twenty-three, Brenton was well aware of the transatlantic constitution.[3]

Several decades later, Brenton had acquired a significant collection of English law books. When he sailed for England in the summer of 1698, he carefully listed his "Law Books left at Boston in Great Trunk in Porch Chamber." The thirty-six volumes were mostly contemporary publications and a notable collection of statutes. Four or five volumes were originally written before the English Civil War; fifteen postdated the Restoration of Charles II; a dozen were less than twenty years old. This collection provided the latest on the laws of England. The *Statutes at Large, Abridgment of the Statutes,* and four books of session laws covering the years 1689 to 1696 gave a working knowledge of the statutes in force in England. Other books provided the basic understanding of the laws of England: Cowell and Rastell on vocabulary; Coke on the statutes, criminal law, and institutions; Wingate on the maxims of the common law. The books covered important subject areas (property, landlord-tenant, minors and executors, contract, and slander), legal officers (Keeble on justices of the peace, Dalton on sheriffs, Meriton on constables), and attorneys (*Compleat Attorney* and the *Practical Register*). Brenton even had the recently available case reports by Coke, Croke, and Vaughan. The collection also addressed the application of these laws in Rhode Island. Several books on recent charter struggles and oaths in England offered information on the laws of England affecting local Rhode Island disputes. Brenton had a wealth of knowledge about the laws of England.[4]

By 1700, Brenton had served both crown and colony and was known to the Board of Trade. Throughout, he played his own game, seeking personal advantage from the transatlantic structure. In 1690 he had displaced Edward Randolph as collector of customs for New England but then ended up in a public fight with the new royal governor of Massachusetts, William Phips, over Brenton's seizure of vessels. In 1698 he journeyed again to London and eventually gained an appointment as the colony's agent. The trip's central purpose, however, was to prosecute two appeals lost in Massachusetts in 1692 while he was customs collector.

Brenton hoped to be reimbursed for his expenses, and his careful records provide an excellent glimpse at the difficulties inherent in managing appeals.[5]

As Brenton's travails reveal, a Privy Council appeal took time. Getting a case heard and decided in England was not an easy process. The appellant had to obtain a Council order agreeing to hear the appeal and then referring it to the Committee for Hearing Appeals from the Plantations. Once the case was argued before the Committee, the appellant had to wait for a report to the Privy Council, which then had to vote on the report and issue the actual order (usually replicating the Committee report). This lengthy process could be prolonged due to difficulties obtaining appropriate papers, briefs, and reports, as well as by delays of the parties or the Committee. Apparently Brenton had previously filed the appeals. On this trip, he first hired a coach in September 1698 to take him to the Council's offices to inquire about his appeal. In June 1699 the case had still not been heard for the first time. Not until mid-July 1700 did Brenton obtain his disappointing Council order.[6]

The appeals process was also financially expensive. Because he was in England, Brenton did not have to employ an agent to make arrangements for the necessary personnel. But he did have to hire a solicitor to prepare the case and write the briefs, as well as a crown law officer to argue it before the Committee. For a solicitor, Brenton chose a Mr. Wharton—presumably William Wharton, a man whose family had land claims in New England and whom Brenton probably knew personally. To argue the appeal, the attorney general (Sir Thomas Trevor) and the solicitor general (John Hawles) were retained. The two men had written an earlier report favoring the appeals. These officers were expensive and had to be paid for multiple appearances when the case was continued. In addition, Brenton had to obtain handwritten copies of various documents for the lawyers and Committee, a process that entailed frequent visits to Whitehall. Each trip required a coach, and Brenton was careful to keep track of all his transportation costs. He had to pay others: the secretary of the Board of Trade (William Popple), the Doorkeeper of the Council, and various clerks and other personnel. Indeed, at one point Brenton even had to pay for someone's wig.[7]

Brenton lost the appeals but had come to understand the advantage of the remedy. Within a year, he had begun to ponder whether the appeals procedure could help him resolve other problems. In September 1701,

Brenton again hired the solicitor general, John Hawles, for his opinion in "cases of Rhode Island about my nephews and about Rhode Island Commons" as well as a "case of R. M." The first cases referred to the large landholdings that Jahleel Brenton and other descendants of William Brenton held in undivided shares as tenants in common. This land would become the subject of a number of future appeals to the Privy Council, including two against Brenton by his great-niece and great-nephew. The case of "R. M." may have referred to the case of the Remington mortgage or redemption of mortgage, the subject of an appeal involving Brenton that was the first successful private appeal to the Privy Council from Rhode Island. Appeal to the Council would become a favorite remedy for Brenton and others in his family.[8]

Conflict over the Appeal

The Assembly was able to postpone appeals to the Privy Council for almost a decade. The crown and the Assembly both cared about the appeal because it ultimately represented authority, both real and symbolic. Appealing depended on a hierarchy of authorities, and the appeal process reflected the relationship of the Assembly to the crown. Since 1680 the Rhode Island Assembly—like the assemblies in Connecticut and Massachusetts—had claimed authority under its charter to hear equitable appeals from colony courts. An appeal to the Privy Council undercut and diminished this authority. The Assembly was anxious to preserve this authority while avoiding any action that could threaten its charter. In the spring of 1700, after complaints from Francis Brinley, who wanted to appeal from the colony, the Board of Trade informed the colony that "it is the Inherent Right of his Majesty to Receive and Determine Appeals" from the colonies. With matters of "inherent right," there was little room for argument—but the Assembly took what little there was. The following year, the Assembly gave a cursory nod to the crown appeal while insisting on its own retained authority. It declared that it gave a "definitive Sentence . . . in all personal actions: except where there shall be Appeals to his Majesty in Council in England." The statement was optimistic with respect to crown appeals. There were none. An appeal by William Harris's son over Pawtucket land was dismissed by the Council. An appeal by Thomas Newton over the title to Hog Island ended up tried in a neighboring colony. The colony successfully blocked an effort by the

Atherton Company, an English and Massachusetts landholding group with claims over the Narragansett region of the colony, by requiring "a rehearing to another court before the appeal be granted." To ensure that only a few would appeal, in 1706 the Assembly increased the burden on would-be appellants by requiring a bond before an appeal could be prosecuted.[9]

In place of a crown appeal, over the next several years the Assembly heard appeals, sitting in essence as an equity court. If a party was "grieved" with the judgment in the General Court of Trials, a rehearing with "new evidences" and a new jury could be obtained. If the litigant was still grieved, an appeal could be taken to the Assembly. The Assembly would hear the plea on both sides with "all their papers and writing." After "some debate," the Assembly would decide the case. As in English equity practice, evidence was given in writing. Equitable claims and remedies were also apparent. In 1702 Stephen Arnold appealed to the Assembly in a case involving claims of a fraudulent deed, a typical equity case. The remedy was the equitable remedy of restitution: Arnold was to give Rhodes a quitclaim deed so that Rhodes "may be in the same capacity he was in before." In 1703 the Assembly heard the appeal of James Bick on behalf of his new wife, Elizabeth Bick, in a traditional area of equitable jurisdiction, the administration of estates. The Assembly adopted a broad approach to fact-finding and, "finding a paragraph" in the will, concluded that it needed more information about funds spent for improvements. The Assembly used its remedial powers with respect to judgments and costs. Andrew Barton's judgment of more than seven pounds was reduced to six pounds. Although Peter Marshall, the co-signer of a bond with Jonathan Barney, had been held individually liable, the Assembly declared that Marshall, Barney, and another man were to bear their own costs for the lower court cases. By hearing appeals, the Assembly appeared as the supreme equitable authority in the colony.[10]

This Assembly authority challenged crown authority. Between 1690 and 1720, the crown and the colonies fought over the right to hear equitable appeals. In England, equity was part of the royal prerogative. The presence or absence of the crown appeal represented the power of the prerogative. With respect to the colonies, the problem was whether equitable authority remained in the crown (in the person of a crown appointee, such as a royal governor or chancellor) or whether it had been delegated in the charter to the highest colonial authority (the elected legislature). Not only did appearance matter, but a crown appointee and legislature would decide certain cases differently—particularly ones involving controversial aspects of the laws of England. By the 1690s, crown officials decisively began to promote a colonial model that placed equitable power in a royal appointee. In southern royal colonies like Maryland, Virginia, and Carolina, the governor sat either with the council as the court of equity or alone as a chancellor. In new royal colonies like Massachusetts and New Hampshire, the crown ended the practice of the assembly sitting as an equity court. The change was not without a fight. The Massachusetts legislature attempted to maintain its equitable authority after the 1691 charter by creating and appointing judges to a new equity court. The crown quickly disallowed the court, noting that "only the crown could establish a court of chancery in the province, it being an exercise of the king's prerogative." In 1704 an opinion by the English attorney general Edward Northey confirmed the matter: the crown could establish a Court of Equity in the province but the Assembly could not. For colonies with royal charters the matter was closed; equity was solely a matter of royal prerogative.[11]

Nonroyal colonies remained more difficult for the crown. In theory, the crown's prerogative powers seemed to have been delegated to the Assembly in the charter. The legislature should then have been permitted to create an equity court. The idea, however, conflicted with the requirement that laws not be repugnant to the laws of England. Given that under the laws of England, equity was a prerogative function, legislative equity courts seemed an anomaly. Charters therefore did not stop the crown from trying to end legislative equity power. In 1701 the Pennsylvania legislature gave equity powers to courts that were to be appointed by it; in 1705 crown officials disallowed the legislation. Neither side could completely convince the other, and the cycle of enactment and disallowance continued for decades.[12]

Disallowance was not an option with respect to the Rhode Island Assembly's equitable practice. Contemporaneously with moves against Assembly practice in Pennsylvania and Massachusetts, other means were sought to accomplish the change in Rhode Island. In 1705 a petition was brought to the Assembly itself suggesting that a court of chancery would be a "great benefit" and implying that the colony was not in compliance with English law. The theory was apparently that any court of chancery had to be a prerogative court. The Assembly acknowledged that the "rules and constitutions" for establishing such a court were of "great weight and concernment." In fact, it concluded, they were of such import that they could not be dealt with at the present. Cleverly postponing any actual dispute over the practice and avoiding even the appearance of explicit authorization, the Assembly concluded that until a "more proper" court of chancery could be "erected and settled," the General Assembly would "be continued a Court of Chancery." As with the contemporaneous struggles over printing the laws, the Assembly avoided a confrontation with the crown at a time when absolute insistence threatened the charter and nonetheless maintained its practice of sitting as a court of equity.[13]

After 1705, perhaps to reduce the power of such petitions within the colony, the Assembly began to behave more explicitly like a court of chancery. When it heard a case, it first "settled a Court of Chancery or Equity." Because the Assembly used both rubrics—*chancery* and *equity*—it blurred the distinction between a court that would provide people with a recourse to equity and one that existed due to prerogative chancery authority delegated within the charter. As a formal matter, the Assembly "resolv[ed] into a committee to hear appeals." This committee of the entire thirty-nine or so deputies, assistants, and governor "maturely" weighed and considered the pleas "with the circumstances and equity of the whole case." Substantively, the Assembly continued to review areas of equitable jurisdiction. In 1706 the Assembly ordered the performance of a will in the appeal of Sarah Carr. In 1709 the Assembly "heard the whole matter and the true circumstances" of William Marsh's appeal from two judgments against him as executor of his father's estate. The Assembly adopted the vocabulary of chancery. When John King appealed from an action of trespass and ejectment, the Assembly concluded that the verdict against him was "good" but decided to "chancerize the charges expended" on the land. Indeed, the Assembly's most common action as an equity court was to reduce, mitigate, or chancerize damages. The remedy proved popular, perhaps too popular. In 1708 the Assembly raised the fee to bring an appeal to three pounds, claiming that appeals had become "a great trouble and charge."[14]

Private petition had not worked to limit the Assembly's power, so a crown appeal was attempted. In 1708 the Assembly's equitable authority was decisively challenged in the first successful private-party appeal to the Privy Council from the colony. The case began as a typical fight over land and in-laws. Jahleel Brenton's father mortgaged 256 acres of land in

Jamestown to his son-in-law, Peleg Sanford. The mortgage was not redeemed for over twenty-five years, suggesting it may have been a gift. In 1674 Brenton's father died. Under the residuary clause of Brenton's father's will, any unaccounted-for land passed to Brenton; Brenton, however, did not sue. That same year Sanford's wife (Brenton's sister) died, and within a year Sanford remarried; eventually he had seven children with his second wife, Mary Coddington. Brenton still did not sue. In 1701 Sanford died, leaving the land to William Sanford, his youngest son by his second marriage. Brenton felt no connection to William, with whom he shared no bond of blood or marriage. In March 1708, Brenton sued the lessee of the land, Captain Stephen Remington.[15]

Brenton's claim was based on equitable redemption. Brenton argued that he should be permitted to redeem his father's mortgage despite the significant passage of time since the loan's due date (likely some thirty years). Equity of redemption was a relatively new development in chancery practice. Occasional chancery decisions had provided relief to mortgagors if they could prove that special hardship had prevented them from paying on time. Out of these developed the right of equitable redemption. Between 1660 and 1671, English chancery cases established a twenty-year equitable right of redemption. In the late 1690s, these cases were printed and became widely known. The idea spread to the colonies, and in 1698 Massachusetts authorized a right of equitable redemption in "An Act for Hearing and Determining of Cases in Equity."[16]

At first Brenton's case did not go well in Rhode Island. He may have handled the suit himself. Sanford, on the other hand, turned to his uncle, Nathaniel Coddington, to serve as attorney. The colony court rejected Brenton's claim, apparently concerned about the more than thirty years' delay in redemption. Brenton appealed to the Assembly "as a Court of Chancery" for relief. Describing contemporary English equity law, the Assembly noted that twenty years was the "time limited in the law for the redemption of mortgages." Nonetheless, it decided in favor of Brenton, for he had "produced several laws which doth plainly hold forth, that upon extraordinary occasion, the mortgagor shall have liberty to redeem a mortgage, notwithstanding the twenty years being past." Which laws these were and what Brenton claimed were the extraordinary facts of his case remain unknown. Brenton had momentarily regained the land.[17]

Brenton's victory was short-lived. Nathaniel Coddington and the

Sanfords successfully appealed to the Privy Council. The efforts of Coddington's uncle, Francis Brinley, had forced the colony to acknowledge a right of appeal. Coddington now made use of it to win both the land and a limit on the Assembly's practice. No records remain regarding the precise argument on appeal, but it likely challenged the Assembly's practice of sitting as a court of equity. Nine months after the Assembly had decided the case, the Privy Council sent back a terse order reversing the decision and declaring it "null and void." The "Court had no jurisdiction." As the Assembly noted, its proceedings had been "utterly condemned." Lacking authority to review directly and disallow the colony's law establishing the Assembly as a court of equity, the Council had taken advantage of the appeal to accomplish the same result.[18]

The Assembly was more unhappy with the outcome than Brenton was. He never again attempted to reclaim the lands. His descendant Benjamin Brenton unsuccessfully resurrected the suit in 1745. The Assembly responded immediately. Obeying the Council's order, the Assembly voided the old act authorizing its appellate equitable jurisdiction and dismissed all appeals. It acknowledged that a legislative body sitting as a court of chancery diverged from the laws of England. Equity came from "executive power or authority," and the Assembly could not "find any precedent that the legislators or Parliament of Great Britain" had ever constituted themselves a "Court of Chancery." The Assembly, however, emphasized the transatlantic constitution. The only requirement "according to the constitution" of the colony was that any courts "be not repugnant, but as near as may be agreeable to the laws of England." Under the charter, the Assembly could "erect, set up and establish a regular Court of Chancery" so long as it followed "the methods and precedents of Great Britain." Until such a court of chancery could be established, the Assembly would continue to hear by petition any matter "cognizable before them." The Assembly had once again reconstituted itself as a court of equity.[19]

The Assembly managed to get away with only rhetorically abolishing its equitable practice by pragmatic calculation. It relinquished exclusive control over cases "respecting title of land" and permitted these cases to be appealed to the Privy Council. Thus, in 1712 it granted the petition of Captain Samuel Greene as attorney to John Knight to appeal to Great Britain in a case "concerning lands." In a local world centered on real property, the Assembly ceded the cases most likely to affect the rich, powerful, and politically connected constituents. In a transatlantic world formed around an English empire defined by property practices, the Assembly gave up the cases over which the Privy Council had the greatest interest. By conceding a small area of jurisdiction, the Assembly reinforced its interpretation of the charter and preserved much of its equitable authority. Moreover, the Assembly did not advertise the availability of an appeal to the Privy Council. *Acts and Laws* (1719) included no reference to appeals to the Privy Council, and the index entry on appeals referred only to appeals to the Assembly. Outside of legal circles, most Rhode Islanders likely considered the Assembly the supreme authority.[20]

Long into the eighteenth century, the Assembly heard equitable appeals in financial matters and debt actions, chancerized damage awards and bonds, and acted as a chancery court in other matters. Throughout, these appeals were heard without reference to the title of the land. Between 1725 and 1751, the Assembly reconvened as a grand committee to hear twenty to thirty appeals a year. Parties wrote their "reasons for appeal," filed the record of the evidence and lower court decisions, and had their attorneys appear and argue before the Assembly. The appeal was sufficiently popular that the Assembly attempted to delegate its authority in 1741 to a committee, a five-man "Court of Equity." The court was to hear appeals in personal actions and give determinations "agreeable to Law and Equity" "in as full and extensive manner as the General Assembly hath been accustomed to do." The Court, however, could not handle the rapidly expanding case load. In 1744 the Assembly abolished the Court and adopted measures to make the lower courts more attractive and to avoid the submission of petitions that had "no other design than to retard and perplex the affair." A new remedy, the writ of review, permitted a new court trial with new evidence to avoid any "failures of justice." In 1747 a new "Superior Court of Judicature, Court of Assize, and General Goal Delivery," composed of five men annually elected by the General Assembly, was instructed to follow the "rules of equity" and enter judgments "as justice and equity requires" in certain cases. The Superior Court came to hear much of the Assembly's prior caseload. Nonetheless, as a 1756 petition to the Assembly noted, when "unjust Advantages are taken by parties and the common law cannot relieve," relief remained available if "the General Assembly is pleased to assist." The Assembly had successfully remained in many respects the supreme equitable authority.[21]

Private Appeals

Although the Assembly was loath to encourage the appeals to the Privy Council and successfully discouraged them for decades, the appeal tentatively reappeared. Between 1718 and 1728, four appeals were brought to the Privy Council from Rhode Island. A small group of attorneys were responsible, in particular Nathaniel Newdigate. As the possibility of appeals increased, the Assembly placed limits on them to protect its authority. These limits momentarily halted the trend, but they did not extinguish it. For certain litigants, the remedy was too attractive. On behalf of clients, attorneys would gradually spread the appeal through Rhode Island legal culture.[22]

Nathaniel Newdigate, as a later Rhode Island attorney noted, was "a Lawyer and a very Ingenious one." By his death in 1746, he had become perhaps the most prominent senior attorney in Rhode Island legal culture. How he acquired his legal training, however, is less than clear. He was born around 1663 and little is known of his early life. In 1707 he was publicly identified as a merchant. He was living in Bristol, a contested part of Massachusetts that would become part of Rhode Island in 1740. At some point in the early eighteenth century, he began to practice as an attorney. He may have initially learned the practice from attorneys Nathaniel Byfield and Nathaniel Blagrove, who also lived in Bristol. Bristol was a good location for a dual-colony practice, and the men took advantage of it. Newdigate would remain interested in attorney culture throughout his career. By 1718 he was calling himself an "Attorney at Law" in a case where he had not been paid. Like other colonial attorneys, Newdigate understood how to argue under the transatlantic constitution—or at least knew how to argue the repugnancy side. He had been denied a jury trial in a case alleging that a client had failed to pay him. He petitioned the Rhode Island Assembly, arguing that such a trial "is the right of every subject by the Statute of Magna Charta" and that denying it "would be contrary to the practice of all courts both of law and equity." Arguing the laws of England was relatively easy.[23]

Newdigate's learning about the laws of England is reflected in his extant "Commonplace Book." The manuscript contains some accounts and fees and a few observations about cases. Most importantly, Newdigate wrote down extensive legal entries arranged in rough alphabetical order ("Admiralty"; "Avoydance of Acts"; "Acts of Parliament") followed by a brief statement of law and citation. Apparently initially compiled prior to 1720, the manuscript may reflect access to the libraries of the Massachusetts attorneys. Whether his commonplace book is original or copied is unclear. Newdigate could have abstracted the entries from books he owned or borrowed, using one of the published guides for creating a commonplace. Alternatively, he may have copied another manuscript or a published commonplace book. A small leaflet in his handwriting, "Explanation of References to Books in this Commonplace Book," contains the works cited. Of course, whether Newdigate actually read all or any of these works is also unclear. Nonetheless, the list indicates the types of books important in understanding the laws of England. Contemporaneousness mattered: although classic works like Coke's volumes appeared, the majority of books were published after 1690. Many of the books were modern abridgments and accounts. The list reflected the growing importance of particular cases. A significant number of references were to case reports from Coke to 1724. Modern chancery practice was well represented, with chancery cases (*Cases in Chancery, Ventris, Modern, Salkeld*) and practitioner books on equitable areas (Ashe's *Law of Obligations*, 1693; *Baron and Feme*, 1700; *Lex Testamentaria*, 1714; *The Orphan Legacy;* the *Practical Register in Chancery*). From these works, Newdigate understood how to argue about repugnancies to the laws of England.[24]

Practicing with colonial Rhode Island's divergences, however, proved at first trickier. Newdigate ran afoul of the Assembly's practice of hearing appeals. In 1716 Newdigate represented Daniel Hodgson in a case brought in admiralty and common-law courts in Massachusetts and Rhode Island. Hodgson had been master of a ship, *The John,* owned by a London merchant, Peter Ford, and several others. The vessel had been chartered to Antigua by another London merchant. *The John,* "proving very leaky," had been forced to return to port in Rhode Island. Declaring the ship "part rotten," Hodgson had sold the ship and freight. In 1716 the Rhode Island Admiralty Court ruled that Hodgson had to repay the owners. Newdigate wrote that this order was "contrary to Law and Equity" because of possible double liability if the charterers also sued Hodgson. Newdigate appealed—but to the Rhode Island governor and assistants (the Council). Unlike Massachusetts, in Rhode Island the Council had no such equitable power. As it informed Newdigate, the Assembly "is the Supreme Court of this Colony and [the body] to whom all other Inferior Courts are Obliged to Answer for any misadministration or Erroneous Judgment etc." The Council, however, generously issued a prohibition stopping the decree until the next Assembly session, when Newdigate could seek proper redress.[25]

Newdigate's error pointed out the danger to the colony from attorneys insensitive to the colony's divergences. The Assembly took measures to ensure that attorneys would understand the colony's local practices. In 1718 it required that one of the "attorneys or lawyers, to speak and plead" had to be a "freeholder, a freeman and an inhabitant in this colony." By 1720 Newdigate had relocated to Newport and been admitted a freeman. The contemporaneous publication of *Acts and Laws* (1719) also made legal practice in the colony easier. No longer did an attorney need to be intimately involved in Rhode Island politics to have access to the laws. In fact, on the very issue of the Assembly's power, *Acts and Laws* (1719) emphasized that the Assembly could "confirm, alter, amend, or reverse such judgments, and give a new judgment thereupon, as to the said Assembly shall appear to be agreeable to law and equity." With the laws of England and Rhode Island available in print, it had become easier for an attorney to argue repugnancy and divergence.[26]

Not only did the boat dispute result in Newdigate's move to Rhode Island, but more importantly it introduced him to the Privy Council appeal. The opposing attorney, Nathaniel Blagrove, decided to appeal to the Privy Council in a related action of account. The client, a London merchant, was unhappy with Rhode Island decisions favoring the Rhode Island defendant and had London connections that facilitated the appeal. In July 1718 the appeal was filed before the Committee for Hearing Appeals from the Plantations. Newdigate, however, had not mastered the procedure. In November, when the Committee met to consider the case, the agent for Newdigate's client appeared and explained that he did not have "instructions to defend the said cause." The Committee postponed the case until May, but emphasized that the parties were to "come prepared to be heard at the said time with their Council learned" in law. A settlement ended the case without further hearings.[27]

Newdigate, however, had already realized the advantage of the Privy Council appeal. In August 1718, one month after the boat appeal was filed, Newdigate filed an appeal to the Privy Council. His clients were the possible heirs of a missing mariner, William Holmes, the son of a second marriage, who had disappeared at sea sometime after his father's

death in 1712. The dispute was between William's sister and his elder
half-brother, John, over a house and land. Under a partition agreement
signed by the children of the father's first and second marriages several
days after their father's death with an incomplete will, William was to
receive the house and land. After William disappeared at sea (likely
drowned), John took possession. John claimed that their father should
be presumed to have died intestate and that, as eldest son, he should get
the house. On behalf of William's sister and her husband, Newdigate argued that the partition agreement should be upheld. Two juries, however, found for John. As an intestate case about partition, the case involved both land title and equity, and Newdigate appealed to the Privy
Council. Newdigate's lack of knowledge about the appeals process still
showed. He sent an incomplete record without the final judgment. The
Committee was concerned that the entire record was unreliable. It asked
"whether there was any other evidence or proofs taken besides what is
recited therein or if the whole proceedings on both sides are therein fully
stated and set forth." The errors did not help, and the Committee dismissed Newdigate's appeal. Although Newdigate had now learned how
to appeal properly—to arrange for a solicitor in England, provide instructions, and send the complete colony record—nothing suggested
that it was a particularly promising procedure.[28]

Even these few appeals discomfitted the Assembly, and it sought to
discourage any more. While the Holmes and Ford cases were pending in
London, in June 1719 the Assembly passed a new law that an appeal
could be made to the Privy Council only when the amount in controversy was at least three hundred pounds. Other colonies had such a re-
striction, but the Assembly's justification bore no relation to reality. The
act depicted a grave problem: in "cases of very small moment" people
would "appeal home" and "many persons of small substance" lost their
"just rights" because they could not defend such a suit. Of course, beyond the two pending appeals, no other appeals seem to appear. The requirement nonetheless further limited appeals. The Assembly managed
to prevent even more by review of claimed damages. In 1728 it thus
barred an appeal by concluding that six hundred pounds in alleged damages were not actually the value of the matter in controversy. Moreover,
not until the *1730 Laws* would there be any indication in the printed colony laws that an appeal to the Privy Council was available.[29]

The appeal continued to promise little for Rhode Islanders but more to those whose interests lay in London. In 1724 and 1729 two additional appeals were brought by parties who had been born in Great Britain, had significant London ties, and had lost before Rhode Island courts. In each case, outsiders had sued Rhode Island families for land and the Rhode Island courts had sided with the residents. In each case, the appellant thought that crown authorities would favor them. These initial litigants were more familiar with crown procedures. In 1724 James MacSparran, a Church of England minister in southern Rhode Island, appealed to the Privy Council. MacSparran had been born in Ireland, had spent time in London, and had only recently moved to the colony. MacSparran's advice may have come from another Scots-Irishman, Robert Auchmuty, who would shortly become the Massachusetts admiralty judge appointed by the crown. In 1728 a second litigant appealed. Eunice Wharton was the London widow of William Wharton, who had served as the agent for the colony and Jahleel Brenton's English solicitor. Because her husband had been a solicitor in matters before the Privy Council, Wharton likely knew of the appeal. Both litigants employed the same English solicitor, John Sharpe, to manage the appeals.[30]

MacSparran and Wharton believed their cases would receive a more sympathetic hearing by the Privy Council under a crown interpretation of the transatlantic constitution. In both cases, they hoped that the Privy Council would see colonial practices as repugnant to the laws of England. MacSparran argued that he deserved certain land given to an "orthodox minister." Under the laws of England, "orthodox" meant Church of England. Therefore, MacSparran believed it could refer only to a minister of the Church of England—that is, himself. MacSparran assumed that crown officials would conclude that the Church of England was "orthodox" in England and the colonies. Wharton's suit for 661½ acres in the Narragansett region also involved the willingness of the colony to follow the laws of England. One of Wharton's relatives, Richard Wharton, had received the deed in 1687. Apparently the deed had been recorded by John Fones, the recorder for the brief controversial government during the Domain of New England. The deeds had eventually been declared illegitimate and the records permanently locked. The Rhode Island judges had refused to allow the deed to go to the jury, and the Assembly refused to reverse the decision. Wharton's suit challenged the colony's right to erase the deeds. Wharton assumed that crown officials would conclude that the colony had to recognize as valid deeds of the prerogative English government. In both cases, to side with the colonial decision was to side with colonial authority. Underlying both claims was a belief in a binary colonial–crown world. Both appellants assumed that legal decisions reflected bias. They hoped that what they perceived as local bias would be overturned by more favorable bias in England.[31]

Despite the seemingly sympathetic nature of their claims under the laws of England, the transatlantic world was not so binary. Neither appellant was vindicated; Rhode Islanders ultimately prevailed in both cases through successful appeal management. Jahleel Brenton and Nathaniel Newdigate defended the appeal of MacSparran. In London, due in part to their efforts, MacSparran was unable to muster support to prosecute the appeal and it was dismissed in 1725. Brenton and Newdigate had learned their earlier lessons well. Although it is unknown who in Rhode Island represented the appellees in the Wharton appeal, that attorney made outstanding transatlantic choices in hiring. He employed a colonial agent, Richard Partridge, as the "correspondent or attorney," and Ferdinando John Paris of the Inner Temple as solicitor. Partridge and Paris managed the case well, and both men came to specialize in colony affairs; Paris, in particular, would be involved in a significant number of future Rhode Island and colonial appeals. Although the Privy Council ordered a new trial in Wharton's case, Paris obtained a copy of Richard Wharton's will from the official records in England. Something in the will proved determinative, and when the case was retried in March 1735, Wharton lost. Although granted an appeal to the Council, she later withdrew it. Neither appeal had hurt Rhode Islanders. For Rhode Island clients, Rhode Island attorneys successfully managed the appeals. The successful defense of these appeals encouraged other litigants, attorneys, and even the Assembly to see the appeal to the Privy Council as a useful remedy.[32]

By 1729, the appeal to the Privy Council had become a realistic remedy in large land cases in the colony. One month after Wharton's appeal was lodged in the Privy Council office, a new appeal by William Wood and John Allen was entered. The extended branches of the Sanford family were fighting, and the litigants all knew of the appeal. Both sides hired attorneys familiar with the appeals process. Henry Bull had overseen MacSparran's case; Nathaniel Blagrove had handled the Ford boat case. Rhode Island attorneys now had the right transatlantic connections to handle the cases in London. Moreover, the appeal no longer posed a threat to the charter and the colony's authority. The Privy Council seemed uninterested in using the appeal to revoke the charter or to rethink the entire structure of colony authority. Instead, the Council seemed to have accepted the transatlantic constitution and seemed interested in deciding cases within its framework: determining, that is, whether a given matter was a legitimate divergence or a repugnancy. With the crown and colony now seemingly on the same page, the Assembly published the availability of the appeal for all to see. *Acts and Laws* (1730) explained that there was an appeal to the General Assembly in "personal actions, and from thence to the King in Council." An Appeal "directly" to the King in Council was permitted in "all causes not cognizable before said Assembly." Both crown and colony had an interest in discouraging small suits and appeals were limited to matters in controversy above 150 pounds sterling. After 1729, approximately sixty-five cases would be appealed from Rhode Island to the Council in the years before the Revolution. The appeal had become part of wealthy Rhode Islanders' system of justice.[33]

5

Women, Family, Property

Litigants and attorneys initially adopted the Privy Council appeal in disputes over inheritance—in particular, female inheritance. Third- and fourth-generation descendants of Rhode Island's first families resorted to the transatlantic constitution to attempt to reacquire remnants of their families' past glory. Between 1729 and 1739, nine of the twelve Rhode Island cases appealed to the Privy Council arose from family disputes over inheritance; only one dealt with customs and trade. These appeals required both motive and means; their pattern reflected litigants' contested beliefs and available legal arguments. In 1730s Rhode Island, the social practices and legal rules relating to inheritance were open to differing interpretations and were worth litigating. The laws of England preferred inheritance practices that were gendered (favoring the eldest son), lineal (favoring keeping land within bloodlines), and ancestral (favoring inherited land). These laws created expectations in certain Rhode Islanders, who channeled their anger about inheritances into specific, formal legal arguments over whether an English statute or common-law principle applied in the colony. As the Rhode Island courts and the Privy Council decided when to diverge or favor uniformity, components of English law were incorporated into Rhode Island law in a subtle, sporadic manner.[1]

Mary Coggeshall's appeal reveals this transatlantic legal culture. When Mary Barker married Joshua Coggeshall, she joined an old Rhode Island family. Her new husband's great-grandfather, John Coggeshall, had left

England in 1632 and, after being disenfranchised in Massachusetts in 1637 over religious differences, had become president of the Rhode Island colony. Over the four generations, the family had kept much of its original land while gradually losing its prominence in colony affairs. Joshua, the eldest son, possessed 140 acres with house, orchard, meadow, pasture, and woodlands in Portsmouth. Joshua had inherited the land entailed. English property law conceptualized land in terms of what rights one had regarding the land. The highest estate someone could hold was known as fee simple. Fee simple conveyed all the land rights—most importantly, the right to use, sell, devise, and otherwise permanently alienate the land. Fee tail, created by entailing land, was a lesser estate. The possessor could use the land, but not sell it or devise it in a will. Instead, the land passed automatically to successive heirs (similar to the way the crown passes in a monarchy). Joshua's grandfather's 1687 will had given land to each son "and to his male heirs lawfully begotten of his body for ever." Under the fee tail provision, the land was to pass to successive male heirs, who would not have the right to alter the descent. After his father's death in 1717, Joshua received the land.[2]

In 1733 Joshua wrote a will to prevent "future trouble in my family and amongst my relations" and to give the land to his "well beloved wife." The will indicated the deteriorated family relations: he left each "loving" sibling only five shillings. The sudden death of his youngest brother had triggered a lawsuit against Joshua by his sister, Phoebe, and her husband, attorney Henry Bull. Litigious siblings likely made Joshua worry about his wife's fate. Because Joshua and his wife had no children, in the absence of a will the land would pass to Daniel, Joshua's only other brother. For reasons that are no longer completely clear, Joshua did not believe that the land remained entailed and assumed that he could devise it to Mary. Under the will, the land would pass to Mary to be "freely possessed and enjoyed by her" and her heirs and assigns forever, "nothing excepted and reserved." In 1735 Joshua took further measures to ensure that the entail was inoperative. The colony's "Act for docking and cutting of Estates Tail, pursuant to the Laws of Great Britain" (1725) adopted common English procedures to break entail, noting that it was the "undoubted right" of people who inherited entailed estates to end the entail by fine or common recovery; legitimate collusive lawsuits could transform fee tails into fee simples. On March 31, 1735, Joshua traveled to court and sued for common recovery. The resulting judgment ended the entail and Joshua held the land in fee simple.[3]

A few days later Joshua died, and Daniel refused to accept Mary's possession. Daniel believed he should have inherited the farm. His feelings of disinheritance reflected assumptions based on gender (the land should not go to a woman), blood and marriage (it should not go to someone outside of the bloodline), and an implicit theory of ancestral land (land that had been owned by three generations of Coggeshalls should not go to non-Coggeshall blood). Moreover, Daniel's anger reflected the threat posed by a childless widow. If Mary remarried, the Coggeshall land would pass to her new husband and any children. Although Joshua had abandoned these traditional ideas of family inheritance for his wife, Daniel was unwilling to respect such a decision regarding land valued at ten thousand pounds.

Daniel hired one of the best young attorneys, Daniel Updike, to void the will. Updike argued that Joshua had died intestate because the will had not been rewritten after the entail had been broken. A will could only devise land that the testator possessed when the will was written; it could not give away land acquired afterward. Because fee simple (land without the entail) carried with it more rights than entailed land, Joshua had gained property by breaking the entail. Thomas Wood's convenient one-volume *Institute of the Laws of England* stated, "Lands purchased after the making of the will cannot pass without a new publication by the devisor." Updike claimed that Joshua's old will was inoperative. At the inferior court, Mary's lawyer, Robert Robinson, lost. Apparently he tried to argue that the land had never been entailed and that therefore Joshua's first will was good. The court, however, concluded that the land had been entailed, and the jury found for Daniel.[4]

For the appeal, Mary hired the other prominent young Rhode Island attorney, James Honeyman. Honeyman was the son of the Episcopal minister of the Newport church. He and Updike were at the center of legal and literary activities in Newport. For years they would alternate service as attorney general. In 1736 they unsuccessfully petitioned the Assembly to regulate the bar as members of a group of "Practicers of the Law" of "all who are that deserve the name of attornies in the colony." In 1745 the two men formed a compact of attorneys, and in 1747 they became members of the new Redwood Library with its outstanding collection of law books.[5]

Honeyman and Updike litigated the case using arguments of the transatlantic constitution. For Mary, Honeyman made a clever argument: Joshua had republished his old will through oral statements "which by law is sufficient without the necessity of writing the same thing over again which at most would be but form." Updike argued, however, that after the introduction of the Statute of Frauds (1677), no evidence could be admitted to show oral publication. A cornerstone of property law reform under Charles II, the statute had systematized inheritance practice and ended much of the diversity of local customs regarding wills and property transfers. As Wood explained, the Statute of Frauds required all devises of lands to be "in writing," emphasizing that "lands cannot pass by words." Although the majority of the court agreed, three judges and the governor disagreed, asserting that oral republication was a Rhode Island custom: "the said Evidences ought to be received, it being consonant to the rules of Law, adjudged cases, and practice of this court." The dissent proved influential. The jury favored Mary; in a second trial granted to Daniel, the Court reversed itself and permitted Mary to introduce her witnesses.[6]

Mary's evidence not only tried to show oral republication but told a story in which terrible fate and attorney error had compromised a husband's love for his wife. Five or six days before his death, Joshua had asked William Sanford to "draw over his will" because he "had been at the charge of getting the entail on his lands docked as some supposed to be on it, in order to take of that scruple that his wife might . . . meet with no difficulty after his decease in the enjoyment." Sanford had procrastinated but, upon meeting Joshua on the highway, had promised he would "do it very speedily." Death, however, "interposed that same evening, so that it was not done." Along with proving republication of the will, the other witnesses emphasized that Joshua had wanted to avoid difficulties. Gideon Cornell, a relative of one of the judges, testified in person that he too had met Joshua on the highway the day before his death. Joshua had said that he had docked the entail that "some had supposed" to exist so that his wife would "meet with no trouble" after his death. Five other men submitted similar evidence. All had met Joshua after he had docked the entail. All noted that Joshua wanted to ensure that the land would go to his wife free and clear. Each witness explained Joshua's divergence from traditional English inheritance patterns because of his love for Mary: "the best friend he had in the world." By emphasizing Mary as best friend and best family, Honeyman hoped to reinforce the idea that a testator could use a will to diverge from traditional inheritance practices.[7]

Updike attempted to deny republication and suggested that Joshua had actually wanted a more traditional inheritance pattern. His witnesses implied that Joshua's preference for his wife was an emotional decision that he had later regretted. Richard Coggeshall, along with Thomas Coggeshall and Nathaniel Coddington, testified that Joshua had said he had made the will "in a passion and gave all his estate to his wife but he would burn that will." Others testified that he had intended to follow more traditional bloodline preferences by giving the land to his sister's children. Another man reported that Joshua had only intended to give his wife her dower—what she deserved as a wife under traditional practices. The last man, Caleb Shreve, offered a reason for traditional practices. He claimed that Joshua planned to alter his will to give his land to his wife only for her lifetime because "a woman has not judgment to dispose of lands but may be sold out of it contrary to her mind."[8]

The Rhode Island attorneys advanced, and the Court considered, both arguments available under the transatlantic constitution. As good attorneys, Honeyman and Updike chose arguments about the application of English law and local Rhode Island practice that furthered their goal—whether Mary or Daniel possessed the Portsmouth farm. Both sides accepted that the Statute of Frauds had been "introduced"; indeed, Mary's attorneys attempted to void the grandfather's will for having only two witnesses. Daniel's side argued for the existence of entail; Mary's side claimed the colony's docking procedures based on modern English law were legitimate. Although both accepted that the colony's "ancient practices" regarding republication mattered, they disagreed whether there had actually been any such ancient practices. For the Court, the challenge was whether permitting witnesses to testify to oral republication was contrary to the Statute of Frauds or an acceptable divergence. The Court went both ways. In the first trial, repugnancy won; in the second trial, divergence. Repugnancy was understood through the lens of the colony's introduction act and phrased as "contrary to the intent and provision of the Statute of Fraud[s] and Perjuries introduction . . . to allow the testimony of witnesses to be sufficient." Divergence was understood through the lens of colonial legal practices and phrased as "ancient Rhode Island practices" and "adjudged cases and practice of the Court." Even the judges who favored repugnancy, conceded the theoretical possibility of divergence. In this case, however, they believed such "loose

parole declaration" would be "contrary to the constant practice of the
colony" and "render Men's inheritances precarious." Ultimately, the
Rhode Island Court followed its own interpretation as to what evidence
the Statute of Frauds permitted.[9]

In the spring of 1739, the case was decided by the Privy Council Committee for Hearing Appeals from the Plantations under a similar argumentative structure. Daniel's petition raised repugnancy and divergence
arguments. Giving the land to Mary was repugnant to Joshua's true intent, which aligned with traditional English inheritance practices. He
had "repented of the rash will he had made and intended to revoke" it
and make another to "his own family and relation." It rebutted the availability of divergence in this case by claiming that "no such practice had
been used in the colony." Moreover, the petition implicitly pointed out
the problem with permitting divergences from the Statute of Frauds by
emphasizing the problem with oral evidence. Sixteen witnesses, no two
of whom "together even spoke with the testator," had been introduced
and not one of them "mentions any one particular word spoke by the
testator." Although the Committee's reports never provided rationales, it
likely decided the case along similar lines. The Statute of Frauds was intended to promote uniform will requirements. Permitting republication
by oral testimony would create uncertainty in the colonies and at home.
Equally importantly, the case had no strong argument for divergence.
The split decisions in Rhode Island indicated the absence of a colonial
policy. Indeed, the decisions seemed more concerned with saving Mary
from attorney error than defending a local policy in favor of oral wills.
The Council did not authorize future divergences from the Statute of
Frauds in order to favor one woman. At the Privy Council, an empire of
uniform land practices was reaffirmed. Daniel won.[10]

Like the Rhode Island judges, the Privy Council was not unsympathetic to Mary's plight. In the order, the Privy Council reminded the colony that the laws of England did not leave a widow without property
rights. The Council granted possession to Daniel "without prejudice to
any demand the respondent may have upon account of her dower."
Shortly thereafter, Mary followed the Council's hint. Daniel had subsequently sold the land to Abraham Redwood, and Mary sued Redwood
for the traditional widow's one-third life estate in the land. Dower was a
far cry from her initial fee simple possession of the entire whole, and she
could not devise the lands. Nonetheless, traditional inheritance prac-

tices and the Privy Council's vision of the English empire at last brought a small and limited victory for Mary. Overall, however, the existence of a transatlantic legal culture had limited a woman's ability to inherit land.[11]

Female and Family Inheritance Practices

Transatlantic legal culture provided a space in which larger social disagreements regarding inheritance practices were literally contested. The very existence of these appeals indicates contrasting assumptions about inheritance in eighteenth-century Rhode Island. The ability to argue about the laws of England often gave Rhode Islanders two sets of possibly applicable laws and practices. From treatises and commentaries, colonial litigants and attorneys made certain assumptions about English practices involving gender, marriage, family blood, and ancestral land. In large part, these expectations were shaped by a vision of English law that was more monolithic and consistent than actual English practice. Yet real or imagined, it was this perceived English inheritance law that created disputes in the colonies.

Gender mattered in traditional English inheritance law, and these appeals reflect gender's relevance. Coke's diagram of descents displayed the pervasive gender disparity of English property law. The left side of the diagram showed "cousins on the part of the father the more worthy in descents, though farther remote." The right side portrayed "cousins on the part of the mother the less worthy in descents, though nearer of kin." The common-law inheritance rules as summarized by William Blackstone included three canons of descent that stated gender preferences: male issue inherited before female; daughters inherited intestate property only as coparceners (taking equal, undivided shares); collateral male heirs were preferred over lineal female heirs (for instance, a father's brother was favored over a daughter). The vulnerability of female inheritance and the unequal status of women before the law appear in these appeals as widows sue to keep land and young women sue to protect inheritances. The significance of gender can be seen in the fact that eight of the nine inheritance-related appeals involved women litigants. Yet the reality that female inheritance was contested did not mean that women always lost—or won. Arranged roughly by gender, the eight appealed cases reveal no strong pattern about the predictive value of colonial and English gender assumptions. Three men and five women win in Rhode

Island; four men and four women win in England. The connection between gender and outcome often required additional factors such as
marital status, relationship to family, and relationship to the land.[12]

Gender mattered the most when women sued by themselves for property for themselves. In two appeals (Mary Coggeshall's case and Ann
Sabeere's case), widows appeared in court, unconnected in any explicit
fashion to male relations. Ann Sabeere's husband had died with a will devising real property in Newport to Ann and their two daughters. As
in Mary Coggeshall's case, Sabeere's husband had left her more than traditional dower (a one-third interest for life). Devising the house as if
it were personal property, Ann's husband gave her one-third "for her
benefit and to be at her own disposal." Both widows thus stood to inherit land that gave them financial independence because they could
manage, sell, and devise it. Yet, like Mary Coggeshall, Ann Sabeere
found her brother-in-law unwilling to respect the will. He claimed that
the house was jointly purchased property and should pass entirely to
him. Ann was forced to sue to attempt to partition the house. Like Mary
Coggeshall, Ann Sabeere won in Rhode Island but lost in England. In
both cases, the Privy Council decision meant that widows did not inherit land in fee simple. In this respect, the extremely small sample of
two appeals seems to hint at a willingness of Rhode Island courts to accept a widowed woman controlling property and a discomfort on the
part of the Privy Council to leave land in the hands of a widow in a form
other than dower. Of course, the Rhode Island decisions were not necessarily pro-female. In the colony, the cases likely remained focused on the
deceased husband, with the court attempting to uphold male intentions
over property. Yet the ability to argue the laws of England and reach the
Privy Council offered brothers-in-law angered at a widowed sister-in-
law's inheritance a greater likelihood of winning a decision against female fee simple inheritances.[13]

For women who were married, the legal conception of married
women complicated the role of gender in inheritance disputes and appeals. Although women in that era can be momentarily pulled out of the
embedded context of their families, they blur inescapably into their husbands and children, fathers and ancestors, former husbands and potential future ones. A married woman was referred to legally as a "feme covert." As a feme covert, a married woman had no separate legal identity
and could not sue or be sued in her own name. If a married woman

wanted to sue, her husband had to participate; if her husband wanted to sue, the married woman may have had no choice but to participate. Married women thus do not appear in cases and legal records in a manner that makes it easy to count them or attribute legal action to them. For example, although Jane Boreland was heir to part of the vast Brenton land fortune through her grandmother, Elizabeth Brenton, only after her marriage did she sue for possession of her share of the land. The cases were entitled "Francis Boreland and Jane his wife" and Francis Boreland "et ux" (*et uxor;* and wife). Was Jane or her husband the motivating force? Husbands like Francis cared about wives' land because the management and use of inherited land passed to husbands *(jure uxoris).* As a popular treatise stated, "if a man take to wife a woman seised in fee of lands, he gaineth by the intermarriage an estate of freehold in her right." Upon the birth of children, the husband gained use of the land for his entire life and the children inherited it *(curtesy initiate).* Indeed, when Peter Coggeshall sued regarding land inherited by his wife, Elizabeth Pelham Coggeshall, he sued solely in his own name. Peter's concern about his wife's property appeared in a related case in which Paul Dudley of Massachusetts wrote that Elizabeth's "present husband has suggested something of that nature to me" regarding Elizabeth's finances. In these cases, husbands may have been self-interested or women may have been determined to keep legacies using the only legal means available to them—their husbands.[14]

The difficulty in separating male interests from those of female family members appears even with unmarried women and widows. Three Sanford sisters inherited land—but it was their stepfather and husbands who sued to protect it. Similarly, in two appeals, widows successfully protected property for their shared grandson, William Gardiner, from his stepfather. The stepfather, James Martin, had been married to William's mother only three years when she died. At her death, Martin ended up in litigation against his wife's mother and former mother-in-law. Martin sued his mother-in-law, Elizabeth Gibbs, arguing that he should receive his wife's inheritance of two-thirds of her father's intestate estate. Gibbs successfully kept the money for her grandson by arguing that her husband had died while their daughter had been married to a previous husband. About the same time, Abigail Gardiner (the previous husband's mother) successfully sued Martin for possession of a house and land, claiming it also descended to the grandson. In both cases, the fact that the property was going to the grandson may have helped ensure the suits' success in the colony and England. Interestingly, however, in both cases the outcomes also likely gave short-term financial control of the property to the widows. Gibbs kept the money and Gardiner likely kept the house until the grandson's majority. Gender in context, not gender qua gender, mattered in these cases' being brought and decided.[15]

Gender often appears in these appeals because transatlantic legal culture supported, indeed encouraged, lawsuits over property moving across bloodlines. Seven of the eight appeals involved a suit across bloodlines in which a litigant sued someone who had married into the family or was descended from a second marriage. Traditional English law offered support for unhappy family members who thought they were more worthy than an in-law. English intestate law strongly disfavored in-laws, attempting to ensure that property would not transfer into an in-law's family or to any children of a subsequent marriage. In the colonies, some shared this vision. While Joshua and Mary Coggeshall thought marriage made her a Coggeshall deserving inheritance, her brother-in-law saw her only as a woman who would remarry and take land from the family. To Daniel Sabeere, his brother's widow presented the same threat.

The concern over bloodline was not necessarily gendered. William Gardiner's grandmothers did not believe that a three-year marriage had given a childless second husband the right to control family property. A male in-law made Edward Pelham so anxious that he prevented his sister, her husband, and children from inheriting family land. In each case, the in-law lost in England or never prosecuted the case.

The success of the blood family member in these appeals reinforced the perception that the Privy Council would favor bloodlines over the marital bond. For Rhode Islanders concerned about in-laws, transatlantic legal culture offered possible recourse from individual decisions to pass land outside the bloodline. The remedy, however, was limited to problems with in-laws. The Privy Council provided little help to those Rhode Islanders who thought they were more worthy members within the bloodline. Jahleel Brenton found no success when he sought to stop his great-niece and her husband from inheriting. Samuel Sanford accomplished nothing when he tried to disinherit his half cousins, descended from a second marriage. In both cases, women prevailed in England because they carried the blood of the ancestor.

These concerns over gender, marriage, and blood reflected deep assumptions about who constituted "family" and the family's relationship to land, particularly ancestral land. Reflecting the special status
accorded land bound to the family, traditional English law distinguished inherited land from purchased land. Land acquired by inheritance could be passed at death only to those who shared the same blood
as the "first purchaser," the person who originally acquired the land. Ancestral land was to remain in the family, defined by blood. Concern over
ancestral land motivated all the appeals except Ann Sabeere's case (land
by purchase) and the case of James Martin against Elizabeth Gibbs (inherited money). In each case, the disputed land had descended from
land purchased at the founding of the colony by Rhode Island's first
English settlers: Benedict Arnold (the case involving Elizabeth Pelham
Coggeshall's land), William Brenton (Francis and Jane Boreland's case),
John Coggeshall (Mary Coggeshall's case) George Gardiner (Abigail
Gardiner's case), and John Sanford (the Sanford sisters' case). This land
connected third- and fourth-generation descendants to the glory and
prominence of their family's past. The English intestate practice of primogeniture reinforced the idea of ancestral land. The land in its entirety preferably descended to "the eldest son as heir, and to his issue."
As eldest surviving grandsons and great-grandsons, Jahleel Brenton,
Samuel Sanford, and Edward Pelham apparently thought the family land
should be reaggregated in their possession. In a world where land still
brought economic and social status, family land was worth fighting family for.[16]

With respect to ancestral land, the laws of England established intestate preferences but affirmed individual divergences by wills. Of the
three men who sued to enforce primogeniture, only one ultimately prevailed. English law was biased toward primogeniture, but it also recognized and upheld the right of individuals to structure a different outcome for property after death. Divergences from intestate practices were
thus authorized by the laws of England. Wills provided an acceptable
method to avoid primogeniture and instead leave land to all children
equally or, if there were no sons, to daughters instead of collateral male
heirs. The Privy Council upheld these individual divergences if they
were accomplished through means available under the laws of England.
Deciding against the eldest male, Jahleel Brenton, the Privy Council
affirmed Rhode Island decisions in favor of Jane Boreland's inheritance

in the Pettaquamscutt Purchase. Her great-grandfather's will had divided the land among his seven children without regard to gender, and Jane had inherited the one-seventh share though a female line: from her grandmother to her mother to Jane. Deciding against Samuel Sanford, the Privy Council similarly protected the Sanford sisters' possession of land that had descended to them through three generations. Female litigants who inherited ancestral land originally devised by will by the family founder still obtained the bias of the Privy Council in favor of ancestral land. By following English wills law, early colonists' divergent preferences for dividing their property among all their children, including daughters, were upheld.[17]

The ability to diverge from traditional practices with a will, however, was gendered under English law. Married women were not supposed to write wills leaving land. Peter Coggeshall's wife, Elizabeth, inherited ancestral land through a will. Because the maker of the will was "Mother Pelham," Elizabeth lost the land when the appeal was never prosecuted in England. "Mother Pelham" was Freelove Arnold Pelham, the "dearly beloved and youngest daughter" of Governor Benedict Arnold. Under her father's 1678 will, Freelove had inherited warehouses in Newport, a mansion house and stone windmill, and 130 acres called Lemmington Farm. In January 1710–1711, Freelove wrote her own will dividing this land among her four children, including a part in fee tail to daughter Elizabeth. On the assumption or hope that her husband's consent would alleviate problems (an acceptable procedure by which a married woman could dispose of personal property), her husband expressly noted that he approved of the bequests and, at her death, relinquished his rights as a tenant in curtesy (the husband's automatic life estate). In September 1730, Elizabeth's brother, Edward Pelham, challenged the town council decision upholding his mother's will and sued for the land as heir under "the common law of England." He argued that a married woman could not write a will and that thus all of the ancestral Arnold land descended to him as the eldest male heir. Edward prevailed before the colony court and Elizabeth and her husband, Peter Coggeshall, never prosecuted the appeal to England. The Privy Council was not likely to uphold the right of a married woman to make a will regarding real property. Ironically, the Arnold land ended up in female hands. Edward had no sons, and, following the colonial preference for lineal heirs over collateral male heirs, Edward left his three daughters the family land.[18]

The perceptions of English law that motivated the litigants were not unique to the early eighteenth century. So what encouraged these inheritance appeals? A combination of changes in Rhode Island society and transatlantic law seem to have fostered the cases. The 1720s and 1730s saw a generational transition from the third to the fourth generation in the families that had originally settled the colony. This transition—likely combined with a growing population that enabled land to be profitably sold, leased, or mortgaged for cash—motivated litigants. Moreover, the passing of family members who personally knew the divergent desires of certain testators opened a space to argue for traditional English practices without jeopardizing family relations (and inheritance). While Joshua Coggeshall was alive, his family did not stop his efforts to break the entail. As long as Edward Pelham's father was alive, Edward made no effort to sue over his mother's will. While John Sanford's sons and grandsons were alive, the children of Sanford's second marriage happily inherited Sanford land. Jane Boreland's mother similarly never sued for her share of the land. Lastly, transatlantic jurisprudence became robust enough to frame legal arguments over these family disputes. By the 1730s, the growing availability of the Privy Council appeal focused the ambitions of third- and fourth-generation Rhode Islanders for ancestral land on legal challenges to family practices.

In each appeal, the transatlantic constitution framed the recurring legal argument: was the law or practice repugnant to the laws of England or a legitimate divergence? This framework was explicit in the litigation. As the Borelands noted, they were "more encouraged therein from the consideration of these words" in the charter that the laws and ordinances should "be not contrary or repugnant unto but as near as may [be] agreeable to the laws of . . . England." They similarly referred to the "wisdom" of the government in passing the law that where no particular law was to decide or determine the same then "the Laws of England shall be put in force." Litigants and lawyers appreciated that transatlantic jurisprudence did not offer a certain answer as to when English law applied. Rhode Islanders picked their way among the laws of England and Rhode Island. Whether confronting a parliamentary statute, English common law, or similar English and Rhode Island acts, lawyers and judges on both sides of the Atlantic struggled to interpret the English law within the particular circumstances of Rhode Island and to apply it to family inheritance.[19]

The Application of Parliamentary Statutes

The majority of issues raised by the eight female inheritance appeals involved the interpretation of English statutes. The central importance of statutes within the laws of England was apparent in Thomas Wood's *Institute of the Laws of England*. Wood included statutory authority for almost every proposition of law. As he explained, to learn the law one needed "only to understand the terms, the definitions and divisions, with some common cases, and the most useful Acts of Parliament." In the colonies, as Rhode Island law libraries reveal, access to English statutes was relatively easy. Through statute books, treatises, and abridgments, a Rhode Island attorney could find specific statutes that would help his client. Of course, when it came to the question of which English statutes applied in the colonies, the answer remained obscure. By 1730, transatlantic legal culture suggested that the statutes that applied were those (1) passed before settlement, (2) passed with the colonies explicitly included in the scope of the statute, (3) adopted explicitly by the colonial legislature, (4) adopted by long colony usage or practice, or (5) introduced because no particular colony law decided the issue.[20]

Both crown and colony agreed that pre-settlement statutes relating to the common law were in force. In 1720 Richard West, counsel to the king and the Board of Trade, explained that all "statutes in affirmance of the Common Law passed in England, antecedent to the settlement of a colony, are in force in that colony, unless there is some private Act to the contrary." Such a statute was at the heart of the dispute over Freelove Arnold Pelham's will devising lands, although the papers from the case no longer survive. The Statute of Wills (1540) made it legal for individuals to devise lands by wills and eliminated the requirement that all lands pass by intestate law. In 1543 a second act explained that the Statute of Wills did not apply to married women: "wills and testaments made of any manors, lands, tenements, or other hereditaments by a woman covert . . . shall not be taken to be good or effectual in the law." Wood's *Institute* particularly summarized the principle: "wills and testaments of manors, lands, &c. by feme-coverts . . . shall not be good in law." Although with respect to personal property, a husband could consent to a married woman's disposition, a married woman's real property was supposed to descend automatically to her heirs. Freelove and her husband, however, adopted the consent requirement for lands, either following the procedure for personal property or seeing her land as akin to a separate estate (a special category in England). The Rhode Island courts, however, were no more sympathetic to a married woman's will than English statute and treatise law were. In 1733 Edward won at both the inferior court and the Superior Court. The Coggeshalls initially appealed to England but, likely sensing the futility of their claim, they never prosecuted the case. Pre-settlement statutes were unquestionably in force in the colony, and colonial practices were not supposed to be repugnant.[21]

With post-settlement statutes, the legal analysis was trickier. According to West, no post-settlement statutes were in force "unless the colonies are particularly mentioned." In essence, the first settlers had brought the law with them. West's theoretically coherent analysis presented practical problems. Many important statutes, such as the Statute of Frauds, had been passed since English settlement in New England. Moreover, because the colonies had been settled at different times, West's theory would lead to nonuniform colonial laws. In 1729 attorney general Philip Yorke modified the theory by stating that the "general Statutes of England" could be in force "if they have been introduced and declared to be laws, by some Act of Assembly . . . or have been received there by long uninterrupted usage or practice, which may import a tacit consent of the Lord Proprietor and the people of the colony, that they should have the force of a law there." A colony act or even long practice could turn a post-settlement English statute into an applicable law. In addition, under the colony's 1700 introductory act, parts of a law of England could be in force without a specific act or practice if "no particular law of this colony is made to decide and determine the same." Nevertheless, under either approach, the English statute had to be introduced somehow into the colony.[22]

Rhode Island attorneys were cautious about arguing for the introduction of entire statutes, and attorneys attempted to introduce only as much of the statute as was necessary for the case. In 1732, in one phase of Jane Boreland's litigation for one-seventh of her great-grandfather's 2,466 acres, her attorney argued for the application of only one paragraph of a statute. William Brenton's will had divided his land among the seven surviving children as tenants in common with undivided shares. Over the years, Jahleel Brenton had acquired a number of the other shares and denied that his great-grandniece Jane still held a share. When the Borelands brought an action for an accounting (to obtain a ruling that Jane and Jahleel held as tenants in common), Brenton argued that Jane was too late: the "neglect of the ancestor [was] . . . ever fatal to the heir." The Borelands, however, pointed to a paragraph in a "plain act of Parliament made in England" that permitted actions of account by one tenant in common against the other as bailiff for receiving more than his "just share or proportion." As "there is no Law of the Colony to the contrary" that "directs in such cases," "the consequence then is from that part of the Charter" that the colony should follow the laws of England. The Borelands, therefore, were "well entitled to an action of account." English law books such as Coke's *Entries* were cited to reinforce the claim. Indeed, in Hobart's *Report,* "the very case before your Honors" appeared in which "it is expressly laid down as a Rule" that "any Man that enters into lands of an infant shall be charged as bailiff." The mélange of colony and charter law, parliamentary statute, and English legal literature eventually persuaded the colony courts and the Privy Council that Brenton was a bailiff and owed an accounting. In March 1739 the Superior Court followed the Privy Council's order and confirmed the judgment that Brenton had lost. A post-settlement paragraph had been successfully introduced for Jane's benefit.[23]

Not every litigant found it as easy as the Borelands to argue that a post-settlement statute should apply in their case. The case between James Martin, clerk of the Superior Court, and his mother-in-law became a fight over the interpretation and application of the English statute, "An Act for the More Effectual Discovery of the Death of Persons Pretended to be Alive to the Prejudice of those who claim estates after their deaths." Martin claimed money that he believed that his deceased wife (Elizabeth Gibbs Gardner) should have inherited from her father, William Gibbs. Gibbs had a "considerable personal estate," valued at 2300 pounds, including three individuals (two Indians, Hector and Tom, and "Rhode Island, a Negro boy so called"). Under the colony's intestate law, two-thirds of the personal estate in theory descended to Elizabeth. Elizabeth's mother, however, claimed that Elizabeth had been married to her first husband, William Gardner, at the time of her father's death in 1729. If so, the personal estate passed at the father's death to Elizabeth and, because she was a married woman, to Elizabeth's first husband, and at his death to his children (two-thirds to Elizabeth's son, William Gardner). The argument was possible because no one knew when Gardner had died. He had last been seen on October 13, 1728 (apparently a

Sunday), when he left Tarpaulin Cove in the Elizabeth Islands in a sloop. Although he had been expected to return that evening, he did not, and on Monday a violent storm had hit. The central issue was whether the husband had died in October (three months before the father's death) or at some later date.[24]

Both sides sought refuge in the English act. For the mother-in-law, the statute was introduced to establish that a person had to have been missing seven years before being assumed dead. Martin's lawyer, James Honeyman, however, argued that Gibbs had obviously died in October. Although "the evidence did not see them perish," yet they must have and "every person . . . hath ever since believed it." Honeyman tried to limit the application of the statute. The "design of that act was never intended to extend to cases of this nature." It was only to apply to cases involving proof of persons lost "beyond the seas," not "in or near a harbour" as in this case. Moreover, it was to "extend only to those cases where grants of land have been made to persons during their lives only," and did not "extend or reach to this case" where there was already strong proof of a person being dead. Honeyman argued that the statute supported his effort to prove the October death. He noted, "presumptive evidence in this case must and ought to be received and allowed of persons being absent and unheard of for presumptive evidence is allowed to be good by the act of parliament to prove a person dead who is absent and unheard of." The argument was somewhat persuasive, and although Martin lost at the inferior court, he was successful at the Superior Court. At the General Assembly, new evidence indicated that Elizabeth had sued in her first husband's name and "by virtue of his power of attorney" after October—and Martin lost. Although he appealed to England, he never prosecuted the case and it was dismissed. The colony had plausibly construed the post-settlement English statute.[25]

The Application of General Laws of England

Rhode Island attorneys did not limit themselves to English statutes but also argued for the application of general English legal principles to the Rhode Island courts. Because English law books provided a wealth of legal maneuvers and procedural actions, the laws of England were particularly useful in matters of pleading. The Coggeshalls argued for the application of English maxims to force Edward Pelham to appeal the town council's probate decision upholding Freelove's will to the colony council before he could sue in court. As they put it, "it is a known Maxim in the Law that where a man has two remedies" he cannot take both. The Borelands justified their action for account as "conformable to the settled law and to the express words of all the Books of Entrys and precedents of right pleading in cases of that nature." Edward Pelham alleged, "Nothing is clearer in the Books of English Law then that the said Edward ought to recover his mesne profits and damages." The three Sanford daughters cited Coke's *Commentary upon Littleton*, page 259B, to support their argument that the "law of the Colony" and "Law of England" saved the "infants" from defaults after the attorney for their tenants missed a filing date. With Rhode Island law relatively thin on procedure, and with little good reason to object in these cases, colony judges seemed comfortable following the laws of England.[26]

When colony legal practices conflicted with the common law of England, however, the colony judges faced a dilemma. Ann Sabeere's case posed such a problem: were co-owners to be classified as tenants in common or joint tenants? In 1716 brothers John and Daniel Sabeere had "purchased jointly" a house and lot. In 1726 John died. Apparently expecting no conflict, he had named his wife and his brother as joint executors of his estate. The two disagreed on the ownership of the house. Claiming it was a joint tenancy that passed automatically on death undivided to the survivor, Daniel seized sole possession. Alleging that it was a tenancy in common and devisable by the dying owner, Ann obtained partition on behalf of herself and her daughters. Daniel's attorney, Nathaniel Newdigate, disputed the partition, arguing for joint tenancy (with right of survivorship) under the "laws of England and Great Britain." On the correct construction of "jointly," the laws of England were somewhat murky. Neither Coke nor Wood clearly articulated a presumption. However, in Salkeld's *Reports, Fisher v. Wigg* (1701) included a dissent by Chief Justice John Holt stating that "joint-tenancies were favoured, for the law loves not fractions of estates, nor to divide and multiply tenures." English law could be read as leaning toward joint tenancies. Newdigate referred to the introductory act and concluded that the "laws of England are established and declared to be in force in this colony" in a case like this one.[27]

The Rhode Island judges appear to have accepted that English law favored joint tenancy but concluded that colony custom had diverged. A majority of the Court decided that, under the colony's "ancient standing custom," estates should go to the "heirs of the purchasers." In short, the colony favored tenancy in common. This decision was not made lightly. *Sabeere* is the only case in which I found any statement of explanation by the majority judges. On a piece of paper in the file and in the court record book, the judges wrote:

> The case being heard and considered: and the Law of Joint tenancy being duly weighted with the Arguments of the Plaintiff who relied on the ancient standing custom in the Colony whereby estates have ever gone to the heirs of the purchasers notwithstanding the Law of England relating to joint tenancy as aforesd. Most of the ancient purchases in the colony at the first settling thereof being made by Purchasers in Joint tenants and their heirs having aid by partition after the decease of their predecessors. And there never appearing to have been any infraction made with the said Custom from time out of mind: so that the same in our judgment hath become equal to a Common Law and is by Ancient Usage the right of the Subject and the only safeguard against an Inexpressible Confusion threatened by the putting in Force the law relied on by the Defendant.

Throughout its short opinion, the majority scattered the buzz phrases of traditional English common law: "equal to a Common Law"; "the right of the Subject"; "ancient standing custom"; "ancient usage"; "time out of mind." Just as English common law was the right of English subjects, Rhode Island common law should be the right of Rhode Island subjects. Divergences were, in essence, examples of ancient customs in the colonies that deserved the same respect as that accorded to ancient customs within various regions of England. Favoring colonial continuity over transatlantic conformity "notwithstanding the Law of England," the majority granted partition to Ann. The three dissenting judges—Joseph Jencks (the governor), John Wickes, and Rouse Helme—succinctly noted that the decision was "contrary to the common law and custom of the Laws of England." Employing transatlantic constitutional rhetoric, they emphasized it was "contrary and repugnant."[28]

Daniel appealed to the Privy Council from the divided vote over whether the colony could follow its own ancient customs or must adhere to the laws of England. Perhaps not surprisingly, the Privy Council reversed the judgment and upheld the apparent English preference for joint tenancy. As Chief Justice Holt had noted, presumptions in favor of joint tenancy kept land aggregated rather than divided. Aggregation seemed to be England's preference. Moreover, the Rhode Island Court's reasons for divergence seemed weak. Confusion within Rhode Island did not seem to offset the confusion within the empire if "jointly" meant noninheritable in England and inheritable in the colonies. Indeed, the governor thought the colony should follow English law, a point emphasized by the Privy Council in its comment that the prior decision was "contrary to the opinion of the Governor and two of the judges." There seemed little reason under the transatlantic constitution to uphold the divergence and every reason to avoid repugnancies.[29]

While the clarity of the judgment of repugnancy is alluring, the case itself is strikingly unusual. Of the eight appeals litigated under the transatlantic constitution, Ann Sabeere's case was the only one in which there was an explicit acknowledgment that colony practice opposed that of England and the only case in which there was a written rationale and dissent. Although in *Appeals to the Privy Council,* Joseph Smith interpreted the case as demonstrating the "gulf which separated American and English opinion," the extraordinary nature of the case hints at how often any such gulf was avoided. Few direct repugnancies were litigated and decided as such. Throughout the late 1720s and early 1730s, when Rhode Islanders sought to invoke English law to their advantage, they rarely attempted to invalidate a widespread colony practice. The arguments were more often efforts to incorporate some aspect of English law (e.g., accounting in tenancy in common) or disagreements over interpreting English statutes (e.g., relating to presumptions) or claims against some recent colony decision (e.g., to permit oral testimony for republication in Mary Coggeshall's case) or even challenges to an individual practice that even the colony was unprepared to defend (e.g., that a married woman could write a will for lands). Because following English law was invoked as an argument to win in a particular case, not as a theoretical goal itself, English law and colony law were not often forced to clash. Unlike statutory review proceedings, challenges by appeal from Rhode Island rarely resulted in wholesale condemnation of important colony practices. Of course, an apparent gulf did exist between England and New England in inheritance laws and common-law presumptions, but the Rhode Islanders did not limit their appeals to such dramatic challenges. In the 1730s they embraced the appeal to litigate more mundane matters. As a consequence, the existence of the appeal did not inherently challenge colony authority.[30]

   In the end, the importance of Ann Sabeere's case lies less in the Privy Council's conclusion of repugnancy than in revealing the colony's effort to craft a persuasive rationale for dramatic divergences. Rhode Island was not the only colony seeking to justify such divergences. At the same time, Connecticut and Massachusetts were facing challenges to their intestate statutes that divided property among all siblings. Like tenancy in common, the intestate statutes promoted an approach to land based on division rather than aggregation and opposed English practices. The Privy Council was not happy with these divergences and struck down Connecticut's intestate law in *Winthrop v. Lechmere*. Instead of abandoning these divergences, the New England colonies sought to articulate a better defense. In June 1728, Connecticut's governor Jonathan Law suggested that one might argue that the intestate law was of "so antient standing" as to have been comparable to the "general and particular customs of England." In adopting this language, Law was attempting to place colony practices into a category of practices that would be treated as law. According to the section "rules concerning customs" in Wood's *Institute*: "Usage and Ancient Custom maketh Law." The claim was to have the divergence treated as an accepted type of English law—custom. Custom, of course, was what permitted practices like gavelkind (equal division) to be upheld within England in areas like Kent. The following year, the claim of ancient colony custom was adopted by the Rhode Island majority in Ann Sabeere's case. This case, however, was not the case in which the Privy Council would accept the argument.[31]

   Five years later, in the Massachusetts case of *Phillips v. Savage*, a "proper defense" was at last successfully made for a divergent colonial law based on the claim of ancient colonial custom. *Phillips* once again raised the issue of an equal division in intestate practices. The English solicitor Ferdinando John Paris had written to the colonists that, if the counsel in *Winthrop* had been prepared with evidence of the act being "daily carried into use," they might have won. In *Phillips*, evidence was introduced to show an ancient colony custom of equal division. In addition to evidence, the existence of the divergent practice was tied to colonial conditions. In England, land conditions might favor aggregation; in New England, differing conditions—perhaps extensive land and fewer people—favored disaggregation. As Paris explained, Mrs. Savage "insisted on the Utility, Convenience and Fitness of those Laws to an Infant Country." He emphasized that the practice of such distribution was the "general Usage of America." Implicit in the legal argument was the claim that in order for the English empire in New England to flourish, more equal division had to be practiced. Persuaded by the improved argument, the Privy Council accepted the divergent intestate practice. Just as English common law fit English conditions, colonial common law would fit colonial circumstance. By the late 1730s, litigants and attorneys had learned how to successfully justify a divergence: prove it an ancient custom, implicitly necessary to the expansion of the empire.[32]

Interpreting Statutes

English law and colonial law were not always opposed. Some appeals involved interpreting parallel English and colony statutes, and in at least several cases the colony and Privy Council agreed. Perhaps the most popular English statute in Rhode Island was the statute of limitations, passed in 1623 under James I, which required that suits over land had to be brought within twenty years from the accrual of the title or cause of action. In a world of uncertain land boundaries and disputed inheritances, the statute provided a reprieve from endless land litigation. In the late seventeenth century, William Harris argued for its application repeatedly in his legal documents and correspondence. In 1712 the colony passed its own version. The version appearing in the Assembly records was to become effective in 1722 and apply to those who had occupied land since 1702. It was aimed at lands given by the Assembly to town persons where the deed had failed to comply with legal formalities. *Acts and Laws* (1719), however, did not specify that it would not apply until 1722. The act applied to any persons claiming land. A claimant had to hold the land for twenty years in "uninterrupted, quiet, peaceable and actual seisin and possession." The statute then barred a suit for trespass and ejectment and permitted the possessor to pass fee simple title. In short, the statutes created what would become known colloquially as "adverse possession." Holding land for twenty years could make it legally one's own. For colonial litigants, the question was how far these statutes extended. In the Sanford sisters' case, the possessor claimed that the statutes barred the suit of a person who held the remainder interest in a fee tail. In Francis and Jane Boreland's case, the possessor claimed that the statutes barred the suit of a co-tenant-in-common. In both cases, the aspiration was to convert property held in the limited estate of fee tail or co-tenancy into the flexible estate of fee simple.[33]

Whether the statute of limitations could be used to end an entail arose in a case over 150 acres in Portsmouth known as Blackpoint Farm, originally owned by Rhode Island founder John Sanford. In a 1653 will, Sanford had divided land among the sons of his first and second marriages, with parcels descending to male heirs in fee tail. If a son had no male issue (sons, grandsons, etc.), the land was to revert to the next eldest son's male heirs. Four generations later, John's great-grandson, Samuel Sanford, sought to claim Blackpoint Farm because that line had run out of male descendants. The farm had come into the possession of three girls, the great-granddaughters of John Sanford. It had descended to them from their grandfather (Peleg Sanford, the eldest son of John's second marriage) and their father (William Sanford) in 1721. In 1726 Samuel brought a suit for trespass and ejectment against two lessees, William Wood and John Allen. Sanford's quite plausible claim to the land under the entail was countered by the girls' claim that their grandfather had been in possession of the lands for over thirty-five years and therefore had title in fee simple. The statute of limitations, in essence, had broken the entail.[34]

In the effort to end entail, the girls were following in the spirit of English and colony law. English law had long provided procedures by which an entail could be terminated. Although entails abounded in English legal practice, the law disfavored the ways in which they bound up land and was sympathetic to efforts to end them. Rhode Island had begun to follow suit. In 1725, the year before Sanford's suit, a new statute permitted the tenant in tail (the person in possession) to end the entail with procedures "as effectual" as those of the "court of common pleas." The act emphasized that ending entails was "the undoubted Right of all his Majesty's Subjects being seized of Estates Tail." Turning fee tail into fee simple was a legitimate "benefit." In both colony and England, Samuel's implicit claim for an unbreakable entail received little sympathy and the girls eventually won.[35]

Indeed, while the case was pending in England, the Assembly reinforced residents' ability to break entail. Modeled on an English statute, a new statute ensured that any want of form in the procedures (for instance, if English was used instead of Latin) would not be considered reversible error. Moreover, it passed a new disability act that could be read to support the idea that the statute of limitations could end fee tail. A person with an estate "in remainder or reversion, expecting or depending" was given a ten-year period to sue. The act emphasized that beyond this disability period there would be no saving of "the right of Persons" who had an estate in remainder or reversion that followed an estate for years, life, or "lives." Their right to the land was extinguished. Although the reference to "lives" likely covered joint life estates in, for example, a husband and wife, it also conceivably covered fee tail. Although the 1725 docking act was repealed in 1737, a large volume entitled *Fines and Recoveries* carefully recorded thirty-six actions largely brought between 1727 and 1750 to end entails. For at least some period, Rhode Islanders were able to break entails as effectively as English landowners were.[36]

Although the colony used the statute of limitations to accomplish an action permitted by English law, it was unwilling to adopt an interpretation that went against English law. Several years after *Sanford,* Jahleel Brenton attempted to use the statute of limitations argument to destroy Jane Boreland's claim of land as a tenant in common. Brenton argued that because he had held the land for more than thirty years, he now owned it in fee simple under the English and colonial statutes. The jury in the inferior court voted for Brenton. On appeal, however, the Borelands argued that statutes of limitations could not end the tenancy-in-common relationship. To support their claim, they described cases from two English law reports. The first, *Smales v. Dale,* involved a complicated story of a one-third share held over several generations, somewhat similar to the Boreland facts. The case demonstrated that a "tenant in common can never be disseised by his fellow but by an actual ouster." The second case, *Reading v. Royston Hill,* was similar in facts and result. In another entangled inheritance dispute, the claim had been made that the statute of limitations ran against a coparcener, a form of female shared ownership similar to tenancy in common. This case showed that "the statute of limitations never runs against a man, but where he is actually ousted and disseised; and true it is, one tenant in common may disseise another; but then it must be done by actual disseisin." Under English law, a tenant in common had to be ousted by actual action, not mere passage of time. As in the Sanford sisters' case, the Rhode Island Court and Privy Council agreed. Statutes of limitations did not apply to co-tenancies. When crown and colony agreed, English and colonial statutes could be used simultaneously to achieve litigation goals.[37]

These eight appeals to the Privy Council reveal the richness and complexity of the transatlantic legal culture. These cases were triggered by differences among third- and fourth-generation Rhode Islanders over the degree of required fidelity to English property and inheritance practices. For the litigants, these cases revealed the politics of family—some colonists continued to value English concerns over blood, marriage, and ancestral land, while others took advantage of local conditions to leave land to wives, younger sons, and daughters. For the attorneys, these cases revealed the politics of the legal community—wealthy appellate practice became dominated by a few attorneys who had access to English legal literature and Rhode Island legal precedent and who were aware of transatlantic practice and precedent in other colonies. For the Rhode Island governing structure and the Privy Council, these cases revealed the politics of empire. The dual authority structure of the colonial world provided encouragement for lawsuits because legitimate, alternative sets of social practices existed. The principles of divergence and repugnancy under the charter and the transatlantic constitution permitted the construction of plausible legal arguments about the necessity to follow or diverge from English law. English law and social practice mattered in the colony—but not in the way it has sometimes been thought. English law was not simply received or rejected; it was introduced, argued over, and interpreted. It was a force in some lawsuits and an ultimate defense in others. The English statutes, pleading principles, maxims, and cases of English law books were a buffet from which colonial attorneys could select the arguments necessary to bring, win, and defend cases for individual litigants.

6

Personnel and Practices

Between the 1730s and the American Revolution, Rhode Island attorneys accepted the Privy Council appeal. Whereas the pre-1729 appeals had largely been brought by English residents hoping to escape perceived bias in Rhode Island, the majority of post-1729 appeals were private-party disputes between Rhode Islanders. For these affluent Rhode Islanders, the emotional and monetary value of the inheritance and commercial disputes justified the cost. This embrace of the appeal may explain the creation of the Court of Equity; it might have been hoped that such a court would diminish the desire to appeal to England. The collapse of that court in 1744, however, hints that the appeal's attraction lay in its transatlantic dimension, not in the mere availability of an additional appeal. In cases that involved disagreements among Rhode Island decisionmakers, the Privy Council could serve as a seemingly neutral arbiter of internal conflicts over transatlantic law or as an authority with a bias in favor of certain English legal principles. After 1745, each year there was at least one, and sometimes there were even four or five, appeals filed with the Privy Council.

Jurisprudential coherence was achieved, not by printed records of court decisions and Council appeals, but by continuity of personnel. On both sides of the Atlantic, a small bench and bar nurtured the transatlantic legal culture. By the 1730s the mechanics of the Privy Council appeal—the participants, the procedure, the rationales behind prosecution and nonprosecution, and the relevance of precedent—were apparent. These practices continued largely unaltered until the Revolution.

116

The Rhode Island Bar and Bench

The legal participants on both sides of the Atlantic were similar. In Rhode Island, a small cohort of four or five attorneys handled most of the cases appealed to the Privy Council. In England, an equally select group of solicitors and crown law officers dealt with the appeals before the Privy Council. The two benches were also strikingly similar in their blending of executive and judicial identities. In Rhode Island, a court composed of the governor and assistants decided most cases headed for appeal. In England, the Privy Council's Committee for Hearing Appeals from the Plantations was made up of members of a select group of the crown advisors. Transatlantic appeals thus incorporated the elite legal thought and governance concerns of colony and crown.

The four attorneys who largely handled appealed cases in the early eighteenth century stood at the center of Rhode Island legal culture. Although Bristol attorneys like Nathaniel Newdigate introduced the appeal, Newport attorneys became the dominant practitioners. In the 1720s, Nathaniel Newdigate successfully fended off an appeal by Henry Bull and Daniel Updike in their first experience with transatlantic legal culture on behalf of James MacSparran. Henry Bull was the grandson of a founder of the colony. After serving for one year as attorney general in 1721, he declined to serve further, devoting himself to private legal practice and eventually becoming chief justice of the newly formed Court of Common Pleas for Newport in 1749. Daniel Updike also traced his family back to the colony's early days and reinforced his family's prominence by marrying Sarah Arnold, the daughter of former governor Benedict Arnold. Updike would serve for many years as attorney general. In the late 1730s two recent graduates of Harvard College, Thomas Ward and James Honeyman, began to handle appeals. Ward's father, Richard, had been the recorder for the colony from 1714 to the 1740s, and Ward inherited his father's law books in 1755. In addition to his private practice, Ward became the colony's secretary. James Honeyman's family was of more recent vintage; he was the son of the episcopal minister of the Newport church. Honeyman and Updike formed a Newport society described as being "for the promotion of Knowledge and Virtue, by a free conversation." Like Updike, Honeyman served for many years as attorney general. Ward and Honeyman began their acquaintance with transatlantic law in representing William Gardner's grandmothers against Bull and Updike's joint representation of James Martin.[1]

The four attorneys perceived themselves to be members of a colony bar. In 1736 they signed a petition brought by "all who are that deserve the name of attornies in the colony" and "Practicers of the Law." First on the list was Nathaniel Newdigate, followed by R. Robinson, Henry Bull, Daniel Updike, James Honeyman Jr., Nathan Townsend Jr., Matthew Robinson, Thomas Ward, John Walton, William Hopkins, and John Cole. The unsuccessful petition aspired to establish a licensing and admission procedure that would exclude attorneys from other colonies (apparently largely Massachusetts). Their desire to limit the practice so that attorneys would be "the more desirous of a just and faithful exercise of their calling to the good of mankind in general" was inextricably linked to economic concerns. The petitioners hoped to obtain a "living and maintenance" through the practice of law, and contended they were "sufficient for the business of the colony." Their legal practices required money and time. An attorney had to know English law with "the expense of procuring Books." An attorney also had to know local law by being "constant in our attendance upon the several courts in the colony." To spend this "great part of our time in the study of the law," the attorneys had to postpone "all other business." The attorneys felt that their devotion to the practice should be rewarded by ensuring that they could make a living from it.[2]

The attorney petition reflected a settled legal culture. There were two types of cases: common and difficult. "Common business" involved matters decided under the "rules of law" and required only the application of well-known legal principles. "Difficult" cases involved disputes over law and required arguments to the bench in "special verdicts, demurrers, pleas in bar, arrest of judgments, etc." In these cases, the attorneys had to subject their "Opinions, Books and Skill in all arduous and difficult cases to the pleasure of the court." The Rhode Island attorneys prided themselves on their advocacy. They criticized the Boston lawyers for thinking "themselves under a necessity of talking a great while and so retard the business of the court by their long flourishes, tire the ears of the judges with their needless repetitions, and sometimes confound and perplex the juries with their circumlocutions and sophistry so as to obscure and darken the case more than if it had not been pleaded at all." This "ill example" had made "long haranguing more fashionable." Rhode Island legal practice aspired to "clear and distinct reasoning."

By the 1740s, legal practice in the colony was going fairly well. A 1745 "agreement among the attorneys" signed by Updike, Honeyman, Ward, and other "brethren" of the "fraternity" sought to regulate "our Practice in Law." Once again, the attorneys wanted to ensure that they could make a living. The agreement set fees "sufficient for our support and subsistence." The structure established a "distinction in fees" between "common uncontroverted cases, and those that are difficult in managing." The attorneys worried, however, about payment. No attorney was to defend a suit for fees against a nonpaying litigant unless "three or more brethren shall determine the demand unreasonable." The attorneys wanted to support practices that involved "a standing client for whom considerable business is done." They sought to discourage practices that decreased client relationships. The compact thus prohibited signing blank writs (legal forms) because it "would make the law cheap." The attorneys wanted to ensure that legal practice in Rhode Island depended on attorneys' full participation.[3]

The attorneys interested in handling the more financially remunerative, difficult cases needed access to newer English law books. In 1747 Updike, Honeyman, and Ward helped found the Redwood Library in Newport. They, along with young attorney Matthew Robinson, drew up the library's governing laws and likely assisted in selecting the library's outstanding law collection of thirty-two titles. The desire for broad knowledge about the laws of England appeared in volumes such as Wood's *An Institute of the Laws of England* and Bohun's *Introduction to the Study and Practice of the Laws of England*. Dominating the list were abridgments and treatises with their promise of compact, coherent descriptions of English law. The prized item was Charles Viner's fourteen-volume *A General Abridgment of Law and Equity* (1742–1748), which cost 420 pounds. Others included Hawkins's *Abridgment of Coke's First Institutes* and *Summary of the Crown Law; The Grounds and Rudiments of Law and Equity, alphabetically digested;* and *Select Trials for Murders.* Rhode Island attorneys were interested in English principles derived from well-established cases; there was little purpose in imagining new interpretations of cases. Other than *Reports and Rules in King's Bench and Common Pleas,* the library did not purchase any of the sizable body of English case reports. Disagreements over the application of modern parliamentary statutes were less common in the colony, and *Statute-Law common-plac'd* was the only edition of English statutes. The library gave evidence of an increasing interest in commercial law, international law, and admiralty. It contained two books on admiralty, a book on customs, one on the exchequer, a treatise on naval trade, Wood's *New Institute of the Imperial or Civil Law,* two versions of Puffendorf's *Law of Nature and Nations,* and *A Digest of all the Laws relating to the Customs, to Trade, and Navigation.* By 1750, the Redwood Library's collection gave Newport attorneys access to the latest knowledge on the laws of England.[4]

The practice of arguing broad legal principles, policies, and facts conformed to the composition of the Rhode Island court. The relatively stable composition of the colony's bench made up for the absence of formal legal study. None of the men who served as colony-wide judges in the first half of the eighteenth century appear to have practiced extensively, if at all, as an attorney. Until 1751, first as the General Court of Trials and then as the Superior Court of Judicature, the colony court was composed of twelve annually elected members: the governor, the deputy governor, and ten assistants. In no year between 1698 and 1745 was the court's membership entirely new. In each year, the Assembly reelected a number of members; in particular, the governor and certain assistants served lengthy terms. As governor, Samuel Cranston served on the court for more than twenty-five years. Joseph Jenckes served on the court at least eighteen years as assistant and deputy governor before serving on it as governor. Many assistants served similar terms: John Wickes for twenty-six years between 1715 and 1741, Rouse Helme for twenty-three years between 1717 and 1744, George Cornell for twenty-three years between 1711 and 1739, William Anthony for twenty-one years between 1717 and 1738, Randall Holden for twenty years between 1705 and 1736, John Wanton for nineteen years between 1715 and 1740. A number of others served for five to ten years. At almost every court session, some judges had served as long, if not longer, than the attorneys who were practicing before it.

Their length of service made the judges legally literate. Prior legal practice was simply not essential to the effective functioning of the court. Judges needed an understanding of the charter and the transatlantic constitution, knowledge of Rhode Island laws, an ability to understand the significance of arguments about the laws of England, an awareness of past decisions and customs, and a sense of equity and judgment. These abilities were as likely to be gained by experience as by study. The attorneys explained the laws of England; the assistants had access to the laws and charter; and long-serving assistants had extensive knowledge of past practices. Although judging necessitated "mature consideration," the contextual nature of repugnancy and divergence made decisions as much political as legal. They depended on a judgment about the history of the colony and a vision of the English empire. They required weighing the colony's commitment to certain laws and practices against England's. In the colony, as in England, judging was an inherently political enterprise under the transatlantic constitution.[5]

Judges with long experience appear to have dominated the Court. In most cases in the late 1720s and 1730s, they agreed on the outcome. As judges and politicians, they tried to negotiate transatlantic legal culture without adopting a pro-colonial or pro-England stance in many cases. In the 1720s, they supported divergences in cases involving Wharton and the Church of England minister, James MacSparran. In the 1730s, they favored English law in cases involving Jane Boreland and Edward Pelham. In the case of the Sanford sisters, the five longest-serving members—Jenckes, Cornell, Anthony, Wickes, and Helme—disagreed with a dissent by three newer members. Nonetheless, in a few cases, two of the longest-serving judges, John Wickes and Rouse Helme, were more cautious about colonial divergences. In 1729, in Ann Sabeere's case, Governor John Wanton, George Cornell, William Anthony, and four others favored a preference for tenancy in common to aid the widow. Wickes and Helme, along with Joseph Jenckes, dissented, advocating the presumption for joint tenancy that the Privy Council would later favor. This division of Wanton, Cornell, and Anthony versus Wickes and Helme reappeared in Mary Coggeshall's case when the two men dissented from a decision to permit republication evidence. Once again, their position was adopted by the Council on appeal. In both cases, the colonial majority claimed that the divergence was justified by ancient colony custom; in both cases, Wickes and Helmes disagreed. What explains the difference is not clear. Perhaps the two were better able to foresee the Privy Council's concern for the underlying English law. Perhaps they did not believe that the divergences really were an ancient custom. Perhaps they were less sympathetic to divergences or customs that empowered unmarried women to hold land outright. This apparent bias in favor of the laws of England, however, does not seem to have been a decisive issue in colony politics. In a world where only men voted, both men were consistently reelected by the Assembly.[6]

The stability of the Court during the 1720s and 1730s in contributing to the internal development of transatlantic jurisprudence can be seen by the absence of appeals during the disruptions of the 1740s. In 1744, King George's War rocked New England as England went to war against France. The colony's resources went toward prosecuting the effort and securing the fortress of Louisbourg on the island of Cape Breton. Experiments with institutional structures such as the Equity Court led to a disarray of personnel. Even after the abolition of the Equity Court in 1744, the Superior Court's membership changed almost entirely at each election. Between 1739 and late 1745, no appeals from Rhode Island were admitted before the Privy Council. Those brought were dismissed for nonprosecution in London. The decade-long absence of appeals is so noticeable that one wonders whether institutional disarray was a deliberate Assembly strategy to limit appeals. In 1747 a new five-man Superior Court was created and, as will be discussed at the end of this chapter, instigated a dispute over English statute precedents. By 1751 the dispute was resolved and the Court began to have a consistent elected personnel. That same year, the Privy Council decided the first three appeals from Rhode Island in more than a decade. Over the next two decades, transatlantic legal culture flourished as the Privy Council regularly considered appealed Rhode Island cases.[7]

The English Bar and Bench

On the other side of the Atlantic, a small group of legal practitioners—London agents, solicitors, and crown law officers—who were interested in "plantation affairs" participated in the transatlantic legal culture. For many litigants, employing an agent and solicitor was the first step in ensuring that the appeal was filed or dismissed, and the proper papers and personnel procured. Some litigants employed a separate agent, such as Thomas Sanford, who appears to have had family connections to the colony. A more popular choice was Richard Partridge, the agent for a number of colonies and individuals. Some agents also served as solicitors; others retained a solicitor. Agent Jeremiah Dummer noted that Partridge "has always an Attorney and Solicitor at his elbow, who know how to make out long bills, whereas I have always done that drudgery myself; but have always had the best Council in the nation." Ferdinando John Paris and Joshua Sharpe reappeared often as solicitors for Rhode Island litigants. Contemporaries referred to Paris as "the famous Mr. Paris, a gentleman of the first caracter *[sic]*" and "a cunning and unscrupulous attorney." Sharpe was described as "one of the ablest Solicitors in England, and imployed by almost all of the Plantations [colonies]. Consistency in procedures was promoted by repeated selection of these men.[8]

The solicitor managed the appeal. His duties can be gleaned from extant bills. In a small matter like a dismissal for nonprosecution, the solicitor read the original papers, took notes and prepared various legal documents, retained counsel to argue the case, regularly visited the Council Office to track the appeal, ensured that the correct papers were filed, and handled necessary payments. In argued appeals, the solicitor often wrote the petitions to the Council. Petitions presented the facts of the case and the general request for relief. In addition to the petition, in one instance solicitor Paris refers to "the printed case," which he drew, suggesting that solicitors also may have prepared the printed briefs to the Committee. Briefs included a statement of the proceedings and facts of the case, the legal and equitable reasons for the appeal, and objections to the other side's arguments. To prepare the arguments, access to colonial law was crucial. Paris owned or had access to law books for Connecticut, Massachusetts, New York, and Pennsylvania, and knew of laws from Rhode Island, New Hampshire, New York, New Jersey, Maryland, Virginia, and Bermuda. Paris remarked that he had been a "bystander" in appeals hearings; solicitors likely sought to improve their understanding of transatlantic legal practice by general attendance on the Committee. The worth of the solicitor lay in his knowledge of both sides of transatlantic legal culture.[9]

For the actual argument before the Council's Committee for Hearing Appeals from the Plantations, the solicitor had to arrange for "learned counsel." The appeals were argued by an elite group of lawyers who held crown law offices: the attorney and solicitor general, men appointed as crown counsel, and men who held patent of precedence (giving royal permission to barristers to argue). Crown law officers earned most of their income by taking the cases of private litigants. The names signed to printed colonial appeals briefs from the 1750s and 1760s reflect this elite bar. While serving as solicitor general or attorney general, Charles Yorke, William de Grey, John Dunning, Fletcher Norton, William Murray, and Dudley Ryder argued appeals. While serving as crown counsel, Charles Ambler, Richard Jackson, Charles Pratt, and Thomas Sewall argued. These same names appear on briefs for prize appeals from the colonies. Without a doubt, colonial appeals were an important component of elite English legal practice.[10]

Securing a counsel who was both a strong legal advocate and knowledgeable about transatlantic legal culture was crucial. Paris advised using the best lawyers in England: William Murray (the future Lord Mansfield) or the solicitor general, John Strange. Usually, strong counsel on one side was matched by equally prominent counsel on the other. In 1752 James MacSparran hired Solicitor General William Murray while Robert Hassard retained Attorney General Dudley Ryder and Alexander Hume-Campbell. Less able counsel could lose an appeal. Paris attributed Connecticut's loss over its intestate statute in *Winthrop v. Lechmere* to inept counsel. The appellant (Winthrop) had been "very well assisted." He had been represented by Attorney General Yorke ("now Lord Chancellor Hardwicke") and the solicitor General Talbot ("late Lord Chancellor Talbot"). They were "two of the ablest Lawyers that I ever did know, or ever am like to know, in those Posts." For the loser, Lechmere, the case had been "so poorly defended." He had been "defended by some body very little acquainted with Plantation Affairs, and in so poor a manner, that, at that time, it gave me, who was only a Bystander & not at all concern'd in that Cause, great Pain, to see a Cause of that Genl Consquence, so wretchedly and poorly conducted." Frances Wilks likewise commented that had the case "been properly Conducted & taken care of on Lechmere's part, that Law wou'd never have been repealed." When partible inheritance was upheld on appeal several years later, Paris considered it a reflection of an improvement in counsel. If the subsequent appeal had "been managed in as bad a manner, sure I am that it would have had the same ill Success." Counsel mattered so much that Paris urged retaining the best lawyers before appeals were even formally filed in London.[11]

Crown law officers may have enjoyed arguing these appeals because they often depended less on the arcane points of English case law (although technical issues did arise) and more on the relationship between the laws of England and colonial circumstances. Little evidence survives to indicate the style of argument. Counsel likely began by stating the facts and proceedings in the case, in the process disagreeing with the opposition's depiction. Pertinent papers under seal could be read as evidence. Marginal notation on some extant briefs suggests that counsel summarized each reason justifying the appeal. These reasons were not long or particularly technical. Paris noted that in the partible intestate appeal, the issue "reduced to that single & great point, whether the Massachusetts law, distributing Intestate real Estates, was a valid law, or not?" "Valid" was a liberal standard, and a broad array of arguments seem to have been legitimate to advance. In a 1760 colonial appeal, Lord Mansfield referred to English chancery practice, the laws of the Province and the "practices" in New England, an act of parliament, and prior decisions by the "Lords of Appeal." Prior Privy Council precedent was relevant. Paris referred to "Mr. Winthrop's Precedent in Connecticut" in describing how the argument had involved the "Distinctions between the two Cases." Precedent, however, was not absolutely binding. Paris recounted how Lord Chancellor Hardwick (Charles Yorke) had explained his decision as a member of the Committee, having been counsel in the Connecticut intestate appeal. He had "offered all that he could for his client" to get the colony law repealed. Although "he had prevailed therein for his Clyent, yet, with the very great Deference to those Lords who judged in that Case, he was not satisfied in his own private Opinion" with that determination—and now concluded the opposite way. Arguing appeals required the best and broadest legal reasoning.[12]

The appeal was formally decided by an order from the Privy Council (the crown and chief ministers). A smaller committee heard the appeal and prepared the report. Although the Committee for Hearing Appeals from the Plantations theoretically sat as a committee of the entire Privy Council, as a practical matter a small core of individuals usually appeared and a three-member quorum was required. In particular, a judicial officer (such as the chief justice of King's Bench, the chief justice of Common Pleas, or the lord chancellor) was almost always present. Because crown law officers were often promoted to cabinet and judicial positions, some members of the Committee had previously argued appeals. In the 1730s, George Lee, brother of Chief Justice William Lee of King's Bench, argued before the Committee and then served on it as dean of the Arches and judge of the Prerogative Court of Canterbury. Charles Yorke similarly argued and then joined the Committee as lord chancellor. Ryder and Murray served on it as chief justices of King's Bench; Pratt and de Grey as chief justices of Common Pleas. With at least one member with legal training and others with political skills, the Committee was well situated to decide appeals over the application of the laws of England.[13]

The Committee decided appeals in a deliberative process. By mid-century, members received printed briefs from appellant and appellee. At least some law officers and Committee members saved the briefs. George Lee saved at least one brief that he argued in 1738, along with the many briefs in appeals that he heard in the 1750s as a member of the Privy Council. Charles Yorke kept a similar collection. Both men made notations on their briefs as to reasoning and result. Notes of a 1760 hearing offer a glimpse at the Committee's decision making. Two members—President Grenville and Lord Mansfield (chief justice of King's Bench)—offered lengthy initial opinions on the appeal. Mansfield noted that he previously had "several conferences about the matter" with certain judges who "were for retaining the old artificial way." The matter was then "much agitated" among the members. One of the lords asked a further question of one of the attorneys. The discussion altered initial opinions. After the agitation, Mansfield stated that "he had received much light, and was relieved from this difficulty from what he had informed that he thought." Appeals were not carelessly decided.[14]

Like the Rhode Island Superior Court, the Privy Council did not write opinions. The Committee's report simply recited the facts and proposed an order. The Committee report sometimes bore a striking resemblance to the petition. In uncontested cases, a solicitor may have drafted documents for the Committee or the Committee used the petition as a template for the report. The Council's subsequent order either affirmed or reversed the colony court or dismissed the appeal. In reversing a colony judgment, the Privy Council usually left the colony with the discretion to arrange a proper response. The order in the Connecticut intestate appeal was atypically specific in requiring legislative repeal. The Council declared the act null and void "as contrary to the laws of England" and reversed all the acts founded on that law. Paris, however, stated that the lords had given a decision that "was never done in any one Case, before or since, to my Knowledge." For most of the eighteenth century, the larger significance and impact of Privy Council decisions was determined by the colony court and Assembly.[15]

The Mechanics of the Appeal

An appeal to the Privy Council began when a colonial litigant obtained permission from the colony to appeal. Not all who threatened to appeal actually did so. The colony required that a bond be posted by the would-be appellant. An appeal also had to fall within subject and monetary jurisdictional requirements of the colony and the Privy Council. Subject matter jurisdiction is somewhat hard to discern but, as will become evident later in this chapter, often appears to have involved issues arising under parliamentary acts affecting the colonies and equitable matters. The monetary jurisdictional limit set by the Privy Council in instructions to a number of colonies was 300 pounds sterling. Although the Rhode Island Assembly set the limit in 1719 at 300 pounds (Rhode Island currency), by 1746 the limited was raised to the more significant sum of 150 pounds sterling (English currency). Inability to meet the requirement, however, did not absolutely bar the appeal. A litigant could petition the Council to admit the appeal, arguing that the case was worth more (for instance, the argument would affect other land titles), the case applied to other similarly situated persons, or the legal issue was intrinsically important. The appeal of George and Mary Taylor was admitted even though it failed the monetary requirements because it asked whether dower could be waived by a revocable jointure in a will. Mary's first husband had left a will that gave her one-half of the house and dwelling lands as long as she remained a widow. If she remarried, she was to receive only the goods and her own estate. After she remarried, she sued for dower. The Rhode Island courts decided against her and in favor of her daughter and then barred the appeal. Jointure and dower interested the Privy Council and it admitted the appeal. Mary, however, never prosecuted the appeal and it was eventually dismissed.[16]

Once an appeal was accepted, the appellant submitted a petition to the Privy Council office. If no petition was filed within a year and a day, an appellee could move for dismissal for nonprosecution. Dismissing an appeal for nonprosecution still took time and money. A petition for dismissal was drafted, copies presumably were made for the Committee, and a copy was filed at the Council Office. The solicitor prepared a brief in support of the petition and attended the Committee to make the motion to dismiss. In one 1739 dismissal, Paris began the process in January 1738 and stopped by the Council Office almost every day for four months (or so he claimed) "to search from time to time if this Appeal is presented." In May he found that the appeal had been dropped, but it took until July to make the motion and have the report and order written and sealed. On more than one occasion, he attended the Committee for six hours only to have the case remain uncalled. Payments to messengers, underclerks, porters, and others added to the expense. This particular dismissal eventually cost Abigail Gardner thirty-seven pounds sterling.[17]

In a prosecuted appeal, once the appellant's petition was submitted, the appeal was set for hearing. The appeal was argued at Whitehall in the Cockpit usually in the late afternoon, at six o'clock. Prior to argument, briefs in the cases likely circulated. By the 1750s the briefs were printed. These large briefs were folded from top to bottom and then in half again, with the case name printed on the outside fold along with spaces for the time and date of the hearing. On occasion the argument stretched beyond one day, and some appeals were continued due to member absences. Once the Committee made a decision, it wrote a report for the entire Council. A final order of the Council was then prepared and sealed copies sent to the colony. Apart from a few extraordinary situations, cases were resolved relatively quickly. Most cases were concluded one to three years after the Superior Court decision in Rhode Island.[18]

Money mattered. Charges for counsel, papers and copies, petitions and briefs, and the solicitor's time added up. Coaches had to be hired, underlings paid, and time billed while cases were continued and delayed. The Council report had to be paid for and stamps and a seal obtained. The cost of prosecuting appeals was at least one reason some went unprosecuted. In February 1735 the Sanford daughters withdrew one appeal and refused to prosecute another. When they petitioned the Assembly instead for a rehearing by writ of review, they explained that the "charge and expense of prosecuting the appeal to the King in Counsel will be very great, and much lessen" their interest. Obtaining a dismissal for nonprosecution was sufficiently expensive that by the late 1730s some appellees were attempting to recover their costs by suing on the bond posted in the colony. By 1750 a colony law permitted some recovery. If an appellant did not get a reversal or "fails to prosecute such appeal," the appellee "may, by action of the case, recover all just and reasonable costs and damages." The appeal's cost, along with the amount-in-controversy requirement, guaranteed that the Privy Council appeal tended to be a realistic legal remedy largely for the affluent.[19]

Jurisdiction: Acts and Equity

Two areas of litigation dominated the Rhode Island appeals to the Privy Council: cases arising under the Navigation Acts and cases that raised equitable issues. In appeals under the Navigation Acts, the crown was enforcing compliance with an act that specifically governed the colonies. In appeals in equity, the Privy Council was exercising the crown's prerogative jurisdiction. Although this equitable jurisdiction is not always readily apparent—many complaints referred on their face only to title to land—almost all of these land disputes involved an equitable area such as fraud, testamentary affairs, or accounts.

In these appeals, the transatlantic advantage of a distant decision-maker was twofold. First, the Privy Council could decide cases in which an appellant was worried about colonial bias in favor of local litigants. In Navigation Acts appeals, the Privy Council attempted both to support crown authority and to prevent Rhode Islanders from using this authority to their personal advantage. Intercolonial trade cases similarly demonstrate the Privy Council's effort to counter local bias in fights among colonial merchants. Second, through appeals the Privy Council could determine whether a law or practice needed to be uniform in London and the colony or could diverge in the colony. Appeals heard by the Council in the 1750s demonstrate these tendencies.

Litigants and the Privy Council used the appeal to regulate potential abuse by Rhode Islanders with crown appointments. Navigation Acts cases such as seizures by crown-appointed custom collectors or privateers, were supposed to be brought in vice-admiralty courts appointed by the crown. Certain cases, however, were brought in colonial courts. Collectors and privateers who lost in a vice-admiralty court were particularly vulnerable when colonial merchants brought suits for inappropriate or illegal seizure. Although the Privy Council wanted to uphold its customs collectors' authority, it also was interested in controlling abuse by Rhode Islanders who held such positions. As early as 1735, two years after the Molasses Act (1733), this issue was apparent. Collector of Customs Peleg Brown seized a ship loaded with foreign molasses. The two Rhode Island owners, James Allen and Ezekiel Chever, successfully sued Brown for 1,848 pounds in colony court, related to a complicated question of whether the required duty had been due before or after the boat landed. On appeal in 1738, the Privy Council concluded that the merchants had owed the custom duty, but insisted that Brown return any amount remaining from the goods after the duty had been paid. The decision prevented undue enrichment by collectors. A similar result occurred in a 1751 appeal involving Joseph Wanton, the deputy collector of customs. Wanton had seized goods from the warehouse of Newport merchant John Freebody. In 1746 Freebody sued Wanton for trespass, and the Rhode Island Court sided with the deputy collector. The Privy Council, however, reversed in favor of the merchant, apparently concluding that the seizure had been inappropriate and the collector owed damages on the profit he had apparently made. In both appeals, the Privy Council used its authority to uphold crown authority but limit private profit.[20]

The Council's willingness to decide in favor of Rhode Island merchants diminished markedly when the crown officials in question were from another colony or England. In March 1741, Massachusetts privateer John Rous seized what he believed was the Rhode Island sloop the *South Kingstown* with a cargo of forbidden rum, molasses, sugar, and indigo. The Rhode Islanders on board, however, claimed that the sloop was French and that their sloop had been lost in December near Jamaica. After Rous lost in the Charleston vice-admiralty court, the Rhode Island owners sued him in Rhode Island for damages. The jury favored the local merchants, although the damages were not as much as they wished. When the sum was further reduced in the colony's equity court, both sides appealed to the Privy Council. Despite the monetary caution of the Rhode Island courts toward the local litigant, the Council reversed, concluding that the Rhode Islanders should have filed the action in the vice-admiralty court. The Privy Council was likely suspicious about the sloop's true identity and wanted to ensure a trial in a forum less inclined to believe Rhode Islanders.[21]

The Privy Council's concern about local bias extended to substantive legal issues. Joseph Powers, a Newport mariner and privateer, had left Jamaican merchants David Vanbrugh and Samuel Carpenter in possession of goods seized on the River Oronoque—including wax candles, arms, a blunderbuss, paper, linen, a feather bed, assorted weapons, two tiger skins, and cocoa—and twelve "Indian slaves." Powers had been concerned that certain jurisdictions might free the captives. Indeed, one captive had died when he had them sailed to London and back "in hopes the dispute would be over and then they might make sale." Nevertheless, when they landed in Jamaica, the governor concluded that the captives were "free persons" and commanded the merchants to set them "at Liberty." Powers brought an accounting action against the merchants, demanding compensation. In Rhode Island, Powers won more than four hundred pounds (Jamaican currency). The Privy Council disagreed. In October 1751 the Council "discharged and set aside" the judgments and "discharged and dismissed" the action. Apparently implicitly accepting the decision of the Jamaican governor in opposition to Indian enslavement, the Council refused to compensate Powers. The seizure was once again regulated by larger imperial concerns.[22]

Beyond Navigation Acts cases, most appeals to the Privy Council raised common-law or statutory issues that applied across the empire. Although this was never explicitly stated, equity was the common thread. Because equity could "order the performance of a will, especially if it concerns land," the Council continued to hear cases over land title. Equitable issues arising over land also included questions about dower, fraud, partition, and accountings between tenants in common. Under such a theory, one of the first post-1751 appeals heard by the Privy Council was another attempt by the Brentons to reclaim the 256 acres in Jamestown. Despite Brenton's claim that there had "been few clearer cases heard in any Court of Law," the effort failed in both Rhode Island and England—with the Privy Council emphasizing that Brenton must relinquish the land if he had come into possession. A significant difference between the post-1751 inheritance appeals and the earlier 1730s appeals was that the Privy Council and Rhode Island courts increasingly agreed. A 1752 appeal raised the tension between blood and nonblood recipients of inheritances. Samuel Potter left a legacy of five hundred pounds to his "loving friend Dorcas Tew." Potter's executor and heir, his nephew John Potter, refused to pay Dorcas, claiming insufficient assets in the estate. Dorcas and her husband sued Potter successfully in Rhode Island. On appeal in England, the Privy Council agreed with the Rhode Island interpretation of the will and even granted Dorcas interest and costs. Another 1751–1752 appeal raised the tension between the eldest son's desire for primogeniture and a younger son's claim under a will. Words had been added to the will of Othniel Tripp after it had been written. The eldest son wanted the will voided so that the land would pass intestate to him; the youngest wanted it upheld. After some disagreement in the colony courts, the youngest son eventually prevailed in Rhode Island, and once again the Privy Council affirmed.[23]

During these years, the Privy Council began to decide commercial appeals arising out of intercolonial trade. These cases often involved accounts, an area where equity could "force men to come to account with each other." Other equitable areas raised by the colonial commercial law involved fraudulent transactions, insurance agreements, partnerships, and dealings by bailiffs, receivers, factors, and agents. The Privy Council was attractive in these appeals because it could appear as an impartial decisionmaker among merchants in different colonies. The constant concern about local bias meant that the Council tended to affirm colony decisions that went against the local party. In two debt cases, Rhode Island courts had favored Charleston merchant William Harvey over Newport merchant Edward Fogg and New York merchant Guilian Verplank over Rhode Island merchant Isaac Polock. Despite having been granted permission to appeal to the Privy Council, the Rhode Island merchants chose not to prosecute either case. When a merchant lost in his own colony, there may have seemed little likelihood of success in England.[24]

The need for an impartial decisionmaker was particularly acute when intercolonial trade went awry and someone was left shorthanded. For example, Rhode Islander Ebenezer Tyler owed Boston merchant Lewis Dumoulin a great deal of money. In December 1743, Tyler signed certain goods—molasses, brandy, indigo, wine, sugar, claret, white wine, and almonds—over to Dumoulin by promissory note. Intending to resell the goods, Dumoulin left them with Tyler. A month later, Boston merchant Nathaniel Wheelwright agreed to buy the goods from Dumoulin. Wheelwright signed a bill of sale and took Tyler's promissory note. Without taking possession of the goods, Wheelwright resold the fifty-five cases of molasses and Tyler delivered them. Assuming Tyler would similarly deliver all the goods, Wheelwright rapidly sold other items to people near Boston. Tyler, however, refused to deliver until Wheelwright paid the freight to Boston. Desperate to get the goods to Boston, Wheelwright offered several compromises and finally sued Tyler for the lost sales. The Rhode Island jury sided with Tyler, perhaps appreciating the cost of moving goods to Boston. Wheelwright appealed to England to have judgment for the "whole damages" or any further order "as shall be agreeable to equity and as the court below ought to have made." The Council accepted the invitation to sit in equity. Not only did it reverse the judgment in 1752, but it recalculated the damages, concluding that Tyler owed Wheelwright the entire value of the promissory note less the fifty-five cases of molasses that had been delivered. Unlike a local jurisdiction that might appreciate, perhaps overly appreciate, local parties' difficulties, the Privy Council could determine the need for universal or local rules in commercial transactions. From a London perspective, an economy based on the interchange of commercial papers could work only if merchants could rely on common rules.[25]

The Council and crown lawyers wanted cases with significant legal issues and were uninterested in cases between Rhode Islanders that rested on factual disputes. In 1740 two Providence men fell out over accusations of fraud. Wood's *Institute* noted that "All frauds and deceits for which there is no remedy at common law" could be heard in equity. Robert Gibbs, owner of the *Hopewell,* had hired Jonathan Sheldon to sail to Jamaica and Honduras and then back to Boston. When Sheldon returned to Rhode Island, he claimed that he had hit a violent gale near Havana and the foresail and mainsail had collapsed. Concluding that he would not make it to Jamaica, he sold the ship in the Bay of Honduras. Gibbs doubted that the *Hopewell* had been unseaworthy. He sued Sheldon for having converted the vessel to his own use and "craftily intending . . . to defraud and cheat." Although one Esek Hopkins testified that he had subsequently seen the ship sailing, two sets of colony jurors believed Sheldon. Gibbs appealed to the Council but did not prosecute the case. A case that depended only on the fate of the *Hopewell* was unlikely to engage the English crown bar.[26]

Reframing a fact-based case into an appeal turning on an interesting legal issue was critical. A factual disagreement lay at the heart of an insurance dispute between John Channing and Arthur Fenner. Insurance agreements fell within equity because equity would "compel men to perform their agreements" and "afford relief when unreasonable engagements are made." Channing had agreed to insure the *Providence,* along with several other men, including James Fenner. In turn, Fenner's father, Arthur, allegedly had promised to indemnify for loss. In 1747 the *Providence* went missing while returning from Surinam. After Channing had to pay £3,000 (Rhode Island current money), he sued Fenner on the alleged promise. Arthur Fenner refused to pay for the loss, claiming that he had "made no such promise." Fenner failed to defend the suit initially and apparently was assessed the complete damages by the jury. He then seems to have had the court reassess the damages to £1,460.4.0 under a writ of inquiry "without the intervention of a jury." The existence of the promise or, indeed, of the ship, was not likely to interest London. The question of whether damages could be assessed without a jury, however, interested the Council. It heard the appeal and ordered that the case be retried with a jury. Because equitable cases often turned on facts, the art of the appeal was to find a specific legal issue that mattered in the empire.[27]

Nonprosecuted Appeals

Many cases appealed to the Privy Council were never heard in England. In some, the petition of appeal was filed but never prosecuted; in others, no papers were even filed in England—the only evidence of a contemplated appeal is the statement at the end of the colony court record. A variety of factors account for nonprosecution. The first four cases appealed from the colony in 1744 and 1745 were dismissed for failure to prosecute, a result perhaps produced by the colony's participation in King George's War (1744–1748). Additional disruptions in transatlantic travel likely caused others. The cost of appealing or a lack of English connections may have barred certain litigants. Intervening settlements may have made others unnecessary. In several instances, the appellant had already lost twice in the colony's courts and may have seen the appeal as a delaying tactic. Indeed, in one dismissed appeal, the petition declared that the appeal had been "for the sake of unjustly delaying the payment." Advice by English agents, solicitors, and law officers may have discouraged other appellants from bringing appeals that were overly dependent on facts. In one case, John Staniford believed that his relative Jeremiah Staniford had not been of sound mind when he wrote his will. Staniford sought to void the will that gave land and a house in Newport to Timothy and Margaret Newell and to have the estate treated as intestate. Staniford lost in the Rhode Island courts, and although he appealed to England, he never prosecuted the case. Whether Jeremiah had been of unsound mind was a factual matter unlikely to interest the Council or the crown bar. Similarly, in 1748 John Angel claimed that the Clemences had sold him three hundred acres in Providence in 1745. The Clemences claimed that the deed was fraudulent. Elizabeth Clemence testified that she "never did write one word in my life" and that her husband had been "often disordered in his mind and out of his head." The courts in Rhode Island sided with Angel, and the Clemences appealed to the Privy Council. Again, however, the fact-based nature of the claim (and the cost) resulted in nonprosecution. Factual disputes among contending colonists did not go far.[28]

The inability to appeal or to achieve rapid dismissal of nonprosecuted appeals in England sometimes had tragic consequences, as shown in two appeals relating to the colony's trustee relationship with the Narragansett tribe. The Assembly had overseen Narragansett affairs since the beginning of the eighteenth century. In 1709 the Assembly had recognized Ninigret (usually referred to as Ninigret II) as the heir with control over lands in the Narragansett region. By 1720, appointed trustees were involved with Ninigret II's affairs. This relationship was fraught with problems. In one instance, the colony sold tribal lands to pay a contested and likely fraudulent mortgage, and some trustees appear to have benefited personally. Ninigret II died in 1727, and the trustee relationship continued in the 1740s between the colony and his son, Charles Ninigret. When Charles died, his widow, Catherine, attempted to appeal to the Privy Council in a 1743 accounting action against the trustees on behalf of her son, also named Charles Ninigret. Although the appeal was granted, no bond appears to have been given and the appeal was not prosecuted. For Catherine, the cost of posting the bond and prosecuting the appeal may have been prohibitive. The inability to appeal left the trustees with authority over the Narragansett lands and shifted tribal power to a family branch that eventually would lose much of the land.[29]

The difficulty in dismissing a nonprosecuted appeal also took its toll on the Narragansett land. In 1746, the other branch of the Ninigret family sued the trustees. The Rhode Island courts were sympathetic to this suit by Sarah, widow of Charles's brother, George, on behalf of her son, Thomas Ninigret, and confirmed that the lands belonged to Thomas Ninigret. Sarah also challenged the appointment of trustees and petitioned the Assembly about the trustees' actions. They had "leased out the land, which was always kept and reserved for the tribe of Indians, for planting of corn and raising other necessaries for their support." Similarly, the trustees had leased two additional areas reserved for the tribe: woodland reserved for firewood and the "sachem's cedar swamp." The trustees appealed to the Privy Council. While the appeal sat in London, Ninigret was unable to take possession of the estates and lost the profits. The loss forced him to rely on the "charitable assistance of some of his friends." Lacking funds and perhaps the connections to move for dismissal in England, Ninigret finally sought relief in the colony. In 1755 Ninigret persuaded the Assembly to drop the appeal, noting that his mother's suit had made his right to the land "so exceeding clear and manifest." The Assembly protected the trustees' failure to prosecute the case by canceling the bond without penalty.[30]

Thomas Ninigret never recovered from his economic debts to various Rhode Islanders, and the tribe continued to lose land. In 1759 he petitioned the Assembly to repeal certain laws that prohibited the purchase of the tribe's lands so that "he [would] have the same liberty of selling and disposing of his estate . . . as others of His Majesty's subjects enjoy." He explained that "having been unhappily engaged in several law suits, in defense of his right, he hath been obliged to advance large sums of money." The Assembly complied, enabling white Rhode Islanders to purchase the land. By 1763 Ninigret's sales had created significant controversy within the tribe, particularly as some had funded a large expensive house for Ninigret and similar expenditures. A "considerable number of the Narragansett tribe" asked the Assembly to prohibit Ninigret from selling any more land without the tribe's consent. The land belonging to the Narragansett had been "reserved by old Ninigret . . . to and for his use, and the use of his said tribe and their children, forever." They were "in danger of being utterly deprived of the means of procuring a maintenance, and must either starve or become a town charge." In August the Assembly attempted to divide the land held by the sachem (chief, currently Ninigret) from that held by the tribe according to English property law. Unable to distinguish lands set off from those that "seem to be in common," however, the committee returned without action. Although members of the tribe soon deposed Ninigret, he continued to sell lands to cover debts. In despair, the tribe sent an agent to England to petition the crown. It did little good. Under the guise of extinguishing debts, an Assembly committee arranged for the sale of the valuable land at Fort Neck, which the tribe used for fishing in the Salt Lake. When Ninigret died in 1769, it was too late for the tribe. Although the Assembly finally agreed with his heir, Esther, that the tribe's land could no longer be liable for the debts, little land remained. The indirect effect of nonprosecuted appeals had taken its toll.[31]

Precedent

Transatlantic legal culture operated with an awareness of past decisions involving the colony. In Rhode Island, attorneys carefully recopied factual evidence introduced or proven in earlier cases for new trials.

Moreover, attorneys introduced prior cases as evidence of the rule that they established. In Mary Coggeshall's case, the attorneys introduced *Honyman v. Dunbar,* an earlier case involving the three-witness rule for wills. After *Martin v. Gardner,* the clerk of the court, James Martin, sought to avoid forfeiting his bond of three hundred pounds for failure to prosecute his appeal by introducing the orders from two prior Privy Council appeals in which dismissals had occurred and apparently no one had sued for the entire bond. Although the outcome of Martin's plea is not clear, past practice was, at a minimum, a relevant argument.[32]

The past decisions of the Privy Council concerning other colonies were also important. The colony's abrupt legislative changes on intestate division resulted from the belief that the Privy Council's decisions regarding Connecticut might apply in the colony. In fact, Francis Wilks wrote to the governor of Connecticut in 1740 that "whatever Appeals come before the Council Board on disputes between Elder & Younger Sons & daugrs. Will be determind according to that Precedent." The Rhode Island Assembly had long attempted to deal with intestate law within the boundaries of transatlantic legal culture. When the colony formally abandoned primogeniture in 1718, it echoed English reformers in saying that it was "very wrongful" for the entire real estate of a person dying intestate to descend to the eldest son, leaving the other children destitute. Balancing traditional English laws with English reform suggestions and colonial divergences, the 1718 law divided the land equitably among male and female children but gave the eldest son a double portion. By including the double portion, the statute attempted to avoid an obvious repugnancy to the laws of England; by dividing the remainder equitably, the statute met local concerns. In February 1728, however, the Privy Council in *Winthrop v. Lechmere* struck down Connecticut's similar intestate act. Upholding John Winthrop's right to inherit the real estate, the Council rejected the claim of his sister, Ann, and her husband, Thomas Lechmere, and voided the colonial law. The decision suddenly cast doubt upon the legitimacy of Rhode Island's act by suggesting that the colony had no power under its charter to alter intestate succession. In February 1729 the colony abruptly repealed the intestate law, noting that it was "destroying inheritances." With the law struck from the statute books, the Rhode Island Assembly avoided the appearance of having any laws repugnant to the laws of England.[33]

Reversing a Privy Council decision was tricky but not impossible. The

New England colonies did not rush to follow *Winthrop*. Connecticut simply stopped deciding intestate estates; by 1730 the governor noted that numerous people had died intestate with nothing decided. The colony considered executive and legislative means to alter the Council result. The governor wanted to petition the crown. Connecticut's agent, Jonathan Belcher, however, wrote "it is the opinion of the best Council" that such a path was unwise. The king could only order prospective relief, and an order might require a new charter: it would be "too dangerous an experiment." The colony's English counsel advocated a special parliamentary bill that would reverse the decision by quieting all estates in the past and the future. The governor, however, thought that path too dangerous as it might lead to an inquiry into additional laws that were contrary to the laws of England and thus "indanger the Charter itself." The colony's agents eventually wrote a petition to the king advocating a parliamentary bill limited to *Winthrop* that would quiet older intestate estates and enable the continuation of similar practices. Reflecting uncertainty within the Council over the result, the report from the Committee for Hearing Appeals showed sympathy to the colony's concern. Unfortunately, by 1731 other Council members were contemplating an effort to force a new charter on the colony. Faced with this threat, the Assembly abandoned parliamentary approaches and turned to draft a new intestate act. Reading *Winthrop* as being only about gender, the new act excluded female issue from inheritance but divided land equally among all sons. English advisors warned that the bill remained a problem. The Privy Council's complaint had not only involved female inheritance. The Council had felt that the act "departed from that Course of Descents, as to Real Estate, which is governed by the Common Law of the Realm"— that is, primogeniture. The theory suggested that real estate was bound by English common law carried over by settlers. Frustrated by the distinctions, Jonathan Law, the deputy governor, advanced a new argument: the colony had "been persuaded" that descents should be governed by "the law of natural equity" (partible inheritance). Despite clever ideas, *Winthrop* remained.[34]

The power of intercolonial precedent eventually solved the situation in New England. In a 1734 Massachusetts appeal, *Phillips v. Savage*, the Council altered the decision that partible inheritance was repugnant to the laws of England. The case was argued based on "Mr. Winthrop's Precedent in Connecticut" and the appeal depended on the "Distinctions between the two Cases." This time, however, colonial intestate law was successfully defended as a legitimate divergence based on proof of the custom and usage in the colony. In 1738 Jeremiah Allen wrote the Connecticut governor suggesting a "method" by which the colony might restore the intestate law. Because a "proper defense" of partible intestate had been advanced in *Phillips,* the colony should simply bring a case under an identical theory. Shortly thereafter, another case was appealed to the Privy Council challenging the original intestate act and adopting the *Phillips* defense of ancient colony custom, discussed in chapter 5. In 1745 the Council dismissed the appeal, in essence upholding Connecticut's original intestate law. *Winthrop* no longer was good law in Massachusetts and Connecticut. In Rhode Island, the Assembly took no chances and refused to print another intestate law until 1770, when it reenacted the 1718 act.[35]

Through appeal precedents, various English statutes relating to the common law had been adopted in the colony. The absence of written reports, however, left the developing doctrine dependent on individual recollection and statutory alteration. In 1749, Rhode Island faced disruption of the system. In 1747 a new annually elected, five-man Superior Court of Judicature had replaced the older, larger colony court; within two years it was composed of an entirely new set of judges. In 1749 this Court suddenly concluded that English statutes "were not in force" unless introduced by colony statute. The decision contradicted the 1729 Attorney General Yorke opinion that colonial usage could introduce English statutes. It gave the Assembly complete control over the introduction of statutory laws of England. The bar was shaken, and a group of attorneys—Daniel Updike, James Honeyman, Matthew Robinson, and John Aplin—petitioned the Assembly. Until this decision, the inferior courts and the Superior Court had "admitted such of the said statutes as relate to the common law to be in force here, and have adjudged upon them as such" without any need for a "formal introduction" of the statutes by Assembly act. The Court's decision seemed to disrupt a half century of transatlantic precedent in which court decisions and Privy Council appeals had introduced various English statutory provisions. Without refuting the decision that only the Assembly could introduce English statutes, the Assembly ordered the "attornies at law" to prepare a bill to introduce "such of the statutes of England as are agreeable to the constitution." Without any extant controversy, the Assembly passed the 1749 act, affirming its authority and the transatlantic constitutional precedents.[36]

The new act contained a selective list of seventeen provisions referring to specific English statutes or categories of statutes that "are, and ought to be in force in this colony." The statute of Merton on dower appeared first, followed by eight statutes to the time of James, criminal statutes, six additional statutes, and statutes relating to the poor. The listed statutes were central to English common law. Reflecting the early eighteenth-century appeals, most related to land and inheritance matters: dower, fee tail, the use (an equitable interest similar to a trust), and intestate distribution; the regulation of joint tenants and tenants in common, partition, leases; the statutes of limitations for land actions, requirements concerning wills and land transactions; and creditors' actions against heirs. A number were among the most famous of the laws of England: *De Donis Conditionalibus* (creating fee tail); the Statute of Uses (largely ending the use); and the Statute of Frauds (regulating wills and land transactions). Two provisions addressed broad criminal matters: bail and the descriptions of crimes in criminal statutes. Two provided for the adoption of the English writs. One introduced statutes relating to the poor and to masters and apprentices. These statutes had been integral to Rhode Island's eighteenth-century legal practice.[37]

The list specifically reflected the precedents of transatlantic jurisprudence. As the drafting committee wrote, these were statutes that "have heretofore been, and still ought to be in force." Some provisions were easily identifiable as laws of England found to apply in the colony in the appeals of the 1730s. Merton's dower provision, the Statute of Frauds, and *De Donis's* acceptance of fee tail had been addressed in Mary Coggeshall's case. The statute on joint tenancy and partition had been raised in Ann Sabeere's case. The statute on limitations had been the issue in the cases of the Sanford sisters and Jane Boreland. An analysis of Rhode Island cases and appeals, and perhaps those in other colonies, likely could match further provisions to decided cases. The list also underscored that colony laws could—indeed, should—diverge for reasons of persons and place. Although many of the definitions set forth in English criminal statutes applied in the colony, some did not because the "nature of the offences mentioned" was "confined to Great Britain." Criminal punishment was also a matter for local decision; the penalty set forth in the English statutes was in force only if the colony had not addressed the issue of punishment. The status of statutes about bastardy was left ambiguous; they were in force only as "applicable to the constitution of this colony." The commitment to the principle of colonial divergence likely explains the curious specificity of certain provisions. Under the act, all of one statute on leases was applicable in the colony, *except* the last paragraph. Similarly, the act included only one part of a statute requiring that a lessee pay double rent in a holdover tenancy. The 1749 act codified the colony's early decisions under the transatlantic constitution and ensured that the Rhode Island legal culture would not lose a half century of transatlantic jurisprudence.[38]

In a world without written reports of colonial or Privy Council decisions, personnel continuities in the bench and bar created a coherent transatlantic jurisprudence. In Rhode Island, the economic interests and professional identity of a small bar encouraged appeals. A relatively constant group of judges accepted a set of boundaries for decisions. In England, economic interest and professional identity also combined to create a colonial practice that funneled appropriate cases to the Privy Council. As crown barristers became, in turn, members on the Committee for Hearing Appeals from the Plantations, transatlantic legal culture flourished. By midcentury, the legal problems of little Rhode Island had become a part of the legal regime of the transatlantic English empire.

III

Visions of the
Transatlantic Constitution

7

Religious Establishment and Orthodoxy

The principles of repugnancy and divergence rested on a vision of the English empire and what it meant to be "English." If the English empire and Englishness required transatlantic uniformity, then some nonuniform colonial laws would be judged repugnant. If the colony could demonstrate that differences related to the nature of the colony and its people, then the colonial laws would be judged divergent. The boundaries of the transatlantic constitution thus shifted as the vision of the English empire changed. The conversation was broader than any one colony because decisions made in one colony could affect other colonies. In the intestate appeals, for example, the New England colonies had wanted similar results diverging from primogeniture. More difficult, however, were cases in which neighboring colonies followed different practices. On matters of religion, Rhode Island disagreed with both England and the other New England colonies. The commitment to these differences gave rise to a thirty-year case regarding three hundred acres. Ultimately, the Privy Council accepted that the New England colonies could diverge from the laws of England that promoted the Church of England establishment. Although the English establishment ended, no uniform colonial religious establishment took its place. A diverse vision of the place of religion in America gradually emerged from the transatlantic constitution.[1]

The case arose from the quest of James MacSparran, minister of the Church of England, to obtain certain land in Rhode Island. In 1668 a group of Rhode Island founders dedicated three hundred acres in the region of southern Rhode Island known as the Narragansett for a minister they described as "orthodox." Initially, no one worried too much about the precise title to the land. By the 1720s, however, a changing political and religious climate raised the question of who counted as an *orthodox* minister. England, Rhode Island, and the neighboring New England colonies promoted different answers.

In England, a minister ordained by the Church of England was *orthodox*. Over the late seventeenth and early eighteenth centuries, England's position on orthodoxy had evolved. In the 1660s the Stuart rulers of England moved to reestablish *the* Church of England. Even with the 1689 Toleration Act, orthodoxy remained linked to the established episcopal church as defined by a diocesan structure, the Thirty-nine Articles, and a liturgy based on the Book of Common Prayer. After 1714, under the Hanoverian Georges, dissenting congregations received more encouragement but the establishment structure remained. In England, orthodoxy mattered because the minister's maintenance was often provided by income from farmland given to the church in perpetuity (a glebe). In the colonies, crown instructions to royal governors since the 1690s had similarly required glebes to be set aside for the ministers of orthodox churches.[2]

In neighboring Massachusetts, however, *orthodox* referred to a minister recognized by the self-proclaimed "Ministers of New England"— ministers aligned with congregational/presbyterian practices who were often called Independents or Dissenters. The group—usually self-described as "congregational or presbyterian"—defined themselves more in opposition to the Church of England's discipline and government rather than its doctrine. Just as the Church of England was the official church on that side of the Atlantic, "Independency" seemed "the religion of the country" in Massachusetts and Connecticut. In these colonies, ministers cited the Act of Toleration to legitimize themselves under the laws of England while also nursing a story in which dissenting principles were justifiable divergences from England because of English religious oppression. Massachusetts statutes supported orthodoxy by requiring contributions to the orthodox congregational and presbyterian ministry. Although a town by majority vote could agree to support a minister of any protestant denomination, in practice the supported minister was the one judged to be orthodox by the New England ministry.[3]

In Rhode Island, orthodoxy was rejected. Founded by religious dissenters and exiles from Massachusetts and England, Rhode Island stood as a living witness to the problem of religious intolerance under the guise of orthodoxy. Followers of English or Massachusetts orthodoxy were few. William McLoughlin estimates that in 1700 "most of the 10,000 people living in Rhode Island . . . may be considered as opponents of the Puritan system." Religiously affiliated Rhode Islanders were for the most part Quakers and Baptists. Moreover, many in the colony avoided firm religious identities or changed their religious identification over time. As a legal matter, the colony explicitly opposed orthodoxy. A 1716 Rhode Island act prevented civil authority from supporting the ministry. According to the Assembly, the "use of the civil power" by churches, congregations, and societies of people was inevitably to endeavor "for preeminence or superiority [of] one over the other." A minister's maintenance had to be "raised by free contribution." The colony left ideas about orthodoxy to individual belief.[4]

The thirty-year case asked which interpretation of *orthodox* applied in Rhode Island: that of (1) the Church of England, (2) the presbyterian/congregationalists, or (3) individual determination. James MacSparran, an ordained minister of the Church of England, thought that Rhode Island should interpret *orthodox* as in England so that the land would support him. Joseph Torrey, a Harvard-educated congregational minister, thought that Rhode Island should follow Massachusetts's divergent interpretation of orthodoxy and that the land should support him. The significance of the decision was great. If Rhode Island had to follow the laws of England supporting the Church of England, Rhode Island's nonestablishment and Massachusetts's religious establishment would both end. If the Massachusetts dissenters were accepted as orthodox, Rhode Island could become an extension of the Massachusetts establishment. The three hundred acres provided a rhetorical space for a battle between the missionary arms of Massachusetts presbyterian/congregationalism and the Church of England, each seeking to define a place in the founding of America. Amid legal machinations, published spin control, and massive fund-raising, accusations flew and history was rewritten.[5]

The Reverend James MacSparran

From the outset, James MacSparran's presence in New England was troubled. Born in 1693 and raised in Ireland in a Scottish Presbyterian family, MacSparran graduated from the University of Glasgow in 1709.

As a minister of the Presbyterian Church of Scotland, MacSparran set off for America, arriving in Boston in 1718. He became pastor of the church in Bristol but the Boston ministry, led by Benjamin Colman, refused to ordain him. Twenty years older than MacSparran, Colman had attended Harvard College and become minister of a new Cambridge church, the Brattle Street Church, after ordination by the English presbytery in 1699. His views were "midway between the Church of England and Dissenters"; his congregation read the Lord's Prayer and had more flexible requirements for full membership and baptism. Committed nevertheless to promoting presbyterian and congregational interests, Colman and other ministers opposed MacSparran. In September 1719, John Danforth wrote Colman that if they ordained a "third-infamous-scotch minister, and then a fourth . . . what will become of Christ Churches and Interests among us?" MacSparran was suspiciously friendly with a notorious minister of the Church of England, John Checkley, and his testimonials seemed not in order.[6]

MacSparran's time in Bristol as a New England minister thus was brief. Colman wrote the Bristol church that MacSparran should not be ordained. In July 1719 a council of church elders convicted MacSparran of "very lascivious and filthy speeches as also of gross, lewd and vile solicitations of women," of "intemperance as to strong drink, in repeated instances," and of "gross profanations of God's Holy name." His response to the charges was found "very defective, superficial, ambiguous, and fallacious, extenuating and excusing all his faults." He was deemed "not qualified for a Gospel Minister" and the church was advised not to complete his ordination. Some in Bristol continued to support him. Attorney Nathaniel Byfield told minister Samuel Sewall that MacSparran was "our Minister." Later that fall, however, MacSparran left for England to obtain confirmation of his credentials as a presbyterian minister.[7]

In England, MacSparran quickly became instead a minister of the Church of England and a missionary of the Society for the Propagation of the Gospel in Foreign Parts (SPG). Later in his life, he attributed his rapid conversion to the Bristol experience: "a false charge in my youth . . . opened me a way into the Christian priesthood in the *most excellent of all churches*." For MacSparran, the appeal of the Church of England was likely its clarity of ordination and the security of the episcopal structure. New England's presbyterian/congregational ministers depended for their legitimacy on the members and other ministers; episcopal authority came from the church hierarchy. In October 1720 the new minister

was assigned to discharge his office in the Narragansett region of southern Rhode Island with a maintenance of seventy pounds. The Church of
England had come to Rhode Island only in 1698. In the Narragansett,
around 1707, the Parish of St. Paul had arisen as a two-story wooden
building with curved windows and broken pediments and pilasters on
the doors. By 1717 the parish had acquired a large folio Bible, a copy of
the Book of Common Prayer, a copy of the Book of Homilies, a chalice,
a carpet for the communion table, and a border for the pulpit—but no
settled minister. Newport's episcopal ministers visited to perform services and baptisms. The parish members had requested a minister of the
"true" religion as "currents of atheism and infidelity" threatened to
"overflow the country." MacSparran was the Church's response.[8]

After a "good deal of hardship," including the ship's being overset
twice in one day and losing its masts, sails, and rigging, MacSparran arrived in New England in late April 1721. On the way to the Narragansett
region, however, he caused himself further difficulty. As a young woman,
Frances Davis, testified, MacSparran spent the night at her father's
house. He apparently hoped that she would come to the Narragansett
and "not come home a maid again." Her affidavit stated:

> He would have me sit on the bed, but I said I would not, but he put his
> hand round my waist, and shove me along, and set me down on the
> bed, and then sat by me, and pulled me down on the bed. I told him I
> did not use to lie on the bed with young men, and he said he would put
> out the candle, but I told him, he should not; yet he did, and he would
> have me put off my hoop petticoat, but I told him I would not. He also
> tried to put his hand into my bosom, but I prevented him. He told me
> he would cut my string, if I did not pull off my hoop petticoat, and he
> tried to untie the string that was round my waist, but I hindered him
> and then he took out his knife and cut my string that was round my
> waist almost in two, which made me very much displeased. I told him I
> would go away if he did so, but I thought it better for my own security
> to pull off [my] hoop coat, and he held me by the hand all the while,
> fearing I should get away . . . He also said let me feel your belly, but I
> was very angry and prevented him, but before I pulled off my hoop pet-
> ticoat, he catched hold of my leg, as high as my knee before I was
> aware, of all which aforesaid actions he knew I resented very ill.

MacSparran declared that he had not taken "up her cloths or to put his
hand under them" and "in general there was nothing morally criminal
either acted or intended." He had "never intended the Lady any dis-

honor, so he never actually attempted her modesty." His response, not entirely disputing her account, fueled doubt as to his ministry.[9]

In the Narragansett, MacSparran strove to be a perfect minister of the Church of England. Within months of settling, he aligned himself with a relatively affluent and established family in Narragansett society. In May 1722 he married Hannah Gardner, the seventeen-year-old daughter of William Gardner. The Narragansett was farming country and during the eighteenth century became the location of one of the largest populations of enslaved Africans and African-Americans in the northern colonies. MacSparran was no exception to the practice of slavery, holding at least four enslaved people, and his diary carefully records his violence against them. After acquiring his new social status, MacSparran turned to church duties. He sought to reclaim various church items and began to recruit. By 1724 he wrote to the SPG that more than 150 people attended the church on Sundays. MacSparran paid particular attention to the SPG's missionary aim of evangelizing Native Americans and African-Americans. He noted that thirty free Indians, as well as a number of Indian and Negroes who were "all slaves," also attended. Attendance did not signal full church membership; MacSparran admitted that only seventeen people took communion. Nonetheless, MacSparran persevered: catechizing the youth, celebrating almost all the holy days, and attempting to establish a borrowing library.[10]

MacSparran lacked only a glebe to prove himself a proper minister of the Church of England. A glebe would follow English practice and make him less dependent on free contributions. Fortunately, a potential glebe was not hard to find. A three-hundred-acre farm existed that some believed had been given to the Church. MacSparran thought the land was worth nine or ten pounds sterling a year and "capable of great improvement." Initially, the parish planned, and the SPG authorized, payment to the "present possessor" of 150 pounds so the land could "be forever secured." In July 1722, however, the parish decided instead to sue. Thus, as MacSparran would recount, "by the advice of my vestry," the lawsuit began.[11]

The Ministry Lands

The three hundred acres lay next to the Great Pond and alongside a cedar and pine swamp within a roughly fifteen-by-seven-mile area known as the Pettaquamscutt Purchase. In 1657 the Purchase had been bought for sixteen pounds from the Narragansett tribe by a group of five men: John Porter, Samuel Wilson, Thomas Mumford, Samuel Wilbore, and John Hull. Later, William Brenton and Benedict Arnold also became co-owners of the original Purchase. Each of these so-called Proprietors received shares of land. In 1668, five of the men voted that three hundred acres would be set apart "as an encouragement, the income or improvement thereof wholly for an orthodox person that shall be obtained to preach God's words to the inhabitants." The land was not fully divided during the lifetimes of the Proprietors and shares passed to heirs and assigns. In 1679, after a majority of the Proprietors had died, a meeting was held to divide land among descendants. The list of lots included one marked "for the Ministry Three Hundred Acres." In 1692, after the last Proprietor (Thomas Mumford) died, the land was finally surveyed. On the survey the three hundred acres were set off and labeled "Ministry."[12]

Although MacSparran's parish thought the land had been given for an episcopal minister, the issue was far from clear. The ambiguity was less the product of dishonest witnesses (though the case would have plenty) than a consequence of the religious practices in the colony. During its first decades, the colony had favored nonhierarchical denominations. Since the 1640s, Baptists had flourished under the leadership of Roger Williams and John Clarke. After sporadic efforts in the 1650s and 1660s, Quaker meetings expanded in the wake of George Fox's 1672 visit. In fact, to early Massachusetts and Church of England observers, the colony's religious societies did not even resemble churches. In 1639 John Winthrop complained that the early Rhode Islanders "gathered a church in a very disordered way." The episcopalian Thomas Lechford similarly concluded that there was no church but a "meeting of some men who there teach one another and call it Prophecy." Congregationalism, presbyterianism, and episcopalianism as established denominations in Rhode Island postdated the 1668 ministry grant and subsequent meetings. Congregationalists and presbyterians first organized, informally, in Newport only in 1695. The Church of England similarly had an institutional presence in the colony only after 1698.[13]

Of what religion were the Proprietors? The five men who made the 1668 grant were three Portsmouth Rhode Islanders, John Hull of Massachusetts, and William Brenton. Hull, the treasurer of the Massachusetts Bay colony, was the only one with a definite religious affiliation—he was a founding member of the congregational/presbyterian Old South Church. Brenton's religious identity in 1668 is murky, although he eventually willed land to the pastor of the Taunton Church. The three Portsmouth men do not appear to have had distinct recoverable religious identities in the 1650s and 1660s. It seems likely that Samuel Wilbore, Thomas Mumford, and Samuel Wilson were not fervent believers of either denomination but instead were comfortable with the loose understanding of Protestantism that was common in the colony. What mattered was a belief in a certain set of core principles about the importance of God's word, not the structure of the religious organization or the precise approach. They were not presbyterians, congregationalists, or episcopalians as those denominations came to define themselves.[14]

When MacSparran sued, the land was held by heirs and assigns of the Proprietors. Twenty of the three hundred acres were in the possession of Henry Gardner (the assign of John Porter). Henry Gardner was a native-born Rhode Islander in his late seventies who appears to have been basically a Baptist. He was the great-uncle of MacSparran's new wife and romantically involved with her grandmother. Years earlier, he had fenced in the acreage with his own land, perhaps hoping to claim it by a statute of limitations argument. By the 1720s, however, Gardner apparently had admitted that he might have been mistaken in fencing the land. Unlikely to gain title, Gardner lost little in transferring the land to his new family member, James MacSparran.[15]

George Mumford (descendant of proprietor Thomas Mumford) held the remaining 280 acres and had nothing to gain by giving up the land. Mumford was acting on behalf of or in concert with another heir, Jahleel Brenton, one of the largest landholders in the Narragansett region. Brenton owned adjacent land and, according to MacSparran, planned to join the tract to his land, giving him a large parcel that backed onto the cedar swamp and the pond. Mumford had acquired the land in 1720 for one hundred pounds from James Bundy, a "poor" man. Mumford and Brenton opposed the establishment of a Church of England glebe, in large part because they wanted the land for themselves. Mumford's religion remains vague; in the later trials he was referred to as "dissenter." By 1732 Brenton was at least a mild congregationalist, for his will left maintenance to Nathaniel Clap, the Newport congregational minister. Brenton had long been concerned that the Church of England might get the land. In 1711 he wrote to Samuel Sewall that some people were "gaping after it already" for a Church of England minister. Brenton was largely uninterested, however, in ensuring that it go to dissenters. Although the grant was wanting in words "of greater force to secure it to a minister of the Presbyterian and Congregational principles," Brenton wanted to add language so that if it were ever taken for any other use, the Proprietors' heirs would regain the land. He would later argue that the grant was no good and should revert to the Proprietors' descendants. Brenton and Mumford wanted the land for themselves; MacSparran's claim upset the plans.[16]

The September 1723 trial between MacSparran and Mumford lacked impartial evidence. MacSparran alleged that he was a minister of the gospel and so "according to the true intent and design" ought to be put in possession of the property. MacSparran unfortunately did not have the original grant (a later trial would reveal that Jahleel Brenton had hid it) and did not know that it used the phrase *orthodox person.* As he acknowledged, the "formality of the grant" was not "so strong as might be." Nevertheless, the farm was known as the ministerial farm or Ministry Farm, the 1679 land list showed it labeled as "for the Ministry Three Hundred Acres," and the 1692 map marked the land "Ministry." In an English colony, a ministry farm should go to a Church of England minister. Three witnesses related to MacSparran's wife supported the claim by stating their belief that the Church of England was the "ministry." A last witness, Henry Gardner, was less help. Gardner noted that in 1692 one person had "insisted" that the land should go to a presbyterian. Jahleel Brenton, however, had pointed out that a three-hundred-acre farm "is a great thing in England and should we give such a farm to the presbyterians here it would be soon noticed at home and would sound ill that the Church of England [was] so much neglected." He added that it "may prove a Disadvantage to our purchase." Brenton's advice was to "[not] express it to the presbyterians but . . . give it to the Ministry and let them dispute who had the best title to it." Accordingly, the surveyor, John Smith, wrote simply "Ministry" on the map. According to Gardner, ambiguity had been deliberate to avoid transatlantic problems.[17]

George Mumford, represented by Nathaniel Newdigate and Jahleel Brenton, offered a string of alternative arguments. MacSparran had no grant and no proof that the land had ever been granted to the ministry. If there had been a grant, it was no good and the land should revert to the heirs. Even if the grant was actually good, the land should go to a

presbyterian or congregational minister because the original Proprietors were of the "presbyterian and congregational persuasion in religion and dissenters from the Church of England." Lastly, a decision for
MacSparran would be a "forced contribution" in violation of the Rhode
Island law requiring free contributions. Mumford also enlisted relatives
for evidence. Eighty-two-year-old Benedict Arnold, son of a proprietor
and Mumford's uncle by marriage, stated that he had often heard the
"original or first Purchasers" state that the land was for presbyterian
ministers. Similar claims were made by a series of "superannuated" men.[18]

MacSparran lost. Although he hired Daniel Updike to handle the rehearing, a second jury reached the same result the following spring. The
verdict was not surprising. MacSparran had no deed. Evidence that the
land had been intended for the Church of England was contradicted
with testimony that it had been for the presbyterians. The only certain
conclusion was that the land had been disputed for decades. As the
colony had no official policy favoring the Church of England or the
presbyterians—indeed, it had instead a policy disfavoring establishments of religion—Mumford kept the land. MacSparran blamed the religious practices of the colony: "the judges are all sectaries and not a bap-
tized person save one Papist in Authority." More importantly, he saw the
verdict as proof of the "progress the presbyterians (as they are called)
are making." The plan had been to "defeat the Church to give it for the
support of an independent teacher." There were too few congregational/
presbyterians to support a minister without the land; with a glebe, Massachusetts religious practices would spread. The spread was threatening, for the previous year MacSparran had visited twelve churchmen
who had been imprisoned in Bristol for refusing to pay ministerial
support. He vowed to "not forget the opposing Spirit of New England
presbyterians."[19]

MacSparran appealed to the Privy Council. MacSparran hoped that in
England "it will appear the justest thing in the world at home that the
land should go to the Church." Moreover, he expected that the head of
the SPG "will espouse that Cause." Having already spent fifty pounds on
the case, he appointed the secretary of the SPG as his attorney to prosecute the appeal because he was "not able to do it at my own charge."
Sending off the copy of the case and the colony's law regarding ministerial support, MacSparran expected good news.[20]

Unfortunately, England was "a great ways off." The SPG never prosecuted the appeal. Rhode Islanders on both sides persuaded London officials to drop the case. Brenton apparently enlisted agent Richard Partridge to explain the weaknesses to the SPG and the bishop of London. Newport's episcopal minister, James Honeyman, simultaneously begged the bishop to render MacSparran "incapable of doing any service here." He had a "scandalous life and conduct" and had been cast out from "the Dissenters for his immoralities" with an "indelible blot cast upon his character by some lewd conversation with and attempts upon the virtue of a young gentlewoman." Perhaps even more importantly, the appeal did not fit the plans of the new bishop of London, Edmund Gibson. During these years, Massachusetts congregational/presbyterian ministers were attempting to hold a synod and claimed that they were "the Legal Establishment" and the "King's Ministers." MacSparran and others in the SPG objected to the effort to create an "established Provincial religion." For the SPG, which was quietly pursuing efforts to have the New England ministry's actions and certain laws found in violation of the laws of England, MacSparran's suit was a distraction. In May 1725, Mumford successfully filed to dismiss the nonprosecuted appeal.[21]

Massachusetts Missionaries

For the next seven years, the dispute lay quiet and MacSparran went about his life as a minister. John Smibert, a Scottish portraitist who painted a number of colonial elites, came to the colony and painted MacSparran and his wife. Visiting dignitary George Berkeley preached at the church, noting "here are fewer quarrels about religion than elsewhere." Then suddenly another minister reawakened the controversy. In May 1732, Joseph Torrey, a twenty-five-year-old Harvard graduate trained as a physician, was installed as the congregational/presbyterian minister in the Narragansett region. Torrey's installation reflected both Rhode Island family machinations to acquire land and Massachusetts's promotion of its religious establishment. Torrey had married Elizabeth Wilson on October 15, 1730, in a ceremony performed by none other than MacSparran. Like the Gardners, Torrey's new in-laws, the Wilsons, sought to gain the land for their daughter. In December, William Mumford (Elizabeth's brother-in-law) and three others wrote to the Boston ministry requesting that Torrey be settled among them as a congregational or presbyterian minister. There was no action on the request until 1732. That spring, religious difficulties returned to Boston. Followers of the Church of England had decided to raise money to once again "lay the sufferings of the churchmen" in New England before the King and the Privy Council. If the New England ministry could acquire the ministry land, the presbyterian/congregational ministry would have a strong toehold in Rhode Island, and the entire New England region would stand as a religious divergence to the Church of England's establishment. MacSparran's nemesis, Benjamin Colman, and another Boston congregationalist minister, Thomas Prince, masterminded the scheme.[22]

Torrey thus became, in MacSparran's eyes, "a missionary sent from Boston & maintained from there." His 1732 ordination was designed with an eye to a subsequent trial. The Boston ministers declared that Torrey was "orthodox" under the doctrine of the Church of England, the presbyterians, and the Independents. The May 22 edition of the *New-England Weekly Journal,* a newspaper controlled by the congregationalists and presbyterians, established each fact necessary to win in court. It also attempted to mollify the Rhode Island Baptists and Quakers who dominated the juries and courts by praising the two groups for their assistance in promoting "universal peace and happiness." In fact, the account singled out "the chief Judge of the County Court"—the person before whom the suit would be heard—as having "very generously" helped them with finding a suitable location for the ordination. To further diminish Rhode Island interference, the Boston ministers hired as their attorney Daniel Updike, who was not only a member of MacSparran's church but his attorney at the rehearing in the earlier trial.[23]

Weeks later, Torrey sued George Mumford for the 280 acres. Mumford once again triumphed. MacSparran claimed that Mumford had wanted, as "a mere layman," to "hold it, as an estate to himself." After losing in the inferior court, Torrey produced stronger evidence for the Superior Court trial: the original 1668 grant with the phrase *orthodox person.* The jury brought in a special verdict: "If it be the opinion of this Honorable Court that the appellant be an orthodox minister according to law, then we find the land" for Torrey, and if not, the jury would confirm the verdict for Mumford. In an apparently five-four decision, the majority concluded that "Joseph Torrey is not an orthodox minister according to law." The dissenters wanted to embrace Massachusetts's divergent interpretation: that under the laws of England ("the Act of Indulgence to dissenting congregations") and Rhode Island's charter a congregational/ presbyterian minister could be *orthodox.* The Quaker judges who formed the majority, however, shied away from orthodoxy and, in so doing, limited the expansion of the congregational/presbyterian ministry. The Quaker majority's concern about a spread of Massachusetts religious practices was understandable. In the 1650s, Massachusetts had enacted laws against Quakers and executed four. Only in the 1730s had the Quakers been able to obtain exemption privileges in Massachusetts so that they were no longer required to support the congregational/presbyterian ministers. Moreover, a decision against Torrey did not make the Church of England the orthodox establishment. The majority decision reaffirmed the colony's attitude toward religious establishments by suggesting that no minister was orthodox according to law in Rhode Island. The colony might successfully continue to diverge from both the English model and the Massachusetts model of orthodoxy and establishment.[24]

In Massachusetts this decision threatened the ministerial establishment. Political and religious leaders leapt into action. If congregational and presbyterian ministers were not orthodox in Rhode Island, they might not be orthodox in Massachusetts—and the establishment could collapse. Without further ado, Torrey and the presbyterians appealed to the Privy Council. Massachusetts governor Belcher wrote to Samuel Holden and Thomas Hollis in London for assistance in prosecuting the appeal "for the cause and interest of the true churches of Christ in this country." In May 1734 the convention of New England ministers appointed a committee composed of Colman, Prince, and several others to ask the General Court to help bear the charge of the appeal and to raise contributions toward the necessary 150 pounds.[25]

The Massachusetts ministry also launched a colonial-style media blitz to promote their claim—compelling but false—that Massachusetts and Rhode Island followed a common divergence from an episcopal establishment. In a June 1733 discussion in the *New-England Weekly Journal,* an anonymous author (most likely the minister Thomas Prince) described the Proprietors as "Dissenters from the Ecclesiastical Order and Discipline as Established in England." For four consecutive weeks, lengthy newspaper columns claimed that the Rhode Island founders were of the same religious persuasion as the Massachusetts dissenters. One angry reader, "W. N.," disagreed with this reconstruction of New England's religious history, reminding readers that "Churchmen as well as Baptists and Quakers had met with hard Usage" from the "Independent or Congregation Interest" in Massachusetts. In his construction of a unified history of New England, however, Prince readily erased Massachusetts religious intolerance and left only the persecution by the Church of England. New England stood for a single proposition: the right to diverge from the *type* of religious establishment found in England, but not the right to diverge from the *idea* of a religious establishment.[26]

In England, Massachusetts officials made an equally deceptive presentation to the Privy Council. The petition replaced the words of the actual grant—*orthodox person*—with the phrase *a Person in their Sentiments Orthodox.* The misrepresentation was crucial. Whereas *orthodox person* required a legal determination of orthodoxy under the laws of England, the later phrase necessitated only a factual decision about the intent of the Proprietors. In theory, the strategy was risky because the Proprietors' religious beliefs were an admittedly murky subject. Curiously, though, Mumford filed no papers in opposition to the appeal and so only one set of facts appeared. Torrey's petition freely presented the Proprietors as unquestionably presbyterian. In July 1734 the Privy Council reversed the judgments and gave Torrey possession of the land. Massachusetts had won.[27]

The victory promised expansion of the New England congregational/presbyterian ministry. Governor Belcher celebrated the "great service" to the "cause of religion in general and of the churches of this country." A year and half later, Thomas Prince's *A Chronological History of New-England* (1736) codified the vision. Massachusetts intolerance and Rhode Island nonestablishment had no place in his triumphant story. In fact, Prince ended his history in 1633 to avoid recounting the religious controversies over Roger Williams and Anne Hutchinson that led to the settling of Rhode Island. Flush with success, the Massachusetts ministry decided that they should acquire the other twenty acres. Colman noted that the remaining acres were "much more valuable than any forty acres of the land recovered, it being laid out in the midst of the town for a Home lot, to build the Ministry House on, and lying near to the Meeting house." Thus, in the fall of 1734, a month after the Council's order had been received, Torrey sued MacSparran's tenant, Ephraim Gardner. Massachusetts members of the Church of England understood the danger. King's Chapel and Christ Church in Boston formed a committee to "defend and promote the interests of the episcopal churches in New England." The New England Episcopalians aligned against a New England ministry increasingly seen as congregationalist.[28]

The central drama of this third trial was the public revelation that Jahleel Brenton, now dead, had hidden the grant. Brenton's nephew, Ebenezer Brenton, recalled visiting his uncle while the first trial, *MacSparran v. Mumford*, was pending. Jahleel had told Ebenezer to open a trunk, remove a file marked "Pettaquamscutt papers," and "take out a small paper marked Ministry." The paper was, as Ebenezer noted, "commonly called the original grant of the proprietors." After Ebenezer read the grant, he was told to "put it into the same file and place from where I took it." With the deception exposed, George Mumford distanced himself from his one-time colleague Brenton and now sided with MacSparran. He declared that the Church of England was "by Law Established" and that, by "construction of law," only episcopal ministers were "truly orthodox." With "utmost sincerity," he insisted that, had he known of the grant or had he "not been forbid by Jahleel Brenton," he would have surrendered the land to MacSparran back in 1723.[29]

Not surprisingly, given the deception, MacSparran and the Church of England won. Although possession of the land had proved again determinative, Colman blamed religion. He pointed to "the disaffection of the judges and jurors at Rhode Island to our ministry, holding us it may be in their very Consciences to be Heterodox." He advised against troubling the King and Council "with another Appeal." Torrey ignored the advice but to no avail. The Rhode Island Court barred the appeal, concluding that the twenty acres fell below the jurisdictional minimum. For the majority of Rhode Islanders—Quakers, Baptists, and non-religiously aligned—the status quo was acceptable. The congregationalists had more land; the episcopalians had the better location. The Privy Council had not defined orthodoxy in the colony, and Rhode Island had preserved its refusal to adopt either Massachusetts or English religious establishments.[30]

Episcopalians versus Congregationalists

Neither the Church of England in New England nor the New England Ministry were content. Pushed by these forces, in 1736 the case became a full battle over the meaning of *orthodoxy* under the transatlantic constitution. MacSparran filed a declaration for trespass against Robert Hassard, who was leasing the 280 acres. According to Colman, the plea by "MacSparran's lawyers was that the english church was the truly and only orthodox [one] through his majesty's Dominions." The Rhode Island Court struggled to avoid a trial. It barred MacSparran's suit against Hassard, claiming that the issue had already been decided, and denied MacSparran's subsequent appeal. MacSparran, however, had learned from his previous travails. He traveled to England to ensure that the appeal would be prosecuted. The Privy Council order in this case, likely drawn from his petition, showed the bias now running in MacSparran's favor. Persons of the presbyterian persuasion and dissenters had lied about the grant, misrepresented its words, and made "overtures . . . to prevent the disputes affecting the Common Cause or interest of the presbyterians." In March 1737 the Council commanded that the Rhode Island Court "hear the merits of the case." In September, during one of the worst heat spells that Thomas Prince could remember, both sides began to prepare.[31]

A year and a half later, in March 1739, MacSparran and the Massachusetts presbyterians and congregationalists had their trial. The evidence had become so lengthy and complicated that the clerk had to construct a four-column chart to list the documents copied into the lengthy (317-page) final record. Page after page testified as to what the "ancient people" had intended. In the decades of trials, the two sides had deposed seemingly every old person in the colony with a passing relation to the Proprietors. The man who as a young boy had carried the chains when the land was surveyed (Ephraim Codners, age 64) and the surveyor's son (Thomas Hassard, age 78) gave testimony. Each side argued that the Proprietors had been of their particular religious persuasion and that no followers of the other religion had even existed in the colony at the time of the grant. Thus for the Church of England, Henry Gardner testified that he "knew of no presbyterians or congregationalist that inhabited this colony" and Peleg Mumford remembered none who inhabited the colony over sixty years ago. For the presbyterians, Jeremiah Wilson said that there had not been a Church of England in the colony "till long since his memory."[32]

The testimony about the three Rhode Islanders was completely contradictory. Peleg Mumford (age 79) said that his father had been brought up in the "way and discipline" of the Church of England and had never joined with any other society. George Mumford also testified that his grandfather "was in the army of King Charles the first when they fought against the parliament army at Edgehill." The presbyterians, however, argued that Mumford was a presbyterian because his son had been one and Mumford had "served in the Army under Oliver Cromwell." With respect to Samuel Wilbore, Henry Gardner stated that Wilbore had professed himself a member of the Church of England, and Wilbore's daughter, Elizabeth Freelove (over 73 years old), agreed. Job Green (age 83), however, testified that Wilbore had been "inclined" to the "presbyterian persuasion." Samuel Wilson was the subject of equally strong disagreement. Peleg Mumford recounted that, when he was 10, the presbyterians and congregationalists came from Connecticut and took his father and Samuel Wilson captives. Therefore, Peleg had "good grounds to believe that said Gentlemen did not mean a presbyterian or congregational minister by the orthodox person" and Wilson "was particularly severe and bitter" against the presbyterians. But Wilson's son, Jeremiah (age 64), a presbyterian who attended Torrey's meetings, stated that he had "always understood" that the farm was for the presbyterians and had "never heard that his father was a churchman" until recently.[33]

Despite the efforts to turn the Rhode Islanders into loyal members of one of the two denominations, the testimony betrayed the ambiguity of the past. Many witnesses ended up using phrases like "brought up" or "inclined" that indicated the speculative nature of Rhode Island religious identity. Indeed, testimony revealed the colony's actual religious history. As Job Green noted, the land was granted "before any Church of England or presbyterian Ministry was settled" in the colony. Moreover, even when denominations began to appear, the differences between the Church of England and the dissenting groups was not as extreme as perceived by the ministry. Some clearly attended whichever church was most convenient in order to take communion and participate in other rituals. As Timothy Cutler, the minister of Christ's Church in Boston noted, "there are and have been many professed members of the Church of England who have communicated not only with the Church of England to which they belonged but occasionally in the dissenting meetings." Neither side could erase the fact that the colony had never favored either establishment.[34]

In April 1739 MacSparran lost. Although the result followed earlier colony decisions in siding with the person in possession, MacSparran blamed religion and politics in the colony. There was "a faction on foot" about the choice of governing officers and the "dissenters" changed "sides all of a sudden." Daniel Abbott, who had deeded land in Providence for the "worship of God in the Presbyterian or Congregational way," joined the court. MacSparran claimed that he lost "in consequence" of the election. He vowed, however, to appeal to the Privy Council. MacSparran's parish wrote to parishes in Massachusetts and Rhode Island "begging their assistance," and a "generous collection" was made. Torrey was similarly supported by "collections abroad" and the "dissenting interests" in New England. Indeed, the Massachusetts General Court at first agreed to financially support the appeal, but after protests it reluctantly concluded that "it could not spend the public money to defend persons or property in another province." Instead, congregations donated close to two thousand pounds. The appeal had become a cause célèbre for both denominations.[35]

If MacSparran's appeal had been successful, it would have set a bad precedent for the Massachusetts establishment. A July 1739 one-page broadside entitled "A Brief Representation" declared: "And that which most affects us is . . . that one of the said McSparran's main pleas was this, that the Ministers of the Church of England are the only orthodox Ministers in New-England: The tendency of which plea is, to pave the way for invading all the ministry lands throughout this country." Now calling themselves congregationalists, the Massachusetts ministry promoted a New England established church. In a ten-page anonymous defense, Thomas Prince declared: "We deny ourselves to be dissenters in New England: for if dissenters signifies the minor part; YOU are the New England Dissenters." Incapable of seeing Massachusetts religious intolerance, Prince claimed that the Proprietors could have only been partial to the Church of England if they had been "hypocrites" and the "most ridiculous and whimsical Religionists that ever were." Determined to promote a uniform New England establishment, Prince denied Rhode Island's religious past.[36]

Yet from Rhode Island came voices determined to preserve the colony's religious history. A pamphlet "A Brief Representation . . . from a Gentleman in Newport, to his Friend in Boston" criticized the "rare art of confounding places," claiming that those "acquainted with the antiquities of New-England in general, and of Rhode-Island in particular" would recall that the Proprietors would not have followed Massachusetts practices. According to even the learned Cotton Mather's *History of New England,* there had been "men of all religions" in Rhode Island. The pamphlet noted that "no congregationalists or independants *[sic]* lived in Rhode Island colony so early as 1668" and the four Proprietors "were driven to Rhode-Island for their disconformity to congregationalism." It was "high abuse and insult" to impose Massachusetts religious history on Rhode Island, "as if that government stood upon higher ground, and her example, as such, were to control us." According to the pamphlet author, there was no New England divergence from the Church of England.[37]

The most accurate description of Rhode Island's approach to religious establishment appeared that same year in Baptist minister John Callendar's *Historical and Religious Discourse, with affairs of the Colony of Rhode Island and Providence Plantations.* The timing of Callendar's book raises the distinct possibility that it was written in part in response to the debates. Rhode Island was a "plantation for religion and conscience sake." Prior to the colony's settlement,

> the *true grounds of Liberty of Conscience,* were not then known, or embraced by any sect or party of Christians; all parties seemed to think, that as *they only* were in the possession of the truth, so *they alone* had a right to restrain, and crush all other opinions, which they respectively called error, and heresy, where they were the most numerous, and powerful; and in other places they pleaded a title, to liberty and freedom of their Conscience.

In Massachusetts, the majority had "soon discovered themselves, as fond of Uniformity" and as reluctant "to allow Liberty of Conscience to such as differed from themselves" as those in England "from whose Power they had fled." It was "the religious Differences among the first Settlers of the Massachusetts Colony, [that] gave Rise to this Colony." Since the outset, the colony had accepted religious fluidity. Some who were "Puritans of the highest form" eventually became Baptists; some Baptists became Quakers. In the colony, the Church of England and the Massachusetts ministry were latecoming minority religions. Only in 1695 had "several Ministers of the Massachusetts-colony" come to preach, and not until 1720 had "a Church in the congregational scheme gathered." Similarly, not until 1706 had the "worship of God, according to the rites of the Church of England" arisen. Currently, Callendar counted eight Baptist churches and seven Quaker meeting houses but only four episcopal churches and three presbyterian/congregational churches. Religious diversity—not establishment—dominated. It was "no uncommon sight, to see Gentlemen of almost every religious persuasion among us" sitting together as magistrates. Political power rested with no religion.[38]

Most importantly, Callendar attacked the very idea of religious establishment and orthodoxy. Although he admitted that "bigots" might call Rhode Island's diverse religious practices "confusion, and disorder," he thought it "no dishonor to the colony, that Christians, of every denomination, were suffered to lead quiet and peaceable lives" without punishment for "speculative opinions" or forms of worship that "they believe God had appointed, and would accept." Orthodoxy and establishments were undesirable. It "must be a mean contracted way of thinking, to confine the favor of God, and the power of godliness, to one set of speculative opinions, or any particular external forms of worship." Moreover, it led inevitably to persecution. As he wrote, "all parties by turns, experiencing, and complaining aloud of the hardships of constraint," should realize that there "is no other bottom but this to rest upon, to leave others the Liberty we should desire ourselves." Rhode Islanders' belief in the "liberty to worship" God "according to their consciences" was the only orthodoxy worth defending.[39]

So Honest and Just a Cause

Despite Callendar's timely plea, orthodoxy and establishment continued to matter to the two sides. In London, episcopalians and congregationalists sought to influence the appeal. The case was scheduled to be heard by the Privy Council in May 1741 but was delayed. According to MacSparran, an "agent of the dissenters" had been at fault. MacSparran's correspondent, Thomas Sanford, however, attributed the delay to the attorney general's absence and added that the delay "may be the better for you, for now, whenever the Hearing comes on, either his Grace of Canterbury, or my Lord of London will attend." He promised to "get as many of your friends of the clergy to be at the hearing as possible as I can." In Rhode Island, MacSparran prayed that the case would be decided soon. He noted the "long suspense I have been under by the delay of my lawsuit (not yet determined)." The endless delay nearly ended the suit. By 1747 Benjamin Colman had died and MacSparran declared he was "at an end of all my hopes." He was "exhausted in person, with this tedious twenty-year suit." Although he had done everything "to serve the church in so honest and just a cause," MacSparran considered dropping the appeal and wanted "strength to bring it fully forth." Filled with "melancholy prospects," MacSparran begged Bishop Gibson to give him "something in your diocese" or in the north of Ireland "where I may spend the small remainder of my days where I began them." By 1751 the appeal had still not been heard. MacSparran's expenses mounted to 350 pounds and he faced tax difficulties.[40]

In the beginning of May 1752 the appeal was finally heard over two nights. Solicitor General William Murray "behaved very well" in representing MacSparran. Dudley Ryder appeared for the congregationalists. The two rejected most of the evidence. Murray sarcastically referred to the evidence as about "what ministry, several particular persons, now living, imagined, or thought those lands should be." He emphasized that most of it had been taken "since the Contest arose" and therefore "is even less to the Purpose (if possible) than the other matters." Ryder agreed and suggested that the only reliable witnesses were those that had testified in 1723. Despite most of the evidence having been abandoned, the case remained framed as a conflict between the Massachusetts and English establishments. The congregationalists' brief recounted English persecution: "the penal statutes against Puritans and Nonconformists being rigorously enforced and put in execution here in England, several presbyterians and Dissenters, to avoid Persecution, and that they might enjoy the free Exercise of their Religion[, fled]." MacSparran's brief recounted Massachusetts persecution: this "Rigor was the very thing which drove the People" to Rhode Island. According to the portrait presented to the Privy Council, New England was awash in persecution for religious belief.[41]

In the end, the Privy Council upheld the Rhode Island Court and accepted divergence on religious establishment: orthodoxy in New England did not have to mean that of the Church of England. The idea of an episcopal establishment across the colonies had ended. The observers for the Church were baffled that under the laws of England the word *orthodox* had not led to a decision in their favor. The SPG's secretary admitted that he was not sure "what Reasons" the Lords had for "the merits of the cause" had seemed "confessedly with us." He concluded that the most plausible explanation was "the common maxim possession is eleven points of the law." Two men familiar with the transatlantic constitution pondered the significance of the divergence. Charles Yorke wrote that, although the case had been affirmed "in favor of a Dissenter," he believed that under the laws of England *orthodox* usually referred to a minister of the Church of England. He noted, "It seemed agreed the word should give it to a Church of England minister if other circumstances had not shown a contrary intent in the Donors." Sir George Lee agreed. In most circumstances, "by law orthodox implies a minister of the established church." The Council had affirmed "principally upon political considerations, because the dissenting minister is in possession of the lands and the dissenters are very numerous in the Northern colonies and must not be disobliged." In England and perhaps in southern colonies, *orthodox* would continue to mean the Church of England; in New England, *orthodox* could have a different meaning. MacSparran, having learned of the "fate of my cause" from the Boston newspapers, concluded that the "thing is over, and I hope, God will give me grace to bear the defeat with a decent equanimity."[42]

MacSparran sought to ensure that people in the colonies and England would understand that the colonies practiced both establishment and nonestablishment. Ironically, he had come to appreciate Rhode Island's divergence. After the appeal, he emphasized that there is "neither local [n]or legal orthodoxy in this colony where the lands lie." Although Massachusetts and Connecticut had "presumed to establish their churches, Rhode Island has not established any religion." In 1753 his history of "English America" in *America Dissected* delineated the colonial practices upheld in the decision. In the southern colonies the Church of England was the established religion. In Virginia it was "legally established." In North Carolina the charter made it "the only established Religion, and entitled to the public Encouragement." In South Carolina it was "established . . . by Provincial Law; as indeed it is, by the Union Act of Parliament, in all his Majesty's Foreign Dominions." In Massachusetts and Connecticut, however, "Presbyterianism, is the Religion of the State." MacSparran emphasized that establishment was not required. Pennsylvania "is an absolute stranger to an uniformity in religion." In Rhode Island, "no Religion is established" and there a "Man may, with Impunity, be of any Society or of none at all." With a note of pride, he added that nowhere else were there so many "heterodox and different Opinions in Religion than were to be found in this little Corner."[43]

Although MacSparran continued with his work—baptizing children and adults, reading prayers, administering the Eucharist, marrying some and burying others—his world was ending. In the summer of 1754 he traveled to England, where the SPG voted a "benefaction of an hundred pounds for his long and faithful services." Unfortunately, Hannah, his wife for over thirty years and "the most pious of all women, the best wife in the world," contracted smallpox and died. Back in Rhode Island, the appeal led the Church to relinquish the twenty acres. The "fatal decree" had "struck such a panic" that "even the Gentlemen of the Law were so awed" as to refuse assistance. The Massachusetts congregationalists seemed to be "in high favor at court" and "upon the point of being upon an equal footing with the church by law." Church members worried that the dissenters "shall soon be uppermost in Britain as they are already in New England." In December 1757, James MacSparran died at home in South Kingstown and was laid to rest beneath the communion table. The funeral sermon came from the book of Revelation, declaring that the dead "may rest from their labours; And their works do follow them." MacSparran's own land became a glebe for the Church of England and remained Church property for more than a century. In 1799 his church was physically moved to Wickford, where it stands today. In a burial ground in woods off a highway in the Narragansett region, a large stone monument to MacSparran endures while those around it crumble. The ministry land itself was sold by the congregationalists in the 1840s for more than five thousand dollars to create a fund to support the Kingston congregational minister.[44]

The ramifications of the case endured. In refusing to reverse in favor of the Church of England, the Privy Council confirmed that the colonies could legitimately diverge from the laws of England on religion. The colonies—and thus the empire—owed their existence in part to dislike of the episcopal establishment, and the Privy Council was willing to recognize this ultimate divergence. Episcopal, congregational, and presbyterian practices would coexist in America. Equally importantly, the Council's decision permitted the abandonment of the Massachusetts establishment that had led to Rhode Island's founding. Nothing about the Privy Council result forced Rhode Island to change its laws on religion, accept a religious establishment, or promote orthodoxy. The English empire in America was also the result of a complete rejection of religious establishment. A colony founded without orthodoxy, without establishment, and without state support for religion could continue. At midcentury, the transatlantic constitution accepted that no relationship of state and religion had to exist across the American colonies.

8

Commerce and Currency

At midcentury, as James MacSparran's appeal was being heard, the boundaries of the transatlantic constitution in Rhode Island began to shift. Although families continued to raise issues of land and inheritance, the Privy Council's interest turned from land to sea and from realty to personal property. In the 1720s and 1730s, running the empire had required bringing uniformity to property laws; by the 1750s the central concern was to ensure that merchants could rely on a uniform set of commercial laws. This transformation followed a larger economic shift in the English empire. The colonial economy was growing rapidly, and colonial merchants increasingly controlled trade among the colonies and between the colonies and England. Particularly in New England, the money to be made from trade and commerce loomed large. The crown's relations with the colony thus focused on the regulation of a commercial vision of the empire. As appeals continued to mark areas of transatlantic discontinuity, commercial disputes gradually gave way to a new pressing concern for the Privy Council: New England currency practices. In the late 1760s, currency regulation became an irreconcilable conflict for the colony and Council.[1]

From Land to Commerce

The appeals to the Privy Council from Rhode Island reflected this transformation toward regulating an empire of commerce in New England.

The Privy Council now seemed more discontent with the colony's approach to commercial law than with its approach to property law. Between 1745 and 1755, twenty-four Rhode Island appeals were referred to the Committee for Hearing Appeals from the Plantations. Whereas one appeal in the 1730s had involved trade, commerce, or navigation, now ten of the twenty-four appeals raised commercial issues. Property appeals were less likely to be pursued fully before the Committee, a fate befalling eight of the fourteen property appeals and four of the commercial appeals. Most importantly, the Privy Council's disposition of these appeals was dramatically different. Of the six argued property appeals, at least four resulted in affirmances of the Rhode Island court, with only one reversal. Of the six commerce appeals, the result was precisely opposite: five reversals and one affirmance. Moreover, this lone affirmance was akin to a reversal, for the colony court was ordered to conduct a new jury trial. After 1755 there was a continued decrease in Rhode Island appeals over land heard by the Privy Council. Over the next two decades, only six land cases involving inheritance and other property disputes were appealed. Three appeals were affirmed and only one reversed. The last two appeals to reach the Privy Council were dismissed for nonprosecution. By the late eighteenth century, most of Rhode Island's property issues fell outside of the body of transatlantic law that the Privy Council was developing.[2]

The disinclination to review property cases was itself a product of the transatlantic constitution. Many of the basic questions about the application of more traditional laws of England in areas like wills, intestate practices, partition, dower, and entail had been already addressed. The appeals and the colony's 1749 act codified which of these areas would follow English law. Newer English property developments had less bearing on Rhode Island legal culture. At midcentury, English property law was absorbed by mastering complex techniques for the wealthy to pass and restrict property. Tricky legal maneuvers involving future interests, trusts, and strict settlements preventing the end of entails perpetuated dynastic family lines and lands. Rhode Island legal culture did not quickly embrace these devices. The reason for the apparent reluctance remains unclear. A distant possibility is that historians less familiar than English scholars with these technicalities simply have not recognized strict settlements in colonial documents and wills. A glance through genealogical records on Rhode Island wills, however, indicates that the majority of testators seem to have given land outright in fee simple or limited it only to a simple life estate. Those who had dynastic desires used entails, but even these appear to diminish into the eighteenth century. The English common law's preference for free alienability of land ironically may have prospered more in the colony than it did at home. Entails and contingent remainders made it difficult to sell or mortgage land to raise money, and they often compromised a wife's dower interest. In will after will in eighteenth-century Rhode Island, testators divided their land among their children (often male) or immediate relations, specifically naming the particular parcels to go to each. With little desire to perpetuate landholdings in one heir, few colonial cases raised legal issues that depended on newer developments in English inheritance law.[3]

From the Privy Council's perspective, the acceptance of partible inheritance practices (that is, the divergence from primogeniture) also meant that other colonial divergences in intestate and probate practices were simply not very relevant. The major issue of difference between England and the New England colonies had already been decided. If partible inheritance had not destroyed the English empire, less significant inheritance issues were unlikely to. To the Privy Council Committee for Hearing Appeals from the Plantations, inheritance cases increasingly raised only factual disputes about interrelated Rhode Islanders and obscure acres of land. In these cases, the Committee deferred to the colony's Superior Court. A younger son, Benjamin Tripp, sued to eject his mother and his elder brother's widow from a house that he claimed under his father's will. Although the will was questionable (allegations suggested that parts had been written and witnessed after being signed), Benjamin won at the inferior court and at the Superior Court on writ of review. The Council, no longer interested in ensuring that land go to an eldest son or in regulating the colonies' probate processes, chose not to intervene and affirmed. As noted by Benjamin's English solicitor, Fortherly Baker, the case was simply an "extraordinary trouble." In another case, the Council affirmed a decision against an eldest male relative by upholding a large monetary legacy to the testator's female friend.[4]

The sections of the appeals briefs that state the "reasons" for appeal demonstrate this disappearance of legal issues in the property and inheritance appeals. In two affirmed appeals, *Potter v. Hazard* and *Stanton v. Thompson,* the appellants' briefs asked the Council to redetermine facts—no specific legal issues were raised. In an effort to make the factual determination seem simple, both briefs were only three pages. In *Stanton,* the disputed inheritance was the Cedar Swamp, some six hundred acres near Westerly. Daniel Stanton, a Pennsylvania resident, claimed that a portion of the swamp had been conveyed by the tribes and now descended to him as heir. His claim was based on "manifest Justice." The three reasons advanced simply claimed that Stanton was the heir to part of "Sosoa's Purchase," land bought from Sosoa, a member of the Narragansett tribe. In *Potter,* the disputed inheritance was the eleven-acre Little Comfort Island. John Potter claimed that he had bought the island and that Jahleel Brenton had not intended to leave Little Comfort to Martha Wanton (a cousin). Again, in the "reasons," Potter claimed the issue was a simple one. Brenton had not intended to leave the island to Martha and she had not been in possession for the necessary twenty years. The Privy Council should reverse the colony courts.[5]

The respondents successfully implied that the Privy Council could not accurately judge the facts and equity from the other side of the Atlantic. Both briefs framed the issues as dependent on complicated purchases, devises, and leases in the colony. Stretched to seven pages, the briefs were filled with exhausting detail. The brief in *Potter* reentered every document relating to the land and included the testimony of elderly Rhode Islanders about whether Little Comfort Island had been an island and how long Martha had lived there. The brief in *Stanton* similarly contained an unbearably complex account of the transfer of the land from the original sachems and the complicated divisions of shares in the colony, as well as lengthy testimony about Stanton's legitimacy. Moreover, both briefs also claimed that reversals would upset settled land titles. The *Potter* brief emphasized Martha's twenty-six years of possession. The *Stanton* brief insisted that, if Stanton were to win, he would claim other lands that had been developed into "two townships and are, consequently, now the property of many hundreds of inhabitants." A reversal would "introduce such infinite mischief, and general inconveniency" to "an indefinite Number of Persons" who had improved a "wild, unsettled Country" for a century. The Privy Council did not intervene in either case. The affirmances deferred to the Rhode Island courts on the history of the colony's land practices, people, and rightful possession.[6]

The Privy Council's reluctance to disturb the existing state of possession was in part reinforced by concerns over English law. Indeed, in an-

other appeal, English advocates argued that altering the colony judgment would upset English law. John Freebody wanted private rights
in a stretch of land (three feet, two inches wide) along an alley from
Thames Street to the Newport wharves. The original ownership of the
way, the parties' usage, and prior agreements were all disputed. Freebody
lost in the Rhode Island courts and appealed. Representing Cook, William Murray argued that Freebody had not shown "any sufficient title in
himself" to the "exclusion of the other inhabitants." "Observations"
made for Cook in a handwritten document, likely by William Murray or
another lawyer or solicitor, noted that the claimed private right in the
way was set on "very insufficient grounds" and had been assumed to be
part of a public way for three or four decades, so an owner should not
be permitted to pretend it "to be a private way or that he has a private
exclusive property" in it. To conclude otherwise, he claimed, would disturb colony practice. Moreover, in a comment that suggested that colonial precedent might even have the power to initiate reconsideration
of broader English law, the argument suggested that a decision for Freebody would throw into question the way that new streets and buildings
had been erected in "this Great Metropolis of London." Just as some
commentators in the *MacSparran* case were concerned about the effect
of the decision in England, it was argued in the somewhat less controversial area of property law that appeals decisions suddenly might detri-
mentally alter property possession in England.[7]

The few property appeals reversed after 1750 involved claims that the
colony ignored key aspects of English law. The land appeal reversed in
the early 1750s, *Walker v. Paget,* was likely framed as a question about
when certain English statutes could apply in the colonies. The appeal
that was reversed in the 1760s, *Larkin v. York,* involved future interests,
the legal classifications that determined how property passed. In 1706
Hannah York's father had given her and her husband land under a tricky
conveyance: "during their natural Lives, and after their Decease, unto
his Daughter Hannah York's Children, and her Heirs for ever." In 1715
the couple sold the land to a son-in-law, who left it to his son, John
Larkin. In 1759, after both had died, another grandson, Edward York,
sued. York argued that the couple had possessed the land for their lives
only; at their death, it was to pass to Hannah's heirs (that is, York)—a
simple life estate with remainder. They could have sold only the possession of the land for their lifetimes. The Rhode Island courts agreed with

this straightforward argument. Larkin appealed, arguing that the decision was "founded upon a Mistake of the legal Import"—the colony had not understood the complexity of English law in which the comma between "children" and "her heirs" was essential. Larkin argued that the land was to go to Hannah's children then living for their lives (a vested remainder) with a contingent remainder in any afterborn children, and then to Hannah and her heirs. Because there was no device such as a trustee to save the contingent remainder, Hannah could destroy it and her reversion. Although some of Hannah's children might have had a claim, the grandson, York, did not. Such subtleties fascinated the English bar, and a decade later Charles Fearne would publish a book on the "abtruse" subject: *An Essay on the Learning in Contingent Remainders and Executory Devises* (1772). The Privy Council agreed with Larkin's more sophisticated reading—and with an interpretation that again left possession where it had been for more than forty years. Although the attorneys could have claimed that the colony should not follow these complicated rules, no such argument appears to have been made. Future interests were to read the same way in Rhode Island and England. After 1750, the Privy Council would hear a property appeal only if it clearly raised an important question of law.[8]

In the 1750s it was commercial appeals that raised questions about which laws were needed to govern the transatlantic commercial empire. In these cases, the Privy Council disagreed with the Rhode Island courts. Three reversed cases raised seizure issues under the trade and navigation acts. In *Rous,* the Privy Council reversed three Rhode Island court decisions that favored Rhode Island merchants over a Boston privateer. In *Vanbrugh,* the Council reversed Rhode Island decisions that had favored a Rhode Island merchant over Jamaican merchants. In *Freebody v. Wanton,* the Council limited the ability of the Rhode Island Collector to privately benefit from the sale of seized goods. These appeals emphasized the Privy Council's commitment to maintaining ultimate control of the enforcement and interpretation of the navigation acts. In *Rous,* a handwritten comment noted that after hearing the case "argued by Common Lawyers," Chief Justice Lee "said he had doubts whether this was not properly a Prize Cause in the original." A prize matter involved a captured vessel and usually belonged in the vice-admiralty courts under crown-appointed judges. Civilian lawyers were then brought in to reargue the matter. After the argument, Lee concluded that it was a prize cause and that it should have been brought in the vice-admiralty court rather than pursued as an act of trespass. The Council acted to guarantee that the crown, not the colonies, would determine the rules.[9]

In ordinary commercial appeals, the Privy Council encouraged predictability in commercial transactions across the trading empire. The Council could not prevent transatlantic trade from occasionally going awry, but it could perpetuate a set of rules that would encourage people to continue commercial transactions. In particular, the Council could reassure third parties that they did not have to worry that earlier transactions would open them to liability in foreign colony courts. In the 1750s, in *Wheelwright v. Tyler,* the Council decided the meaning of promissory notes for delivery of goods when used as payment for debts. The Council reversed a colony decision that was sympathetic to the Rhode Islander's desire for separate freight payment before delivery. The Committee report emphasized that the note had not made mention of freight or other charges. The decision upheld that promissory notes would be interpreted strictly, permitting greater reliance and transferability. The Privy Council similarly protected a third party in *Rodman v. Banister.* Noble Park, part owner of the ship *Noble Jane,* borrowed money for repairs from Newport merchant John Banister. Park gave Banister bills of exchange and a bond of hypothecation (a note that pledged the ship as the collateral for the loan). Park's London correspondents refused to pay the bills. Banister turned to the ship, but it had been destroyed in a storm near New York and the hull sold to Jacob Isaacs. When the rebuilt ship (now the *Jacob*) arrived in Newport, sailed by Robert Rodman, Banister sued for the ship in trover (a cause of action to obtain damages for the wrongful appropriation of property). Although the Superior Court found for Banister, the Privy Council reversed. As William Murray argued, Banister was never "entitled to the value of the ship, which was merely a pledge, but to the money lent." If the "ship was lost," the obligation was only to pay the money. The risk of loss of the security remained with the lender. A similar conviction may have underlain the only reversed appeal in the 1760s (*Stead v. Hart*) involving a third-party endorsed note, although the case was likely as much a matter of depreciating currency as of commercial paper.[10]

The appeal, however, was not a particularly good vehicle for regulating commercial law. The majority of Rhode Island appeals involving commercial trade brought between 1755 and 1774 were never pursued or were dismissed for nonprosecution. This may have been partly because commercial appeals depended on the commercial economy. After 1755 the perils and privateering of the Seven Years War caused a number of Newport merchants extreme losses. The business of running commercial ventures may have made prosecuting appeals seem an unnecessary waste of resources. Settling cases with other merchants may have produced a more satisfactory outcome. Moreover, in many of the cases, no one seems to have been desperate to have an overarching legal issue decided. Thus, an accounts case was dismissed at the parties' request, an appellant's solicitor confessed to having no orders, a reversed case on book debt was heard *ex parte* with no appearance by the respondent (*Laycock*), and another reversed case was decided without prejudice so that the appellant could pursue a more appropriate defendant (*Isaacs*). Beyond regulating the navigation acts, ensuring against local bias, and occasionally protecting third-party reliance, the Privy Council did not obsess over the colony's commercial appeals.[11]

The Concern over Currency

Of more distress to the Privy Council were Rhode Island's practices regarding paper currency. Throughout the late 1750s and 1760s the Privy Council heard appeals that provided the opportunity to shape monetary policy. Since the beginning of the century, paper currency had been a low-level concern of transatlantic law. Having a scarcity of gold and silver coins, the New England colonies had attempted to ensure sufficient circulating currency by setting the value of the silver dollar at an increasing number of colonial shillings. In London the silver dollar was worth four shillings, six pence, but in Massachusetts and Rhode Island a silver dollar was used to back a larger number of shillings. In 1707 a parliamentary act prevented the colonies from setting the dollar above six shillings. For the next forty years, this act established the only limit on colonial monetary policy.[12]

Under these minimal restrictions, in 1715 the Rhode Island Assembly adopted a scheme to create paper currency known as "old tenor." Old-tenor notes were bills of credit issued by the colony through institutions known as land banks. These bills worked much like the modern home equity loan. The government issued the bills as loans to residents, secured by land usually worth at least twice the loan. The loan was to be paid back over ten years with 5 percent interest. The annual interest payments would provide the government with income, and at the end the bills were to be returned and burned. Within the first decade, however, the requirements were altered. In 1724 a still shrinking currency supply and a large number of borrowers induced the colony to reschedule repayments and permit borrowers to redeem their mortgages even after initially defaulting. Although occasional crises plagued the system, nothing diminished the ardor for paper currency. As James MacSparran noted, "the Rhode-Islanders . . . are perhaps the only People on Earth who have hit on the Art of enriching themselves by running in Debt." The old-tenor currency supported the Rhode Island economy and spread to neighboring colonies. Addicted to the system, the colony created eight successive land banks between 1715 and 1744.[13]

Throughout the 1720s and 1730s, Rhode Islanders remained confident that their monetary policy was relatively insulated from English interference under the transatlantic constitution. In 1732, after an investigation into the colony's currency practices under the fourth land bank, crown officials concluded that they held "no discretionary power of repealing laws." The validity of the colony's acts rested only on the charter command. The "validity thereof depends upon their not being contrary but as near as may be agreeable to the laws of England, regard being had to the nature and constitution of the place and people." Because the colony's acts could be vacated only if they were repugnant to the laws of Great Britain, "a very wide field is left open for enacting many things contrary to good policy." The colony's laws regulating paper money did not seem repugnant to the 1707 act. Moreover, the Rhode Island government took steps to placate crown officials. In the 1740s, when crown officials complained that the colonial bills had no real worth, the Assembly set the face value of old-tenor notes at six shillings, nine pence for an ounce of silver. Rhode Island managed to control its monetary practices.[14]

After 1750 the crown's tolerance for colonial paper currency grew thin. Troubled by the continual depreciation of the colonies' currencies, Parliament began to consider reinforcing the 1707 act with new parliamentary legislation applying to the colonies. Massachusetts rapidly abandoned its paper currency and replaced it with the silver dollar. The Rhode Island Assembly, however, ignored the warnings and created a ninth land bank. These new bills of credit barely became legal currency.

In June 1751 the new parliamentary act limited the colony's discretion over monetary practices. The act essentially barred the creation of future land banks and required existing bills to be retired on schedule. No longer could Rhode Island postpone loan repayments or keep bills in circulation past retirement. The new act, however, did not provide guidance for dealing with already depreciated currency. It stated only that contracts should be settled according to the "true intent and meaning." The colony established a set exchange rate for the bills in circulation and placed the risk of depreciation on those who continued to hold older notes. In June 1754 an Assembly law stated that judges should not take depreciation into account in calculating judgments. The colony was determined to treat its currency at the declared face value.[15]

With London authorities concerned about depreciation and the colony's law set against recognizing depreciation, appeal to the Privy Council offered holders of depreciated bills a potentially sympathetic venue. Between 1757 and 1770, at least four Rhode Island cases reached the Privy Council raising issues of paper currency. In all four appeals, the Council reversed the Rhode Island courts. The most celebrated of these currency appeals, *Freebody v. Brenton,* reflected the slow deterioration in the transatlantic relationship. Historian David Lovejoy writes that by the 1770s the case was linked to "the patriot cause by colonists who were not inclined to accept interference in their internal affairs by the government abroad." Yet what is remarkable about the appeal was how long the Rhode Island courts and the Privy Council attempted to decide the case in a manner that preserved mutual legal respect and recognition.[16]

The case involved a typical Rhode Island mortgage transaction based on paper currency. When the borrower went bankrupt, the lender's demand to be compensated for the currency's depreciation triggered a twenty-year battle. It began with two Rhode Island merchants angling for advantage over the loan of paper currency. Aware of the value fluctuations in paper currency and the disapproving attitude of crown officials, both borrower and lender hoped to gain. Neither man was an innocent in commercial transactions; both were familiar with the Privy Council appeal. The borrower was Joseph Whipple, a well-known merchant and politician whose family had been in Rhode Island since the founding. He held two lots in Middletown, adjacent to Newport: one of 520 acres with two houses, the other of 289 acres with three houses. In October 1752, Whipple mortgaged this land to another Newport merchant, Captain John Freebody. Freebody had warehouses in Newport, and his mercantile business included profits gained from reselling goods and enslaved people acquired from privateering.[17]

Whipple mortgaged the land to raise cash. He conveyed the deeds to Freebody with the provision that the deeds would be void if the money was repaid within two years. The loan provisions specified repayment partially in silver coins and partially in pre-1748 old tenor. Although the finer aspects of the deal are hard to decipher, uncertainties over the validity and stability of paper currency made it somewhat risky and somewhat advantageous for both sides. Whipple likely planned to pay back the loan with currency that had further depreciated. Freebody, however, had acquired the old-tenor notes he used for the loan at already depreciated rates. If Whipple never was able to repay the loan, Freebody would gain the land at the cost of already depreciated bills. If Whipple attempted to pay back the loan, Freebody assumed the 1751 act would constrict the money supply as old-tenor notes were destroyed. In the absence of such notes, creditors could hold debtors to repayment in another form of currency at the undepreciated face value of the notes.[18]

Unfortunately for Freebody, events did not proceed as he had expected. The colony continued to retire the bills and the value of the currency fell, but even though the supply contracted, the colony never completely abandoned its earlier paper currency. While Whipple's financial situation was worsening, the colony passed a bankruptcy act under which the borrower's equity of redemption (the right to redeem the land after the loan date) was vested in the bankruptcy commissioners. In August 1753, immediately after the act's passage and less than a year after the mortgage, Whipple declared bankruptcy. Jahleel Brenton (the nephew of the earlier Jahleel Brenton), Benjamin Wickham, and George Gardiner were appointed commissioners to oversee the estate. In October 1754, when the loans came due, the commissioners apparently were selling assets to pay creditors and did not tender the money. A little over a year later, however, on January 2, 1756, the commissioners exercised their equity of redemption and tendered pre-1748 old-tenor notes to Freebody with interest. Nathaniel Mumford recalled the tender. Jahleel Brenton said, "Capt. Freebody, here is your Money" and added "Give us your answer whether you will receive it or not, for at this minute your interest ceases." As the old-tenor notes had continued to depreciate, Freebody replied, "I won't touch it; I won't have anything to do with it."

To extinguish the equity of redemption, Freebody sued the commissioners for the land in November 1756.[19]

In 1757 both sides argued in court that Rhode Island law and practices favored them. Freebody claimed that merchants had a custom of making compensation for depreciation in reconciling accounts. The commissioners, however, argued that the courts had always discharged old-tenor loans without accounting for depreciation and that the new law codified this procedure. Prominent merchants Abraham Redwood and Samuel Vernon, as well as the clerk of court, Thomas Ward, testified to this point. Persuaded by the merchants and their own clerk, the Rhode Island courts barred Freebody's action. In 1758 Freebody appealed to England, but he died the following year before the Privy Council could hear the appeal. Through fortuity, the colony seemed to have avoided confrontation with England.

By 1763, monetary politics had become more heated. Within the colony, confrontation over currency abounded as opposing political groups argued for different currency policies. Although the colony continued to use old tenor to set prices, fewer old-tenor notes were left. Allegations of profiteering raged as creditors charged increasing amounts in new currency to pay off the nominal value of old-tenor debts, already overstated because of depreciation. An author in the *Providence Gazette* claimed that "quoting either the Act of Parliament or our own Laws, is only a sham pretence of a set of avaricious money jobbers. . . ." Under Governor Stephen Hopkins, the Assembly passed a controversial act to stabilize the situation—but with significant dissent. It abandoned paper money for coin, prevented creditors from arbitrarily raising the amount due, and established the silver value of old tenor for each past year. Although the opposition wanted depreciated values taken into account from the date of the debt, the act discharged old-tenor debts upon the debtor's payment of the established value of the nominal sum that was due in the year when the debt was to be repaid. Ignoring depreciation remained the official colony policy.[20]

By the late spring of 1764, signs suggested that the Privy Council was willing to protect depreciation, and Freebody's sons (John, Thomas, and Samuel) revived his appeal. In appeals from New Hampshire in 1760 and 1762, the Council had made some allowance for the depreciation of colonial currency. Moreover, Parliament was debating a new bill (the Currency Act of 1764) that would regulate colonial paper money and seemed likely to make all paper money void. The Freebodys used the same legal arguments as their father on appeal but adopted an even more extreme rhetoric. Arguing that "he who comes for Equity must himself do Equity," their Privy Council brief characterized the commissioners' position as unfair. The colony's paper currency was similarly "fluctuating and precarious": £100 sterling equaled £1,200 bills in 1752, £1,700 bills in 1756, and £2,200 in 1765. They claimed that the colony's 1751 issuance of paper money was deliberately contemptuous of Parliament, and that the 1754 law that courts could not allow depreciation was "a barefaced Endeavour to establish a public fraud by law." The Freebodys' brief argued that colonial practices were completely repugnant to English currency policy.[21]

The commissioners' brief to the Privy Council sought to depoliticize the case and disassociate it from transatlantic currency debates. As argued by Charles Yorke and Charles Ambler, depreciation was not an issue that should matter to English law. The problem was simply a financial risk taken by two Rhode Islanders. Here "two inhabitants" had made the bargain. The lender had had "his eyes open" and, regardless of the depreciation, was receiving 6 percent interest. The appeal was no different from "a Case that happens here daily" in England when people made risky stock purchases, sometimes losing the value of the original purchase. The case, they claimed, simply did not need to concern the Council; the colony should be permitted to follow the "universal practice" of its courts. Yorke recast the appeal as one in which the Council should not bother to get involved.[22]

The Yorke and Ambler argument was remarkably successful. The Council's decision in late summer 1764 reversing the colony court was, in substance, a victory for the commissioners. Freebody could bring his ejectment action, but if the commissioners paid the principal in old-tenor bills with interest and costs, they could redeem the property. The order rejected the idea that the loans had to be paid taking depreciation into account. Moreover, the order carefully sidestepped the form of currency in which the interest should be paid: it was to be paid in "such manner as payments ought to be paid by law." On the implicit question of which "law"—England's or the colony's—governed the manner of payments, the Council was silent. The Council's order avoided direct conflict with the colony's governing authority.[23]

By the fall of 1764 when the order became known, Rhode Island was embroiled in transatlantic politics. In July it had resolved to confer with other colonies on measures to repeal the Sugar Act and prevent the passage of the Stamp Act. In the newspaper and private correspondence, a small group of Newport men were reasserting the old argument for revocation of the charter and greater parliamentary control. By November the Assembly sought to defend the charter by authorizing the circulation and transmittal to England of copies of the pamphlet *The Rights of the Colonies Examined* by former chief justice and governor Stephen Hopkins. After detailing the colony's charter provisions, Hopkins noted that the colonists had used their rights "to their own advantage, in dutiful subserviency to the orders and interests of Great-Britain." He claimed that Rhode Islanders "have long enjoyed, and not abused or forfeited their liberties." Dutiful subservience, however, was not particularly evident that summer when Newport was racked by riots over the Stamp Act's passage.[24]

In the fall of 1765, when the Rhode Island Court executed the Council's order in *Freebody,* it attempted to balance liberty and subservience. The majority ordered interest paid to the year 1765 in the same currency as the principal (old tenor). The Court may have hoped that the Freebodys would see the additional decade of interest as some compensation for the depreciation and drop the case. Indeed, Benjamin Wickham had the original old-tenor money preserved in bundles in a large iron chest ready to be tendered. The Freebodys remained unplaced. Once again they appealed to the Privy Council, this time claiming that the interest had to be paid in coin, not old tenor. The commissioners' counsel repeated their arguments from the first appeal. Charles Yorke's almost illegible extant handwritten notes summarized the essential point: the "universal practice and usage" of Rhode Island courts was that the principal and interest should be paid in old tenor without depreciation. Rhode Island ought to be permitted to govern its own court practices.[25]

When the Privy Council finally heard the appeals in April 1769, crown and Parliament had become less willing to defer to colonial practice. In 1766 Parliament had passed the Declaratory Act, which stated that "in all cases whatsoever" Parliament could make laws binding on the colonies. The colony's complaints about duties and taxes in subsequent years had not improved the situation. The Council's new order reflected uninterest in deferring to the colony. Both interest and costs were now to be paid in sterling. Even more troublesome, the interest was to be recalculated. Instead of computing the interest in old tenor and then converting it to silver as the Rhode Island court had done, the Council stated that the principal should be converted into silver at the rate set by the original proclamation of 1704 and then the interest should be calculated. The Council's method gave the Freebodys their interest with depreciation taken into account. Rhode Island law and practices were swept away.[26]

By late 1769 when the Privy Council order arrived in the colony, conflict seemed unavoidable. In Rhode Island, the Council's order appeared to violate the long understood transatlantic relationship under which the colony had a sphere of self-governance. The Assembly made its position clear: the Court was to execute the Council's decrees according to the "laws, custom, usage and practice" of Rhode Island courts. To the Court, Henry Marchant, twenty-eight-year-old attorney for the commissioners, argued that the Council's order was contrary to local practice; he cited depositions by Stephen Hopkins and other judges. Although an initial narrow decision by the Court was favorable to the Freebodys, it was quickly altered when Stephen Hopkins once again became chief justice. Under Hopkins, the Court refused to grant depreciation on the interest. The Court concluded that the original 1756 tender had been sufficient "according to the constant invariable practice of tenders made in said colony" for the redemption of mortgaged estates. The commissioners could retender the principal and interest in old tenor. The Rhode Island Court reasserted its commitment to local practice.[27]

Remarkably, the colony once again managed to preserve respect for local authority. The Freebodys once again petitioned the Council, arguing that the Court had violated the transatlantic constitution. According to them, the orders were "altogether repugnant" and "illegal and not warranted by the Constitution of the colony." The Court had "frustrated" the Council's orders by its "direct disobedience." The matter was not confined to these facts. As they pointed out in a letter to the Earl of Hillsborough, the secretary of state for the colonies, "too many in this charter colony . . . think themselves under no obligation to pay any obedience to the authority of Great Britain." The colony and the commissioners decided to deal directly with London. Attorney Henry Marchant sailed to meet English authorities about the colony's affairs. In the spring of 1772 Marchant met Hillsborough and discussed "a late affair of the Judges Conduct" in a manner "as clearly as so long an affair and that shortness of time would admit." Marchant also spoke with many members of the board, apparently impressing a number of them. Once again the Council stepped back from the confrontation. In the summer of 1772 it decided to interpret the Freebody petition as a "complaint against the Judges" and asked for an explanation of the Court's decision. The request preserved the Council's authority while paying respect to the Rhode Island judiciary. The transatlantic relationship struggled on.[28]

The Collapse of the Transatlantic Constitution

Time was not improving the situation. On June 9, 1772, even as the Privy Council contemplated its order, on the other side of the Atlantic a British schooner, the *Gaspee,* was set afire off the Narragansett coast near Warwick, allegedly by Rhode Islanders. After Rhode Island failed to make arrests, the crown appointed an intercolonial commission to meet in January 1773 to investigate the incident. In December 1772, amid uncertainty over the investigation, the Rhode Island judges crafted their explanation of the *Freebody* case to the Privy Council. The lengthy reply by Chief Justice Stephen Hopkins spent considerable time on the equities of the case as a matter of ensuring "equal justice" to the commissioners and Freebody, a man of "design." The letter itself reflected a century-long conviction that the crown could be persuaded to tolerate, if not respect, the colony's authority.[29]

The letter bespoke a continued commitment to the transatlantic constitution. As Hopkins noted, they were "judges, under a peculiar constitution." The premise of the letter was that Rhode Island had the authority to have divergent laws and practices. The "local situation" had created a "necessary and unavoidable difference in our modes of practice, laws & customs." Hopkins hastened to add that these differences were "not in any essential point whatever repugnant to the laws of Great Britain." The reality of dual authorities, he said, placed the judges in a "delicate" situation. They were not mere inferior officers who executed orders; instead, they were judges and their power of "making or giving judgment implies some consideration." Hopkins explicated the judges' responsibilities. To simply obey the Privy Council without consideration of local differences would be to fail in judicial duties. Although they had an "obligation of duty and respect" to the Privy Council's "right . . . of hearing and determining all Matter of Appeal," they also had an obligation under their oath to the colony to maintain its laws, usages, and practices. Hopkins's phraseology underscored the crucial distinction. To the Privy Council, the Rhode Island judges owed a certain attitude; to the colony, the judges owed a legally binding oath.[30]

Nevertheless, throughout the letter Hopkins sought to avoid casting the colony and Council as irreconcilably opposed authorities. For more than a century these two obligations had been balanced by discretion and flexibility. Hopkins argued that "literal execution" of the order was not required, that a judgment that complied with the "most substantial part and essentials" of the Council's order could not be considered repugnant. In this instance, the Court had followed the decree as "to the most substantial part" and in "very near compliance." The earlier Council orders had all been written this way, allowing interest to be set by the "law here" and holding the parties to the "laws, customs and usages of the country where they contracted." It was the Council's recent decision to "vary" the order that had produced the difficulty, he argued. Ever the good attorney, Hopkins offered a path by which the Council could uphold the judges without compromising its authority. Blaming the parties for not having provided the "proper information of the laws, customs & usages" of the colony, he attached affidavits of two men who had practiced in the colony for more than forty years to show that the colony had never treated interest differently than principal. Given that the Court's decisions had been founded upon "the customs, practice and usage immemorial of the courts" and the "positive and declarative law of our legislature," he said, he hoped that a "right understanding" and a "true understanding" could be reached by the Council. The Freebodys had had "justice done them" by the Rhode Island judges and "injustice would issue" to the commissioners if the Council in its "wisdom and justice" did not uphold the colony.

The underlying tension of dual authorities, however, could not be ignored. Hopkins's final plea was that the "peculiar situation" in Rhode Island would "never be the least impediment to the most entire and ready obedience to his royal will and pleasure signified to us either as judges of the superior court of his loyal colony of Rhode Island, or as faithful subjects to the best of Princes." Remaining a Rhode Island judge *and* a faithful subject became impossible as events pushed judge and subject, colony and prince, apart. In March and April 1774 a Parliament furious at Boston for dumping tea in Boston Harbor passed the Coercive Acts. Rhode Island towns responded with resolves proclaiming that Parliament's ability to make laws for the colonies was "inconsistent with the natural, constitutional and charter rights and privileges" of the colony. They would oppose any "unconstitutional" measures.[31]

In June 1774 the Privy Council issued its response to the *Freebody* judges without even bothering to acknowledge the judges' letters. In substance and style, transatlantic legal culture came crashing to an end. In the order, the king and Council did not attempt a conversation with the colony, but used the words "peremptorily order, require and command." Rhode Island could not use time and distance to avoid a direct conflict, as it had so often in the past, but was to "comply punctually," "forthwith and without delay" with the order. Rejecting Hopkins's claim, the colony's judges were not to interpret the Council orders; they were to carry them "literally into execution." The draft of the final order reveals the dramatic change in transatlantic legal culture. For decades the Privy Council's orders had ended with the polite request that the colony and its officials "govern themselves accordingly." In the *Freebody* draft order, these words are literally scratched out. In their place, inserted words described a new relationship: the colony's officials and judges were to "yield due obedience." The tension-laced respect for dual authority that had characterized the colonial period was no more.[32]

With this final order in *Freebody v. Brenton,* appeals to the Privy Council came to an end. Even as the Council had penned the order, Rhode Island was appointing Stephen Hopkins as a delegate to the new continental congress with the command to establish "the rights and liberties of the colonies upon a just and solid foundation." In June 1775 in one final appeal from the colony, Charles Dudley, the collector of customs, had an unsympathetic Rhode Island judgment regarding his seizure of molasses reversed. It was the last time the colony's courts were reviewed in England. That same month the Assembly repealed its act regulating appeals to the Council. A year later in 1776, the colony crossed the king's name out of the charter. Stephen Hopkins decisively chose his role as judge over his role as subject and signed the Declaration of Independence. The peculiar transatlantic constitution that had governed the colony for a century and a half had collapsed.[33]

9

The Transatlantic Constitution and the Nation

Although the formal structure of the transatlantic constitution ended in 1776, its legal arguments and cultural practices continued to influence the American nation. Transatlantic legal culture had been like an enormous American chestnut tree that had permanently affected the development of all in its shade. Erasing this legal culture proved more difficult than repealing the appeals law and excising the king's name from the charter. The legal culture of the colonies had grown to maturity as part of a conversation about when the laws of England applied and when local laws and practices could diverge because of the people and place. This culture came to revel in the existence and tension of dual authorities; it understood the advantages and disadvantages of having a distant decisionmaker, and linked constitutional interpretation to the changing substantive concerns of the empire. The loss of the transatlantic relationship was dramatic. Although Americans rejected the tree, they planted new saplings to cast similar shade. In the new Republic's development of federalism and judicial review, the vestiges of the rhetoric and practices of transatlantic legal culture remained. This last chapter briefly considers certain critical moments in this transformation.[1]

By definition, the American Revolution overthrew the "repugnant to the laws of England" standard. The principle of repugnancy, however, had served well as a boundary by which to judge laws. Post-Revolutionary American legal culture retained repugnancy but replaced the laws of England with constitutions. This substitution appears in the early writ-

186

ten state constitutions. Several states flipped the constitutional comparison by prohibiting laws of England repugnant to a state constitution. In the summer of 1776 the New Jersey Constitution declared that "the common law of England, as well as so much of the statute law, as have been heretofore practiced in this Colony, shall still remain in force" until legislatively altered except for parts "repugnant to the rights and privileges contained in this Charter." The 1776 Delaware Constitution used similar language in establishing that adopted English common and statute law remained in force "such parts only excepted as are repugnant to the rights and privileges contained in this constitution, and the declaration of rights." The 1777 New York Constitution similarly used repugnancy to sort out the acceptable adopted aspects of English common and statute law and colonial New York law. Abandoning the laws of England that were a part of colonial law was inconceivable to these constitutions' framers. With the repugnancy standard now ensuring the promotion of an American identity, English laws could continue.[2]

A second substitution caused greater difficulty. Just as colonial legislation had been judged against the laws of England, state legislation now was to be judged against the state constitutions. Being repugnant to the state constitution became the boundary for ordinary state legislation. The 1777 Georgia Constitution gave the Assembly lawmaking power "provided such laws and regulations be not repugnant to the true intent and meaning of any rule or regulation contained in this constitution." The 1780 Massachusetts Constitution similarly provided that the legislature could make "all manner of wholesome and reasonable orders, laws, statutes, and ordinances, directions and instructions" so long as "the same be not repugnant or contrary to this constitution." Although this semantic and theoretical substitution was straightforward, the consequences were not.[3]

Attorneys were confronted with the practical difficulties of adapting the argumentative structure of transatlantic legal culture to the non-transatlantic world. Interpretation of a single written document replaced the flexible idea of "the laws of England." Moreover, courts and legislatures derived from the same authority no longer had a higher tribunal like the Privy Council to decide disputed matters. Attorneys, judges, and state legislators struggled to adapt older arguments to new institutions. These efforts produced at least some of the cases that have been seen as foundations for the American doctrine of judicial review (the belief that courts can void legislative acts that violate the constitution). One of the most famous of these cases, *Trevett v. Weeden,* arose in Rhode Island.[4]

The facts were straightforward. On September 13, 1786, Newport butcher John Weeden had refused to accept John Trevett's paper currency. In August the state had passed a law that a refusal to accept paper money constituted a criminal act that would be tried "without any jury." The penalty was a fine. Under the statute, Trevett immediately brought an action against Weeden in Superior Court. Henry Marchant joined James Varnum to defend Weeden. The two attorneys had impeccable credentials as colonial attorneys and revolutionaries. Marchant had argued the *Freebody* case on behalf of the colony, served as the Rhode Island Attorney General, and represented the colony in England, and he was a Rhode Island delegate to the Continental Congress. Varnum, eight years younger and born in Massachusetts, had studied law in Rhode Island with Oliver Arnold and headed the Rhode Island troops during the Revolution. He had also been a delegate to the Continental Congress.[5]

That a colonial legislature could not deny a jury trial would have been a relatively easy argument in colonial Rhode Island. The right to a jury was a central tenet of the laws of England, set forth in Magna Carta. A statute denying a jury trial was seemingly repugnant to the laws of England and most likely not a matter on which the colony could diverge. But was this conclusion still true after the collapse of the empire? The importance of the right to a jury trial under the laws of England helps explain the frequency of such cases among the early judicial review precedents. It was the perfect test issue to discover whether rights accepted under the transatlantic constitution survived. Did the right to a jury trial disappear merely because a state was no longer bound by the earlier repugnancy principle and the state constitution did not include any explicit mention of such a right? The question was of particular interest in Rhode Island because the state retained the colonial charter as its new "constitution."[6]

In 1786 the two attorneys argued for the continued existence of a right to a jury trial by substituting the phrases "laws of the land" and "constitution" for "laws of England." The arguments left it somewhat ambiguous whether "constitution" was being used to refer to the charter as the written Constitution of Rhode Island or to the unwritten and written body of fundamental laws and practices that the state inherited from its colonial period. They declared that the absence of a jury trial made

the statute "unconstitutional, and repugnant to the Law of the Land."
The Assembly had directed judges to execute a law "by a mode of trial
repugnant to the constitution." According to Varnum, trial by jury had
been "a first, a fundamental, and a most essential principle, in the English constitution." In colonial Rhode Island, trial by jury had been a
"fundamental right, a part of our legal constitution." After the Revolution, he argued, it remained "fundamental, a constitutional right—ever
claimed as such—ever ratified as such—ever held most dear and sa-
cred." The Revolution and independence had made "no change" to the
legislature's inability to pass laws repugnant to such a fundamental part
of "our legal constitution." The act was "unconstitutional and void."
The judges should continue to act as they had during the colonial period. Just as the Court had judged repugnancy with respect to colonial
laws and the laws of England, the "court has power to judge and determine what acts of the General Assembly are agreeable to the constitution." Varnum declared that the judges were "under the most solemn obligations to execute the laws of the land."[7]

The loss of the transatlantic empire placed tensions on these claims.
The nature of the British empire had mandated the repugnancy principle. What justified it within a state? Similarly, the Privy Council had determined ultimately whether a Rhode Island law was repugnant, while
the colonial courts had been able to seek refuge in controversial situations by aligning themselves with the legislature in the claim that a statute was a legitimate divergence. What gave Rhode Island judges, elected
by the legislature, the power to find laws repugnant? Repugnancy and
judicial power needed new explanations. In the new nation, Varnum
could not argue that judges could strike down laws because the empire
had always worked in this way, but he made a very similar claim. He proposed that judges had always had the ability to not enforce repugnant
laws. The power to declare laws repugnant to the constitution was not a
special function of judges in a transatlantic empire but of all judges. To
bolster the contention, Varnum cited Chief Justice Coke in *Dr. Bonham's
Case* (1610), where he said that "if a statute be against common right or
reason, or repugnant, or impossible to be performed, the common law
shall controul it, and adjudge it to be void." Whatever Coke had actually
meant was irrelevant. Pulled from the case, the quotation's use of the repugnancy principle blurred common-law practices into constitutional
ones. It implied that the use of the repugnancy principle owed more to

English common law than to, as was more correct historically, imperial practice. To reinforce local authority, Varnum argued that the state judicial oath inherently required this judicial authority. In *Trevett*, transatlantic practice became English common law practice, which in turn became state judicial practice.[8]

Varnum's recasting proved persuasive. On September 26 the judges decided in favor of Weeden. According to reports in the *Providence Gazette* and *Newport Mercury*, Judge David Howell explained that the court could not take cognizance because the law was "repugnant and unconstitutional." Judge Thomas Tillinghast replaced the phrase *laws of England* with the nicely ambiguous *laws of the land* and emphasized that the act had allowed action "without trial by jury, according to the laws of the land." Two other judges explicitly agreed. The third, Chief Justice Paul Mumford, offered no explicit opinion but was assumed to have agreed because he had "always shown himself to be a good whig, a friend to trial by jury, and the fundamental rights of the citizens." Seen through the judicial lens, the case was not difficult. The right to a jury trial had been a fundamental right under the laws of England, and under the laws of the land it must continue to be one. The *Trevett* decision was consistent with Rhode Island's colonial judicial practice.[9]

The Assembly, however, found the decision outrageous, given its colonial practice. For more than a century the Assembly had worked to preserve its authority as the supreme power in the colony. When necessary, it had sought to prevent divergent laws from being found repugnant by the Privy Council. The absence of direct Council review had increased the Assembly's perception that Rhode Island laws were never explicitly struck down as void. In *Trevett*, however, the state court had adjudged "an act of the supreme legislature of this state to be unconstitutional, and so absolutely void." The decision tended "directly to abolish the legislative authority." The Rhode Island Assembly had thought itself limited only by English institutions. With that authority removed by the Revolution, the Assembly considered itself supreme and could not understand the judiciary's behavior. The practices of the Rhode Island Court and Assembly were inconsistent, not because either institution had altered its behavior, but because the loss of the Privy Council had changed their relationship. In the ebb of the colonial era, the theoretical problem appeared: Could two practices developed under the transatlantic empire—the judiciary's standard of repugnancy and the legislature's commitment to supremacy—continue within the border of a single state?[10]

The confusion inherent in the transition made each institution hesitant to insist upon its position. Just as the Privy Council had asked the *Freebody* court to explain its decision, the Assembly asked the judges "to render their reasons for adjudging an act of the General Assembly unconstitutional, and so void." Judge David Howell recognized that the problem lay in the judges' comments declaring voidness. He thus stated that the judge's opinions were immaterial and should be ignored. Although the Assembly found the reason unsatisfactory, it did not remove the judges for cause. The following spring, the Assembly did what it had often done: it elected four new judges. The election was less dramatic than often has been supposed. Between 1776 and 1792, the entire court was reelected on only three occasions, and the *Trevett* court itself had been composed of four new justices. With the Court reluctant to assert its authority to void legislation and the Assembly unwilling to prove its supremacy by removing the judges outside of annual election, the conflict remained unresolved in Rhode Island. The Assembly's view of its supremacy remained ascendant for another half century. In states with legislatures less committed to supremacy, state judicial review of legislation would be more quickly accepted.[11]

The difficulty in relinquishing transatlantic practices also appeared at the national level. Was the type of control over the states that had been exercised by the Privy Council to continue? Refusing to attend the 1787 Philadelphia Convention, Rhode Islanders had no part in the initial conversation. Nonetheless, many colonies had dealt with direct Privy Council statute review; although, as Joseph Smith pointed out, "in the field of common law civil jurisdiction only the courts of Rhode Island, Virginia, and Massachusetts of the continental colonies were subject to fairly well-sustained control by the King in Council." The Virginians favored continuation of certain transatlantic practices. They proposed a "Council of revision" (formed by executive and judicial branches) to examine "every act of a particular Legislature." Although there were similar state councils, James Madison's justification drew on transatlantic practice for the "negativing" power. It had been one of "the most mild & certain means of preserving the harmony" in the "British System" and had maintained "harmony & subordination of the various parts of the empire." The problems that had arisen when the power had been "sometimes misapplied thro' ignorance or a partiality" would not reappear, according to Madison. Although Virginia, Massachusetts, and North Carolina liked the idea, the other states rejected it. Instead, the Convention adopted the supremacy clause that simply asserted that the "Legislative acts of the U.S." were "the supreme law." The final version recast the phrase *laws of England* by describing the "supreme Law of the Land" as "this Constitution, and the Laws of the United States." Interestingly, the clause paralleled some early colonial charters' provisions on repugnancy, including the absence of an ultimate enforcement institution as well as exclusion of the divergence principle. Despite Madison's continued efforts, the Constitution never included an institution parallel to the Privy Council. Just as the institutional framework to enforce the charters' phrases and the argument for divergence had developed over time, the enforcement mechanisms and theories of divergence under the supremacy clause would also evolve.[12]

That the repugnancy principle proved hard to abandon can be seen in how its terminology floats through comments on the relationship of state to national laws under the U.S. Constitution and the role of judges in reviewing laws. In one of the few Convention remarks regarding judicial review, Rufus King of Massachusetts (a state with experience in Privy Council appeals) noted, "the Judges will have the expounding of those Laws when they come before them: and they will no doubt stop the operation of such as shall appear repugnant to the constitution." In the *Federalist Papers,* Alexander Hamilton responded to criticisms that federal authorities or courts might find legislative actions continually repugnant. As Bernard Bailyn points out, Hamilton claimed that "repugnance was not inevitable" between federal and state authorities. Underlying Hamilton's use of the term repugnance was his belief, fostered by decades of transatlantic practice, that disagreement between federal and state authorities was not the same thing as constitutional repugnancy. He insisted that constitutional repugnance should not be confused with "a mere possibility of inconvenience in the exercise of powers" or "occasional interferences" in *"policy."* Indeed, he referred to the federal government varying state intestate laws as an obvious example of federal overreaching—the very aspect of authority that the Privy Council had surrendered to the New England colonies. A similar thought appeared in *Federalist 78* where Hamilton noted the claim that "courts, on the pretense of a repugnancy, may substitute their own pleasure to the constitutional intentions of the legislature." Hamilton's distinctions between true constitutional repugnancy and pretences, inconveniences and interferences admittedly lacked a certain theoretical rigor but revealed the inability to imagine a world without a repugnancy principle.[13]

Despite the absence of the word in the U.S. Constitution, repugnancy quickly came to govern federal review of state statutes. In this development, Rhode Island—which had been comfortable with Privy Council appeals—took the leading role. In giving effect to the supremacy clause, section 25 of the 1789 Judiciary Act stated that federal courts had jurisdiction over state courts in matters where "the validity of a statute" is drawn into question "on the ground of their being repugnant to the Constitution, treaties or laws of the United States." Federal courts slowly began to assume the place of the Privy Council. The first case heard by the United States Supreme Court, *West v. Barnes,* was from Rhode Island. In August 1791 the justices concluded that they had no power to take the case because of procedural problems with the writ of error. Nonetheless, federal judicial review had begun.[14]

The first instance of federal judicial review of state legislation took place in Rhode Island in June 1792. Henry Marchant, the U.S. district judge, joined Chief Justice John Jay and Associate Justice William Cushing to hold a Rhode Island law void. In *Champion & Dickason v. Casey,* Rhode Island merchant Silas Casey owed money to London merchants Alexander Champion and Thomas Dickason. The Rhode Island Assembly gave Casey a three-year period to settle his accounts, during which he would be exempt from attachments. Champion and Dickason nonetheless successfully sued in the federal circuit court to collect the debt. The Court concluded that the Rhode Island law was "contrary to the Constitution of the United States" for "the individual states are prohibited from making laws which shall impair the obligation of contracts." Three years later, Justice William Paterson wrote, "Whatever may be the case in other countries, yet in this there can be no doubt, that every act of the Legislature, repugnant to the Constitution, is absolutely void." With the replacement of the U.S. Constitution for the laws of England, the federal courts assumed a position over the states analogous to that of the Privy Council over the colonies.[15]

Rhode Island continued to be the primary agent in the development of federal judicial review of state legislation. The first cases "to be fully adjudicated by the Supreme Court" under section 25 of the Judiciary Act

arose in that state. *Olney v. Arnold* and *Olney v. Dexter* were reminiscent
of the customs cases that had drawn the attention of the Privy Council
after passage of the Navigation Acts. Jeremiah Olney was the Providence
collector under the new 1790 federal customs laws. Olney's enforcement
clashed with the interests of Providence merchant Welcome Arnold over
bonds given to the customs collectors for payment of duties. Olney and
Arnold had disagreed before over Olney's particularly strict enforcement
of the due dates on the bonds. After Olney rendered Arnold incapable
of receiving credit, Arnold began to transfer his goods to other merchants in an effort to legally evade the problem. Frustrated by the seemingly collusive transfers, Olney eventually detained a cargo of Arnold's
goods that had been given to merchant Edward Dexter. Arnold and Dexter sued Olney in state court for damages from the detention. Carefully pleaded by Rhode Island and Massachusetts attorneys, the case depended on interpretation of the 1790 federal law. Finally in 1794 the
Superior Court decided against Olney. In the fall, he appealed to the U.S.
Supreme Court, where he "[doubted] not of a Just and favorable Decision." After delay and debate over whether the Superior Court was the
highest court of law in Rhode Island, in the late summer of 1796 the U.S.
Supreme Court reversed the judgments and decided in favor of the custom collector. Like the Privy Council, the Supreme Court used its power
to protect federal interests, here the act of Congress. In deciding these
cases, the Supreme Court and other federal courts would use appeals to
define where uniformity to federal law was required and where states
could diverge for local conditions. Just as the Privy Council's perception
of repugnancy and divergence had changed as the empire developed, so
too the boundaries of federalism would shift as the demands of the nation altered.[16]

With the acceptance of federal judicial review of state legislation came
a final possibility: federal judicial review of federal legislation. In 1801,
Chief Justice John Marshall in *Marbury v. Madison* recognized the existence of such review. His opinion framed the question in the same language that had been used to discuss repugnancy under the transatlantic
constitution: "The question, whether an act, repugnant to the constitution, can become the law of the land, is a question deeply interesting to
the United States; but, happily, not of an intricacy proportioned to its interest." Indeed, the question was not hard if one followed the pattern of
keeping the idea of repugnancy and substituting the written U.S. Consti-

tution for the laws of England. After all was said and done in the complicated opinion, Marshall founded his conclusion upon this commitment.
In the final paragraphs of the opinion, Marshall four times used the
phrase "repugnant to the constitution," saying that legislative acts "repugnant to the constitution" were void. As he declared, the United
States Constitution "confirms and strengthens the principle, supposed
to be essential to all written constitutions, that a law repugnant to the
constitution is void." Believing that the repugnancy standard was essential, Marshall could not imagine what other choice the United States Supreme Court had.[17]

Although the transformation of the repugnancy standard led to that
conclusion, judicial review of congressional legislation presented theoretical difficulties. Federal judicial review of state legislation looked like
a continuation of Privy Council practice. Although state judicial review
of state legislation faced controversy in states like Rhode Island with supreme assemblies, it at least looked like what state judiciaries had always
done. Federal judicial review of congressional legislation, however, had
no historic parallel in the colonial experience. It was a possibility produced by the new institutional structure of the nation in which a national legislature and judiciary appeared as separate and equal branches.
Analogous traditional institutional practices seemed to cut in the opposite direction. The English belief in legislative supremacy at the parliamentary level and the attitude of certain colonial legislatures suggested
that the U.S. Supreme Court should not reject congressional acts. Although Justice Marshall insisted five times in *Marbury* that the nature of
the "written constitution" required such a conclusion, coming to terms
with the practice was sufficiently difficult that more than fifty years
would pass before the Supreme Court once again decided to strike down
congressional legislation.[18]

Federal judicial review of congressional legislation eventually became
part of American culture. Over the years, lawyers, judges, politicians,
and legal scholars came up with justifications: A written constitution
was superior to both legislature and judiciary; in a democracy the people
were above all three branches; the courts were better at representing certain unrepresented minority interests and fundamental values; the legislature had institutional failures. The list would grow longer and longer.
None of these explanations would prove completely satisfying because
federal judicial review had been the product, not of theory, but of the

empire. As the product of practice, the eventual acceptance also owed relatively little to theoretical rationales. The legal culture that surrounded the transatlantic constitution had created judicial review.[19]

American legal culture inherited from the colonial period a set of arguments and practices that related to repugnancy to and divergence from the laws of England. This transatlantic constitution framed the development of the legal profession, statutory publication, legal institutions, and substantive law in the colonies. The legal developments of the Revolutionary and early national periods were pragmatic efforts to relocate this 150-year-old practice to new state and national institutions. Internal debates that long had been displaced and decided abroad had to be decided within the state and nation. Disputes that had been debated with the vague luxury provided by the phrase *the laws of England*—encompassing cases, statutes, custom, and the idea of the English unwritten constitution—had to be decided within the more constrained bounds of written constitutions. Legislatures and judiciaries that had never needed to be clear about their authority, beyond justifying their very existence under a charter, now had to fight for supremacy among themselves.

These replacements were by necessity artless and awkward, their consequences unclear and unimagined. Constitutions replaced charters; federalism succeeded the dual authorities of the imperial relationship; federal judicial review of state legislation displaced the Privy Council and the practice of appeals; and federal judicial review of federal legislation became a necessary, albeit not completely planned, consequence. As a vision of a changing nation enveloped the vision of a developing empire, the transatlantic constitution faded slowly, but incompletely, from view.

Notes

Manuscript materials are cited in the endnotes in a variety of ways consistent with the cataloging used in the various archives. Though some forms of citation may appear unusually compressed, they contain the information necessary for a reader to find the information in that archive. Some citations for case files from the Rhode Island Supreme Court Judicial Records Center (JRC) are less precise. This inconsistency arises from the arrangement of these records when I did this research. I was the first researcher to use many of the case records. The JRC subsequently has been reorganizing its case materials. The citations to JRC case files contain as much information as was available when I did this research and should be adequate for the researcher to find the JRC records. While the names of the parties in the case names are correct, the order may not always correctly reflect the respective position of appellant and appellee.

Abbreviations

APC	*Acts of the Privy Council, Colonial Series* (1908; Nendeln: Kraus Reprint, 1966)
BL	British Library, London
CHS Coll.	*Collections of the Connecticut Historical Society* (Hartford: Connecticut Historical Society, 1892)
CO	Colonial Office (Records classification at National Archives [PRO], UK)
Earliest Acts	*The Earliest Acts and Laws of Rhode Island and Providence Plantations*, ed. John D. Cushing (Wilmington: Michael Glazier, 1977)
GCT	General Court of Trials, Rhode Island
GCT Recs.	Records of the General Court of Trials (1671–1724) (JRC), Rhode Island
GCT/SCJ Recs.	Records of the General Court of Trials (1725–1730) and Superior Court of Judicature (1730–1741) (JRC), Rhode Island
ICCP	Inferior Court of Common Pleas, Rhode Island

JCB	John Carter Brown Library, Providence
JRC	Rhode Island Supreme Court Judicial Records Center, Pawtucket
LPL	Lambeth Palace Library, London
MHS	Massachusetts Historical Society, Boston
NHS	Newport Historical Society, Newport, Rhode Island
PC	Privy Council (Records classification at National Archives [PRO], UK)
Portsmouth Recs.	*The Early Records of the Town of Portsmouth* (Providence: E. L. Freeman & Sons, 1901)
Providence Recs.	*Early Records of the Town of Providence* (Providence: Snow & Farnham, 1892–1915)
R.I. Ct. Recs.	*Rhode Island Court Records: Records of the General Court of Trials of the Colony of Providence Plantations, 1647–1670* (Providence: Rhode Island Historical Society, 1920–1922)
R.I. Recs.	*Records of the Colony of Rhode Island and Providence Plantations in New England*, ed. John Russell Bartlett (Providence: A. C. Greene, 1856–1865)
RIHS	Rhode Island Historical Society, Providence
RISA	Rhode Island State Archives, Providence
SCJ	Superior Court of Judicature, Rhode Island
SCJ Recs.	Superior Court of Judicature Records (JRC) (includes Books C, D, E, and Books for Providence, Kent, and South Kingston)
Smith, *Appeals*	Joseph Smith, *Appeals to the Privy Council from the American Plantations* (1950; repr. New York: Octagon Books, 1965)
TNA(PRO)	National Archives (Public Record Office), Kew, UK
Warwick Recs.	*The Early Records of the Town of Warwick* (Providence, 1926)

Introduction

1. Letter of Stephen Hopkins et al. in *Freebody v. Brenton* (Dec. 1772), PC 1/60/10.

2. For an excellent discussion of early understandings of *constitution,* see Daniel Hulsebosch, "The Constitution in the Glass Case and Constitutions in Action," 16 *Law and History Review* 397–401 (1998); Hulsebosch, *"Imperia in Imperio"*: The Multiple Constitutions of Empire in New York, 1750–1777," 16 *Law and History Review* 319–326 (1998); Bernard Bailyn, *The Ideological Origins of the American Revolution,* rev. ed. (Cambridge, Mass.: Harvard University Press, 1992), pp. 184–192 (orig. pub. 1967); John Phillip Reid, *Constitutional History of the American Revolution,* abridged ed. (Madison: University of Wisconsin Press, 1995), pp. xviii–xx,

3. For Thomas Paine, see his *Common Sense* (Philadelphia: W. & T. Bradford, 1776), appendix.

3. *R.I. Recs.*, vol. 2, p. 9; Board of Trade to the House of Lords (Jan. 23, 1733/34), *CHS Coll.*, vol. 5, pp. 446–447. On the origins of the Rhode Island charter, see Sydney V. James, *John Clarke and His Legacies: Religion and Law in Colonial Rhode Island, 1638–1750,* ed. Theodore Dwight Bozeman (University Park: Pennsylvania State Press, 1999), pp. 59–83; James, *Colonial Rhode Island: A History* (New York: Scribner's, 1975), pp. 67–70; and Patrick T. Conley, *Democracy in Decline: Rhode Island's Constitutional Development, 1776–1841* (Providence: RIHS, 1977), pp. 22–23 n. 3. For meanings of *repugnancy,* see *The Oxford English Dictionary,* 2nd ed. (New York: Oxford University Press, 1989), vol. 13, pp. 675–676.

4. Elizabeth Gaspar Brown, *British Statutes in American Law, 1776–1836* (Ann Arbor: University of Michigan Law School, 1964), p. 9 (quoting Sir William Jones's opinion). Brown's first chapter remains the most succinct description of the colonial transatlantic legal relationship; see pp. 1–22. See also Brown, "British Statutes in the Emergent Nations of North America: 1606–1949," 7 *American Journal of Legal History* 95–135 (1963). An unpublished essay by Alan Ford, "Ireland and England in the Early Seventeenth Century: Power and Distance," and Richard R. Johnson's *Adjustment to Empire: The New England Colonies, 1675–1715* (New Brunswick: Rutgers University Press, 1981), were helpful in clarifying some of these ideas.

5. After Rhode Island, Virginia and Massachusetts had the next largest numbers of appeals, particularly if one includes civil and chancery appeals. Joseph Smith reported total appeals during 1696–1783: Rhode Island (76), Virginia (54), Massachusetts (33) (Smith, *Appeals,* pp. 667–671). I count 70 to 80 Rhode Island appeals, depending on how one classifies pre-1709 appeals. See Mary Sarah Bilder, "Salamanders and Sons of God: Transatlantic Legal Culture and Colonial Rhode Island" (Ph.D. diss., Harvard University, 2000), pp. 530–532. Even beyond appeals, discussions of the legal history of colonial Rhode Island are somewhat paltry. See, for example, Thomas Williams Bicknell, *The History of the State of Rhode Island and Providence Plantations* (New York: American Historical Society, 1920), vol. 3, pp. 935–971; Thomas Durfee, *Rhode Island Historical Tract No. 18, Gleanings from the Judicial History of Rhode Island* (Providence: S. S. Rider, 1883); Amasa Eaton, "The Development of the Judicial System in Rhode Island," 14 *Yale Law Journal* 148 (1904); Stephen O. Edwards, "The Supreme Court of Rhode Island," *Green Bag,* pp. 525, 527 (1890); John T. Farrell, "The Early History of Rhode Island's Court System," parts 1–3, *Rhode Island History,* vol. 9, pp. 65–71 and 103–17 (1950), and vol. 10,

pp. 14–25 (1951). For nice discussions of Rhode Island as the "most understudied of England's mainland colonies," see the editors' preface and the author's introduction in Sydney V. James's posthumous *The Colonial Metamorphoses in Rhode Island: A Study of Institutions in Change,* ed. Sheila L. Skemp and Bruce C. Daniels (Hanover: University Press of New England, 2000), pp. vii–xi, 1–12. Both Sydney V. James and William G. McLoughlin noted the repugnancy principle in the charter. See James, *John Clarke and His Legacies,* p. 81, and William G. McLoughlin, *Rhode Island: A Bicentennial History* (New York: W. W. Norton, 1978), pp. 38–39. Other recent historical accounts focus largely on town authority. See Bruce C. Daniels, *Dissent and Conformity on Narragansett Bay: The Colonial Rhode Island Towns* (Middletown: Wesleyan University Press, 1983); James, *Colonial Metamorphoses;* David S. Lovejoy, *Rhode Island Politics and the American Revolution, 1760–1776* (Providence: Brown University Press, 1958).

6. For discussion of the 1720s Connecticut litigation, see *CHS Coll.*, vols. 4–5. Census figures place Rhode Island's population at 7,181 in 1708, at 40,536 in 1755, and at 59,678 in 1770; see John Blanchard MacInnes, "Rhode Island Bills of Public Credit, 1710–1755" (Ph.D. diss., Brown University, 1952), pp. 554–555, 573. The estimated population figures for New England and the British North American colonies are: 22,900/55,000 in 1650; 92,400/265,000 in 1700; 360,000/1,206,000 in 1750; and 581,100/2,283,0000 in 1770. John J. McCusker and Russell R. Menard, *The Economy of British America, 1607–1789* (Chapel Hill: University of North Carolina Press, 1991), pp. 103, 54. For recent work discussing racial issues, see Joanne Pope Melish, *Disowning Slavery: Gradual Emancipation and "Race" in New England, 1780–1860* (Ithaca: Cornell University Press, 1998); John Wood Sweet, "Bodies Politic: Colonialism, Race and the Emergence of the American North, Rhode Island, 1730–1830" (Ph.D. diss., Brown University, 1995); Robert K. Fitts, "Inventing New England's Slave Paradise: Master/Slave Relations in Eighteenth-Century Narragansett, Rhode Island" (Ph.D. diss., Brown University, 1995); Joshua Micah Marshall, "'A Melancholy People': Anglo-Indian Relations in Early Warwick, Rhode Island, 1642–1675," in *New England Encounters: Indians and Euroamericans ca. 1600–1850,* ed. Alden T. Vaughan (Boston: Northeastern University Press, 1999), pp. 84–108; John A. Sainsbury, "Indian Labor in Early Rhode Island," in ibid., pp. 259–275.

7. On statutes, charters, and repugnancy, see "The Case of William Bradford" in David P. Brown, *The Forum, or, Forty Years Full Practice at the Philadelphia Bar* (Philadelphia: R. H. Small, 1856), vol. 1, p. 272 (courtesy of Kathryn Preyer); David D. Hall, *Cultures of Print: Essays in the History of the Book* (Amherst: University of Massachusetts Press, 1996), p. 111 (John

Winthrop declared that "the Puritan laws, if fixed in a printed book of statutes, would show up at once as repugnant to English law and hence violations of the charter"). For other colonies and issues, see Smith, *Appeals,*
pp. 487–582. Future scholarship in this area will be greatly assisted by a
forthcoming reprint of the *APC, Colonial Series* with an introduction by
Morris Cohen, and by Sharon O'Connor's forthcoming guide to documen-
tation, *Appeals to the Privy Council before American Independence.*

8. On the imperial approach, see Charles Andrews, *The Colonial Period of
American History,* 4 vols. (New Haven: Yale University Press, 1934), and
R. L. Schuyler, *Parliament and the British Empire: Some Constitutional Con-
troversies concerning Imperial Legislative Jurisdiction* (New York: Columbia
University Press, 1929). On the "imperial constitution," see Charles H.
McIlwain, *The American Revolution: A Constitutional Interpretation* (Ithaca:
Great Seal Books, 1923); Schuyler, *Parliament and the British Empire;* Julius
Goebel Jr., "The Matrix of Empire," in Smith, *Appeals,* p. xxi; Barbara
A. Black, "The Constitution of Empire: The Case for the Colonists," 124
University of Pennsylvania Law Review 1157 (1976); Bailyn, *Ideological Ori-
gins;* Thomas C. Grey, "Origins of the Unwritten Constitution: Fundamen-
tal Law in American Revolutionary Thought," 30 *Stanford Law Review*
843 (1978); Reid, *Constitutional History;* Martin Stephen Flaherty, "Note:
The Empire Strikes Back: *Annesley v. Sherlock* and the Triumph of Imperial
Parliamentary Supremacy," 87 *Columbia Law Review* 593 (1987); Liam
Seamus O'Melinn, "Note: The American Revolution, Constitutionalism,
and the Seventeenth-Century West Indies," 95 *Columbia Law Review* 104
(1995); L. Kinvin Wroth, "Notes for a Comparative Study of the Origins of
Federalism in the United States and Canada," 15 *Arizona Journal of Inter-
national and Comparative Law* 93 (1998); David Thomas Konig, "Coloniza-
tion and the Common Law in Ireland and Virginia, 1569–1634," in *The
Transformation of Early American History,* ed. James A. Henretta et al. (New
York: Knopf, 1991), pp. 70–92. For recent work on law and the empire, see
Christine A. Desan's "Remaking Constitutional Tradition at the Margin of
the Empire: The Creation of Legislative Adjudication in Colonial New
York," Hulsebosch's *"Imperia in Imperio,"* and comments and responses in
"Constitutions on Edge: Empire, State, and Legal Culture in Eighteenth-
Century New York," all in 16 *Law and History Review* 257–401 (1998);
Jack P. Greene, *Negotiated Authorities: Essays in Colonial Political and Con-
stitutional History* (Charlottesville: University Press of Virginia, 1994), particularly chaps. 1–4. On appeals, see Smith, *Appeals,* pp. v–vi; see also
Smith, "Administrative Control of the Courts of the American Plantations," 61 *Columbia Law Review* 1210–53 (1961). Smith's work was pre-
ceded by that of historians John Franklin Jameson, Paul L. Ford, Arthur

Schlesinger, Harold Hazeltine, and Charles Andrews. For an outstanding early Columbia University dissertation on the subject, see George A. Washburne, *Imperial Control of the Administration of Justice in the Thirteen American Colonies, 1684–1776* (New York: Columbia University, 1923).

9. For discussion of these matters, see Peter Charles Hoffer, *Law and People in Colonial America*, rev. ed. (Baltimore: Johns Hopkins University Press, 1998), pp. 165–168, 178–179, 183; Stanley N. Katz, "The Problem of a Colonial Legal History," in *Colonial British America: Essays in the New History of the Early Modern Era Development*, ed. Jack P. Greene and J. R. Pole (Baltimore: Johns Hopkins University Press, 1984), pp. 457–489; John Murrin, "The Bench and Bar of Eighteenth-Century Massachusetts," in *Colonial America: Essays in Political Social Development*, ed. Stanley N. Katz (Boston: Little, Brown, 1971), p. 415; Joseph H. Smith, "New Light on the Doctrine of Judicial Precedent in Early America: 1607–1776," in *Legal Thought in the United States of America under Contemporary Pressures*, ed. John H. Hazard and Wenceslas J. Wagner (Brussels: Emile Bruylant, 1970), pp. 9–39; and George Lee Haskins, *Law and Authority in Early Massachusetts: A Study in Tradition and Design* (New York: Macmillan, 1960), pp. 163–188.

10. On the difficulty of sources, see Brown, *British Statutes in American Law,* pp. 19–20; Jack P. Greene, "Colonial Origins of Constitutionalism," in *Negotiated Authorities,* p. 34.

11. For examples of Rhode Island attorney libraries, see Mary Sarah Bilder, "The Lost Lawyers: Early American Legal Literates and Transatlantic Legal Culture," 11 *Yale Journal of Law & the Humanities* 45 (1999), and "Salamanders and Sons of God," pp. 159–161, 233–234, 317–318, 413.

1. Legal Practitioners and Legal Literates

1. Report of the Earl of Bellomont, on the irregularities of Rhode Island, in *R.I. Recs.,* vol. 1, p. 386. On Bellomont, see Frederic de Peyster, *The Life and Administration of Richard, Earl of Bellomont* (New York: New York Historical Society, 1879). For versions of the myth, see Anton-Hermann Chroust, *The Rise of the Legal Profession in America* (Norman: University of Oklahoma Press, 1965), vol. 1, pp. 6–7; and Charles Warren, *A History of the American Bar* (Boston: Little, Brown, 1913), pp. 3–19. For various recent interpretations of "attorney," see Cornelia Hughes Dayton, *Women before the Bar: Gender, Law, and Society in Connecticut, 1639–1789* (Chapel Hill: University of North Carolina Press, 1995), pp. 47–48; Bruce H. Mann, *Neighbors and Strangers: Law and Community in Early Connecticut* (Chapel Hill: University of North Carolina Press, 1987), pp. 93–96; William Offutt,

*Of "Good Laws" and "Good Men": Law and Society in the Delaware Valley,
1680–1710* (Urbana: University of Illinois Press, 1995), p. 119; and A. G.
Roeber, *Faithful Magistrates and Republican Lawyers: Creators of Virginia
Legal Culture, 1680–1810* (Chapel Hill: University of North Carolina Press,
1981), p. 53. On two early attorneys, see Thomas G. Barnes, "Thomas
Lechford and the Earliest Lawyering in Massachusetts, 1638–1641," in
Law in Colonial Massachusetts, 1630–1800, ed. Daniel R. Coquillette
(Boston: Colonial Society, 1984), p. 3; and Barbara A. Black, "Nathaniel
Byfield, 1653–1733," also in Coquillette, *Law in Colonial Massachusetts,*
p. 57. For a further discussion, see Mary Sarah Bilder, "The Lost Lawyers:
Early American Legal Literates and Transatlantic Legal Culture," 11 *Yale
Journal of Law & the Humanities* 47–55 (1999).

2. C. W. Brooks, *Pettyfoggers and Vipers of the Commonwealth: The "Lower
Branch" of the Legal Profession in Early Modern England* (Cambridge: Cam-
bridge University Press, 1986), pp. 162 (quoting the 1614 order), 165;
Robert Robson, *The Attorney in Eighteenth-Century England* (Cambridge:
Cambridge University Press, 1959), p. 3; and Wilfrid R. Prest, *The Rise
of the Barristers: A Social History of the English Bar, 1590–1640* (Oxford:
Clarendon Press, 1986), p. 13. On attorney backgrounds, see Brooks,
Pettyfoggers, pp. 115–116, 275–276. On the growth from 150 attorneys in
1560 to 1,400 by 1640, see C. W. Brooks, "Litigants and Attorneys in the
King's Bench and Common Pleas," in *Legal Records and the Historian,* ed.
J. H. Baker (London: Royal Historical Society, 1978), p. 53. In general, see
J. H. Baker, "The English Legal Profession, 1450–1550," in *The Legal Pro-
fession and the Common Law* (London: Hambledon Press, 1986). On the
later eighteenth-century barristers, see David Lemmings, *Professors of the
Law: Barristers and English Legal Culture in the Eighteenth Century* (Oxford:
Oxford University Press, 2000) and *Gentlemen and Barristers: The Inns of
Court and the English Bar, 1680–1730* (Oxford: Oxford University Press,
1990).

3. Brooks, *Pettyfoggers,* pp. 152, 17, 142; see pp. 18–19 and 114 on attorney
training; see p. 144 on the 1633 rule.

4. For the laws, see *Earliest Acts,* pp. 52, 74. On the towns, see *Providence
Recs.,* vol. 2, p. 86; *Warwick Recs.,* p. 69; *Portsmouth Recs.,* p. 164.

5. For notations, see *R.I. Ct. Recs.,* 2 vols. For the attorney list and details, see
Bilder, "Lost Lawyers," pp. 104–107. More than half of these men had
wills. On the agreement between Uselton and Greene, see *Warwick Recs.,*
p. 270.

6. *R.I. Recs.,* vol. 1, p. 417 (1659). For details, see Bilder, "Lost Lawyers,"
pp. 108–110. Even if little evidence still exists to verify the label, thirteen
men had sufficient legal literacy to act as attorneys: William Almy, Francis

Brinley, Henry Bull, William Coddington, John Coggeshall, William Dyer, Nicholas Easton, Samuel Gorton, Randall Houlden, Richard Knight, Richard Morris, Richard Smith, and James Rogers, the general sergeant (though he may not have been literate throughout the entire period).

7. On Calverly, see *Warwick Recs.,* pp. 186, 1145 (1657); Glenn W. LaFantasie, ed., *The Correspondence of Roger Williams* (Providence: Brown University Press for RIHS), vol. 2, p. 544 n. 7. On Porter, see *Winthrop Papers* (Boston: MHS, 1929–1947), vol. 4, p. 296; ibid., pp. 330–333. For handwriting, see the William Harris Papers (1638–1846) (hereafter, Wm. Harris Papers) (Harris and Sherman) (RIHS), Box 1, and *Portsmouth Recs.* (Sherman). Roger Williams and John Clarke also may have obtained attorney or clerk training. On Providence town clerk Gregory Dexter, a prominent London petition printer, see LaFantasie, *Correspondence of Roger Williams,* vol. 1, p. 231 n. 2; Howard M. Chapin, "Gregory Dexter, Master Printer, A Checklist of Books Printed by Gregory Dexter," *Rhode Island Historical Society Collections,* vol. 13, pp. 105–113, 114 (1919).

8. Harris's Account of New England (Apr. 29, 1675), in *Harris Papers,* in *Collections of the Rhode Island Historical Society* (Providence, 1902), vol. 10, pp. 142, 146. On Sanford, see ibid., vol. 2, 459 n. 1; John Osborne Austin, *The Genealogical Dictionary of Rhode Island* (1887; repr., Baltimore: Genealogical, 1969), p. 171; *R.I. Recs.,* vol. 1, p. 300. On John Sanford Sr., see *Winthrop Papers,* vol. 3, pp. 112–113. On Greene, see Louise Clark, *The Greenes of Rhode Island* (New York: Knickerbocker Press, 1903), pp. 52–58; LaFantasie, *Correspondence of Roger Williams,* vol. 1, p. 109 n. 2.

9. For Richmond proceedings, see *R.I. Ct. Recs.,* vol. 1, pp. 18–19, 22, 31, 37–38, 45–46; *R.I. Recs.,* vol. 1, pp. 348–349, 358–360.

10. *Harris Papers,* pp. 80–81; *R.I. Recs.,* vol. 1, pp. 195–196; see ibid., vol. 2, p. 147.

11. On the recorder's work for the Court and Assembly, see *R.I. Recs.,* vol. 1, pp. 232, 304, 316, 326. The recorder also served as secretary to the Council. See ibid., vol. 1, p. 405; vol. 2, pp. 192, 563.

12. On the governor, see ibid., vol. 2, p. 151.

13. On individual matters, see, e.g., *Warwick Recs.,* pp. 68, 98. In 1659 the law stated that the town was sued by arresting the treasurer. *R.I. Recs.,* vol. 1, p. 424.

14. Harris's Bill against Calverly and others (Nov. 17, 1677), in *Harris Papers,* p. 213. For table of fees, see ibid., pp. 207, 226–227, 244, 280. For Harris references, see Letter from William Harris to William Arnold and others (Dec. 25, 1657), in ibid., p. 49; Letter from William Harris to his Family (Apr. 6, 1680), in ibid., pp. 324, 325; Letter from William Harris to his Family (Aug. 22, 1680), in ibid., p. 336.

15. Letter from William Harris to the Court (Oct. 1, 1678), in *Harris Papers,* pp. 250, 259. For Williams's views, see Letter from Roger Williams to the Governor and Council (Aug. 31, 1668), in *Providence Recs.,* vol. 15, p. 122 (punctuation added); *Harris Papers,* p. 78. For Calverly quote, see ibid., pp. 90–91. For views on Harris, see Sydney V. James, *Colonial Rhode Island: A History* (New York: Scribner's, 1975), pp. 88–89. For speculation on attorney background, see Henry C. Dorr, *The Proprietors of Providence and Their Controversies with the Freeholders, Collections of the Rhode Island Historical Society* (Providence, 1897), vol. 9, p. 7. On the Harris lawsuit, see Charles M. Andrews, *The Colonial Period in American History* (New Haven: Yale University Press, 1934), vol. 2, pp. 57, 62–66. On Harris's service, see *R.I. Recs.,* vol. 2, pp. 150, 180, 184, 191, 375. Harris was also the agent for the Atherton Associates, a group including the Winthrops, Simon Bradstreet, Elisha and Edward Hutchinson, Richard Wharton, both Richard Smiths, and Francis Brinley. See J. M. Sosin, *English America and the Restoration Monarchy of Charles II* (Lincoln: University of Nebraska Press, 1980), p. 255.

16. On Harris's captivity and death, see *Harris Papers,* pp. 321, 324, 330, 341. The library included the following law books: "Cookes Comentarey upon littlton" (Edward Coke, *First Part of the Institutes of the Lawes of England: or, Commentarie upon Littleton,* first published 1628); "The Compleat Clarke" (*Compleat Clerk; containing the best Forms of all sorts of Presidents for Conveyances and Assurances, etc.,* first published 1655); "The Touchstone of wills" ([George] Meriton, *Touchstone of Wills, Testaments, and Administrations; a compendium of Cases and Resolutions,* first published 1668); "Lambaths preambulations" (William Lambarde, *Perambulation of Kent: Conteining the description, Hystorie, and Customes of that Shyre,* first published 1576); "The Statute booke by poulton" ([Ferdinando] Pulton, *Collection of sundrie Statutes frequent in use, with notes and references,* published 1661); "Declerations & pleadings" (Richard Brownlow, *Declarations and Pleadings in English; the Forme of Proceeding in Courts of Law,* first published 1652); "The Exsecutors office" (Thomas Wentworth, *Office and Duty of Executors; or treatise of Wills and Executors directed to Testators in the choice of their Executors and contrivance of their Wills,* first published 1641); "The Exposition of termes of law" (William Rastell, *An Exposition of the termes of the lawes of England,* first published in 1563); "The lay mans laywer" (Thomas Forster, *Lay-Mans Lawyer; or, Second Part of the Practice of the Law. Relating to the Punishments of Offences committed against the public peace, with presidents [precedents],* first published 1654); "The law Concerning juryers" ([Giles Duncombe], *Tryals per Pais: or Law concerning Juries by Nisi Prius, etc.,* first published 1665); "Justice restored" (*Justice restored: or Guide for His Majestie's Justices of Peace, both in Sessions and out*

of Sessions, according to the antient Laws of the Kingdom, first published 1660); "Dallons Countrey justice" (Michael Dalton, *The Countrey Justice, the Practice of the Justices of the Peace out of their sessions,* first published 1618); "The Lawes Resolution of Women's Rights" (*Lawes Resolution of Women's Rights: or, Lawes Provision for Woemen; a methodical collection of such statutes and customes, with the case, opinions, arguments, and points of learning in the law as doe properly concerned woemen,* first published 1632). He also owned "New Englands Memoriall" (Nathaniel Morton, *New-Englands Memoriall,* published in Cambridge, Mass., 1669). A copy of the Rhode Island charter can be found in Harris's papers. In addition, the inventory noted that there were "another book" and "several books" on loan. It also included the following nonlaw books: "Dixionary"; "The London Despencettorey"; "Chururgions mate"; "Norwoods Tryangles"; "Bible"; "Contemplations, Morall, & devine" (Matthew Hale, *Contemplations moral and divine,* first published 1676); and "a great Bible"; "Naturs Explecation"; "Treatise of faith"; "Treating of the Effect of war"; "The Gentleman jocky"; "The Gospell preacher"; "The Method of Phissick"; "A short Introduction of the Grammer"; "The Book of Artillery." See *Providence Recs.,* vol. 6, pp. 76–86, 88–89. *The Lawes Resolution of Women's Rights* and *The Book of Artillery* are listed in a receipt given to John Whipple Jr. from Susan and Howlong Harris (June 1682). See RIHS Manuscripts, vol. 1, p. 34. Bibliographic information has been drawn from *A Legal Bibliography of the British Commonwealth of Nations,* 2nd ed., ed. W. Harold Maxwell and Leslie F. Maxwell (London: Sweet & Maxwell, 1955), vol. 1.

17. [Giles Duncombe], *Tryals per Pais* (London: John Streater, James Flesher & Henry Twyford, 1665), introduction; Richard Brownlow, *Declarations and Pleadings in English* (London: Thomas Roycroft, 1652), title page; John More, *The Lawes Resolution of Women's Rights* (London: [printed by the assigns of John More], 1632), title page; *The Compleat Clerk, and Scriveners Guide* (London: Thomas Roycroft, 1655), title page.

18. William Hamilton Bryson, *Census of Law Books in Colonial Virginia* (Charlottesville: University Press of Virginia, 1978), p. xx. On colonial law libraries, see Warren, *History of the American Bar,* at p. 71.

19. On Providence clerk Thomas Olney, see LaFantasie, *Correspondence of Roger Williams,* vol. 2, p. 518 n. 5. Both Pocock and Whipple borrowed "several" books.

20. *Providence Recs.,* vol. 15, p. 80 (1660). Cases unfolded according to the "progress of law" or "legal progress": (1) the plaintiff filed a declaration; (2) a writ was filed for the defendant's arrest; (3) the defendant posted bond, promising to appear on the trial date; (4) the defendant answered

the declaration and entered a plea; and (5) the trial proceeded before a jury. See "Touching Pleaders," *R.I. Recs.*, vol. 1, pp. 200–207. For Providence references, see *Providence Recs.*, vol. 15, p. 34 (1650); vol. 2, p. 67 (1652); ibid., p. 85 (1655). On literacy, see Kenneth A. Lockridge, *Literacy in Colonial New England* (New York: W. W. Norton, 1974), p. 15. Rough literacy rates are based on available printed sources. On English legal literacy, see Brooks, *Pettyfoggers,* p. 19, and J. H. Baker, "Counsellors and Barristers: A Historical Study," 27 *Cambridge Law Journal* 205, 221 (1969). In 1671 the colony passed a law that "for the future" no person shall be elected or employed as general sergeant "unless such a one as can read and write." *R.I. Recs.*, vol. 2, p. 400.

21. *Providence Recs.*, vol. 2, p. 87. Extant Warwick court records reveal at least one case with an illiterate plaintiff and another with illiterate defendants. See *Records of the Court of Trials of the Town of Warwick, 1659–1674* (Providence, 1922), pp. 2, 11, 15. People who could not sign their names regularly appeared on jury rosters. See Bilder, "Lost Lawyers," p. 58 nn. 45, 47. On *nihil dicit,* see John Rastell, *Les Termes de la Ley: or Certain Difficult and Obscure Words and Terms of the Common Law and Statutes . . .* (London: John Streater, James Flesher, & Henry Twyford, 1667), p. 474; see also Rastell, *An Exposition of Certain Difficult and Obscure Words* (1579; New York: Da Capo Press, 1969), p. 151. For examples in the colony, see *R.I. Recs.*, vol. 1, p. 224 (1650). The 1657 law appears at ibid., p. 356. For a 1662 denial of a motion for *nihil dicit,* see *R.I. Ct. Recs.*, vol. 2, pp. 5–6. For the 1698 case, see *Samuel Stibbins v. Thomas Durfee, Jr.,* in *GCT Recs.*, Book A, p. 126 (JRC).

22. For the 1669 statute, see *R.I. Recs.*, vol. 2, pp. 238–239. The criminal side of the General Court of Trials operated in part as an oral culture in which women and men, literate and illiterate, participated. Indictments, pleas, the jury verdict, and the defendant's punishment and bonds were orally conveyed. See *R.I. Ct. Recs.*, vol. 1, pp. 5–80.

23. *Providence Recs.*, vol. 2, p. 59. In 1649, fees "for preparing the cause and for pleading" were 6 shillings, 8 pence. In 1656, the fee was reduced to 3 shillings, 4 pence. See ibid., p. 92. In 1677, the colony reset fees so that drawing a declaration was two-thirds of the old fee. See *R.I. Recs.*, vol. 2, pp. 590–591. For cases, see *R.I. Ct. Recs.*, vol. 1, p. 19 (1656) (action in detinue); *John Greene, Jr. v. Mathias Harvey, Records of the Court . . . of Warwick,* pp. 1, 13–15. On declarations, see *Providence Recs.*, vol. 2, pp. 85–89.

24. On the four actions, see Brooks, *Pettyfoggers,* p. 66. On the writ system with "a less than highly skilled population," see David Thomas Konig, *Law and Society in Puritan Massachusetts: Essex County, 1629–1692* (Chapel

Hill: University of North Carolina Press, 1979), pp. 114–115. For slander, see *R.I. Ct. Recs.*, vol. 2, p. 33 (Sept. 1664); *Cowland v. Earle,* ibid., vol. 1, p. 20 (June 1656); *Katherine Mills v. Ralph Earle, Sr.,* ibid., p. 33 (Sept. 1664). On the Brinley suit, see ibid., vol. 2, p. 99.

25. On Easton's case, see *R.I. Recs.*, vol. 1, pp. 387–389; see also, ibid., pp. 314, 321, 346–347, 425, 430, 440; *R.I. Ct. Recs.,* vol. 1, pp. 56, 67–68, 70–71. For a formal definition, see Rastell, *Les Termes de la Ley,* p. 244; Rastell, *Exposition,* p. 63. For laws about demurrers, see *R.I. Recs.*, vol. 1, pp. 237 (1651), 356 (1657), 479 (1662); vol. 2, p. 523 (1674). On Carpenter's appearance, see *Records of the Court . . . of Warwick,* pp. 7–8; *R.I. Ct. Recs.,* vol. 2, pp. 29–30 (1664). On removal, see *Providence Recs.,* vol. 15, p. 58 (1652). For a case in which the assistant had posted bond for the opposing side and would later represent him as an attorney, see *R.I. Ct. Recs.,* vol. 1, pp. 19–20.

26. *Providence Recs.,* vol. 2, p. 88; see also *R.I. Recs.*, vol. 1, pp. 266–267. On Arnold's appeal, see *Providence Recs.,* vol. 15, pp. 49–50. For three appeals, see *Garriardy v. Westcott, R.I. Ct. Recs.,* vol. 1, p. 69 (Oct. 1660); *Field v. Carpenter,* ibid., vol. 2, p. 20 (Oct. 1663); *Harvey v. Greene,* ibid., p. 29 (Dec. 1663). A 1652 law stated that no more evidence could be used on appeal than in the town court. *R.I. Recs.,* vol. 1, p. 242.

27. For early references to discretionary rehearings, see *R.I. Recs.,* vol. 1, pp. 222, 237; *R.I. Ct. Recs.,* vol. 1, pp. 11–12, 13–15. For the Brenton-Coddington case, see *R.I. Recs.,* vol. 1, pp. 337–338, 348, 361; *R.I. Ct. Recs.,* vol. 1, p. 20, 22–23. On the new law, see *R.I. Ct. Recs.,* vol. 1, p. 24; *R.I. Recs.,* vol. 1, p. 357. For the quote, see Letter from William Harris to King Charles II (June 11, 1675), in *Harris Papers,* p. 153.

28. For rehearings, see Bilder, "Lost Lawyers," p. 111. Reductions ranged. See *R.I. Ct. Recs.,* vol. 1, pp. 48, 52 (reduced from £150 to £60), pp. 62–63, 68 (reduced by 10 shillings). During these years, defendant attorneys had the sentence reversed or damages reduced in eight of the eleven requests. On Torrey, see ibid., pp. 41–42, 52. On 1698 rehearings, see *GCT Recs.,* Book A, pp. 122, 123, 126 (JRC).

29. For the report, see "Rhode Island: State of the Constitutions & proceedings of the Courts of Tryals & goal deliveries both in Civil and Criminall Cases. . ." (Apr. 18, 1701), in Erwin C. Surrency, "Report on Court Procedures in the Colonies—1700," 9 *American Journal of Legal History* 234–238 (1965). For *Gereardy v. Scarbrough,* see *R.I. Ct. Recs.,* vol. 2, p. 76. The court stated that the issue was, first, whether the tobacco attached was in Scarbrough's estate and, second, how much he was indebted. Ibid., p. 80 (Oct. 1669). For *Gereardy v. Westcott,* see *R.I. Ct. Recs.,* vol. 1, p. 69 (Oct.

1660); ibid., vol. 2, pp. 14–15, 18–19. For a similar hung jury, see *Elles v. Bull, R.I. Recs.,* vol. 2, pp. 139, 224; *R.I. Ct. Recs.,* vol. 2, pp. 42, 43–44, 48–49.

30. For the 1680 law, see *R.I. Recs.,* vol. 3, p. 87. For case, see *Christopher and John Almy v. Mary Almy Pococke,* ibid., vol. 3, pp. 86–87 (May 1680). For appeal, see ibid., vol. 3, pp. 91–92. For another early appeal, see *Pococke v. Edmund Calvery, R.I. Recs.,* vol. 3, p. 118 (Oct. 1682). On appeals, see Mary Sarah Bilder, "The Origin of the Appeal," 48 *Hastings Law Journal* 913, 949–951 (1997).

2. The Laws of England

1. See Elizabeth Gaspar Brown, *British Statutes in American Law, 1776–1836* (Ann Arbor: University of Michigan Law School, 1964), p. 1. On medieval empire and law, see Julius Goebel Jr., "The Matrix of Empire," in Smith, *Appeals,* pp. vvi, xlii–xlv. On the early balance of custom and common law, see J. H. Baker, *An Introduction to English Legal History,* 3rd ed. (London: Butterworth, 1990), pp. 1–43.

2. "Concerning the laws to be used in Wales," 27 Hen. 8 26 (1535). The act granted the Welsh the benefit of English liberties, rights, privileges, freedoms, and laws. The English King and Council were to decide which divergent Welsh laws were "expedient, requisite and necessary." Baker, *Introduction,* pp. 36–37.

3. The three quoted sentences appear in Daniel R. Coquillette, *Francis Bacon* (Edinburgh: Edinburgh University Press, 1992), pp. 71 (quoting *Discourse touching the Happy Union* [1603]), 74 (quoting *Preparation for the Union of Laws*), 73 (quoting *Certain Articles or Considerations Touching the Union of the Kingdoms of England and Scotland* [1604]). On the Succession Act of 1604, see "Succession Act (1604)" in *Sources of English Constitutional History,* ed. Carl Stephenson and Frederick George Marcham (New York: Harper & Row, 1972), vol. 1, pp. 431–432; Brian P. Levack, *The Formation of the British State: England, Scotland, and the Union, 1603–1707* (Oxford: Clarendon Press, 1987).

4. Edward Coke, *The First Part of the Institutes of the Lawes of England, or, a Commentary upon Littleton, not the name of a Lawyer onely, but of the Law it selfe* (1628; repr., New York: Garland, 1979), preface, p. 7; Coke, *The Second Part of the Institutes of the Laws of England, containing the Exposition of Many Ancient, and Other Statutes* (1797; repr., Buffalo: William S. Hein, 1986), pp. 3–4; Coke, *The Third Part of the Institutes of the Laws of England concerning . . . pleas of the crown and criminal causes* (1797; repr., Buffalo:

William S. Hein, 1986); Coke, *The Fourth Part of the Institutes of the Laws of England concerning the jurisdiction of courts* (1797; repr., Buffalo: William S. Hein, 1986), intro., p. 2.

5. Coke, *Institutes, First Part,* p. 11, verso. Throughout, Coke noted where different regions followed particular customs regarding property law. Ibid., preface, p. 11. This section is treated as "Chapter II—of the Laws of England" in the nineteenth-century arrangement of Coke. See J. H. Thomas, *Systematic Arrangement of Lord Coke's First Institute of the Laws of England* (1836; repr., Buffalo: William S. Hein, 1986), pp. 6–7. The *Case of Tanistry,* Dav. Ir. 78 (1608), decided the same year as *Calvin's Case,* permitted customary rules of inheritance in England to continue in certain cases. See Baker, *Introduction,* p. 39. For discussion of Coke's belief that "common law was custom," see Donald Veall, *The Popular Movement for Law Reform, 1640–1660* (Oxford: Clarendon Press, 1970), p. 66.

6. Matthew Hale, *The History of the Common Law of England,* 5th ed. (1794; repr., Holmes Beach, FL: Gaunt, 1993), vol. 1, pp. 130, 131, 60; vol. 2, pp. 1, 7, 28, 40. On Hale, see Alan Cromartie, *Sir Matthew Hale, 1609–1676: Law, Religion, and Natural Philosophy* (Cambridge: Cambridge University Press, 1995), p. 13; see also pp. 12, 37, 41, 49–50, 106. On the laws of England and Blackstone, see David Lieberman, *The Province of Legislation Determined: Legal Theory in Eighteenth-Century Britain* (Cambridge: Cambridge University Press, 1989), pp. 31–55. For a discussion of common-law publication, see Richard J. Ross, "The Commoning of the Common Law: The Renaissance Debate over Printing English Law, 1520–1640," 146 *University of Pennsylvania Law Review,* pp. 323, 395, 436–48 (1998).

7. Hale, *History of the Common Law,* vol. 1, p. 130; vol. 2, pp. 28, 40, 2.

8. L. Kinvin Wroth, "Notes for a Comparative Study of the Origins of Federalism in the United States and Canada," 15 *Arizona Journal of International and Comparative Law* 93, 97 (1998); Donald W. Sutherland, *Quo Warranto Proceedings in the Reign of Edward I, 1278–1294* (Oxford: Clarendon Press, 1963), p. 5; Cecil T. Carr, ed., *Select Charters of Trading Companies, 1530–1707* (London: Selden Society, 1913), p. xxvii. On the Privy Council, see Edward Raymond Turner, *The Privy Council of England in the Seventeenth and Eighteenth Centuries, 1603–1784,* 2 vols. (Baltimore: Johns Hopkins University Press, 1927–1928). For a general discussion, see Brown, *British Statutes in American Law,* pp. 1–6; and Goebel, "Matrix of Empire" in Smith, *Appeals,* p. xxiii. On the timing of imperial parliamentary supremacy after the Glorious Revolution of 1688 and the relevance of the changing understanding of the prerogative, see Barbara A. Black, "The Constitution of Empire: The Case for the Colonists," 124 *University of Pennsylvania*

Law Review 1157 (1976); Martin Stephen Flaherty, "Note: The Empire Strikes Back: *Amnesty v. Sherlock* and the Triumph of Imperial Parliamentary Supremacy," 87 *Columbia Law Review* 593 (1987); Martin S. Flaherty, "More Apparent than Real: The Revolutionary Commitment to Constitutional Federalism," 45 *Kansas Law Review* 993, 1002 (1997); Wroth, "Origins of Federalism," p. 97.

9. See Black, "Constitution of Empire," p. 1157; Brown, *British Statutes in American Law,* pp. 4–20; Flaherty, "More Apparent than Real," pp. 999–1000; Flaherty, "Empire Strikes Back," p. 618; Smith, *Appeals,* pp. 464–522; Joseph H. Smith, "New Light on the Doctrine of Judicial Precedent in Early America: 1607–1776," in *Legal Thought in the United States of America under Contemporary Pressures,* ed. John N. Hazard and Wenceslas J. Wagner (Brussels: Emile Bruylant, 1970), pp. 14–20.

10. *Calvin's Case,* 7 Coke 1a, 2a (Trinity, 6 Jac. 1) (1608), 77 English Reports 377. The case originally appeared in law French. It reappeared in a 1651 abridgement and in a 1658 English-language edition of Coke's *Reports.* See W. Harold Maxwell, *A Legal Bibliography of the British Commonwealth of Nations* (1955; repr., London: John Rees, 1989), vol. 1, pp. 295–297. On the case and the colonies, see Smith, *Appeals,* p. 468; Goebel, "Matrix of Empire," in Smith, *Appeals,* pp. lx–lxi; Black, "Constitution of Empire," pp. 1175–98; Flaherty, "Empire Strikes Back," pp. 597–618; Liam Seamus O'Melinn; "Note: The American Revolution and Constitutionalism in the Seventeenth-Century West Indies," 95 *Columbia Law Review,* 104, 110–114 (1995). The interpretation here has benefited from these scholars and a discussion with Charles Donahue. For a very recent discussion of the case emphasizing British legal thought, see Daniel J. Hulsebosch's "The Ancient Constitution and the Expanding Empire: Sir Edward Coke's British Jurisprudence," *Law and History Review,* vol. 21 (2003), pp. 439ff.

11. *Calvin's Case,* pp. 397–398.

12. Ibid., p. 398. Coke explicitly noted that the argument against Calvin might be made against anyone in Ireland, but that "all men know that they are natural-born subjects, and capable of and inheritable to lands in England." Ibid., p. 405. Coke conveniently ignored the fact that John had extended the laws after inheriting Ireland.

13. *Blankard v. Galdy,* 2 Salkeld 411, 91 English Reports 356 (King's Bench 1693). The immediate impact of the decision is unclear. Holt did not apply the category in the case, deciding instead that Jamaica had been acquired by conquest. The opinion remained available only by manuscript until the publication of William Salkeld's *Reports of Cases in the Court of King's Bench* [1689–1712] (London: Elizabeth Nutt and R. Gosling, 1717–1718). On its publication, see Maxwell, *Legal Bibliography,* p. 308. For the 1720 West

opinion, see George Chalmers, *Opinions of Eminent Lawyers on Various Points of English Jurisprudence* (1858; repr., Buffalo: William S. Hein, 1987), p. 206. For the 1722 memo, see 2 Peere Williams 75; Brown, *British Statutes in American Law,* pp. 11–12. In the 1826 report of *Calvin's Case,* the editor, John Frager, inserted the 1722 memorandum stating that "if there be a new and uninhabited country found out by English subjects, as the law is the birthright of every subject, so wherever they go, they carry their law with them, and therefore such new found country is to be governed by the laws of England, though after such country is inhabited by the English, Acts of Parliament made in England, without naming the foreign plantations, will not bind them." *Calvin's Case,* p. 398 n. K. On Connecticut, see Instructions to Our Agent, Jonathan Belcher (Dec. 19, [1728]), *CHS Coll.,* vol. 4, pp. 143–158. Smith notes that the case was cited in 1670 in *Craw v. Ramsey* when "Vaughan for the first time injects the conception of a dominion acquired by plantation." Smith, *Appeals,* p. 469.

14. *Calvin's Case,* p. 404; R. T. Barton, ed., *Virginia Colonial Decisions: The Reports by Sir John Randolph and by Edward Barradall . . . 1728–1741* (Boston: Boston Book, 1909), vol. 2, p. B-1; Chalmers, *Opinions,* p. 208. Brown summarizes, the "position of the Crown law officers automatically insured a wide variety in the degree to which both Common and Statute law were 'received' into the colonies." Brown, *British Statutes in American Law,* p. 14.

15. William Blackstone, *Commentaries on the Laws of England* (1765–1769; repr., Chicago: University of Chicago Press, 1979), vol. 1, pp. 104–105; Brown, *British Statutes in American Law,* pp. 13–14 (quoting 1775 seventh edition).

16. Francis Newton Thorpe, *The Federal and State Constitutions, Colonial Charters, and Other Organic Laws of the States, Territories and Colonies Now or Heretofore Forming the United States of America* (1909; repr., Buffalo: William S. Hein, 1993), vol. 1, pp. 50, 54. On locking, see John Russell Bartlett, ed., *Records of the Colony of Rhode Island and Providence Plantations in New England* (Providence: A. C. Green, 1856), vol. 1, p. 196; John Dykstra Eusden, *Puritans, Lawyers and Politics in Early Seventeenth-Century England* (New Haven: Yale University Press, 1958), p. 53. For pre-1608 examples, see the Levant Company ("the said laws [etc.] be reasonable and not contrary or repugnant") and the Newfoundland Company Charter ("statutes, ordinances, and proceedings as near as conveniently may be shall be agreeable"), in Carr, *Select Charters,* pp. 30, 34, 51, 60. On the formula and the 1606 Virginia instructions that permitted the king or the Council of Virginia to alter or void ordinances, as long as the alterations were "in substance consonant unto the lawes of England or the equity thereof," see Smith, *Appeals,* pp. 465, 468–469. Affirmative examples

include: the 1609 Virginia charter ("as near as conveniently may be, be agreeable"); the 1621 Virginia Ordinances ("as near as may be"); the 1629 Mason Grant ("as shall be agreeable as near as may be"); the 1622 Gorges and Mason grant in Maine ("agreeable, as near as may be"). Thorpe, *Federal and State Constitutions*, vol. 7, pp. 3801, 3812; vol. 4, p. 2436; vol. 3, p. 1624. Negative examples include: the 1611 Virginia charter ("be not contrary"); the 1629 Massachusetts Bay charter ("be not contrarie or repugnant"); the 1641 Piscataqua River settlers statement ("not repugnant"). Ibid., vol. 7, pp. 3806; vol. 3, pp. 1853, 1857–58; vol. 4, p. 2445. Examples with both affirmative and negative phrases include: the 1620 Massachusetts charter ("so always as the same be not contrary" and "as near as conveniently may be, agreeable "); the 1629 patent to Robert Heath for Carolina ("be consonant to reason and not repugnant or contrary but (as conveniently as may be done) consonant"); the 1632 Maryland grant to Baltimore ("be consonant to Reason, and be not repugnant or contrary, but (so far as conveniently may be) agreeable"); the 1639 Maine grant to Gorges (be "reasonable and not repugnant and contrary but agreeable (as neere as conveniently may bee)" and a similar grant to Gorges himself to make ordinances under the same phrase); the 1664 Maine charter to the Duke of York and assigns ("be not contrary to but as neare as conveniently may be agreeable"); the 1662 Connecticut grant ("not contrary")." Ibid., vol. 1, p. 71; vol. 3, pp. 1832–33, 1680–81, 1629–30, 1638; vol. 1, p. 533. For discussion, see Jack P. Greene, *Peripheries and Center: Constitutional Development in the Extended Polities of the British Empire and the United States* (Athens: University of Georgia Press, 1986), pp. 19–42.

17. For 1644 charter, see *Earliest Acts*, p. 2; Sydney V. James, *Colonial Rhode Island: A History* (New York: Scribner's, 1975), pp. 57–60. On its legality, see Patrick T. Conley, *Democracy in Decline: Rhode Island's Constitutional Development, 1776–1841* (Providence: RIHS, 1977), p. 18, n. 24. For 1663 charter, see *R.I. Recs.*, vol. 2, p. 9. On Clarke and the charter, see James, *Colonial Rhode Island*, pp. 67–70; Conley, *Democracy in Decline*, p. 23 n. 3; William G. McLoughlin, *Rhode Island: A Bicentennial History* (New York: W. W. Norton, 1978), p. 39. For Williams's quotes, see Glenn LaFantasie, ed., *The Correspondence of Roger Williams* (Providence: Brown University Press, 1988), vol. 2, p. 535–536 (spelling modernized).

18. For post-1663 examples, see the 1663 Carolina charter ("be consonant to reason, and as near as may be conveniently"); the 1664 New Jersey charter ("be consonant to reason, and as near as may be conveniently agreeable"); the 1680 Cutt Commission ("as the present state and condition of our subjects inhabiting within the limit aforesaid, and the circumstances of the place will admit"); the 1688 crown charter to Sir Edmund Andros in Mas-

sachusetts ("as consonant and agreeable . . . as the present state and condition of our subjects inhabiting . . . and the circumstances of the place will
admit"); the 1691 Massachusetts charter ("so as the same be not repugnant
or contrary"); Thorpe, *Federal and State Constitutions,* vol. 5, pp. 2746,
2538; vol. 4, p. 2447; vol. 3, pp. 1864, 1882. The same repugnancy standard appeared in the Act for Preventing Frauds and Regulating Abuses in
the Plantation Trade, 7 & 8 Will. III, c.22 (1695–1696), reprinted in *Statutes of the Realm* (Buffalo: William S. Hein, 1993), vol. 7, pp. 103, 105
("That all Lawes By-lawes Usages or Customes . . . in practice . . . in any of
the said Plantations which are in any wise repugnant to the before mentioned Lawes . . . or which are wayes repugnant to this present Act or to
any other Law hereafter to bee made . . . soe farr as such Laws shall relate
to and mention the said Plantations are illegall null and void to all Intents
and Purposes whatsoever").

19. William Harris Papers (1638–1846) (hereafter, Wm. Harris Papers)
    (RIHS), Box 1, folder 16. For books, see Nathaniel Morton, *New England's
    Memorial* (1669; repr., Boston: Congregational Board of Publication,
    1856); William Lambarde, *The Perambulation of Kent* (London: Mathew
    Walbanke, 1656).

20. For his will, see *Providence Recs.,* vol. 6, pp. 48–51; Harris Family Papers,
    Box 1 (1641–1720), folder 2 (RIHS). On his estate, see Letter from William
    Harris to Newport Town Council (July 3, 1676), in *Harris Papers,* p. 161.
    For statute references, see Ferdinando Pulton, *A Collection of Sundry Stat-
    utes Frequent in Use, With Notes in the margent, and References to the Book
    Cases, and Books of Entries and Registers . . .* (London: J. J. Bill & C. Baker,
    1661), copy annotated by William Harris in the Early Imprint Collection
    (RIHS), end of volume flyleaf i (recto) (citing 21 James 16); Harris's Decla-
    ration against John Towers (Nov. 17, 1677) in *Harris Papers,* pp. 205–206.
    For 21 James 16, see "An Act for Limitation of Actions, and for Avoiding of
    Suits in Law" (1623) in Danby Pickering, ed., *The Statutes at Large* (Cam-
    bridge: Joseph Bentham, 1763), vol. 7, p. 273.

21. Pulton, *Sundry Statutes* (RIHS), end of volume flyleaf i (recto) (on execu-
    tors); p. ii (verso) (duties of sheriff); p. ii recto (matching the citation re-
    garding forcible entries in *R.I. Recs.,* vol. 2, p. 513); end of ii (verso) (ses-
    sions); end of volume flyleaf ii, (recto) (special commissions); end of
    volume flyleaf i (verso), ii (recto), iii (recto), verso of title page, end of vol-
    ume flyleaf ii (verso), end of volume flyleaf iii (recto) (many of the cita-
    tions are at edge of pages and have been torn) (juries and judgments). On
    equity of the statute, see ibid., end of flyleaf i (recto-verso).

22. See Pulton, *Sundry Statutes* (RIHS), p. iii (verso) (citing 42 Edw. 3, chap. 1;
    tempore Edw. 1, chap. 4; [illeg.] Edw. 1, chap. [illeg.]); Letter from Wil-

liam Harris to Providence Town Meeting (Dec. 15, 1669), in *Harris Papers,* pp. 93, 94; Harris, concerning Connecticut (dated by editors to Feb. 1672), in *Harris Papers,* pp. 104–105. Harris cited to 6 Hen. 8, chap. 15 (relationship among charters); 13 Car. 2, chap. 15 (orders of parliament void without royal consent); 18 Hen. 6, chap. 1 (petitions to the king in cases of patents); 34 & 35 Hen 8., chap. 21 (favorable construction given to grantees); 21 James 3 (monopolies void in certain cases); 13 Rich. 2, chap. 2; 7 Eliz. chap. 1; 1 Edw. 6, chap.1, and 5 Eliz. chap. 1 (statutes relating to English law contrary to Rhode Island patent); 9 Hen. 3, chap. 1 (Magna Carta). See also *Harris Papers,* pp. 107–117, for additional discussion of statutes.

23. *Providence Recs.,* vol. 6, pp. 50–53.

24. *R.I. Recs.,* vol. 2, p. 19. The viability of the entail is unclear. Harris's son, Andrew, died intestate, and his estate "by the clear incontestable law of the colony in the 96 page of our lawbook descended in equal proportion to his relations in equal degree." Wm. Harris Papers, Box 1, at 98 (Aug. 18, 1727) (RIHS). According to a later family genealogist, Andrew's son, Toleration, "forget the entailment and made a will." Ibid., p. 105. For other entails, see Will of John Sanford (June 22, 1653), in *Sanford v. Wood & Allen* (Mar. 1726) (JRC); Will of John Coggeshall, in *Coggeshall v. Coggeshall* (Mar. 1737) (JRC).

25. *R.I. Recs.,* vol. 2, pp. 504–505 (1673), 522. On executor, see ibid., vol. 3, pp. 13–14 (calling "executor" the "improper term"), 75–76 (probate). On forcible entry, see ibid., vol. 2, p. 513. Harris seems a likely catalyst for the adoption. He had noted these same statutes in a flyleaf and was sitting as an assistant that session.

26. Letter from William Harris to Richard Nicolls (July 1667), in *Harris Papers,* pp. 83–86; Letter from Richard Nicolls to Gov. William Brenton (July 24, 1667), in *R.I. Recs.,* vol. 2, pp. 233–234; see ibid., pp. 236–37 (remitting fine); Letter from William Harris to Sergeant Steele (Aug. 15, 1678), in *Harris Papers,* pp. 249, 250.

27. Letter from William Harris to Thomas Hinckley (Apr. 15, 1678), in ibid., pp. 231–232; Letter from William Harris to the Court (June 18, 1678), in ibid., pp. 242–243; Letter from Court [Hinckley] to Connecticut Jurors (June 19, 1678), in ibid., pp. 244–245; see Return of the Commissioners to the King (Oct. 5, 1678), in ibid., pp. 261–263. On the statute, see ibid., 232 n. ‡; "Of what things an Assize shall lie" (1285), in Pickering, *Statutes at Large,* vol. 1, pp. 199–201.

28. John Cowell, *The Interpreter or Booke Containing the Signification of Words* (Cambridge, 1607); Coke, *Institutes,* Fourth Part, p. 340. On the Henry VIII legislation, see "For the Restraint of Appeals" 24 Hen. 8, chap. 12

(1532); see also "The Submission of the Clergy and Restraint of Appeals," 25 Hen. 8, chap. 19 (1533). On the history of the appeal, see Mary Sarah Bilder, "Salamanders and Sons of God," in *The Many Legalities of Early America,* ed. Christopher L. Tomlins and Bruce H. Mann (Chapel Hill: University of North Carolina Press, 2001), pp. 47–77; Bilder, "The Origin of the Appeal in America," 48 *Hastings Law Journal* 913–968 (1997).

29. On Jersey and Guernsey, see William S. Holdsworth, *A History of English Law,* 7th ed., rev. (1956; repr., London: Methuen, 1982), vol. 1, p. 520; Smith, *Appeals,* pp. 3–38. For quotes, see Letter from Edward Winslow to John Winthrop, Jr. (June 22, 1636), in [John Winthrop], *Winthrop Papers* (Boston: MHS, 1929–47), vol. 3, p. 274 [John Winthrop], *Winthrop's Journal: History of New England,* ed. James Kendall Hosmer (New York: Scribner's, 1908) (hereafter, Winthrop, *Journal*), vol. 1, p. 240; Thomas Lechford, *Plain Dealing or News from New England* (Boston: J. K. Wiggin, 1867), p. 64; Thomas Hutchinson, *The Hutchinson Papers* (1865; repr., New York: Burt Franklin, 1967), pp. 214, 216. The Remonstrants suggested that these measures were a "good means to prevent divers unnecessary Appeals into England." Ibid., p. 218. Winthrop referred sarcastically to this theory as Dr. Robert Child's "logic": "every corporation of England is subject to the laws of England" and "this was a corporation of England, ergo." Winthrop, *Journal,* vol. 2, p. 304. Winthrop wrote to his son in 1646 that the Child petitioners "did presently appeal to the Parl[ia]ment, etc: so as we are like to proceed to some Censure for their appeal, if not for the Petition." Letter from John Winthrop to John Winthrop, Jr. (Nov. 16, 1646), in *Winthrop Papers,* vol. 5, pp. 119, 120. Child referred to his "Appeal before Parliament" and hoped that his "Cause may be heard before indifferent Arbiters." Letter from Robert Child to John Winthrop, Jr. (May 14, 1647), ibid., p. 160.

30. Winthrop, *Journal,* vol. 1, pp. 239–240; Winthrop, "A Short Story," in *The Antinomian Controversy: 1636–1638, A Documentary History,* 2nd ed., ed. David D. Hall (Durham: Duke University Press, 1990), pp. 256–257. In his journal entry on Wheelwright's appeal, he likewise argued that the patent denied appeals. Winthrop, *Journal,* vol. 1, p. 240. For more detail, see Bilder, "Salamanders and Sons of God," pp. 74–76.

31. On charters, see John Wheeler, *A Treatise of Commerce,* ed. George Burton Hotchkiss (1601; repr., New York: New York University Press, 1931), p. 156. On the King's Merchants, see Carr, *Select Charters,* p. 88. The appeal language may date back to the Elizabethan 1564 charter of the King's Merchants. Ibid., pp. xxi–xxii. On Winthrop's petition, see Winthrop, *Journal,* vol. 2, pp. 312, 337. A 1661 General Court order stated that the governor and officials in Massachusetts had "full power and authority" over "ec-

clesiastics and civils, without appeal." Nathaniel B. Shurtleff, ed., *Records of the Governor and Company of the Massachusetts Bay in New England* (Boston: W. White, 1853–1854), vol. 4, pp. 24–25.

32. For Gorton quotes, see Samuel Gorton, *Simplicitie's Defence against Seven-Headed Policy* (London, 1646), pp. 40, 55. For Williams quotes, see *Correspondence of Roger Williams,* vol. 2, p. 618. On Gorton, see Philip F. Gura, *A Glimpse of Sion's Glory: Puritan Radicalism in New England, 1620–1660* (Middleton, Conn.: Wesleyan University Press, 1986), pp. 194–195, 280–282, 276–303; Lewis G. Janes, *Samuell Gorton: A Forgotten Founder of Our Liberties; First Settler of Warwick, R.I.* (Providence: Preston & Rounds, 1896), p. 55.

33. Richard R. Johnson, *Adjustment to Empire: The New England Colonies, 1675–1715* (New Brunswick: Rutgers University Press, 1981), p. 52. For the Maine charter, see Thorpe, *Federal and State Constitutions,* vol. 3, pp. 1638–39 (Mar. 12, 1664), and vol. 3, p. 1642 (June 1674) ("bee not contrary to but as neare as may bee agreeable to the Lawes Statutes and Government of this our realm of England and saving and reserving to Us our heirs and successors the receiving hearing and determining of the appeal and appeals"). Earlier grants differed in this respect. For example, the 1622 Maine grant to Mason and Gorges stated that if the men or their assigns did not make laws agreeable, any aggrieved inhabitant could "appeal to the chief courts of justices of the President and council" of New England. Ibid., vol. 3, p. 1624. The 1639 Maine grant gave Gorges the right to hear appeals within forty days and to "proceede in such Appeals as in like case of Appeals within this our Realme of England." Ibid., vol. 3, p. 1629.

3. The Laws of Rhode Island

1. The case is *James Honyman, Jr. v. George Dunbar* (Sept. 1725), UB21, F9 (JRC). For the act, see "An Act for the Probate of Wills, and Granting of Administrations," in *Acts and Laws, Of His Majesties Colony of Rhode-Island, and Providence-Plantations, In America* (Boston: Printed by John Allen for Nicholas Boone, 1719) (hereafter, *Acts and Laws* [1719]), p. 13, in *Earliest Acts,* p. 140. On Honeyman (c. 1710–1778), see Wilkins Updike, *Memoirs of the Rhode-Island Bar* (Boston: Thomas H. Webb, 1842), pp. 26–31. I have attributed it to Honeyman, given his later use of the evidence in 1737 in another case. On the evidence, see "List of 2 Wit to Wills," *Honyman, Jr. v. Dunbar* (Sept. 1725) (No. 6), in *Coggeshall v. Coggeshall* (Newport, Sept. 1737), Folder 2 (JRC); "Protest of Samuel Cranston," *Honyman* (Sept. 1725), UB21, F9 (JRC) (language silently corrected); "Memorial" in ibid.

2. For an act for the probate of wills dating to "the Orders made 19, 20, 21 May 1647," see *Coggeshall v. Coggeshall* (Mar. 1736), No. 4, Folder 1 (JRC). For English requirements, see Henry Swinburne, *A Brief Treatise of Testaments and Last Wills* (1590; repr., New York: Garland, 1978), pp. 18–19; The Statute of Frauds, 29 Car. 2, c.3 (1677); William Nelson, *Lex Testamentaria: Or, a Compendious System of All the Laws of England, as well before the Statute of Henry VIII as since, concerning Last Wills and Testaments* (1714; repr., New York: Garland, 1978), pp. 530–532; Thomas Wood, *An Institute of the Laws of England*, 3rd ed. (1724; repr., New York: Garland, 1978), p. 294. On the 1704–1705 committee, see "Copy of Act of Probate of Wills by Major Coddington" in *Honyman* (Sept. 1725), UB21, F9 (JRC). This language matches the 1705 transcript reprinted in *Earliest Acts*, p. 71. On the 1704–1705 committee, see *R.I. Recs.*, vol. 3, pp. 493 (Jan. 1703/1704), 507 (May 1704). The committee to look over the transcription included Coddington. Ibid., pp. 534–535 (June 1705).

3. *R.I. Recs.*, vol. 2, p. 27 (Mar. 1663/1664) (related to courts of commissions and the towns' repeal of General Assemblies). On the committees, see *R.I. Recs.*, vol. 2, pp. 64, 147, 184, 191. The laws appear in *Rhode Island General Assembly Records* (hereafter, *R.I.G.A. Records*) (Colony Records), pt. 2, vol. 1, pp. 161–192 (manuscript edition) (RISA). Page 160 is in the hand of John Sanford and is dated September 1, 1666.

4. On the 1647 Code, see the editorial note by John D. Cushing in *Earliest Acts*, p. vii. The specific 1647 acts and orders are labeled as such and the laws are numbered: "Acts and Orders made and Agreed upon at the General Court of Election . . . 19, 20, 21 of May anno 1647." They are followed by the Providence agreement. Last are the post-1647 laws ("For the Province of Providence"). Further support for this interpretation is given by a notation in the 1647 section of the composure (in what appears to be Harris's handwriting) that some specific laws were confirmed in "1657/58." *R.I.G.A. Records*, pt. 2, p. 164 (RISA).

5. The quote is from Peter Charles Hoffer, *Law and People in Colonial America*, rev. ed. (Baltimore: Johns Hopkins University Press, 1998), p. 173. On women, see John More, *The Lawes Resolutions of Women's Rights* (London, 1632), pp. 381–382 (discussion of rape involving 6 Rich. 2, c. 6); *R.I. Recs.*, vol. 2, pp. 186–187. On criminal law, see *Earliest Acts*, pp. 12–13, n. *. On archery, see ibid., p. 41. G. B. Warden pointed out that the English appearance of the code is deceptive because passages were drawn from Dalton's *Countrey Justice* and many of the English statutory citations were a later addition to the drafted and approved 1647 document. See G. B. Warden, "The Rhode Island Civil Code of 1647," in *Saints and Revolutionaries: Essays on Early American History*, ed. David D. Hall, John M. Murrin, and

Thad W. Tate (New York: Norton, 1984), pp. 142–149. John Farrell made a similar argument in 1950, although he also accepted the 1647 dating for the entire set of laws. Farrell described much of the material in the Code as influenced by Walter Young's *A Vade Mecum and Cornu Copia* (London: L. Blaiklock, 1642). See John T. Farrell, "The Early History of Rhode Island's Court System," *Rhode Island History* 9 (1950), pp. 103, 107. For Staples's comment, see William R. Staples, ed., *The Proceedings of the First General Assembly of "The Incorporation of Providence Plantations," And the Code of Laws Adopted by That Assembly in 1647* (Providence, 1847), p. 19.

6. On review, see Elmer Beecher Russell, *The Review of American Colonial Legislation by the King in Council* (New York: Columbia University, 1915), pp. 16–40; Smith, *Appeals*, pp. 70–71. "An Act prohibiting Trade with the Barbadoes, Virginia, Bermuda and Antego" (1650) stated that these and other plantations and colonies had been and ought to be "subject to such Laws, Orders and Regulations as are or shall be made by the Parliament of England." C. H. Firth and R. S. Rait, eds., *Acts and Ordinances of the Interregnum, 1642–1660* (London, 1911), vol. 1, p. 425. Bliss reads this act as a "sweeping assertion of a new legislative supremacy over all colonies." Robert M. Bliss, *Revolution and Empire: English Politics and the American Colonies in the Seventeenth Century* (Manchester: Manchester University Press, 1990), p. 61. Lawrence Harper concludes that colonists tried to evade the law rather than deny its validity. Lawrence A. Harper, *The English Navigation Laws: A Seventeenth-Century Experiment in Social Engineering* (New York: Columbia University Press, 1939), p. 151.

7. Russell, *Review*, pp. 23 (quoting from Calendar of State Papers and Board of Trade proceedings), 25–31. For the 1680 conclusion, see ibid., p. 27 (quoting Board of Trade, 3, 167 (Apr. 27, 1680)) (italics added). The Committee asked, "what right the people of Jamaica have to the laws & government of England" or "how far English laws and methods of government ought to take place in Jamaica." Bliss, *Revolution and Empire*, p. 186; see Russell, *Review*, p. 26 (quoting *APC*, 2:6). As Robert Bliss suggests, "what was at issue was not whether English common law extended to Jamaica, but which statute laws and, more importantly, who chose which laws." Bliss, *Revolution and Empire*, p. 182. Richard Dunn terms the Jamaican episode a "losing struggle against imperial centralization." Richard S. Dunn, "Imperial Pressures on Massachusetts and Jamaica, 1675–1700," in *Anglo-American Political Relations, 1675–1776*, ed. Alison Gilbert Olson and Richard Maxwell Brown (New Brunswick: Rutgers University Press, 1970), pp. 62, 60.

8. *Records of the Governor and Company of the Massachusetts Bay in New England, 1628–86* (Boston, 1854), vol. 5, p. 200; John Winthrop, *History of*

New England, ed. James K. Hosmer (New York, 1908), vol. 1, p. 324, both cited in Michael Garibaldi Hall, *Edward Randolph and the American Colonies* (Chapel Hill: University of North Carolina Press, 1960), pp. 25, 28. The last quote is in Hall, *Edward Randolph,* p. 40. On the episode, see ibid., pp. 33–45; Russell, *Review,* p. 33; Randolph, "Report to the Committee for Trade and Plantations" (Oct. 1676) in Hall, *Edward Randolph,* vol. 2, pp. 225–234. On Randolph, see Robert Noxon Toppan, ed., *Edward Randolph; including his letters and papers . . .* (Boston: Prince Society, 1898), 5 vols.

9. "William Jones . . . Opinion about Col. Burnham's Will" (1681), in *Virginia Colonial Decisions: The Reports of Sir John Randolph and Edward Barrandall,* ed. R. T. Barton (Boston: Boston Book, 1909), vol. 2, p. B1. Debate over lawmaking also arose over parliamentary legislation. In 1689, some worried that the Corporations Restoration Bill would not necessarily apply to the plantations. Although the bill was to restore corporate charters "in all of England's dominions and territories," colonial supporters "felt it necessary to tack on an amendment—'and *New England,* and other Plantations'—to ensure the colonies' inclusion." Richard R. Johnson, *Adjustment to Empire: The New England Colonies, 1675–1715* (Newark: Rutgers University Press, 1981) p. 161 (quoting *Commons Journals,* vol. 10, p. 51). Johnson discusses the Massachusetts debate over the bill. On this period in Massachusetts, see Philip S. Haffenden, *New England in the English Nation, 1689–1713* (Oxford: Clarendon Press, 1974), pp. 1–119.

10. *R.I. Recs.,* vol. 3, p. 284 (Andros quote, n.d.). On review, see Russell, *Review,* pp. 31–33, 37. On the 1695–1696 disallowance, see ibid., pp. 35–36. New Hampshire had become subject to review as a royal colony in 1681.

11. On Randolph, see Hall, *Edward Randolph,* p. 159. On the Dominion in Rhode Island, see Sydney V. James, *Colonial Rhode Island: A History* (New York: Scribner's, 1975), p. 107. On the colony's response to the Dominion, see Johnson, *Adjustment to Empire,* pp. 109–114. The Rhode Island charter had been threatened with confiscation in 1685 and 1686. Hall, *Edward Randolph,* pp. 91, 108–109. On the charter confirmation, see "Attorney General's Opinion upon the Address from Rhode Island," *R.I. Recs.,* vol. 3, p. 294 (Aug. 2, 1692). For related documents, see ibid., pp. 288–300 (Aug. 2, 1692–Aug. 21, 1694).

12. On the reorganization, see Russell, *Review,* p. 45; Hall, *Edward Randolph,* p. 166; Charles M. Andrews, *The Colonial Period in American History* (New Haven: Yale University Press, 1934), vol. 4, pp. 292–293, 296. For the request, see PC 2/76/585 (Feb. 25, 1696/1697). For the 1696 navigation act, see "An Act for Preventing Frauds, and Regulative Abuses in the Plantation Trade," 7 & 8 Will. III, chap. 22 (1695–1696), reprinted in *Statutes of*

the Realm (Buffalo: William S. Hein, 1993) vol. 7, pp. 103, 105. On the act, see Andrews, *Colonial Period,* vol. 4, p. 300. For crown letter and appointments, see "King William III to Rhode Island, on the Plantation Trade," *R.I. Recs.,* vol. 3, pp. 326–327 (Aug. 26, 1697), 329–331. In general, see Hall, *Edward Randolph,* pp. 172–179. For the quote, see "Peleg Sanford to the Board of Trade" (Jan. 31, 1697/98), *R.I. Recs.,* vol. 3, p. 329. Clarke soon resigned, and his nephew, Samuel Cranston, governed to 1727.

13. Brinley's suit was for three acres against Charles Dyer. Brinley appealed to obtain a Privy Council order permitting him to try his "title upon a new ejectment." PC 2/77/302 (Feb. 23, 1698/1699). Brinley alleged the colony denied the appeal. The Committee for Hearing Appeals concluded that Brinley and "all other persons whatsoever who may think themselves aggrieved by sentences given in the courts of that colony be likewise allowed to appeal unto your majesty in council, and that authentic copies of records, and other proceedings" be transmitted. PC 2/77/331 (Apr. 21, 1699). The Privy Council told the governor to permit the appeal and added that it is "the Inherent Right" of the king to "Receive and Determine Appeals." Ibid. An earlier appeal by Daniel Pierce may have also implicated the charter. PC 2/77/205 (July 16, 1698). The case was referred to the attorney general who was to inspect the charter to see what it permitted. PC 2/77/223 (Sept. 2, 1698). For the Randolph and Board quotations, see *R.I. Recs.,* vol. 3, pp. 339–340 (May 30, 1698) and pp. 363–364. For the Board's inquiry, see also ibid., vol. 3, p. 330 (Feb. 23, 1697/98) (Board of Trade to Rhode Island).

14. On Brenton, see Samuel Green Arnold, *History of the State of Rhode Island and Providence Plantations* (Providence: Preston & Rands, 1894), vol. 1, p. 539. For the report, see *R.I. Recs.,* vol. 3, pp. 329–330 (Jan. 31, 1697/1698) (Sanford, Brinley, and Brenton to Board of Trade); CO 5/1257/447 (Jan. 31, 1697/1698). For the agent appointment, see *R.I. Recs.,* vol. 3, p. 375 (May 27, 1699). Brenton was also distantly related to Brinley through the Byfields. See Barbara A. Black, "National Byfield, 1653–1733" in *Law in Colonial Massachusetts,* ed. Daniel R. Coquillette (Boston: Colonial Society of Massachusetts, 1984), p. 61 n. 5. For the quoted Brenton letter, see *R.I. Recs.,* vol. 3, p. 331 (Brenton to Board of Trade, Mar. 8, 1697/1698); Arnold, *History of Rhode Island,* vol. 1, p. 539.

15. Andrews, *Colonial Period,* vol. 4, p. 380 (quoting *Calendar of State Papers, Colonial Series, 1701,* pp. 286, 420, 422). On these efforts between 1698 and 1701 when the bill was heard, see ibid., p. 378; I. K. Steele, "The Board of Trade, the Quakers, and Resumption of Colonial Charters, 1699–1702," *William and Mary Quarterly,* 3rd ser., vol. 23, issue 4 (1966), pp. 603, 618.

16. *R.I. Recs.,* vol. 3, p. 396 (Dec. 22, 1699) (Cranston to Bellomont). On com-

mittees, see ibid., pp. 346 (Aug. 2, 1698), 350–351 (Oct. 26, 1698), 374 (May 27, 1699), 378 (Oct. 25, 1699), 382 (Nov. 21, 1699), 396 (Dec. 22, 1699). At the beginning of October, Cranston apologized to Bellomont and noted that he was still accomplishing "the perfecting thereof." Ibid., vol. 3, p. 394 (Oct. 5, 1699). For Bellomont quote, see ibid., vol. 3, p. 399 (Jan. 5, 1699/1700) (Bellomont to Board of Trade). See also ibid., pp. 396–397 (Dec. 23, 1699) (Brinley, Sanford, and Coddington to Bellomont), 394–395 (Nov. 8, 1699) (Sanford to Bellomont).

17. For the quoted language, see *R.I. Recs.,* vol. 3, pp. 330 (Feb. 23, 1697/1698), 342 (Oct. 25, 1698), 376 (Aug. 11, 1699) (Board of Trade to Gov. and Co.). For similar language, see ibid., vol. 3, pp. 389–393 (Sept. 20, 1699) (Lord Bellomont's Journal).

18. Sidney Rider, "A Historical Introduction to the Laws and Acts of the Colony of Rhode Island 1705" in Sidney S. Rider, ed., *Laws and Acts of Her Majesty's Colony of Rhode Island and Providence Plantations . . . 1636 to 1705* (Providence: S. S. Rider & B. Rider, 1896), p. v. On committees, see *R.I. Recs.,* vol. 1, p. 278 (Aug. 1654); vol. 2, pp. 64 (Oct. 1664), 184 (Oct. 1666); vol. 3, pp. 86 (May 1680), 188–189 (May 1686).

19. On Massachusetts and New York, see John Cotton, *An Abstract of Laws and Government of New England as they are now Established* (London, 1655); William H. Whitmore, ed., *The Colonial Laws of Massachusetts . . . containing also the Body of Liberties of 1641* (Boston, 1889); John D. Cushing, ed., *The Laws and Liberties of Massachusetts, 1641–1691* (Wilmington: Michael Glazier, 1976); and John D. Cushing, ed., *The Earliest Printed Laws of New-York, 1665–1693* (Wilmington: Michael Glazier, 1978), pp. 109–110. On Connecticut, see John D. Cushing, ed., *The Book of the General Laws for the People within the Jurisdiction of Connecticut collected out of the Records of the General Court,* in *The Earliest Printed Laws of the New Haven and Connecticut Colonies, 1639–1673* (Wilmington: Michael Glazier, 1977), pp. 71, 72. In 1656, New Haven's governor arranged to have printed in London "some Lawes for Government." The title page emphasized tentativeness: "Though some of the Orders intended for present convenience, may probably be hereafter altered, and as need requireth other Lawes added." Cushing, ed., *Earliest Printed Laws of the New Haven,* p. 1. The notoriously incomplete London editions of Virginia laws reveal that comprehensive accounting of statutes was not always the goal of publication. See John D. Cushing, ed., *Colony Laws of Virginia, 1619–1660* (Wilmington: Michael Glazier, 1978), vol. 1, pp. v–vi (describing the "incomplete and defective" edition by Frances Morison, *Laws of Virginia now in Force* (1662) and the "very poorly done" edition by John Purvis, *A Complete Collection of all the Laws of Virginia Now in Force* (1684)). On Chesapeake manuscript and

print editions, see David D. Hall, *Cultures in Print: Essays in the History of the Book* (Amherst: University of Massachusetts Press, 1996), pp. 97–150. On the codes, see J. H. Baker, *Introduction to Legal History*, 3rd ed. (London: Buttersworth, 1990), pp. 249–250; George Haskins, "Codification of the Law in Colonial Massachusetts: A Study in Comparative Law," 30 *Indiana Law Journal* 1–17 (1954). For examples of English abstracts, see *Abstract of the Laws in Force against Profaneness, Immorality, and Debauchery, etc. Together with the Laws and Ordinances by the Parliament; also by Oliver and His Council from 1640 to 1656 . . . Digested by way of Alphabet for the ease of those that are to know them, and put them in Execution* (1698); *Abstract of all the Statute Laws of this Kingdom now in force, made against Jesuits, Seminary Priests, and Popish Recusants* (n.d.); *Abstract of all the Penal Laws now in force* (1679); all in *Legal Bibliography*, pp. 358, 159, 160.

20. William Bradford's 1694 printing of the New York *Laws* marks the shift to session laws. *The Laws and Acts of the General Assembly of Their Majesties Province on New York as they were enacted in divers Sessions. . . .* (New York: William Bradford, 1694). The dramatic alteration of legislation during the English Civil War, Restoration, and Glorious Revolution may have reinforced the importance of attributing legislation to specific dates. On English statute printing, see Percy H. Winfield, *The Chief Sources of English Legal History* (1925; repr., Buffalo: William S. Hein, 1983), pp. 90–91; Katherine F. Pantzer, "Printing the English Statutes: Some Historical Implications," in *Books and Society in History: Papers of the Association of College and Research Libraries Rare Books and Manuscripts Preconference*, ed. Kenneth E. Carpenter (New York: R. R. Bowker, 1983), pp. 69–114. For Brenton's library, see Jahleel Brenton Papers, Notebook, Mss. 306 (RIHS). *"An Abridgement"* was likely either *An Abridgment of the Statutes in Force* (London: Streater, 1663) or Washington, *Abridgment of the Statutes of King William and Queen Mary* (multiple publication dates). "Keble" was Keble's *Statutes at Large* (London: 1676). For 1690 publications, see Cushing, *Earliest Printed Laws of New-York*, p. viii, *Acts and Laws of . . . Massachusetts Bay* (Boston: Printed by Bartholomew Green & John Allen, 1699); John D. Cushing, ed., *The Earliest Printed Laws of New Hampshire, 1680–1726* (Wilmington: Michael Glazier, 1978), p. vii; John D. Cushing, ed., *The Earliest Printed Laws of New Jersey, 1703–1722* (Wilmington: Michael Glazier, 1978), pp. vii–viii.

21. On the laws, see *R.I. Recs.*, vol. 3, pp. 346 (Aug. 1698), 350–351 (Oct. 1698), 378–379 (Oct. 1699), 382–383 (Nov. 1699). For the Board's reaction, see ibid., vol. 3, pp. 376–377 (Aug. 11, 1699). For other comments, see ibid., vol. 3, pp. 397 (Dec. 23, 1699) (Brinley, Coddington, and Sanford to Bellomont), 398–399 (Dec. 31, 1699) (Brinley to Bellomont). In 1700, a

new committee was to transcribe the laws "in a regular manner" "into a true form and method" to be sent under seal "as soon as possible." Ibid., vol. 3, p. 415 (May 4, 1700).

22. For Board to Bellomont, see *R.I. Recs.*, vol. 3, p. 363–364 (Mar. 9, 1698/1699). For Gov. Samuel Cranston to Board of Trade, see ibid., vol. 3, p. 374 (May 27, 1699) *[sic]*.

23. *R.I. Recs.*, vol. 3, p. 425 (Aug. 1700). For a recent description of the state's reception statutes, see Ernest G. Mayo, "Rhode Island's Reception of the Common Law," 31 *Suffolk University Law Review* 609 (1998).

24. "Rhode Island: State of the Constitutions & proceedings of the Courts of Tryals & goal deliveries both in Civil and Criminall Cases . . ." (Apr. 18, 1701), in Erwin C. Surrency, "Report on Court Procedures in the Colonies—1700," 9 *American Journal of Legal History* 235, 238 (1965). For the 1719 version, see "An Act, for putting in force the Laws of England in all cases, where no particular law of this colony hath provided a remedy" (dated in the 1719 edition as April 30, 1700). in *The Charter and the Acts And Laws of His Majesties Colony of Rhode-Island And Providence-Plantations in America*, p. 45 (1719), in *Earliest Acts*, p. 181 ("That in all actions, matters, causes and things whatsoever, where no particular law of this colony is made to decide and determine the same; that then and in all such cases the laws of England shall be put in force to issue, determine and decide the same. Any usage, custom or law to the contrary hereof notwithstanding").

25. *R.I. Recs.*, vol. 3, pp. 493 (Jan. 4, 1703/1704), 507 (May 3, 1704), 534–535 (June 19, 1705). The Reunification bill would have restored all the charter and proprietary colonies to the crown. See Hall, *Edward Randolph*, pp. 203–213, 216–217.

26. For Coddington references, see *Honyman* (Sept. 1725), UB21, F9 (JRC). The Rider quote appears in *Laws and Acts . . . to 1705*, p. viii. Compare *Laws and Acts . . . to 1705* with the compilation in *Earliest Acts*, pp. 12 and 59. Other examples include the 1705 omission of the requirement that all persons between age 17 and age 70 to learn to shoot a bow and arrow, and an alteration in the section on oaths to exclude solemn professions. Other alterations include the sections on marriage, the omission of the laws on the public administration of justice, and the addition of an act on special courts and an alteration to lessen the punishment for fornication.

27. For the defense, see *R.I. Recs.*, vol. 3, p. 548 (Aug. 28, 1705) (Weston Clarke to Board of Trade). They also noted that they have allowed appeals when applied for even when only twenty pounds was at stake, an amount that was "frivolous and vexatious." On the charges, see ibid., vol. 3, p. 543 (Nov. 2, 1705) (Dudley to the Board of Trade). On the laws, see *R.I. Recs.*,

vol. 3, p. 558 (May 1706). On the new bill, see PC 1/46/7 (bill and Feb. 1705/1706 Council order on proprietary governments' misfeasance); *APC*, vol. 2, pp. 475–476 (Aug. 1704, complaint about Rhode Island), 480 (Nov. 1705, Attorney and Solicitor Generals' report). For the Cornbury (Edward Hyde) quotes, see "Lord Cornbury to the Board of Trade," *R.I. Recs.*, vol. 3, p. 544–546 (Nov. 1705). On 1706, see Oliver Morton Dickerson, *American Colonial Government, 1696–1765: A Study of the British Board of Trade in its Relation to the American Colonies, Political, Industrial, Administrative* (Cleveland: Arthur H. Clark, 1912), p. 213. On the manuscript publication, see *R.I. Recs.*, vol. 4, p. 86 (Feb. 1709/1710).

28. "The opinion of the Attorney-General, Northey, of the bad effects of temporary acts of Assembly, which in his judgment could only be remedied by an act of parliament" (Edward Northey, July 22, 1714), in George Chalmers, *Opinions of the Eminent Lawyers on Various Points of English Jurisprudence* (1858; repr., Buffalo: William S. Hein, 1987), pp. 338–340.

29. *R.I. Recs.*, vol. 4, pp. 194–195 (July 1715), 209 (May 1716), 225–226 (Oct. 1717). The 1716 and 1717 committees included attorney Nathaniel Newdigate. On the Ward appointment, see ibid., p. 234 (June 1718). Richard Ward (1689–1763) had been attorney general in 1712 and then general recorder from 1714 to 1730. His father, Thomas, had been on the 1680 law printing committee. At Richard's death in 1755, he left all his law books to his son. James Savage Austin, *A Genealogical Dictionary of the First Settlers of New England* (Boston: Little, Brown, 1861), p. 407.

30. For the order, see *R.I. Recs.*, vol. 4, p. 240 (Sept. 1718). For title pages, see *Acts and Laws* (1719), in *Earliest Acts*, pp. 125, 135. Twenty-nine books were distributed to the towns to use as they saw fit. *R.I. Recs.*, vol. 4, p. 248 (1719).

31. *R.I. Recs.*, vol. 4, p. 258–260 (Sept. 7, 1719) (Caleb Heathcote to the Lords Commissioners for Trade and Plantations). In November 1718, Nathaniel Kay, the collector of customs, similarly complained that the charter governments had laws repugnant to laws of England relating to trade. Ibid., pp. 244–245 (Nathaniel Kay to Popple) (Nov. 24, 1718).

32. For the explanatory act, see *R.I. Recs.*, vol. 4, pp. 257–258 (Sept. 1719). For the original act, see "An Act for Distributing and Settling Intestates Estate," in *Acts and Laws* (1719), in *Earliest Acts*, pp. 229–232. Concern over the effect of the act may explain why Daniel Coggeshall reentailed land in his will in a case discussed in chapter 5.

33. On the disallowance, see Francis M. Fane, *Reports on the Laws of Connecticut*, ed. Charles M. Andrews ([New Haven: Tuttle, Morehouse & Taylor Press], 1915), p. 18; Charles M. Andrews, "The Influence of Colonial Conditions as illustrated in the Connecticut Intestacy Law," in *Select Essays*

in *Anglo-American History* (Boston: Little, Brown, 1907), vol. 1, pp. 431–463. On the committee, see *R.I. Recs.,* vol. 4, pp. 408 (June 1728), 417 (February 1728–1729). For the laws, see *Acts and Laws, Of His Majesty's Colony of Rhode-Island, and Providence-Plantations, In America* (Newport: Printed by James Franklin, 1730), pp. 167–169. For intestate repeal, see ibid., pp. 163, 182; *R.I. Recs.,* vol. 4, p. 417 (Feb. 1728/1729).

34. Fane, *Reports,* pp. 20–21 n. 39 (Rip Van Dam to Board of Trade, Dec. 29, 1731). For an example of a statute that appeared "agreeable," see law related to dowry, ibid., p. 74. For comments, see ibid., pp. 85–86 (houses), 96–97 (intestate). For other comments accepting divergences in the 1734 report, see ibid., pp. 116 (trained bands), 118 (posts), 119 (military officers), 120–121 (trespasses), 122 (domestic issues), 124 (exemptions for ministers), 125. Fane objected to a law not permitting husbands and wives from living separately from each other. Ibid., p. 86. He objected to a law branding A's on the forehead in cases of adultery because the "stigmatising . . . is more liable to make them incorrigible than to reform them." Ibid., p. 59. He objected that inflicting corporal punishment on men for wearing women's apparel and vice versa "seems likewise a little hard." Ibid., p. 102.

35. On Paris, see Paris to Jeremiah Allen (July 26, 1738), in *Collections of the Connecticut Historical Society,* vol. 5, pp. 85–86. For the Board request, see *APC,* vol. 4, p. 153 [167] (January/April 1752).

4. The Transatlantic Appeal

1. On the early appeals, see Smith, *Appeals,* pp. 72–74, 121–127. On boundary matters, see *APC,* vol. 1, pp. 1025, 1222–24, 1233–34, 1236, 1244, 1291; vol. 2, pp. 273, 512, 560. On claims relating to the Council of Plymouth, see Samuel Greene Arnold, *History of the State of Rhode Island and Providence Plantations* (Providence: Preston & Rounds, 1894), vol. 1, pp. 305–306, 362–363, 469, 474, 479–480, 529, 537–538.

2. On the 1696 restructuring, see Smith, *Appeals,* pp. 134–135; PC 2/76/559 (Dec. 1696); *APC,* vol. 2, p. 310 (Dec. 1696). On the appeal of Daniel Peirce, the tenant of William and Benjamin Brown, regarding Prudence Island, see *APC,* vol. 2, p. 324 (Sept. 1698). In the 1670s, Prudence Island briefly became an independent government held by John Paine. See Arnold, *History of Rhode Island,* vol. 1, pp. 362–363. In 1694, the son of the Duke of Hamilton petitioned over the Narragansett. Ibid., p. 373.

3. On "the ubiquitous Jahleel Brenton," see Richard R. Johnson, *Adjustment to Empire: The New England Colonies, 1675–1715* (New Brunswick: Rutgers University Press, 1981), p. 299; John Osborne Austin, *The Genealogical Dictionary of Rhode Island* (1887; repr., Baltimore: Genealogical, 1969),

pp. 253–254. On the bankruptcy matter, see *R.I. Recs.*, vol. 3, pp. 9 (May 1678), 11–12 (June 1678).

4. The list appears in his journal of his voyage to England. Jahleel Brenton Papers, Jahleel Brenton Notebook and Workbook, Mss. 306 (RIHS). The Account lists: "Statute at Large" (Keble, *Statutes at Large . . . from Magna Charta until this time*, first published 1676); "Cokes Reports" (Edward Coke, *Reports*, 2nd ed. published in English 1680); "Crooks Reports" (Croke, *Reports of Cases in King's Bench and Common Bench [1582–1641]*, first published 1669); "the 2d, 3d & 4th part of Cooks Institutes" (Edward Coke, *Institutes of the Laws of England*, set first published 1644); "Keebles Justice" (Keble, *Assistance to Justices of the Peace*, first published 1683); "Pleading against the Cytty Charter" (likely *Pleadings and Arguments and other Proceedings in the Court of Kings-Bench upon the Quo Warranto . . . Which Points do not only concern the City of London but all other Corporations in England*, first published 1690); "Cowells interpreter" (Cowell, *Interpreter; or, Booke containing the Signification of Words*, first published 1607); "Vaughans Reports" (Vaughan, *Reports and Arguments in the Common Pleas*, first published 1677); "Daltons office of Sherriffs" (Michael Dalton, *Officium Vicecomitum; the Office and Authoritie of Sheriffs*, first published 1623); "Wingates Maxims" (Edmund Wingate, *Maximes of Reason: or, Reason of the Common Law of England*, first published 1658); "Compleat Clerk" (*Compleat Clark; containing the best Forms of all sorts of Presidents for Conveyances and Assurances*, first published 1664); "Terms de la lay" (Rastell, *Termes de la Ley; or, Certain Difficult and Obscure Words, and Termes of the Common Lawes of this Realme expounded*, first published 1624); "Sheppard of Deeds" (Sheppard, *Actions upon the Case for Deeds*, first published 1663); "Greenwood of Courts" (Greenwood, *[Bouleutērion]: or Practical Demonstration of County Judicatures*, first published 1659); "the Practicall Registr" (William Style, *Regestrum Practicale, or the Practical Register; or, Accomplish'd Attorney*, first published 1675); "the office of Clerk of the Assize" ([W. T.], *Office of the Clerk of the Assize*, first published 1676); "Book of Oaths" ([Richard Garnet], *Book of Oaths*, first published 1649); "March's Actions for Slander" (March, *Actions for Slander*, first published 1647); "Compleat Minor"; "Royal Charter" ([T. Bayly], *The Royal Charter*, first published 1656); "Lex Londinensis" (*Lex Londinensis: or City Law*, first published 1680); "Mystery of Clerkship" ([G.] Billinghurst, *Arcana Clericalia; or, Mysteries of Clarkship. A sure way of selling Estates by Deeds, Fines and Recoveries*, first published 1674); "Argument Ante Norman" (*Argumentum Antinormanicum*, first published 1682); "The office & Duty of Executor" ([T.] Wentworth, *Office and Duty of Executors; or treatise of Wills and Executors directed to Testators . . .* , first published 1641); "Ten-

ants Law" (*Tenants Law; a treatise of great use for Tenants and Farmers,* first published 1666); "Landlord Law" ([G.] Meriton, *Land-Lords Law,* first published 1665); "Compleat Attorney" (*Complete Attorney,* first published 1654); "A Guide for Constables" (G. Meriton, *Guide for Constables, Church-Wardens, Overseers of the Poor* . . . , first published 1669); "Abridgment of the Statutes" (*An Abridgment of the Statutes in force* [16–18 Car. & 12–14 Car. 2] or Washington, *Abridgment of the Statutes of King William and Queen Mary*); "Court Leet" (Kitchin, *Jurisdictions; or, Lawful Authority of Courts Leet, Courts Baron,* published 1651–1701); "Statutes from the first of KW & QM to the 27 of Jan 1689 . . ."; "in a paper book unbound Acts began the 14 of April 1690 . . . & ending with an Act of the three and twentieth day of May 1690 . . ."; "in a Bound Book Acts began the 18 Day of November 1690 . . . & ending . . . the 12th Day of November 1694"; "in a Bound Book Acts begun the 22 Day of November 1695 . . . & to the 20th day of October 1696. . . ." For titles, see W. Harold Maxwell and Leslie F. Maxwell, *A Legal Bibliography of the British Commonwealth of Nations,* 2nd ed. (London: Sweet & Maxwell, 1955), vol. 1; John D. Cowley, *A Bibliography of Abridgments, Digests, Dictionaries and Indexes of English Law to the Year 1800* (London: Quartich, 1932). On the oath dispute, see *R.I. Recs.,* vol. 3, pp. 329–30.

5. On Brenton's actions, see Johnson, *Adjustment to Empire,* pp. 182–184, 278–281, 288 n. 88; Michael Garibaldi Hall, *Edward Randolph and the American Colonies* (Chapel Hill: University of North Carolina Press, 1960), pp. 133–134. Johnson describes Brenton's actions as intended "to undermine the colony's independence," but adds, "Brenton seems to have played a lone hand, playing off one side against the other." Johnson, *Adjustment to Empire,* p. 300 and n. 112. For the Board, see *R.I. Recs.,* vol. 3, p. 327 (Aug. 1697). Brenton also acted for the colony in the Connecticut boundary dispute in the fall of 1697. Ibid., vol. 1, p. 539. For his appointment and activities as agent from May 1699 to 1703, see *R.I. Recs.,* vol. 3, pp. 402–403 (Feb. 1699/1700), 409–410 (May 1700), 464 (Feb. 1702/1703). For references to the appeals, see *APC,* vol. 2, p. 325; Jahleel Brenton Notebook (Aug. 10, 1700). On September 1, 1698, Elizabeth Shrimpton, the widow of a claimant, moved to have the appeals dismissed because he had not prosecuted them within the appropriate time. There had been disagreement over the right of appeal where the crown had lost. For discussion of Brenton's arguments and the Board of Trade's decision to permit appeals, see Smith, *Appeals,* pp. 138–139.

6. On the customs appeal, in 1700 the Committee concluded that Brenton had "acquiesced" in the judgment. *APC,* vol. 2, pp. 324–325. Brenton received £67.14.6 from the Receiver General of the Custom "being for so

much disbursed by me about Appeals from New England in the case of the Brigantine Mary & Lading of Tobacco and the Case of the Spanish Iron." Jahleel Brenton Notebook (Aug. 10, 1700).

7. For the records, see Jahleel Brenton Notebook. On Wharton as the solicitor for Rhode Island and Pennsylvania, see Arnold, *History of Rhode Island,* vol. 2, pp. 24–25, 36, 45. On the Board of Trade, see Charles M. Andrews, *The Colonial Period in American History* (New Haven: Yale University Press, 1934), vol. 4, p. 298. On law officers, see John Christopher Sainty, *A List of English Law Officers, King's Counsel and Holders of Patents Precedence* (London: Selden Society, 1987), pp. 47, 64. On the case, see Smith, *Appeals,* p. 139. Expenditures included: coach payments to inquire after various petitions, including to the petition from New England against appeals, to visit the Council's clerk, and to obtain copies of "Presidents" about appeals for Chief Justice Holt (£00.01.0–00.03.0); payments for numerous summons (£00.10.0 each), Council order about appeals (£00.01.6) and a Council order allowing the appeal (£3.02.6); payments for copies from the attorney and solicitor generals' clerks of the Address of Massachusetts Bay against Appeals, the report on appeals, and a copy of a Massachusetts law and Massachusetts laws allowed and disallowed (£00.05.0–00.10.0); payments to the solicitor for the briefs (£1.00–1.05.0); payments to the attorney and solicitor generals to attend Chief Justice Holt on the appeals (£2.03.0 and 3.04.6) and for various committee hearings; payments to clerks (£00.05.0–00.10.0); fees to the doorkeeper of the Council chamber (£00.15.0 each time); and payment for a wig (£7.10.6).

8. Jahleel Brenton Notebook (Sept. 1701).

9. On internal appeals, see Mary Sarah Bilder, "The Origin of the Appeal," 48 *Hastings Law Journal* 913, 949–951 (1997). On Connecticut's Act for a Court of Chancery (1686), see Solon Wilson, "Courts of Chancery in the American Colonies," in *Select Essays in Anglo-American Legal History,* vol. 2 (Boston: Little, Brown, 1908), p. 791; Bruce H. Mann, *Neighbors and Strangers: Law and Community in Early Connecticut* (Chapel Hill: University of North Carolina Press, 1990), pp. 156–159. For the Board of Trade's response to Brinley, see *APC,* vol. 2, p. 328. For the Assembly's response, see "Rhode Island: State of the Constitutions & proceedings of the Courts of Tryals & goal deliveries both in Civil and Criminall Cases. . . ." (1701), in Erwin C. Surrency, "Report on Court Procedures in the Colonies— 1700," 9 *American Journal of Legal History* 234, 237 (1965). For the Harris appeal, see *APC,* vol. 2, p. 980; for Newton, see ibid., p. 497. For the Atherton claim (1704), see *GCT Recs.,* Book A, p. 155 (JRC). For a few other appeals during this period, see "Appeals Recorded, Rhode Island Colony Records (no file papers)," RISA folder (list prepared by RISA). For the

complaint, see "Governor Dudley to the Board of Trade, with charges against Rhode Island," *R.I. Recs.*, vol. 3, p. 543 (1705). The Assembly insisted that it had even granted an appeal for twenty pounds, "which with humble submission, we conceive to be frivolous and vexatious." "Answer to the several charges . . ." (1705), ibid., p. 548. For bond, see ibid., p. 562 (1706).

10. For a description, see "Rhode Island: State of the Constitutions . . .," pp. 234–238. See *Stephen Arnold v. Zachariah Rhodes* (1701–1702), *GCT Recs.*, Book A, pp. 141, 142 (JRC); *R.I. Recs.*, vol. 3, pp. 444–445; *James and Elizabeth Bick v. Jonathan Sprague* (1703–1704), *GCT Recs.*, Book A, pp. 146, 150 (JRC), *R.I. Recs.*, vol. 3, pp. 481–482, 494–495; Andrew Barton's appeal (1704), *GCT Recs.*, Book A, p. 154 (JRC), *R.I. Recs.*, vol. 3, p. 512; Peter Marshall's appeal (1702–1704), *GCT Recs.*, Book A, pp. 146, 149, 152, 155 (JRC), *R.I. Recs.*, vol. 3, p. 513. Appellants lost in *Isaac Ayres v. John Easton* (1704), *GCT Recs.*, Book A, pp. 150, 152 (JRC), *R.I. Recs.*, vol. 3, p. 507; Josiah Arnold's appeal, *R.I. Recs.*, vol. 3, p. 507; *Lawrence Clinton v. Peleg Chamberlain* (1704), *GCT Recs.*, Book A, pp. 153, 154 (JRC), *R.I. Recs.*, vol. 3, p. 512; *Richard Sherrin v. Rowland Robinson* (1704), *GCT Recs.*, Book A, pp. 153, 154 (JRC), *R.I. Recs.*, vol. 3, p. 512. My work with *GCT Recs.*, Book A, was greatly assisted by the availability of a transcript of Book A in Jane Fletcher Fiske's *Rhode Island General Court of Trials, 1671–1704* (Boxford, Mass.: 1998).

11. On English equity, see Henry Horwitz, *Chancery Equity Records and Proceedings, 1600–1800* (Kew, UK: National Archives, Public Record Office, 1998), pp. 5–6. On colonial equity courts, see Peter Charles Hoffer, *Law and People in Colonial America,* rev. ed. (Baltimore: Johns Hopkins University Press, 1998), pp. 38, 49–51, 236 n. 18. On equity in Massachusetts, see William J. Curran, "The Struggle for Equity Jurisdiction in Massachusetts," 3 *Boston University Law Review* 271 (1951). For the Northey opinion, see "The opinion of the Attorney-General Northey" (Apr. 21, 1703/1704) in George Chalmers, *Opinions of the Eminent Lawyers on Various Points of English Jurisprudence* (1858; repr., Buffalo: William S. Hein, 1987), pp. 194–195.

12. In Pennsylvania, acts and repeals relating to equity occurred in 1690–1693, 1701–1705, 1710–1713, and 1715–1719. See Spencer R. Liverant and Walter H. Hitchler, "A History of Equity in Pennsylvania," 37 *Dickinson Law Review* 159–161 (1933); Peter Charles Hoffer, *The Law's Conscience: Equitable Constitutionalism in America* (Chapel Hill: University of North Carolina Press, 1990), pp. 50–51; Sidney George Fisher, "The Administration of Equity through Common Law Forms in Pennsylvania," in *Select Essays in Anglo-American History,* vol. 2, pp. 810, 812; Thomas A.

Cowan, "Legislative Equity in Pennsylvania," 4 *University of Pittsburgh Law Review* 1–43, n. 2 (1937).

13. *R.I. Recs.*, vol. 3, pp. 550–551 (Oct. 1705).

14. For language, see *Brenton v. Remington*, *R.I. Recs.*, vol. 4, pp. 80–81 (Oct. 1709). For substantive appeals, see *Sarah Carr v. Jonathan Carr, R.I. Recs.*, vol. 3, p. 556 (1706–1709); Marsh appeal, ibid., vol. 4, p. 72. For reductions of damages, see *Joseph Carpenter v. John King* (1707), ibid., vol. 4, pp. 29–30, *GCT Recs.*, Book A, p. 171 (JRC). For other cases, see *Col. Samuel Cranston v. Samson Batty* (1706), *R.I. Recs.*, vol. 3, p. 556, *GCT Recs.*, Book A, pp. 160, 162 (JRC); *Samuel Albro v. Weston Clarke . . .* (1709), *R.I. Recs.*, vol. 4, pp. 80–81, *GCT Recs.*, Book A, p. 180 (JRC); *Joseph Knowlton v. John Pellet* (1710), *R.I. Recs.*, vol. 4, p. 90, *GCT Recs.*, Book A, p. 183 (JRC); *Lydia Checkley and Samuel Checkley v. Thomas Hix* (1711), *R.I. Recs.*, vol. 4, p. 115, *GCT Recs.*, Book A, p. 190 (JRC), *John Pellet v. Joseph Knowlton* (1711), *R.I. Recs.*, vol. 4, pp. 115–116. By 1708, the recorder had fallen into the pattern of discussing the appeals as enactments by the Assembly. See *Richard Mew v. Jahleel Brenton* (1708), *R.I. Recs.*, vol. 4, pp. 39–40; *Caleb Carr v. John Ward* (1708), *R.I. Recs.*, vol. 4, p. 40. It dismissed an appeal for failure to file "reasons of appeal." *Samuel Wait v. Abraham Anthony* (1705–1706), *R.I. Recs.*, vol. 3, p. 569, *GCT Recs.*, Book A, pp. 160, 161, 165 (JRC). For an exception for a man "of but mean estate," see *R.I. Recs.*, vol. 3, p. 570 (1706). On appeal legislation, see ibid., vol. 4, pp. 52–53 (1708). Not all appeals requested in the General Court of Trials actually were appealed to the Assembly. See, e.g., *Josiah Wascott v. John [Albro]* and *William Coddington & Richard Mew v. Patience Coggeshall* (1708), *GCT Recs.*, Book A, p. 175.

15. Austin, *Genealogical Dictionary,* pp. 254 (will of William Brenton), 172 (will of Peleg Sanford). An earlier appeal to the Privy Council between private parties for trespass and ejectments had been granted in 1706 but never prosecuted in England. *Albro v. Mr. James Noyes* (1706–1706), *R.I. Recs.*, vol. 3, p. 556; *GCT Recs.*, Book A, pp. 159, 161 (JRC).

16. By the late seventeenth century, "practically all questions connected with mortgages were dealt with by Chancery to the exclusion of its rival." R. W. Turner, *The Equity of Redemption: Its Nature, History and Connection with Equitable Estates Generally* (Cambridge: University Press, 1931), p. 49; J. H. Baker, *Introduction to English Legal History,* 3rd ed. (London: Buttersworth, 1990), p. 121. On chancery cases setting twenty-year limit, see Turner, *Equity of Redemption,* pp. 28–29, 30. They appeared in 1696–1697 in the first volume of *Chancery Cases* and the second volume of *Ventris*. Ibid., pp. 56, 58. On right, see Thomas Wood, *An Institute of the Laws of England,* 3rd ed. (1724; repr., New York: Garland, 1978), p. 141

("Mortgages are not redeemable in Chancery after twenty years, no demand being made, or interest paid."). The Massachusetts act appears in *Acts and Resolves, public and private, of the Province of Massachusetts Bay* (Boston: Wright & Potter, 1869–1922), vol. 1, pp. 356–357. Brenton may have learned of the claim from Nathaniel Byfield and Nathaniel Blagrove, two Bristol attorneys who practiced in Rhode Island and had dealt with the claim. Barbara Black, "Nathaniel Byfield, 1653–1733" in *Law in Colonial Massachusetts,* ed. Daniel R. Coquillette (Boston: Colonial Society, 1984), pp. 83–85.

17. For 1708 case, see *GCT Recs.,* Book A, pp. 173, 175 (JRC); *R.I. Recs.,* vol. 4, p. 48. It appears that Brenton sued for the land circa 1705 but the court threw out the action. *GCT Recs.,* Book A, p. 159 (JRC).

18. PC 2/82/334–335 (June 1709); PC 2/83/23 (July 1710, Comm. hearing), 46 (July 1710, Order); *APC,* vol. 2, p. 605. For copies of the order, see Jahleel Brenton Papers (RIHS); Governor and Council Records (RISA), p. 74 (entered by Weston Clarke on July 15, 1711); *Benjamin Brenton v. Gersham Remington* (SCJ, Newport 1745) (JRC).

19. *R.I. Recs.,* vol. 4, pp. 136–137 (Feb. 1711/1712).

20. *John Knight v. Job Babcock* (1712), *R.I. Recs.,* vol. 4, pp. 138–139. For the absence of appeals to the Privy Council, see *Acts and Laws, Of His Majesties Colony of Rhode-Island, and Providence-Plantations, In America* (Boston: Printed by John Allen for Nicholas Boone, 1719), reprinted in *Earliest Acts.*

21. For cases, see *William Coggeshall v. Bolston Coggeshall* and *John Langford v. Evan Henry, R.I. Recs.,* vol. 4, p. 157–158 (1713); *Edward Pelham v. John Lancaster, Daniel Ayrault v. Samuel Davis,* and *John Scott v. Thomas Peckham,* ibid., vol. 4, pp. 185, 199 (1715). For 1720s cases on debt or chancerizing, see *John Russell v. Aaron Milliman, Edward Mott v. Jahleel Brenton, Jahleel Brenton v. Thomas Pelham,* ibid., vol. 4, pp. 268, 289, 294–294 (1720–1721); *James Arnold v. Charles Whitfield* and *Benjamin Ellery v. John Wanton,* ibid., vol. 4, pp. 312–313, 320 (1722); *Brenton v. Samuel Brown,* ibid., vol. 4, pp. 346, 362 (1724). The Assembly confirmed the judgment in some cases, e.g., *Christopher Almy, Jr. v. Eunice Greenman, spinster,* ibid., vol. 4, p. 313. Not everyone who requested an appeal during these years received one. *Ralph Chapman & Benjamin Norton v. William Rouse, R.I. Recs.,* vol. 4, p. 199 (Oct. 1715). For appeals emphasizing title to land exception, see *Thomas Hazard v. George Mumford* and *Christopher Champlin v. Benjamin Perry,* ibid., vol. 4, pp. 217, pp. 224–225 (1717). For the creation of the Court of Equity, see *R.I. Recs.,* vol. 5, pp. 23–24 (May 1741); "An Act for appointing and erecting a Court of Equity, to hear and determine all Appeals in Personal Actions, from the Judgments of the Superior Court," *Acts and Laws, Of His Majesties Colony of Rhode-Island, and Providence-*

Plantations, In New-England (Newport: Printed by the Widow Franklin, 1745), pp. 239–240. The committee members represented the three county courts. For a discussion of this court that somewhat misunderstood it, see Zechariah Chafee, "Records of the Rhode Island Court of Equity, 1741–1743," *Publications of the Colonial Society of Massachusetts, Transactions, 1942–1946* (Boston: Colonial Society of Massachusetts, 1951), vol. 35, pp. 91–118. The published Rhode Island General Assembly records for 1725–1741 are misleading because they exclude the Assembly record of appeals after 1717 as "business of a private character." *R.I. Recs.,* vol. 4, p. iii. The Equity Court's docket increased: 29 cases (September 1741); 65 cases (1742); 43 cases (April and May 1743); 46 cases (October 1743), 29 cases (December 1743). For repeal, see "An Act for Repealing an Act . . . entitled, An Act for Appointing and Erecting a Court of Equity . . .," *Acts and Laws* (1745), pp. 282–284. After the repeal in 1744, the Assembly briefly permitted undecided equity cases to be appealed to England. *R.I. Recs.,* vol. 5, pp. 76–78, 86. For the quote, see "An Act directing the Method of receiving Petitions into, and acting thereon by the General Assembly," *Acts and Laws* (1746 session laws), in *Acts and Laws, Of His Majesty's Colony of Rhode-Island, and Providence-Plantations, In New England* (Newport: Printed by J. Franklin, 1752), pp. 22–24. For the new court, see "An Act for the more regular establishing a Superior Court of Judicature, Court of Assize, and General Goal Delivery, throughout the Colony," *Acts and Laws* (1746 session laws), pp. 27–30. On petitions to the Assembly, see *R.I. Recs.,* vol. 5, p. 365. For the 1756 petition, see R.I. State Record Collection Misc. (RIHS).

22. The only apparent appeal between 1708 and 1717 was the appeal of John Knight, *R.I. Recs.,* vol. 4, p. 139 (Feb. 1711/1712). The four appeals and attorneys are: *Ford v. Hodgson* (1717) (Blagrove/Newdigate); *Carr v. Holmes* (1718) (Newdigate/Robinson); *MacSparran v. Mumford* (1724) (Bull & Auchmuty/Newdigate & Brenton); *Wharton v. Northrup* (1728) (file papers missing).

23. For the quote, see Matthew Robinson to Ebenezer [Brenton?] (June 10, 1754) in Box 5, folder 4A (NHS). On Newdigate, see *R.I. Recs.,* vol. 4, p. 26 (1707); Sydney V. James, *Colonial Rhode Island: A History* (New York: Scribner's, 1975), pp. 137–138. On another aspect of Newdigate's legal life, see William T. Marvin, *The Newdigate Fine* (Boston: George G. Marvin, 1914). On the effort to regain a thousand acres in West Jersey, see Box 5, folder 4A (NHS). On Blagrove and Byfield, see *R.I. Recs.,* vol. 4, pp. 4, 29 (1707). For the 1718 petition, see Petition of Nathaniel Newdigate (May 1718) in *Newdigate v. Richardson,* UB5 (JRC).

24. The commonplace book is in the Rhode Island Historical Society.

Newdigate likely had a guide at least for the headings. The book seems to have been compiled largely in one piece prior to 1720, with later books and entries added after page 159 (e.g., "Admiralty" appears on pages 1, 164, 165, 180, 183, 198). For published commonplace books, see *A Brief Method of the Law being an Exact Alphabetical Disposition of all the Heads Necessary for a Perfect Common-Place* (London: Assignees of Richard & Edward Atkins for John Kidgell, 1680); *A Collection of Heads and Titles proper for a Common Place-Book in Law and Equity, . . . which renders the whole a Copious Index to the Law* (London: E. & R. Gott & R. Gosling, 1733). He may have also relied on William Sheppard, *A Grand Abridgement of the Common and Statute Law of England* (London: E. Flesher, J. Streater, and H. Twyford, 1675). Nathaniel Newdigate's Commonplace Book List included: "Cooke's Reports" (*Coke's Reports* [English], first published 1658); "Compleat Solicitor" (perhaps *Compleat Solicitor, Entring-Clerk, and Attorney,* first published 1683); "Shepard Abridgment 1st–2d–3 & 4th parts" (William Sheppard, *A Grand Abridgment of the common and statute law of England,* 4 vols., first published 1675); "Crook 1st is Crook Eliz" ([Sir. G] Croke, *Reports of Cases in King's Bench and Common Bench, Part I, Elizabeth,* first published 1661); "Crook 2d Is Crook Jac" (*Part 2, James,* first published 1657); "Crook 3d Is Crook Carols" (*Part 3, Charles,* first published 1657); "Canc—Is Cases in Chancery 1st-2d-3d parts" (*Reports of Cases in chancery . . .,* first published 1715–1716, 3 vols.); "Law oblig Is Law of Obligations" (T. Ashe, *Law of Obligations and Conditions . . . ,* first published 1693); "Co. Lit—Is Cook upon Littleton" (Coke, *First Part of the Institutes . . . or, Commentarie upon Littleton,* first published 1628); "Bar & Fem Is baron & Feme" (*Baron and Feme; Common Law concerning Husbands and Wives,* first published 1700); "Instit Is Cookes Institutes 2d–3d & 4th part" (Coke, *. . . Institutes of the Lawes of England,* 3 vols., first published 1644); "Law Exex Is law of Executors" (*Law of Executors and Administrators,* first published 1701); "Shower Is part of Shower Rept" (Shower, *Reports, King's Bench [1678–1694],* first published pt. 1, 1708); "Ventris Is Ventris Rept 1st & 2d part" (Ventris, *Reports in two parts* [King's Bench, Common Pleas and "many remarkable and curious cases in the Court of Chancery"], first published 1696); "Modern Repts Is 1st of Modern Repts" (*Modern Reports; or, Select Cases adjudged in the Courts of K. B., Chancery, C. P. and Exchequer,* first published 1682); "Wingat is Wingath maximes" (E[dmund] W[ingate], *Maximes of Reasons: or, Reason of the Common Law of England,* first published 1658); "IC Is Instructor Clericalis 1st -2d -3 & 4th pts" (*Instructor Clericalis: or, precedents in the Court of King's Bench and Common Pleas,* first published 4 pts. 1714); "Salk Is Salkelds Repts 1st & 2d part" (Salkeld, *Reports of Cases in the Court of King's Bench, with some*

*special cases in the Courts of Chancery, Common Pleas and Exchequer . . .
[1689–1712],* first published 1717); "Salk 3d Is Salkelds Repts 3d part"
(first published 1724); "Orphans Legacy—sometimes refers to the old edition and some times to the new" (Godolphin, *Orphans Legacy; or, Testamentary Abridgment,* first published 1674); "Repts Anne Is 6 Modern Repts
in the 3d & 4th years of the Reign of Queen Anne" (*Modern Reports; or, Select Cases adjudged in the Courts of K. B., Chancery, C. P. and Exchequer
[1703–4],* first published 1713); "Couber batch Is Comberbatches Rept"
(Comberbach, *Report of several Cases, King's Bench at Westminster* [1685–
98], first published 1724); "L Wills is Law of Last Wills" (*Of last wills and
testaments . . . ,* first published 1703); "Lex Test Is Lex Testimentaria" (Nelson, *Lex Testamentaria; or, System of the Laws of England . . . concerning Last
Wills and Testaments,* first published 1714); "Tryalls in parl Is Tryalls in
parliamt"; "Keylings Is Keylings Repts" (Kelyng, *Report of divers Cases in
Pleas of the Crown [1662–69] . . . ,* first published 1708); "Hawkins Is
Hawkins pleas of the Crown 2 Volumes" (Hawkins, *Pleas of the Crown,*
published 1716–21); "Pract Reg Is practical Register" (*Practical Register in
Chancery . . . ,* first published 1714). For titles, see Maxwell and Maxwell,
Legal Bibliography; Cowley, *Bibliography.* All volumes except Croke's *Re-
ports,* the Coke volumes, *Instructor Clericalis,* Salkeld's *Reports, Orphan's
Legacy, Modern Reports,* Keyling's *Reports,* and Hawkins's *Pleas* contained
the notation "printed AD."

25. For the 1717 case, see *GCT Recs.,* Book A, pp. 246, 255. For the Assembly's
    decision, see *R.I. Recs.,* vol. 4, p. 224 (Oct. 1717). For Newdigate's com-
    ments, see his Commonplace Book, p. [iv recto], "Judgments by Judge
    Menzies December 1716." For the order, see Council Order (Dec. 1716) in
    Records of the Vice-Admiralty Court of Rhode Island, 1716–1752, ed. Doro-
    thy S. Towle (Washington D.C.: American Historical Association, 1936),
    pp. 105–107. Earlier file papers appear in UB1, F13 (GCT, June 1714)
    (JRC); Petition of Daniel Hodgson to General Council (Dec. 1716), Gover-
    nor and Council Records (RISA), pp. 82–85, 90 (Dec. 1716) (order to
    stay); General Assembly Records 1715–1729 (RISA), pp. 158, 165 (Privy
    Council appeal granted).

26. *R.I. Recs.,* vol. 4, pp. 243–244 (1718); *Acts and Laws* (1719), p. 169. On
    Newdigate in Rhode Island, see *R.I. Recs.,* vol. 4, pp. 262 (1719), 289
    (1720).

27. For the 1718–1719 appeal, see PC 2/86/153, 187, 189, 287–288; *APC,*
    vol. 2, pp. 743–744. For Ford's account of the suit, see *Peter Ford v. Daniel
    Hodgson* (1716–1717), UB4, F12 (JRC); *GCT Recs.,* Book A, pp. 241, 246
    (JRC). The underlying legal issue may have involved whether Hodgson
    was a bailiff.

28. See Declaration (filed Aug 1717) and Answer in *William Holmes v. John Holmes and John Martin,* UB5, F3 (JRC) (GCT, Mar. 1718) (JRC); *GCT Recs.,* Book A, pp. 258 (Sept. 1717), 266 (Mar. 1718) (JRC). For the order about the record, see PC 2/86/194–195 (Dec. 1718). For the second order, see PC 2/86/351 (Nov. 1719), 2/86/364 (Jan. 1719/1720; order); *APC,* vol. 2, p. 747–748. Another copy of the committee report in the case appears in *APC,* vol. 6, p. 119. Newdigate had to have the statutes amended so that the sister could sue. *Acts and Laws* (1719), p. 217; *R.I. Recs.,* vol. 4, p. 219. On the Holmes family, see Austin, *Genealogical Dictionary,* p. 104.

29. "An Act for regulating Appeals to His Majesty in Council in Great Britain" (June 1719) in *Acts and Laws, Of His Majesty's Colony of Rhode-Island, and Providence-Plantations, In America* (Newport: Printed by James Franklin, 1730) (hereafter *Acts and Laws* [1730]), p. 106. For the case, see *R.I. Recs.,* vol. 4, pp. 412–413 (Oct. 1728) (*Jahleel Brenton v. John Stanton*). There were at least four admiralty appeals during these years. *Records of the Vice-Admiralty Court; APC,* vol. 3. The 1706 act requiring a bond in appeals mysteriously did not appear in *Acts and Laws* (1719).

30. Thomas Wood's *Institute* mentioned the appeal: "for the controversies arising in point of law amongst the king's subjects" of Jersey and Guernsey, "etc.," the King and the Privy Council "are the proper Judges without Appeal." The "etc." may have been intended to cover the ambiguous situation involving the colonies. Wood, *Institute,* p. 458. The Connecticut case of *Winthrop v. Lechmere* in 1728 also likely influenced the development of the appeal. On MacSparran's case, see chapter 7. On Wharton, see *R.I. Recs.,* vol. 4, pp. 63–64 (1709); Sydney V. James, *The Colonial Metamorphoses in Rhode Island: A Study of Institutions in Change,* ed. Sheila L. Skemp and Bruce C. Daniels (Hanover: University Press of New England, 2000), pp. 133–134. Although MacSparran hired a Newport attorney, Henry Bull, Wharton employed Polycarp Wharton, presumably a relative. On Auchmuty's 1735 opinion, see *CHS Coll.,* vol. 5, pp. 426–467.

31. The Wharton case is complicated and file papers are missing. For the trial, see *GCT/SCJ Recs.,* Book B, p. 149 (Sept. 1727) and (March 1728) (JRC); *Wharton v. Northrups* (1735) (JRC). Two assistants dissented because the deed had been permitted in an earlier case. For the Assembly petition, see Petition of Polycarp Wharton, attorney for Eunice Wharton, to Hon. Joseph Jencks, et al. (June 1728) in Petitions, vol. 1, p. 35 (RISA). The Wharton complaint appears in PC 2/91/302. The lands seem to have been held by the Atherton Company. See *R.I. Recs.,* vol. 3, pp. 225–226; Arnold, *History of Rhode Island,* vol. 1, passim. In 1712, an attorney for Richard's "heirs" sold the land to the Northrups. J. R. Cole, *History of Washington and Kent Counties, Rhode Island* (New York: W. W. Preston, 1889), p. 392.

On William and Richard Wharton, see *R.I. Recs.*, vol. 3, p. 184; Elisha R. Potter, *The Early History of Narragansett* (Providence: Marshall, Brown, 1835), pp. 104–105; Mellen Chamberlain, *A Documentary History of Chelsea* (Boston: MHS, 1908), vol. 1, p. 400 n. 14.

32. On Wharton's appeal to the Privy Council (1730), see PC 2/90/436, 2/91/ 192, 302, 305; *APC,* vol. 3, p. 214. On the will, see Affidavit of Ferdinando John Paris (June 1731, London), *Wharton v. Northrup* (JRC). On the new trial, see *GCT/SCJ Recs.*, Book B, p. 508 (Sept. 1735) (JRC). For earlier proceedings, see ibid., pp. 420 (Mar. 1732, reversal by his Majesty in Council), p. 500 (Mar. 1735). On Paris, see Michael Kammen, *Empire and Interest: The American Colonies and the Politics of Mercantilism,* (Philadelphia: Lippincott, 1970), p. 69.

33. "An Act for Regulating Appeals to His Majesty in Council in Great-Britain, and for Repealing the former Act . . .," *Acts and Laws* (1746 session laws), p. 30 (raising the 1719 amount in controversy limits); *Acts and Laws* (1730), p. 192 (regulating appeals). In 1729–1730, the Assembly restructured the court system with new fees for attorneys and clerks. See *Acts and Laws* (1730), pp. 188–189, 190–198, 202–204, 208. In appeals, both sides were to "have the benefit of any further or new evidence relating to the case." Except for a brief period during which judges held their office "bene gesserint," judges were elected annually under "the Constitution of this Government." Ibid., p. 251.

5. Women, Family, Property

1. The trade case related to molasses duties under the Navigation Acts. See *Brown v. Allen & Chever* (SCJ, Newport, Mar. 1737) (JRC); *GCT/SCJ Recs.*, Book B, p. 570 (Mar. 1737) (JRC); *Rhode Island Law Cases* (RISA) (hereafter, *R.I. Law Cases),* vols. 7 & 9; *Rhode Island General Assembly Records* (hereafter, *R.I.G.A. Recs.*), *1729–1745* (RISA), pp. 274 (May 1737), 361 (Aug. 1739); PC 2/94/481, 536, 556–558, 591; *APC,* vol. 3, p. 603. The three other appeals include two involving glebe land (discussed in chapter 7) and one case that paralleled a female inheritance case. See *Brenton v. Brenton* (SCJ, Mar. 1736) (JRC); PC 2/95/95, 96–98, 143 (1738–1739); *APC,* vol. 3, p. 563. For discussion of the tension between Dutch inheritance practices and English ones, see David E. Narrett, *Inheritance and Family Life in Colonial New York City* (Ithaca: Cornell University Press, 1992), particularly chapter 3. For discussion of cognate and in-law inheritance practices, see Toby L. Ditz's *Property and Kinship: Inheritance in Early Connecticut, 1750–1820* (Princeton: Princeton University Press, 1986). For a summary of the conventional theory of English and colonial practices,

see Carole Shammas, Marylynn Salmon, and Michael Dahlin, *Inheritance in America from Colonial Times to the Present* (1987; repr., Galveston: Frontier Press, 1997), pp. 23–62; Roger Thompson, *Women in Stuart England and America: A Comparative Study* (London: Routledge & Kegan Paul, 1974), pp. 161–186. For a social history approach, see Philip J. Greven, *Four Generations: Population, Land, and Family in Colonial Andover, Massachusetts* (Ithaca: Cornell University Press, 1970), pp. 72–99. For additional genealogical information on the families involved in these cases, such as the Arnold-Pelhams, see John Osborne Austin, *The Genealogical Dictionary of Rhode Island* (1887; repr., Baltimore: Genealogical, 1969), pp. 149, 242–245; on the Brentons, see ibid., pp. 252–256; on the Gardiner/Gardners, see ibid., p. 81; on the Sanfords, see ibid., pp. 171–172; on the Sabere/Sabeer/Sabeeres, see ibid., p. 169; on the Coggeshalls, see ibid., p. 49; Charles Pierce Coggeshall & Thellwell Russell Coggeshall, comps., *The Coggeshalls in America* (Boston: C. E. Goodspeed, 1930) pp. 1, 12, 28, 50–51. Greater detail on cases and analysis can be found in Mary Sarah Bilder, "Salamanders and Sons of God: Transatlantic Legal Culture and Colonial Rhode Island" (Ph.D. diss., Harvard University, 2000), pp. 340–379.

2. For Joshua's will, see Austin, *Genealogical Dictionary,* p. 49. For Daniel's will, see Last Will and Testament of Daniel Coggeshall (May 1717), *Mary Coggeshall v. Daniel Coggeshall* (SCJ, Mar. 1736) (JRC), Copy Case, 5–13. Joshua's brother, Daniel, was left only ten pounds, having inherited land from his mother's family. The entail was rewritten in Daniel's will and conditioned on Joshua's paying his youngest brother six hundred pounds.

3. For Will of Joshua Coggeshall (Nov. 1733), in Mary *Coggeshall v. Daniel Coggeshall* (*SCJ,* Mar. 1736). For earlier suit, see Copy of Deposition, *Bull et Uxor v. Joshua Coggeshall,* No. 6 (Oct. 1733) and Copy of Judgment in *Bull et Uxor v. Joshua Coggeshall,* No. 7 (Nov. 1733), in ibid. On breaking entail, see "An Act for docking and cutting of Estates Tail, pursuant to the Laws of Great Britain" (June 1725), *Acts and Laws, Of His Majesty's Colony of Rhode-Island, and Providence-Plantations, In America* (Newport: Printed by James Franklin, 1730) (hereafter, *Acts and Laws* [1730]), p. 138, and "An Act for recording fines and common recoveries," ibid., 156–157. For record book, see *Rhode Island Fines and Recovery* (1727–1750) (RISA). For Coggeshall's common recovery, see *Peleg Rogers v. Thomas Ward,* Fines and Recovery, pp. 188–196. His initial belief that the land was not entailed may have arisen because the grandfather's will had only two witnesses; the land had been mortgaged in a fashion that may have served as a fine and recovery; he failed to pay Peleg under the will; or the twenty-year statute of limitations broke it. Some of these arguments were raised on appeal in 1736.

4. On Updike (c. 1693–1757), see Austin, *Genealogical Dictionary,* p. 397; Wilkins Updike, *Memoirs of the Rhode Island Bar* (Boston: Thomas H. Webb, 1842), pp. 34–64. For the quote, see Thomas Wood, *An Institute of the Laws of England,* 3rd ed. (1724; repr., New York: Garland, 1978), p. 294. For Daniel's argument, see Declaration of Daniel Coggeshall, *Mary Coggeshall v. Daniel Coggeshall* (SCJ, Mar. 1736) (JRC). For the inferior case, see Copy Case (ICCP, Newport, Nov. 1735), in *Mary Coggeshall v. Daniel Coggeshall* (SCJ, Mar. 1736) (JRC) (special verdict involving whether, as a matter of law, Daniel Coggeshall's will had created fee tail; if not, the jury found for her).

5. On Honeyman (c. 1710–1778), see Updike, *Memoirs,* pp. 26–31; *R.I. Recs.,* vol. 4, pp. 447, 469. For attorney petitions, see Petition of Nathaniel Newdigate et al. (Oct. 1736) in Petitions to the General Assembly (RISA), vol. 3, p. 74; "Agreement among Attorneys" (Sept. 1745) (JRC). On the library, see *The 1764 Catalogue of the Redwood Library Company at Newport, Rhode Island,* ed. Marcus A. McCorison (New Haven: Yale University Press, 1965), pp. ix, 8, 14.

6. For Honeyman's arguments, see Reasons of Appeal (Mar. 1735/1736) and Notes of James Martin in *Mary Coggeshall v. Daniel Coggeshall* (SCJ, Mar. 1736) (JRC). For use of the introduction act, see "An Act to put Laws of England in Force" (Apr. 1700), in *Coggeshall v. Coggeshall* (SCJ, Mar. 1737) (JRC). On the Statute of Frauds, see 22 & 23 Car. II, c. 10; Wood, *Institute,* pp. 294, 317. On republication, see Thomas E. Atkinson, *Handbook of the Law of Wills* (St. Paul: West, 1953), p. 19; S. J. Bailey, *The Law of Wills,* 6th ed. (London: Sir Isaac Pitman & Sons, 1967), pp. 21–25. For dissent in the first trial, see Protest of John Wanton, Governor, George Cornell, William Anthony, and Phillip Arnold, Assistants, *Mary Coggeshall v. Daniel Coggeshall* (SCJ, Mar. 1736) (JRC). For the final jury decision, see *GCT/SCJ Recs.,* Book B, p. 526 (Mar. 1736) (JRC). For Daniel's request for a new trial, see Writ of Review (Sept. 1737), *Daniel Coggeshall v. Mary Coggeshall* (SCJ, Mar. 1737) (JRC).

7. See William Sanford (Nov. 1735), No. 10 in *Daniel Coggeshall v. Mary Coggeshall* (SCJ, Mar. 1737) (JRC); Gideon Cornell Evidence (sworn in court), No. 11 in ibid. For other evidence, see Gideon Wanton, No. 12 in ibid.; Martin, Brightman, & Cornell, Nos. 15, 16, 17 in ibid.; Francis Brayton, No. 14 in ibid. For the "best friend" comment, see, in ibid., Nicholas Easton, Brayton ("for he had no greater friend to give it to"), and Cornell ("his wife was the best friend he had in the world").

8. For the quote, see Richard Coggeshall Evidence, No. 24 in ibid; see also, in ibid., Thomas Coggeshall ("did it in a heat") and Nathaniel Coddington ("made the same when he was angry") (both sworn in court). For other evidence, see, in ibid., Peter Easton (sworn in court), John Coggeshall, and

William Brown (sworn in court). For the final quote, see Caleb Shreve, No. 25 in ibid.

9. On the second trial, see *GCT/SCJ Recs.*, Book B, pp. 569 (Mar. 1737) (JRC) (retried because of jurors related to Daniel), 588 (Sept. 1737) (juror dismissed by Daniel for prejudging the case). For the majority, see ibid, Book B, p. 588 (Sept. 1737); No Endorsement, No. 3 in *Daniel Coggeshall v. Mary Coggeshall* (SCJ, Mar. 1737) (JRC). For the dissent, see Protest of John Wickes and Rouse Helme (Sept. 1737) in *Daniel Coggeshall v. Mary Coggeshall* (SCJ, Mar. 1737) (JRC).

10. PC 2/95/164, 166, 167–177 (Apr. 1739). John Sharpe represented Mary Coggeshall. PC 2/95/5 (Oct. 1738). Unfortunately, no briefs have yet been found.

11. For the order, see PC 2/95/209–210 (June 1739); *SCJ Recs.*, Book C, p. 18 (Sept. 1741) (JRC). For the probable dower suit, see *Coggeshall v. Redwood* (ICCP, Newport, May 1741) (JRC) (slightly different acreage).

12. Edward Coke, *The First Part of the Institutes of the Law of England* (1628; repr., New York: Garland, 1979), vol. 1, diagram at p. 19; William Blackstone, *Commentaries on the Laws of England,* (1765–1769; repr., Chicago: University of Chicago Press, 1979), vol. 2, pp. 212, 214, 234.

13. See *Sabere v. Sabere,* UB46, F7 (1729) (JRC). "Sabeere" and "Sabere" both appear as spellings.

14. For the treatise, see *Baron and Feme: A Treatise of the Common Law concerning Husbands and Wives* (1700; repr., New York: Garland, 1979), p. 52. For the quote, see Paul Dudley to Edward Pelham (Roxbury, Nov. 1736), *R.I. Law Cases* (RISA), p. 43. On Jane Boreland, see *Boreland v. Brenton* (SCJ, May 1731), (SCJ, Sept. 1731), (SCJ, Mar. 1732), (SCJ, Sept. 1732), (SCJ, Mar. & Sept. 1735), (SCJ, Mar. & Sept. 1737) (JRC); *GCT/SCJ Recs.*, Book B, pp. 417, 431, 432, 509, 656 (JRC). On *Pelham,* see *Pelham v. Coggeshall* (SCJ, Sept. 1731) (2 folders), (SCJ, Sept. 1733), (SCJ, Mar. 1735), (SCJ, Sept. 1735) (two folders), (SCJ, Sept. 1736) (four folders on accounts) (JRC); *R.I. Law Cases* (RISA), vol. 6, pp. 39, 40–43; *GCT/SCJ Recs.*, Book B, pp. 408, 425, 443, 452, 522, 535, 541 (JRC).

15. On the Sanford sisters, see *Sanford v. Wood & Allen* (SCJ, Mar. 1732), (SCJ, undated folder) (JRC); *GCT/SCJ Recs.*, Book B, pp. 83, 107, 143, 404, 422, 437 (JRC); and *Arnold v. Johnson* (SCJ, Mar. 1734?) (2 folders), (SCJ, Sept. 1735), (SCJ, Sept. 1737) (JRC); *GCT/SCJ Recs.*, Book B, pp. 475, 508, 601 (JRC); Petition of Grizzel Cotton, Petitions (RISA), vol. 3, p. 41 (1734). The colony's intestate act was repealed in 1728, but provisions for widows (one-third of personal estate) and children (the remaining two-thirds) likely remained the same. See "An Act, for Distribution and Settling of Intestates Estate," *Acts and Laws, Of His Majesties Colony of Rhode-Island,*

and Providence-Plantations, In America (Boston: Printed by John Allen, for Nicholas Boone, 1719) (hereafter, *Acts and Laws* [1719]), reprinted in *Earliest Acts,* pp. 95–98; "An Act for repealing an Act . . ." (Feb. 1728) in *Acts and Laws* (1730), pp. 163–164. On James Martin's cases, see *Gardner v. Martin* (SCJ, 1739), (SCJ, Sept. 1739), (SCJ, Sept. 1741) (JRC); *R.I. Law Cases* (RISA), vol. 8, p. 38, vol. 9, pp. 55–56 (Oct. 1739); *GCT/SCJ Recs.,* Book B, pp. 527, 656, 666, Book C, p. 13 (JRC); *Martin v. Gibbs* (SCJ, Mar. 1737), (SCJ, Sept. 1737) (JRC); *R.I. Law Cases,* vol. 7, pp. 36–37; *R.I.G.A. Recs.,* 1729–1745, p. 286 (Oct. 1737); *GCT/SCJ Recs.,* Book B, pp. 572, 583.

16. On English law, see Wood, *Institute,* p. 218; Blackstone, *Commentaries,* vol. 2, pp. 220–222; William Nelson, *Lex Testamentaria: Or, a Compendious System of All the Laws of England . . . concerning Last Wills and Testaments* (1714; repr., New York: Garland, 1978), pp. 364–371; Tapping Reeve, *A Treatise on the Law of Descents* (New York: Collins & Hannay, 1825), p. 364.

17. For a similar suit brought by the daughter of Sarah Brenton Eliot, see *Wheeler et ux. v. Brenton,* Box 5, folder 7 (NHS). For final settlement of family claims, see the Indenture (1740) between Jonathan Law, Jahleel Brenton, Francis Boreland, Benjamin Brenton, Thomas Noyes and Ann Mason, reprinted at rootsweb.com/~rigenweb/article67.html.

18. I assume that the appeal involved Elizabeth's land but the colonial records are not clear. It could also have involved Thomas's land, which came into the Coggeshall's possession. For a related case involving Edward's brother-in-law, John Banister, discussed in a letter referring to "Mother Pelham's affair," see Box 45A, folder 14 (NHS). For the father's will, see "Will of Gov. Benedict Arnold," *Rhode Island Historical Magazine,* vol. 6, pp. 20, 25–26 (1885–1886). Peter Coggeshall and Elizabeth married in 1719. On relevant property law, see Wood, *Institutes,* pp. 295–296; J. H. Baker, *Introduction to English Legal History,* 3rd ed. (London: Buttersworth, 1990), p. 552. For a letter on tenant by curtesy and eldest son permissibly disposing of inherited land, see Roger Mopesson (Oct. 1709), Box 7, folder 22 (NHS). In 1742 and 1743, Hermione and Elizabeth destroyed any contingent interests by suffering a fine and recovery in the Rhode Island court. Hermione's husband, John Banister, became a wealthy merchant, privateer, and smuggler. Elizabeth's husband, Englishman Peter Harrison, would design the Redwood Library and King's Chapel, and become a loyalist and Connecticut custom collector. On the husbands, see Sydney V. James, *Colonial Rhode Island: A History* (New York: Scribner's, 1975), pp. 237, 240. On the daughters' suits, see *Fines and Recovery* (1727–1750) (RISA); *R.I.G.A. Recs.,* 1729–1745, pp. 510 (Sept. 1742), 564 (June 1743).

19. Petition of Francis Boreland and Jane (Oct. 1732), Petitions (RISA), vol. 2, p. 70.

20. Wood, *Institute*, pp. ii, v.

21. For West, see "Mr. West's opinion" (1720) in George Chalmers, *Opinions of Eminent Lawyers on Various Points of English Jurisprudence* (1858; repr., Buffalo: William S. Hein, 1987), p. 206; Smith, *Appeals*, pp. 482–483, 548 n. 119. On West's appointment, see William Lambarde, *A List of English Law Officers, King's Counsel and Holders of Patents Precedence* (London: Selden Society, 1987), p. 91. For Copy of Freelove Pelham's Will, see *Pelham v. Coggeshall* (SCJ, Sept. 1733) (JRC). On the law, see "An Act for the explanation of the Statute of Wills," 34 & 35 Hen. 8, c. 5 (1542–1543), *The Statutes of the Realm* (London: G. Eyre and A. Strahan, 1816–1828), vol. 3, pp. 901, 903; Wood, *Institute*, p. 293; *A Treatise of Feme Coverts* (1732; repr., New York: Garland, 1978), pp. 79–80; Nelson, *Lex Testamentaria*, p. 299. On exceptions (e.g., separation, specific consent, and separate estate), see Maria L. Cioni, *Women and Law in Elizabethan England, with Particular Reference to the Court of Chancery* (New York: Garland, 1985), p. 163. On case, see *GCT/SCJ Recs.*, Book B, pp. 452 (Sept. 1733), 541 (Sept. 1736) (JRC); *APC*, vol. 3, p. 340 (Apr. & May 1735).

22. For West's opinion, see "Mr. West's Opinion" (1720), in Chalmers, *Opinions*, p. 206. For Yorke's opinion on Pennsylvania, see "The Attorney-General Yorke's opinion" (1729) in Chalmers, *Opinions*, p. 208. For other opinions, see "The opinion of the Attorney and Solicitor-General . . . how far the Statute of Monopolies extends to the Colonies" (1720) in ibid., p. 213; "The opinion of the Attorney and Solicitor-General . . . on the extension of the Laws of England to the colonies, and on other analogous topics of Law" (c. 1724) in ibid., pp. 215, 229. Such opinions were on occasion sent by English solicitors to the colonies. See the opinion of Attorney General Yorke (1726) sent by J. Sharpe. Box 5, folder 2 (NHS).

23. For *Boreland* argument, see Petition of Francis Boreland, Petitions (RISA), vol. 2, p. 70. For earlier related case, see Copy Case, *Boreland v. Brenton* (SCJ, May 1731) (JRC); Reasons of Appeal, in *Boreland v. Brenton* (SCJ, Sept. 1731) (JRC); Plea and Answer of Brenton, in Copy Case, *Boreland* (May 1731). For statute, see "An Act for the Amendment of the Law and the better Advancement of Justice" (4 & 5 Ann, c. 3), *Statutes of the Realm*, vol. 8, pp. 458, 461; Wood, *Institute*, p. 148 (citing as 4 & 5 Ann, c. 16). Coke's *Entries* and Hobart's *Report* referred to E. Coke, *Book of Entries* (1614) and H. Hobart, *Reports in the reign of James I with some few cases in the reign of Queen Elizabeth* (King's Bench, 1603–1625; originally published in 1641; 5th ed. published in 1724). For Brenton's argument, see Reasons of Appeal of Brenton (Sept. 1732) in *Boreland* (SCJ, Mar. & Sept.

1735) (JRC). The Borelands attributed an earlier "error" to the "suddenness" of the decision, which "in the books of reports appears to beget many erroneous judgments and which afterwards on more mature consideration and solemn arguments by other judges declared not to be law." Petitions, vol. 2, p. 70. For the final Superior Court order, see *GCT/SCJ Recs.,* Book B, p. 656 (Mar. 1739) (JRC). The appeals in England are a bit confusing. See PC 2/92/184, 196 (1733 dismissal); 2/92/308, 309, 319, 418, 428, 456, 496, 519 (1733–1734 hearing). In April 1735, the Privy Council declared that the Borelands should have a trial, as the case had been "properly brought." Order in Council (Apr. 1735) in *Boreland* (SCJ, Mar. & Sept. 1735) (JRC). In September, the jury found for the Borelands. *GCT/SCJ Recs., Book B,* p. 509 (Sept. 1735). In January 1737/1738, the Privy Council upheld the verdict. Order in Council (Jan. 1737/1738) in *Boreland* (SCJ, Mar. & Sept. 1739).

24. For value, see Inventory of William Gibbs (Feb. 1728/1729) in Copy Case, *Martin v. Gibbs* (SCJ, Sept. 1737) (JRC). For case, see Declaration, Copy Case, *Martin* (SCJ, Mar. 1737) (JRC). Gardner's death apparently had been litigated before in *Town Council v. Godfrey Malbone* (1736?).

25. For Honeyman's argument, see Reasons of Appeal, *Martin* (SCJ, Sept. 1737). For the statute, see "An Act for the More Effectual Discovery of the Death of Persons Pretended to be Alive to the Prejudice of those who claim estates after their deaths," in *Statutes of the Realm,* vol. 8, pp. 830–831 (6 Ann c. 18) (the statute dealt with married women and infants); Wood, *Institutes,* pp. 127–128. For the 1738 Privy Council proceedings, see PC 2/95/5, 48, 62 (dismissal for nonprosecution), 64 (Martin ordered to pay Gibbs £20). Elizabeth Gibbs died after the decree, and her administrator, Matthew Stewart, applied for execution.*R.I.G.A. Recs.,* 1729–1745, p. 361 (Aug. 1739).

26. Answer, Copy Case, *Pelham v. Coggeshall* (SCJ, Sept. 1731) (JRC); Petition of Frances Boreland and Jane (Oct. 1732), Petitions (RISA), vol. 2, p. 70; *R.I. Law Cases* (RISA), vol. 6, p. 39 (Oct. 1736); Cotton, Wood, Allen Petition (Aug. 1727), Petitions, vol. 1, p. 12, and *Wood v. Allen* (SCJ, undated); *APC,* vol. 3, pp. 227–228. The petition noted that in England, the default could be reversed upon writ of error, "which our rehearings in this colony are in lieu of." For Assembly agreement, see *Wood v. Allen* (SCJ, undated).

27. For Assembly approval of writ of partition, see Petition of Ann Sabere (June 1727?), Petitions (RISA), vol. 1, p. 39. For arguments, see Plea and Answer (Aug. 1728), *Sabere v. Sabere* (1729), UB46, F7 (JRC). On law, see Coke, *Institutes,* First Part, vol. 1, §292; Wood, *Institutes,* pp. 145–147; *Fisher v. Wigg,* 1 Salkeld 391–392, 91 E. R. 339–340. Blackstone cited *Fisher* as establishing the presumption for joint tenancy. On joint tenancy,

see R. H. Helmholz, "Realism and Formalism in the Severance of Joint Tenancies," 77 *Nebraska Law Review* 1, 4 (1998).

28. Paper without endorsement, *Ann Sabere v. Daniel Sabere,* UB 46, F7 (1729) (signed John Wanton, William Wanton, Richard Waterman, George Cornell, William Anthony, Job Green, and William Hall); *GCT/SCJ Recs.,* Book B, p. 302 (JRC).

29. For 1730–1731 Council proceedings, see PC 2/91/229, 351, 373, 380, 388; *APC,* vol. 3, p. 283.

30. Smith, *Appeals,* p. 561. The Privy Council decision of repugnancy in Ann Sabeere's case may not have been significant. The case involved a purchase only ten years old, and the Privy Council's decision could easily be limited to recent purchases. Moreover, many large purchases already had been partitioned or protected by the statue of limitations.

31. For law comment, see Law to J. Belcher (June 1728) in *CHS Coll.,* vol. 4, pp. 120–123. For Wood, see Wood, *Institute,* p. 7.

32. On *Phillips,* see Allen to Talcott (Nov. 13, 1728) in *CHS Coll.,* vol. 5, pp. 71–72; Allen to Talcott (Jan. 25, 1738/39) in ibid., pp. 72–73. For an excellent discussion of the cases (*Winthrop, Sabeere,* and *Phillips*) by Joseph Smith with far greater subtlety than can be addressed here, see Smith, *Appeals,* p. 531–577. For Paris comments, see *CHS Coll.,* vol. 5, p. 78–87. Similar comments occur throughout the Talcott Papers. See, e.g., Wilks to Talcott (Nov. 27, 1740) in *CHS Coll.,* vol. 5, pp. 330–331.

33. For the English version, see "An act for limitation of actions, and for avoiding of suits in law," 21 James c. 16 (1623). Minors, feme coverts, persons non compos mentis, imprisoned persons, and persons beyond the seas had ten years after losing their disability to sue. See Blackstone, *Commentaries,* vol. 3, pp. 177–178, 192. The manuscript records for the Assembly contain the 1712 act, "Possessions Quieted." The 1712 act blamed a "want of Scribes" and noted that the lands were now cultivated and improved. The act stated that people who had held ten years and continued to hold for ten years would have land quieted. The act noted that it did not prejudice minors, feme coverts, persons non compos mentis, or those imprisoned or beyond the seas. *Rhode Island Colony Records, 1686–1715,* pp. 453–455 (RISA). For the Rhode Island version, see "An Act, for Quieting Possessions, and avoiding Suits at Law" (1712), *Acts and Laws* (1719), p. 67. Curiously, there is no record of the act in the printed Assembly records during these years. See *R.I. Recs.,* vol. 4, p. 381 (1726) (act limiting personal actions). On the Borelands' case, see note 23 above; on the Sanfords' case, see notes 15, 34, 35.

34. For Sanford's claim, see Declaration (Mar. 1725/1726), *Sanford v. Wood and Allen* (SCJ, undated) (JRC). For dispute over whether the entail was "spe-

cial" or "general," see Answer (Mar. 1725/1726); Declaration (Aug. 1726); Answer (Sept. 1726), *Sanford v. Wood and Allen* (SCJ, undated) (JRC). Samuel was the eldest son of the eldest son of a son of the first marriage.

35. For the act, see "An Act for docking and cutting of estates tail, pursuant to the laws of Great Britain" (June 1725), *Acts and Laws* (1730), pp. 138–139. Peter Coggeshall and Daniel Sabeere both signed a petition for the act. Petitions (RISA), vol. 1, p. 15. In September 1726, Wood and Allen won on a general verdict. In March 1727, the jury reversed. They requested a third rehearing. After the case there appears the notation "the plaintiff allows the defendants to be in possession of premises sued for thirty five years or thereabouts." *GCT/SCJ Recs.*, Book B, p. 107 (Mar. 1727) (JRC). After some complexity, the Rhode Island courts concluded in the girls' favor in 1727, although procedural problems left the land in Sanford's hands. Attorney Nathaniel Blagrove failed to post bond and pay the costs within ten days, and an execution was entered against them. Petition to Gov. and Asst. (June 1727); Act granting rehearing (Aug. 1727), *Sanford v. Wood and Allen* (SCJ, undated). For further proceedings, see *GCT/SCJ Recs.*, Book B, p. 143 (Sept. 1727); Order of the General Court (Sept. 1727). On English law, see Joseph Biancalana, *The Fee Tail and Common Recovery in England, 1176–1502* (Cambridge: Cambridge University Press, 2001); John Habakkuk, *Marriage, Debt, and the Estates System: English Landownership, 1650–1950* (Oxford: Clarendon Press, 1994); Lloyd Bonfield, *Marriage Settlements, 1601–1740* (Cambridge: Cambridge University Press, 1983).

36. For the recording act, see "An Act for recording of fines and common recoveries" (May 1728) in *Acts and Laws* (1730), pp. 156–157. For the disability act, see ibid., p. 166. In 1737, the Assembly repealed the 1725 act. See "An Act for repealing an Act, entitled, An Act for docking and cutting off estates tail" (1737), in *Acts and Laws, Of His Majesty's Colony of Rhode-Island, and Providence-Plantations, In New-England* (Newport: Printed by the Widow Franklin, 1745), p. 197. For the *Fines and Recoveries* volume, see *Fines and Recoveries* (1727–1750) (RISA). Eventually the Privy Council also sided with the girls. For 1729–1731 Privy Council proceedings, see PC 2/90/467; PC 2/91/69, 160, 191, 379, 387–388; Copy of Order from King in Council (May 11, 1731), *Sanford v. Wood & Allen* (Mar. 1732); *GCT/SCJ Recs.*, Book B, pp. 404 (Sept. 1731), 422 (Mar. 1732), 437 (Sept. 1732) (JRC). Whether the young girls eventually received the land is unclear.

37. *Smales v. Dales*, 12 Jac. Rot. 2141, in *Hobart's Reports*, p. 120, and *Reading v. Royston Hill*, Ann. B. R., in *Salkeld's Reports*, vol. 2, p. 423, in *Boreland* (Sept. 1731). The cases were attested as copied correctly by the clerk. For appeals from 1732–1738, see PC 2/92/49, 184, 196, 308, 309, 319, 418,

428, 456, 496, 519, 308; PC 2/94/2, 343, 367; Order in Council in *Boreland* (Mar. & Sept. 1739); *APC,* vol. 3, p. 365.

6. Personnel and Practices

1. On Bull, see Wilkins Updike, *Memoirs of the Rhode Island Bar* (Boston: Thomas H. Webb, 1842), pp. 23–26. On Updike, see ibid., pp. 34–66; Edward Peterson, *History of Rhode Island* (New York: John S. Taylor, 1853), p. 155; John Osborne Austin, *The Genealogical Dictionary of Rhode Island* (1887; repr., Baltimore: Genealogical, 1969), p. 397. Honeyman graduated from Harvard in 1729 and Ward in 1733. See Clifford K. Shipton, *Sibley's Harvard Graduates* (Boston: MHS, 1951), vol. 8, pp. 587–589; Shipton, *Sibley's Harvard Graduates* (Boston: MHS, 1956), vol. 9, pp. 360–365. On Richard Ward (1689–1763), see *R.I. Recs.,* vol. 4, pp. 142, 169, 469, 584; Austin, *Genealogical Dictionary,* p. 407. On Ward and Honeyman, see Updike, *Memoirs,* pp. 27–33; Peterson, *History of Rhode Island,* pp. 154–155. On the Society (SPG), see Records of the Society (Feb. 2, 1735?), reprinted in *Newport Mercury* (Nov. 23, 1833), in Henry Bull, *Memoir of Rhode Island* (Newport: C. E. Hammett, 1888), vol. 2, pp. 161–163. Attorneys for appealed cases 1725–1740: *MacSparran v. Mumford* (Bull/Updike vs. Newdigate); *Wharton v. Northrups* (Wharton vs. unknown attorney); *Sanford v. Wood & Allen* (Bull vs. Blagrove); *Sabeere v. Sabeere* (J. Wilson vs. Newdigate); *Boreland v. Brenton* (Bull vs. Updike; Newdigate for Brenton); *Torrey v. Mumford* (Updike vs. unknown); *Pelham v. Coggeshall* (Updike vs. Bull); *Arnold v. Johnson* (Updike vs. Bull); *MacSparran v. Hassard* (Bull vs. Ward); *Brenton v. Brenton* (Ward vs. Updike); *Brown v. Allen & Chever* (Updike vs. Bull); *Coggeshall v. Coggeshall* (Updike vs. Honeyman & Robinson); *Gardner v. Martin* (Bull & Updike vs. Ward); *Martin v. Gibbs* (Bull & Updike vs. Honeyman).

2. Petition of Nathaniel Newdigate et al. (Oct. 1736) in Petitions to the General Assembly (RISA), vol. 3, p. 74. The petition wanted to replace the old rule that one of the two attorneys had to be an inhabitant with a requirement that both should be.

3. "Agreement among Attorneys" (Sept. 1745) (JRC); Updike, *Memoirs,* pp. 294–295. Other attorneys were John Aplin, John Walton, Matthew Robinson, David Richards Jr., and John Andrews. Walton and Andrews had both served as the attorney for Providence County during 1741 and 1742. Updike, *Memoirs,* p. 21. The fees were: an inferior court case necessitating an answer, forty shillings "or more"; a case pled in the Superior Court, at least three pounds; one requiring a writ of review, four pounds. If an unreasonable attorney continued to demand fees, "the whole Fraternity shall rise up against him."

4. Marcus A. McCorison, ed., *The 1764 Catalogue of the Redwood Library Company at Newport, Rhode Island* (New Haven: Yale University Press, 1965), pp. ix, 8, 14. Law Books in the Redwood Library (c. 1750): Roger Acherley, *The Britannic Constitution*, 1741, 2nd ed.; Hugo Grotius, *The Rights of War and Peace,* 1739; *The Grounds and Rudiments of Law and Equity, alphabetically digested;* Matthew Hale, *Historia Placitorum Coronae: The History of the Pleas of the Crown,* 1736, 2 vols.; William Hawkins, *A Treatise of the Pleas of the Crown,* 1739, 3rd ed.; Giles Jacob, *A New Law-Dictionary;* Giles Jacob, *The Common Law Common-plac'd,* 1733; Job Mill, *The present practice of Conveyancing,* 1745; Samuel Pufendorf, *Of the Law of Nature and Nations,* 1729, 4th ed.; Charles Viner, *A General Abridgment of Law and Equity* (Aldershot), 1742–1748, 14 vols.; Thomas Wood, *An Institute of the Laws of England,* 1738, 6th ed.; Thomas Wood, *A New Institute of the Imperial or Civil Law,* 1730, 4th ed.; Matthew Hale, *The History of the Common Law of England,* 1716, 2nd ed.; Giles Jacob, *The Statute-Law Common-plac'd: or, a General table to the statutes,* 1748, 5th ed.; William Bohun, *Institutio Legalis; or, Introduction to the study and practice of the laws of England,* 1724, 3rd ed.; William Bohun, *The English Lawyer . . .,* 1732; William Hawkins, *A Summary of the Crown Law . . .,* 1728, 2 vols.; Edward Coke, *An Abridgment of the First Part of . . . Coke's Institutes,* ed. William Hawkins, 1742, 6th ed.; *The Law of Evidence,* 1744, 3rd ed.; Giles Duncombe, *Trials per Pais: or, the Law concerning juries by nisi prius, etc.,* 1725, 6th ed.; William Nelson, *The Office and Authority of a Justice of Peace,* 1729, 10th ed., 2 vols.; Joseph Higgs, *A Guide to Justices,* 1734; *The Compleat Sheriff . . .* and *A Methodical Treatise of Replevins, Distresses, Avoweries, &c.,* 1710, 2nd ed. and 1718; Samuel Forster, *A Digest of all the Laws relating to the Customs, to Trade, and Navigation,* 1727; *General Treatise on Naval Trade and Commerce* (1753), 2 vols.; *Reports and Cases of Practice in the Court of Common Pleas,* 1747, 2nd. ed., 2 vols.; Geoffrey Gilbert, *The History and Practice of the Court of Common Pleas,* 1737; *Laws, Ordinances and Institutions of the Admiralty of Great Britain, Civil and Military,* 1746, 2 vols.; Francis Clerke, *Praxis Curiae Admiralitatis Angliae. Lat. & Angl.,* likely 1722; Geoffrey Gilbert, *An Historical View of the Court of Exchequer . . .,* 1738; Christopher St. German, *Two Dialogues in English, between a Doctor of Divinity, and a Student in the Laws of England . . .,* 1709, rev. ed.; *Tenants Law: or, the Laws concerning landlords, tenants and farmers,* 1750, 13th ed.; Christopher Tancred, *An Essay for a General Regulation of the Law,* 1727, 2nd ed.; *The Complete Constable; Directing constables . . .,* 1728, 8th ed.; Samuel Pufendorf, *Of the Law of Nature and Nations,* ed. J. Spavan, 1716, 2 vols.; *Select Trials at the Session-House of the Old Bailey,* 1742–1743, 4 vols.
5. Petition of Newdigate et al. (Oct. 1736), in Petitions to the General Assembly (RISA), vol. 3, p. 74.

6. See *Sanford v. Wood and Allen* (Wanton, Coddington, and Willett in dissent); Mary Coggeshall's case (Helme & Wickes in dissent); Ann Sabeere's case (Wickes, Helme, Jencks, and Cranston in dissent). These cases are discussed in detail in chapter 5. The problem of split decisions on legal issues in the evenly divided inferior courts caused problems. When the "Court is divided in Opinion" on a plea in abatement or bar, the action proceeded to the jury to the disadvantage of the defendant; when the jury returned a special verdict and the court was divided on the opinion of "determination agreeable with law," the case was continued from one term to another. In 1737 a fifth justice was added, resolving the problem. "An Act appointing a Fifth Justice in each of the Inferior Courts" (Nov. 1737) in *Acts and Laws, Of His Majesty's Colony of Rhode-Island, and Providence-Plantations, In New-England* (Newport: Printed by the Widow Franklin, 1745) (hereafter, *Acts and Laws* [1745]), p. 201.

7. J. Fred Parker, *Manual with Rules and Orders for the Use of the General Assembly* (Providence: E. L. Freeman, 1910), pp. 244–245.

8. Jeremy Dummer to Gov. Talcott (Middle Temple, Aug. 24, 1726), *CHS Coll.*, vol. 4, pp. 79–80. On Paris, see James Allen to Talcott (Boston, Jan. 25, 1738/1739), ibid., vol. 5, pp. 72–73, 74 n. * (quoting Palfrey). On Sharpe, see Belcher to Talcott (Apr. 23, 1730), ibid., vol. 4, p. 197.

9. Paris to Allen (July 28, 1734), *CHS Coll.*, vol. 5, pp. 74, 85–86.

10. For positions, see *A List of English Law Officers King's Counsel and Holders of Patents Precedence,* (London: Selden Society), pp. 48–49, 65, 93–94, 277. For discussion of salary, see J. L. J. Edwards, *The Law Officers of the Crown* (London: Sweet & Maxwell, 1964), pp. 4, 32, 70–72, 119. For discussion in prize appeals, see James Oldham, "The Work of Ryder and Murray as Law Officers of the Crown," in *Legal Record and Historical Reality*, ed. T. G. Watkin (Ronceverte: Hambledon Press, 1989). Law officers on extant briefs include: *Rous v. Hassard* (1750) (D. Ryder & W. Murray for appellant); *MacSparran v. Hassard* (1752) (W. Murray vs. D. Ryder, A. Hume-Campbell); *Potter v. Freeborn* (1752) (Al. Forrester for respondent); *Rodman v. Banister* (W. Murray & Al. Forrester for appellant); *Freebody v. Cook* (1754) (Al. Forrester vs. W. Murray); *Whipple v. Bowen* (1757) (Al. Forrester for respondent); *Isaacks v. Merrett* (1758) (Al. Forrester vs. C. Pratt); *Stanton v. Thompson* (1759) (Al. Forrester & Fredk. Campbell vs. C. Pratt & C. Yorke); *Larkin v. Yorke* (1761) (C. Pratt & Al. Forrester vs. C. Yorke & Tho. Sewall); *Potter v. Hazard* (1763) (Fl. Norton & J. Gardiner vs. C. Yorke & Al. Forrester); *Freebody v. Brenton* (1764) (Tho. Sewall & Al. Forrester vs. C. Ambler & C. Yorke); *Shearman v. Cornell* (1766) (C. Yorke & Al. Forrester for appellant); *Lewis v. Wilkinson* (1766) (Al. Forrester & Rd. Jackson vs. C. Yorke & J. Dunning); *Freebody v. Brenton*

(1769) (Wm. De Grey & Rd. Jackson vs. C. Yorke & C. Ambler). From [Charles Yorke] briefs in the British Library, Additional Mss. 15489, 36216–38220, and [George Lee] briefs, Great Britain, Privy Council, Judicial Committee, Library of Congress, Law Division, Rare Books. For similar names on prize appeals held by William Lee and George Lee, see Prize Appeals, 1736–1758, 2 vols. (New York Public Library); Paul Leicester Ford, *List of Some Briefs in Appeals Causes . . . 1736–1758* (n.d.; repr., New York: Burt Franklin, 1971).

11. On *Winthrop,* see Paris to James Allen, *CHS Coll.,* vol. 5, pp. 74, 77–78, 84 (July 26, 1738). On retention of Strange and Murray, see ibid., p. 84. For Wilks comment, see Wilks to Talcott (Nov. 27, 1740), ibid., p. 330.

12. Paris to Allen, *CHS Coll.,* vol. 5, pp. 78, 81. For 1760 appeal, see *Dering v. Packer* (1760), Box 173, folder 1, Malbone/Brinley Collection (NHS).

13. Edward Raymond Turner, *The Privy Council of England in the Seventeenth and Eighteenth Centuries* (Baltimore: Johns Hopkins University Press, 1928), vol. 2, pp. 295, 297, 377. The Committee practice began in 1696 and was continued in 1714 and 1727. Ibid., pp. 357–358, 381, 383, 394–395, 421–423. On Lee, see John Campbell, *The Lives of the Chief Justices of England* (London: John Murray, 1899), vol. 2, p. 214. For example, in *Wood v. Allen* (1729), the Committee consisted of the Privy Seal, the Earl of Sussex, Viscount Townshend, the Bishop of London, Lord Wilmington, and the Speaker. PC 2/91/69. In March 1730, the Committee consisted of the Privy Seal, Townshend, Viscount Lonsdale, Wilmington, and Chief Justice Raymond. Ibid., p. 191. In December 1730 the Committee consisted of the Privy Seal, the Earl of Islay, the Bishop of London, Chief Justice Raymond, and Horatio Walpole. Ibid., p. 302. In December 1766 the Committee consisted of the President, the Duke of Queenbury, the Earl of Marchant, and the Earl of Hillsborough, Lord Sandys, and Chief Justice Wilmot. PC 2/112/104. In 1768 the Committee consisted of the President, Hillsborough, the Master of the Rolls and Chief Justice Wilmot. Ibid., p. 244.

14. For Lee, see *Boyde v. Johnson* (St. Christophers, June 19, 1738) (W. Murray, G. Lee) and *Rous v. Hassard* (Rhode Island, April 2, 1750) (G. Lee's notes on brief as Lord Chief Justice), [George Lee] Briefs, Great Britain, Privy Council, Judicial Committee, Library of Congress, Law Division, Rare Books. On Mansfield comments, see *Dering v. Packer* (1760), Box 173, folder 1, Malbone/Brinley Collection (NHS).

15. Paris to James Allen, *CHS Coll.,* vol. 5, pp. 78–79 (July 26, 1738).

16. "An Act for Regulating Appeals to His Majesty in Council in Great-Britain, and for Repealing the former Act made for that Purpose," in *Acts and Laws* (1746), p. 30 (raising the 1719 amount-in-controversy limit to 150

pounds sterling); "An Act for Establishing of Inferior Courts . . .," in *Acts and Laws, Of His Majesty's Colony of Rhode-Island, and Providence-Plantations, In America* (Newport: Printed by James Franklin, 1730) (hereafter, *Acts and Laws* [1730]), p. 192 (regulating appeals). For Smith's discussion of the various minimums, see Smith, *Appeals,* pp. 216–234. On Mary Taylor's case, see Copy Case (June 1748), *Taylor v. Clark* (Providence, Sept. 1748) (JRC); *SCJ Recs.,* (Providence) (JRC), p. 29 (Sept. 1748), pp. 33–35 (Mar. 1748/1749); *APC,* vol. 4, pp. 92–93.

17. "Thomas Sanford of London, Merchant in William Gardner, an Infant, by Mrs. Abigail Gardner, his Grandmother & Guardian, Respondent to the Appeal of Mr. James Martin, Appellant from Rhode Island (1738)," *Gardner v. Martin* (SCJ, Sept. 1739) (JRC).

18. For correspondence relating to a 1728 Connecticut case and a "print" being shown in Boston about a decision, see Talcott to Belcher (May 29, 1728), *CHS Coll.,* vol. 4, pp. 116–117. One extant handwritten brief survives in *Freebody v. Cook* (1754) but it may be a copy. The Privy Council briefs are identical to those for appeals in admiralty and the House of Lords.

19. On the Sanfords, see Petition of Grizzel Cotton et al. to Governor and General Assembly (Feb. 1734/1735) in Petitions to the General Assembly (RISA), vol. 3, p. 41, and *E. Johnson* (SCJ, Sept. 1735) (JRC); *R.I.G.A. Recs.,* (RISA), 1729–1745, p. 214. The Council dismissed the appeal for nonprosecution, and Johnson's later appeal was withdrawn in 1736. *Arnold v. Johnson* (SCJ, Newport, Sept. 1737) (JRC); *GCT/SCJ Recs.,* Book B, pp. 475, 508 (JRC). Johnson's bond was given to Arnold in 1737. Ibid, p. 601. On the writ of review, see "An Act for Review in real Actions relating to Titles of Lands" in *Laws and Acts* (1730), pp. 247–248 (permitting trial of land titles with "new and further Evidence" for the defense). On bond, see *Gardner v. Martin* (SCJ, Sept. 1739) (JRC); *GCT/SCJ Recs.,* Book B, pp. 656, 666 (ordering Martin's bond of £300 to Gardner) (JRC). For argument, see Declaration (July 1739) in Copy Case, *Gardner v. Martin* (SCJ, Sept. 1739) (JRC); *R.I. Law Cases* (RISA), vol. 9, pp. 55–56 (Oct. 1739). For the 1750 act, see *R.I. Recs.,* vol. 5, pp. 311 (Oct. 1750), 316 (Dec. 1750) (act not retrospective).

20. On the Molasses Act, see Charles M. Andrews, *The Colonial Period in American History* (New Haven: Yale University Press, 1934), vol. 4, pp. 242–243. For first appeal, see *Allen & Chever v. Brown* (SCJ, Newport, Mar. 1737) (JRC); *R.I. Law Cases,* vol. 7, pp. 1, 2, 34; vol. 9, p. 22; *R.I. Recs.,* 1729–1745, pp. 274 (May 1737), 361 (Aug. 1739); PC 2/94/481, 536, 556–558, 591 (1738). On the second appeal, see *SCJ Recs.* (Newport), Book C, pp. 243–244 (Oct. 1744), 444 (Sept. 1746) (JRC); PC 2/100/274,

PC 2/102/177, 178, 186–187, 210. On Wanton, see Dorothy S. Towle, ed., *Records of the Vice-Admiralty Court of Rhode Island, 1716–1752* (Washington D.C.: American Historical Association, 1936), pp. 224–226, 473–474. A few other cases after 1750 involved molasses and privateers: *Grant & Heatley v. Dyre* (1753–1755) (molasses conversion), *Moss v. Hopkins* (1757–1759) (privateer), as well as possibly *Whitfield v. Creaugh* (1758–1760) and *Simons v. Wanton* (1758–1762). After 1760 these cases disappear, but they reappear again briefly before the Revolution.

21. See "The Overzealous Privateer," in Zechariah Chafee Jr., "Records of the Rhode Island Court of Equity, 1741–1743," in *Publications of the Colonial Society of Massachusetts, Transactions, 1942–1946* (Boston: Colonial Society of Massachusetts, 1951), vol. 35, pp. 108–110; *Hazzard et al. v. Rous* (SCJ, Newport, 1743) (JRC); PC 2/99/369 (Feb. 1745/1746); *APC,* vol. 4, p. 14 (Apr. 1750).

22. Powers's intent comes from John Rous, who recounted that the captain stated that he had "all nations aboard" as slaves and had said that some were "of poor Powers Indians." Deposition of John Rous, Copy Case, *Power v. Vanbrugh & Carpenter* (SCJ, Newport, Mar. 1744) (JRC). The 1741 order of the Jamaican governor, Edward Trelawny, is in Deposition of David Vanbrugh (Mar. 1741/1742), ibid. The admiralty court had initially awarded the captives to one John Bargos. Vanbrugh and Carpenter apparently were in charge of prosecuting the suit to keep the Indians but never appealed the judgment against Powers. It is not clear that the Rhode Island damages (£459.13.4 Jamaican currency) were for the Indians; however, it seems conceivable, as one group of Rhode Island auditors completely refused to audit the accounts. For the 1751 case, see *APC,* vol. 4, p. 24; PC 2/102/240, 262, 330–332, 352. For an earlier 1746–1748 appeal by Powers, dismissed for nonprosecution, see PC 2/99/534; *Powers v. Vanbrugh* (SCJ, Newport, Mar. 1748) (JRC). Rhode Island had banned Indian slavery in 1675–1676. Barbados and Jamaica banned importation in 1676. See Margaret Ellen Newell, "The Changing Nature of Indian Slavery in New England," in *Reinterpreting New England Indians and the Colonial Experience,* ed. Colin G. Calloway and Neal Salisbury (Boston: Colonial Society of Massachusetts, 2003), pp. 106–136.

23. For the quote, see Maria L. Cioni, *Women and Law in Elizabethan England, with particular reference to the Court of Chancery* (New York: Garland, 1985), p. 18. On the Brenton family case, see Reasons of Appeal, Copy Case, *Benjamin Brenton v. Gersham Remington* (SCJ, Newport, Sept. 1745) (JRC); *SCJ Recs.* (Newport), Book C, p. 389 (Mar. 1746) (JRC); PC 2/102/142–143, 208–209. On the legacy case, see *Potter v. Freeborn* (SCJ, Newport, Mar. 1744) (JRC); *SCJ Recs.* (Newport), Book C, p. 113 (Mar. 1743)

(JRC); 188 (Mar. 1744); Reasons of appeal, *R.I. Equity Cases* (RISA), vol. 7, case 1 (April 1744); PC 2/103/155, 158, 177. For the refusal to probate the Tripp will, see *Benjamin Tripp v. Town Council of Newport* (1741), Governor and Council File Records (RISA), Folder 4, p. 158 (Aug. 1741). For case, see *Tripp v. Tripp* (SCJ, Newport, Mar. 1745) (two files) (JRC); *SCJ Recs.* (Newport), Book C (JRC), pp. 171 (Sept. 1743), 246 (Oct. 1744), 282 (Mar. 1745); PC 2/102/403–405, 427–428; *APC,* vol. 4, pp. 36–37; *Tripp v. Redwood* (SCJ, Newport, August 1755) (JRC) (suit by Benjamin on the bond). As solicitor, Fortherly Baker had drawn a "long brief for council of observations on the whole affair" with a fee of fifty-seven pounds for the "extraordinary trouble in this affair." See bill of account of Fortherly Baker to Mathew Robinson (1753), *Tripp v. Redwood* (SCJ, Newport, Aug. 1755) (JRC). For the 1755 bond dispute, see *SCJ Recs.* (Newport), Book E, p. 27 (JRC).

24. For the quote, see Thomas Wood, *An Institute of the Laws of England,* 3rd ed. (1724; repr., New York: Garland, 1978), p. 462. Blackstone noted, "it would be endless to point out all the several avenues in human affairs, and in this commercial age, which lead to or end in accounts." William Blackstone, *Commentaries on the Laws of England* (1765–1769; repr., Chicago: University of Chicago Press, 1979), vol. 3, p. 437. For Fogg's case, see Copy Case, *Fogg v. Harvey* (SCJ, Newport, Mar. 1744) (JRC), *SCJ Recs.* (Newport), Book C, p. 189 (Mar. 1744) (JRC); *R.I. Law Cases,* vol. 7 (RISA). In 1745, Harvey argued that Fogg appealed "for the sake of unjustly delaying the payment." PC 2/99/225, 242, 260–261, 268; *APC,* vol. 4, p. 10. On Polock, see Order in Council, *Verplank v. Polock* (SCJ, Newport, Mar. 1746) (JRC); *APC,* vol. 4, p. 36.

25. See *Wheelwright v. Tyler* (SCJ, Newport, Mar. 1747/48) (JRC); *SCJ Recs.* (Newport), Book D, p. 76 (Mar. 1747/48) (JRC); PC 2/102/391, 427; *APC,* vol. 4, pp. 84–85.

26. For the quote, see Wood, *Institute,* 3rd ed., p. 462. On the case, see *Sheldon v. Gibbs* (SCJ, Newport, Mar. & Sept. 1744), (SCJ, Providence, Mar. 1744) (eight folders) (JRC); *SCJ Record Book* (Providence), pp. 45 (Sept. 1749), 65–66 (Sept. 1750) (JRC).

27. For the quote, see Wood, *Institute,* 3rd ed., p. 462. On the case, see *Channing v. Fenner, SCJ Recs.* (Providence) (JRC), p. 23 (Sept. 1748); PC 2/102/444, 456–459, 464 (Jan. 1752/1753).

28. On the colony's participation, see Sydney V. James, *Colonial Rhode Island: A History* (New York: Scribner's, 1975), pp. 267–76. The four dismissed cases were *Fogg v. Harvey* (appealed 1744); *Staniford v. Newell* (appealed 1744); *Gibbs v. Sheldon* (appealed 1744); *Polock v. Verplank* (appealed 1745). The accusation of delay comes from the Committee Report in *Fogg*

v. Harvey, a commercial paper case. For facts, see *Fogg v. Harvey* (SCJ, Newport, Mar. 1744) (JRC); *SCJ Recs.,* Book C (JRC), p. 189; *R.I. Equity Cases* (RISA), vol. 7, cases 10 and 18; PC 2/99/225, 242, 268; *APC,* vol. 4, p. 10. On Staniford, see Reasons of Appeal (Mar. 1744), *Staniford v. Newell* (SCJ, Newport, Mar. 1744) (JRC); *SCJ Recs.* (Newport), Book C (JRC), p. 179 (Mar. 1744). On the Clemences, see Deposition of Elizabeth Clemence (daughter), Copy Case, *Angel v. Clemence* (SCJ, Providence, 1744) (JRC); *SCJ Recs.* (Providence), pp. 36–37 (Mar. 1748/1749) (JRC). For appeals never filed, see, e.g., *Job Briggs* (Mar. 1744), *SCJ Recs.* (Newport), Book C, pp. 227–228 (requesting appeal) (JRC); *Nathan Nathans & Israel v. Frances Lewis* (1744), *SCJ Recs.* (Newport), Book C, pp. 227–228 (granting appeal to Privy Council).

29. On the Ninigrets, see James, *Colonial Rhode Island,* pp. 82, 94–99, 142–143, 256; Sydney V. James, *The Colonial Metamorphoses in Rhode Island: A Study of Institutions in Change,* ed. Sheila L. Skemp and Bruce C. Daniels (Hanover: University Press of New England, 2000), pp. 141–143. For a 1718 discussion of whether statutes of limitations applied to the sachem lands, see *R.I. Recs.* vol. 4, pp. 229–233. On trustees, see ibid., vol. 4, pp. 316, 344, 390–391, 397, 450–451, 550; vol. 5, pp. 25–26, 38. For the family relationship, see *R.I. Recs.,* vol. 5, pp. 122–123, 156. On Catherine's suit, see *SCJ Recs.* (Newport), Book C, pp. 148–149 (JRC).

30. For Sarah's suit, see *SCJ Recs.* (Newport), Book C, p. 439 (Sept. 1746) (appeal granted) (JRC). For the petition, see *R.I. Recs.,* vol. 5, pp. 221–224 (Aug. 1747). For Ninigret's petition, see *R.I. Recs.,* p. 378 (1753). For the canceled bond, see *Ninigret v. Shish & Tindal* (SCJ, Washington, Aug. 1755). For an excellent discussion of Thomas Ninigret and the role of attorney Matthew Robinson, see John Wood Sweet, "Bodies Politic: Colonialism: Race and the Emergence of the American North, Rhode Island, 1730–1830" (Ph.D. diss., Princeton University, 1995), pp. 16–156; *R.I. Recs.,* vol. 4, p. 232 (1718).

31. For the petition, see *R.I. Recs.,* vol. 6, p. 221 (1759). For the tribal petition, see ibid., p. 357 (June 1763). For Assembly action, see ibid., pp. 366 (Aug. 1763), 402 (1764). On further debt, land sale, and tribal matters (1767–1768), see ibid., pp. 530, 533, 564, 574–575, 589. On the Fort Neck sale, see ibid., vol. 6, pp. 599–600, and vol. 7, p. 46. On post-Ninigret negotiations, see ibid., vol. 7, pp. 9–10, 15 (petition of Esther Sachem), 17–18, 214–215, 223.

32. See *Gardner v. Martin* (1739) (JRC) (Council Order dismissing appeal); *Gardner v. Martin,* in *R.I. Law Cases* (RISA), vol. 9, p. 56; *R.I.G.A. Recs.* (RISA), 1729–1745, p. 377 (Jan. 1739/1740) (introducing orders from *Pelham v. Coggeshall* [1735] and *Arnold v. Johnson* [1735]).

33. For the Wilks quote, see Wilks to Talcott (Nov. 1740), *CHS Coll.*, vol. 5, p. 330. For Rhode Island law, see "An Act, for Distribution and Settling of Intestates Estates" (May 1718) in *Acts and Laws, Of His Majesties Colony of Rhode-Island, and Providence-Plantations, In America* (Boston: Printed by John Allen, for Nicholas Boone, 1719), reprinted in *Earliest Acts*, pp. 95–98. For the February 1728/1729 repealing act, see *Acts and Laws* (1730), p. 182; *R.I. Recs.*, vol. 4, p. 417. On the larger English and colonial debate, see Carole Shammas, *Inheritance in America from Colonial Times to the Present* (New Brunswick: Rutgers University Press, 1987), pp. 32–34. On *Winthrop*, see the note in *CHS Coll.*, vol. 4, pp. 4, 94–97; Smith, *Appeals*, pp. 569–572. For the letter about vacating and voiding intestate law, see Talcott to General Assembly (May 1728), *CHS Coll.*, vol. 4, pp. 114–115. For another account, see Extracts from Hempstead's Diary, *CHS Coll.*, vol. 4, p. 389 ("May 31, 1729: "hear the news from Great Britain, wch is that the King & Council hath Repealed our Law for Dividing Intestate Estates"). For comment that the issue was lack of power in the charter "to make laws for the dividing of property, and the descent of real estate," see Talcott to Belcher (May 1728), ibid., pp. 116–117. For Jonathan Law's argument that the law might be of "so antient standing" as to have been comparable to "the general and particular customs in England, which are unalterable by any thing, short of an Act of Parliament," see Law to Talcott (June 1728), ibid., pp. 118–120; Law to Talcott (June 1728) (discussing *Chancery Cases* and Coke), ibid., pp. 120–123 (quote at p. 122). For arguments that the colony should have the right to make its own laws not contrary to the law of England and citing *Blankard*, see Instructions to Belcher (Dec. [1728]), ibid., pp. 143–158. The double portion to the eldest son also was briefly mentioned in the Bible; the standard reference is Deuteronomy, chapter 21.

34. For post-case practice, see Talcott to Council (Sept. 1729), *CHS Coll.*, vol. 4, pp. 172–174; Talcott to Dummer (July 1730), ibid., pp. 203–204; Talcott to Wilks (Oct. 1730), ibid., pp. 210–211. For Belcher's comments, see Belcher to Talcott (London, May 1729), ibid., pp. 167–168; see also other 1729 letters, ibid., pp. 169–175. For the governor's concern, see Talcott to Dummer and Belcher (Nov. 1729), ibid., pp. 174–180. On petition, see ibid., (Feb. 1729/1730), pp. 187–190; Belcher to Talcott (Apr. 1720), ibid., pp. 197–198. On 1730 Committee report, see ibid., pp. 200–201. On threat to charter, see Letters among Wilks, Dummer, and Talcott (Feb.–Apr. 1731), ibid., pp. 216–223. For new plan, see Talcott to Wilks (June 1731 [draft]), ibid., pp. 232–234 (noting that the attorney general had acknowledged that they did not have to transmit their laws). On primogeniture concern, see Wilks to Talcott (Oct. 1731), ibid., pp. 240–242.

For Law's comment, see Law to Wilks [draft] [1732?], ibid., pp. 260–261. For the distinction between real estate and personal estates covered by statute laws in force before the first settlements, as well as any that were expressly mentioned or enacted, see Wilks to Talcott (Apr. 1733), ibid., pp. 272–276. Talcott disagreed: "it's a thing not generally received that the Statute Laws of England, as to such as were in force prior to the first settlement of the Plantation" are laws "any more than those made subsequent" to the settlement. Talcott to Wilks (Nov. 1733), ibid., p. 293.

35. For Paris, see Paris to James Allen, *CHS Coll.,* vol. 5, pp. 72, 78, 81 (July 1738). On Allen comment, see Allen to Talcott (Nov. 1738), ibid., p. 71; Allen to Talcott (Jan. 1738), ibid., pp. 72–73. On *Clark v. Tousey,* see Smith, *Appeals,* pp. 572–578. On history of intestate statutes of 1718 and 1770, see *Smith v. Smith,* 4 R.I. 1, 8–10 (1854).

36. Quotations are from the Assembly record (Oct. 1749), Rhode Island Colony Records, 1746–1757 (RISA), p. 175; *R.I. Recs.,* vol. 5, pp. 276–277. For the petition, see Petition to General Assembly (Oct. 1749) in Petitions to the General Assembly (RISA), vol. 7, p. 35. The petition did not identify the case, but it was likely from the March or September 1749 term. Two possibilities are *Taylor v. Clark* (March 1749) or *Walker v. Paget* (September 1749), both appealed to the Privy Council. *Taylor* involved dower and jointure and has been discussed above. *Taylor v. Clark* (SCJ, Providence, Sept. 1748) (JRC). *Walker* asked whether a recent English statute could be read to the jury. The widow of a deceased debtor had moved to England and sued for her dower in Rhode Island. The defendant had acquired the lands through a foreclosure sale pursuant to English and colonial statutes. In 1736, the colony passed notification procedures to attach real estate of people who moved out of the colony. "An Act for making the Real Estates of Persons that have left this Colony, or conceal themselves therein; or do not live in this Government liable to the Payment of debts" in *Acts and Laws* (1730), pp. 278–280. The colony courts concluded that her dower right could not be defeated by her husband's debts or the foreclosure sale. The widow's attorney successfully prevented the defendant's attorney from reading an English act to the jury. The case file has been lost, but the act may have been a 1732 English statute providing that "houses, lands, negroes, and other hereditaments and real estates" in the plantations "shall and may be assets for the satisfaction" of debts as were "real estate . . . by the law of England." "An Act for the more easy recovery of debts in his Majesty's plantations and colonies in America," 5 Geo. II, c. 7 (1732). The Superior Court, however, barred the widow's action. In 1754, the Privy Council heard the case without the appellee's appearance. It reversed, finding that the widow and her son should have the lands. For debt judgments,

see copy case, *Walker v. Paget* (JRC). On the 1747–1749 dower suit, see
SCJ Recs., (Providence), pp. 2, 13, 28–29, 4 (JRC). On the Council proceedings, see PC 2/103/74, 78, 110, 169, 188; *APC,* vol. 4, p. 164. On
a 1754 suit by the widow against Paget, see *SCJ Recs.* (Providence), p. 133
(JRC). On Paget, see Gertrude Selwyn Kimball, *Providence in Colonial
Times* (Boston: Houghton Mifflin, 1912) pp. 170–177. *Peirce v. Rice* would
be a good candidate but appears to have been argued in 1750. Sydney V.
James, "Why Is There a Kent County?" *Rhode Island History,* vol. 47, no. 3,
pp. 96–106 (1989).

37. For the act, see Rhode Island Colony Records, 1747–1757 (RISA), p. 183;
R.I. Recs., vol. 5, p. 289 (Feb. 1749/50); Updike, *Memoirs,* pp. 54–58. The
provisions according to the manuscript version were: "The statute of Merton concerning dower" (Henry III, 20; the first two chapters); the statutes of "Westminster the first as far as it concerns bail" (3 Edw. 15);
"Glocester" (6 Edw. 1 [1278], writs for property, damages done to property, waste, trespass, and other judicial writs); "Westminster, the second,
de donis conditionalibus" (the Statute De Donis, 13 Edward 1 [1285], creating fee tail); "First Henry the 5th, chap. 5th, of additions" (requirements
for writ pleading); "partition, in general"; "Thirty-second of Henry the 8th,
concerning leases, saving and excepting the last paragraph"; "Twenty-first
James 1st Chap. 16 for limiting real actions: and that of 32 of Henry 8th,
chap. 2" (the statutes of limitations); "James & Elizabeth, and all other
statutes that concern bastardy, as applicable to the constitution of this colony"; "All statutes that are against criminal offenders, so far as they are de-
scriptive of the crime, and where the law of this colony hath not described
and enjoined the punishment, then that part of the statute that relates to
the punishment, also; always saving and excepting such statutes, as from
the nature of the offences mentioned in them, are confined to Great Britain, only"; "The statute of Henry III, commonly called the Statute of Uses"
(27 Hen. 8 [1536], executing the uses; "The statute of 29 Charles 2d,
chap. 3d, commonly called the Statute of Frauds and Perjuries" (1677)
(land transactions to be in writing); "The statutes of the 22d & 23d Char.
the 2d, chap. 10, for distributing the estates of intestates" (the Statute of
Distribution); "The statute of 3 & 4 William & Mary, c. 14" (a 1691 act for
relief of creditors against fraudulent devises, permitting creditors to attach
the land of deceased debtors); "The statute of 4th & 5th Anne, chap. 16th,
relating to joint tenants, and tenants in common" (permitting actions of
account among such tenants; the statute is 4 & 5 Anne, c. 3 (1705) (annexed to the act on a separate schedule), *The Statutes of the Realm* (1822;
repr., London: Dawsons, 1966), vol. 8, p. 461; Wood's *Institute* cited it as 3
& 4 Ann., c. 16, Wood, *Institute,* 3rd ed., p. 148.; "that part of the statute of

[regnal year omitted] Ann[e], that subjects lessees that hold over their terms against the will of the lessor, to the payment of double rent, during the time they hold over" (the standard citations for the double rent hold-over statute are 4 Geo. 2, c. 28 (1730) and 11 Geo. 2, c. 19 (1738); 8 Anne, c. 18 (1709) involved the "better security of rents" but stated nothing explicit about double rents for tenants at sufferance, *The Statutes of the Realm* (1822; repr., London: Dawsons, 1966), vol. 9, pp. 247–248); "all statutes relating to the poor, and relating to masters and their apprentices; so far as they are applicable in this colony, and where we have no law of the colony." For treatise citations, see Edward Coke, *The Institutes of the Laws of England* (1797 ed.), Second Part, vol. 1, pp. 78–100, 184–186, 330, 664–665; Wood, *Institute,* 3rd ed., pp. 122, 125, 148, 557–558, 609. For a discussion of the statutes, see J. H. Baker, *Introduction to English Legal History,* 3rd ed. (London: Butterworth, 1990), pp. 311–312, 322–328, 338, 342, 396–398, 436. The similarity between the property law issues debated under the transatlantic constitution and the modern distinction between "English" and "American" rules in common-law property doctrine suggests that the transatlantic constitution is the origin for many of these controversies.

38. The concern over the colony laws and the laws of England continued in other legal areas. In 1750, the new county courts were made as "subject to all the laws of this colony, now in force, and the laws of England, in every respect, as fully and effectually, to all intents and purposes" as the other courts. *R.I. Recs.,* vol. 5, p. 303. In 1712, South Carolina had put in force a list of statutes, and in 1715, North Carolina passed a general act. On the acts, see Elizabeth Gaspar Brown, *British Statutes in American Law, 1776–1836* (Ann Arbor: University of Michigan Law School, 1964), pp. 17–18; "An Act to put in Force in this Province the several Statutes of the Kingdom of England . . .," in *Laws of the Province of South-Carolina,* ed. Nicholas Trott (Charlestown: Printed for Lewis Timothy, 1736), p. 37; "An Act for the more effectual observing of the Queen's Peace . . .," in *Laws of North Carolina,* ed. James Iredell (Edenton: Printed by Hodge and Wills, 1791), p. 17. In 1749, North Carolina passed another act, disallowed by the Privy Council in 1754. Brown, *British Statutes in American Law,* pp. 360–377.

7. Religious Establishment and Orthodoxy

1. For accounts of the case, see Wilkins Updike, *A History of the Episcopal Church in Narragansett, Rhode Island,* ed. Daniel Goodwin, 2nd ed. (Boston: D. B. Updike, Merrymount Press, 1907), vol. 1, p. 82; Clifford K. Shipton, *Sibley's Harvard Graduates: Biographical Sketches of Those Who Attended*

Harvard College in the Classes 1726–1730 (Boston: MHS, 1951), vol. 8, pp. 498–507. For more details, see Mary Sarah Bilder, "Salamanders and Sons of God: Transatlantic Legal Culture and Colonial Rhode Island" (Ph.D. diss., Harvard University, 2000), 416–503.

2. The description of the Church of England is drawn from Sydney E. Ahlstrom, *A Religious History of the American People* (New Haven: Yale University Press, 1972), pp. 96–97, 218–220; John Walsh and Stephen Taylor, "Introduction: The Church and Anglicanism in the 'Long Eighteenth Century,'" in *The Church of England c. 1689–c.1833: From Toleration to Tractarianism,* ed. John Walsh, Colin Haydon, and Stephen Taylor (Cambridge: Cambridge University Press, 1993), pp. 1–64. For the instructions, see Leonard Woods Labaree, ed., *Royal Instructions to British Colonial Governors, 1670–1776* (New York: Appleton-Century, 1935), vol. 2, p. 482–483. Although it is anachronistic, I use MacSparran's term *episcopal* to emphasize the difference in church structure.

3. For the quote, see John Frederick Woolverton, *Colonial Anglicanism in North America* (Detroit: Wayne State University Press, 1984), p. 88 (quoting Thomas Bray, *A Memorial Representing the Present State of Religion on the Continent of North America* [1700], p. 9). For contemporary correspondence over Massachusetts's practices, see Daniel Neal, *The History of New-England Containing an Impartial Account of the Civil and Ecclesiastical Affairs of the Country to the Year of Our Lord, 1700* (1720); J. Watts to Benjamin Colman (Feb. 11, 1719/1720), in Benjamin Colman Papers, 1641–1763 (MHS) (hereafter, Colman Papers). On the congregational church, see J. William T. Youngs, *The Congregationalists* (New York: Greenwood Press, 1990), p. 3. On the presbyterians, see Randall Balmer and John R. Firzmier, *The Presbyterians* (Westport: Greenwood Press, 1993); Alexander Blaikie, *A History of Presbyterianism in New England* (Boston: Alexander Moore, 1881); Ahlstrom, *Religious History,* p. 267. The religious history of early New England is more complicated and nuanced than can be properly addressed in this limited discussion.

4. William G. McLoughlin, *New England Dissent, 1630–1833: The Baptists and the Separation of Church and State* (Cambridge, Mass.: Harvard University Press, 1971), vol. 1, p. 10. The law is An Act, Regulating the Maintenance of Ministers within this Colony (May 1716), in *Acts and Laws, Of His Majesties Colony of Rhode-Island, and Providence-Plantations, In America* (Boston: Printed by John Allen, for Nicholas Boone, 1719) (hereafter, *Laws and Acts* [1719]), p. 80, reprinted in *Earliest Acts,* p. 216.

5. Evidence was mostly presented through documents and depositions. The Rhode Island Supreme Court Judicial Records Center (JRC) is missing files for *Torrey v. Mumford* and *Torrey v. Gardner.* The Massachusetts Historical

Society (MHS) could not find *Torrey v. Gardner* when this work was researched. For copy, see Letters and Papers to and from Rhode Islanders, or relating to Rhode-Island Differences copied chiefly from the Originals, belonging to, or deposited with the MHS, Mss. Codex Eng. 121–126 (JCB), vol. 1, pp. 135–204.

6. For biography, see James MacSparran, *A Letter Book and Abstract of Out Services, written during the years 1743–1751,* ed. Daniel Goodwin (Boston: Merrymount Press, 1899), pp. xvii–xxi; Updike, *History,* vol. 1, pp. 66–67. On MacSparran in Bristol, see MacSparran's *Letter Book,* p. xx. On Colman, see Clifford K. Shipton, *Sibley's Harvard Graduates: Biographical Sketches of Those Who Attended Harvard College in the Classes 1690–1700* (Cambridge, Mass.: Harvard University Press, 1933), vol. 4, pp. 120–126; John Von Rohr, *The Shaping of American Congregationalism: 1620–1957* (Cleveland: Pilgrim Press, 1992), p. 133; McLoughlin, *New England Dissent,* vol. 1, pp. 217–218; Woolverton, *Colonial Anglicanism,* p. 122; John T. O'Keefe, "Family of God, Family of Man: Liberal Religion in Eighteenth-Century New England" (Ph.D. diss., Harvard University, 1999). The quote comes from Shipton, *Sibley's Harvard Graduates,* vol. 4, p. 124 (quoting from Henry Newman to the Bishop of London). On the complaints, see John Danforth to Colman (Sept. 28, 1719), Colman Papers (MHS); John Checkley to MacSparran (June 26, 1721), in Edmund F. Slafter, *John Checkley or the Evolution of Religious Tolerance in Massachusetts Bay* (1897; repr., New York: Burt Franklin, 1967), vol. 2, pp. 154–156; M. Halsey Thomas, ed., *The Diary of Samuel Sewall, 1674–1729* (New York: Farrar, Straus & Giroux, 1973), vol. 2, p. 922 n. 21. I use the spelling "MacSparran," although his name was also spelled "McSparran."

7. For the quote, see Elders of Churches in Bristol County as an Ecclesiastical Council (July 1, 1719), Fulham Papers (LPL), vol. 8, p. 121. On the controversy, see Colman to Church at Bristol (1719), Colman Papers (MHS); Thomas, *Diary of Samuel Sewall,* vol. 2, p. 928 (Sept. 7, 1719); Letter from Members of the Church in Bristol to the Second Church in Boston, respecting the Ordination of James McSparran, Oct. 6, 1719, and Letter from Messrs. John Carry and John Throope to the Ministers of Boston and vicinity relative to Mr. McSparran (1719), Letters, Codex Eng., 121–126, vol. 2, pp. 77–78.

8. For the quote, see James MacSparran, *America Dissected,* quoted in MacSparran, *Letter Book,* pp. xxi–xxii. On the parish, see Updike, *History,* vol. 1, pp. 32–38. For the parish request, see Narragansett to Bishop Robinson (Oct. 20, 1715) in Fulham Papers (LPL), vol. 8, p. 100.

9. On the trip, see Narrative of Lawsuit relating to Glebe Land at Narragansett (n.d., 1752?), Ms. 1123, Part I, doc. 82 (LPL). On the items,

see William Guy to Bishop Robinson (Dec. 17, 1717), Fulham Papers (LPL), vol. 8, p. 108. On Davis, see Affidavit of Frances Davis and Affidavit of MacSparran, ibid., vol. 8, pp. 125–126 (punctuation added).

10. On marriage, see Updike, *History,* vol. 1, pp. 70, 369 n. 89. On the Gardners (Gardiners), see ibid., pp. 135–137, 373 n. 100; John Osborne Austin, *The Genealogical Dictionary of Rhode Island* (1887; repr., Baltimore: Genealogical, 1969), p. 81. On slavery, see Joanne Pope Melish, *Disowning Slavery: Gradual Emancipation and "Race" in New England, 1780–1860* (Ithaca: Cornell University Press, 1998), pp. 11–49; John Wood Sweet, "Bodies Politic: Colonialism: Race and the Emergence of the American North, Rhode Island, 1730–1830" (Ph.D. diss, Princeton University, 1995), pp. 297–299. On the items, see MacSparran's letters from 1723–1726 to SPG officials, Fulham Papers (LPL), vol. 8, pp. 138, 142, 177, 184, 214. On the congregation, see MacSparran's Answers to SPG Questionnaire (Apr. 1724), ibid., vol. 8, p. 189.

11. MacSparran to Bishop Gibson (June 9, 1724), Fulham Papers (LPL), vol. 8, p. 184; MacSparran's Answers, ibid., p. 189; David Humphreys to Church Wardens and Vestry (June 5, 1722) in *The Register Book,* in Updike, *History,* vol. 2, pp. 468; ibid., p. 466.

12. For the grant, see *Torrey v. Mumford* (1734) in Copy Case, *McSparran v. Hassard* (SCJ, Mar. 1736), p. 36 (JRC); Declaration (Jan. 1735), ibid.; also Meeting (June 4, 1668) in Elisha R. Potter, *The Early History of the Narragansett* (Providence: Marshall, Brown, 1835), pp. 278–279. Benedict Arnold became a partner at the meeting when the grant was made; John Porter was not present. On the purchase, see ibid., pp. 275–277. Porter's shares ended with the Gardners. Wilbore (Wilbur) left his to his daughters. Some of Brenton's shares were given to Jahleel Brenton. Mumford's shares descended to his sons. Hull's shares descended to his daughter Hannah, who married Judge Samuel Sewall. Proprietors Meeting (Apr. 8, 1692), ibid., p. 279; Meetings of the proprietors and legal representatives of the proprietors of the Pettaquamscutt Purchase (1704), ibid., pp. 284–286; Howard M. Chapin, *Documentary History of Rhode Island* (Providence: Preston & Rands, 1919), vol. 2, p. 66; Austin, *Genealogical Dictionary,* pp. 227–228; Updike, *History,* vol. 1, pp. 73, 370 n. 93.

13. For the quotes, see Samuel Greene Arnold, *History of the State of Rhode Island and Providence Plantations* (Providence: Preston & Rounds, 1894), vol. 1, pp. 139–140 (quoting John Winthrop, *History of New England from 1630 to 1649,* vol. 1, p. 297); Thomas Lechford, *Plain Dealing on News from New England* (Boston: J. K. Wiggin, 1867), p. 94. On Rhode Island religious history, see Ahlstrom, *Religious History,* pp. 172–174, 178–180, 181.

14. On Porter, see Austin, *Genealogical Dictionary,* p. 155; Updike, *History,* vol.

1, p. 370 n. 92. On Wilbore, see Austin, *Genealogical Dictionary,* pp. 81, 155; Chapin, *Documentary History,* vol. 2, p. 34; Arnold, *History of Rhode Island,* vol. 1, pp. 124, 127. On Brenton, see Chapin, *Documentary History,* vol. 2, p. 71; Updike, *History,* vol. 1, pp. 371–372 n. 97; Arnold, *History of Rhode Island,* vol. 1, pp. 128, 132. On Mumford, see Austin, *Genealogical Dictionary,* p. 136; Updike, *History,* vol. 1, pp. 370–371 n. 94. On Wilson, see Austin, *Genealogical Dictionary,* pp. 230, 392–393; Updike, *History,* vol. 1, p. 371 n. 95. Wilson appears in the records by 1644. *R.I. Recs.,* vol. 1, p. 80 (May 1644). On Wilson and Mumford against Connecticut, see Arnold, *History of Rhode Island,* vol. 1, p. 347. On Hull, see Updike, *History,* vol. 1, p. 371 n. 96; *Dictionary of American Biography* (New York: Scribner's, 1928–1958) (hereafter, *DAB*), vol. 9, pp. 362–363. On Arnold, see Austin, *Genealogical Dictionary,* p. 242; Updike, *History,* vol. 1, p. 372 n. 98; Chapin, *Documentary History,* vol. 1, p. 11.

15. On Gardner, see *New-England Weekly Journal,* Aug. 13, 1732; Austin, *Genealogical Dictionary,* pp. 81, 161.

16. On Bundy, see Appellant's Brief, *McSparran v. Hassard* (1752, W. Murray), Additional Mss., 36217 (BL). On Brenton, see Austin, *Genealogical Dictionary,* p. 254. For Brenton letter, see Brenton to Sewall (Aug. 9, 1711) in Potter, *Early History,* pp. 129–130. MacSparran cautioned that the gentleman who bears Mumford's charges (likely Brenton) "intends if he can defeat the church to give it for the support of an Independent [minister]." MacSparran to Bishop Gibson (June 9, 1724), Fulham Papers (LPL), vol. 8, p. 184. On the claim, see Updike, *History,* vol. 1, pp. 341–345 nn. 44, 45. On Brenton's motivations, see Narrative, Ms. 1123, pt. 1, doc. 82, p. 2, verso (LPL).

17. *MacSparran v. Mumford,* UB16 F4 (1724) (JRC); Petition and complaint of James MacSparran (Sept. 1723) in Copy Case, Fulham Papers (LPL), vol. 8, p. 152. On the references, see *The Register Book,* in Updike, *History,* vol. 2, p. 466. For concern about the grant, see MacSparran to Gibson (June 9, 1724), Fulham Papers (LPL), vol. 8, p. 184. For the evidence, see Depositions of Philip Briggs, Mary Bundy and Samuel Bundy, and Henry Gardner in Copy Case, Fulham Papers (LPL), vol. 8, p. 152. A newspaper article claimed that Nathaniel Niles, attorney for Samuel Sewall, favored the presbyterians. *New-England Weekly Journal,* Aug. 13, 1733.

18. Plea of George Mumford in *MacSparran v. Mumford* (1723) in Copy Case, Fulham Papers (LPL), vol. 8, p. 152. For the quote about age, see *New-England Weekly Journal,* Aug. 13, 1733. For the evidence, see Samuel Tist, Joseph Case, Thomas Mumford, Nathaniel Niles, and Benedict Arnold in Copy Case, Fulham Papers (LPL), vol. 8, p. 152. Only Niles had been at the 1679 meeting. On the family, see Austin, *Genealogical Dictionary,*

p. 243. MacSparran noted that Brenton appeared as an attorney when the court would not allow him to defend Mumford. Narrative, Ms. 1123, Part I, doc. 82, p. 2, verso (LPL).

19. On the first trial, see *GCT Recs.,* Book A, p. 409 (Sept. 1723) (JRC); Judgment (Sept. 1723) in Copy Case, Fulham Papers (LPL), vol. 8, p. 152. On the rehearing, see Judgment (March 1723/1724) in Copy Case, Fulham Papers (LPL), vol. 8, p. 152; *GCT Recs.,* Book A, p. 421 (Mar. 1723/1724) (JRC). On the practices, see MacSparran to Bishop Gibson (June 9, 1724) in Fulham Papers (LPL), vol. 8, p. 184. On presbyterians, see MacSparran to Bernon (Oct. 5, 1721) in Updike, *History,* vol. 1, p. 46. For the vow, see *The Register Book,* in Updike, *History,* vol. 2, p. 477; ibid., vol. 1, pp. 85–86. For other conflicts, see Ahlstrom, *Religious History,* pp. 223–225.

20. MacSparran to Bishop Gibson (June 9, 1724), Fulham Papers (LPL), vol. 8, p. 184. On the transmittal, see MacSparran to Bishop Gibson (June 16, 1724), ibid., p. 185.

21. MacSparran to Bishop Gibson (Dec. 1, 1724), Fulham Papers (LPL), vol. 8, p. 186. On Partridge, see *New-England Weekly Journal,* Oct. 22, 1733. On MacSparran, see Honeyman to Robinson (Dec. 12, 1724), Fulham Papers (LPL), vol. 8, p. 129. For MacSparran's concern about bond liability if the case were not prosecuted, see MacSparran to Bishop Gibson (Dec. 1, 1724), ibid., p. 186. For dismissal, see Petition of George Mumford (May 15, 1725), PC 1/58/3. On the 1725 synod, see *The Register Book,* in Updike, *History,* vol. 2, pp. 478–480; Ms. 1123, Part I, docs. 6–14 (LPL); Lord Justices to Lt. Gov. Dummer (Oct. 7, 1725), in *The Register Book,* in Updike, *History,* vol. 2, pp. 482–485. For Colman's establishment claim, see McLoughlin, *New England Dissent,* vol. 1, pp. 217–218. Although no decision was made on the laws, the synod was found in violation of the prerogative. Woolverton, *Colonial Anglicanism,* p. 129; McLoughlin, *New England Dissent,* vol. 1, p. 221. In 1727 the colony passed a tax measure exempting Church members. Ibid. For the order from England in October 1725, see Updike, *History,* vol. 1, pp. 91–92. In 1727 Henry Newman explained that the Society declined "to concern themselves with the Controversy between the Established Church and the Dissenters." Craig Rose, "The origins and ideals of the SPCK, 1699–1716," in Walsh et al., *Church of England,* pp. 189–190.

22. On church activities, see MacSparran's *Letter Book,* pp. xxix–xxx; *The Register Book,* in Updike, *History,* vol. 2, pp. 495–498. MacSparran's portrait is at Bowdoin College; that of his wife, Hannah, at the Boston Museum of Fine Arts. Smibert's portrait of Benjamin Colman is at Harvard. Shipton, *Sibley's Harvard Graduates,* vol. 4, p. 128. For the Berkeley quote, see McLoughlin, *Rhode Island,* pp. 70–71. On the marriage, see Updike, *History,* vol. 1, p. 123. On Torrey (1707–1791), see Shipton, *Sibley's Harvard*

Graduates, vol. 8, p. 498. On the Wilsons, see Austin, *Genealogical Dictionary,* p. 230. On the new efforts, see *The Register Book,* in Updike, *History,* vol. 2, pp. 504–505; McLoughlin, *New England Dissent,* vol. 1, p. 222–224, 236–237; William Wilson Manross, *A History of the American Episcopal Church* (New York: Morehouse, 1935), p. 98. On episcopal efforts to appeal a lawsuit from Massachusetts to the Privy Council, see McLoughlin, *New England Dissent,* vol. 1, pp. 236–237. On Prince, see Thomas Prince, *A Chronological History of New England, in the form of Annals* (Boston: Kneeland & Green, 1726; Boston: Cummings, Hilliard, 1826), p. iv; Potter, *Early History,* p. 123; Clifford K. Shipton, *Sibley's Harvard Graduates: Biographical Sketches of Those Who Attended Harvard College in the Classes 1701–1712* (Boston: MHS, 1937), vol. 5, p. 341.

23. Narrative, Ms. 1123, Part I, doc. 82, p. 3, recto (LPL). For the article, see *New-England Weekly Journal,* May 22, 1732, p. 2.

24. On layman comment, see Narrative, Ms. 1123, Part I, doc. 82, p. 3, recto (LPL). For the case, see Declaration of Joseph Torrey (June 1732), *Torrey v. Mumford* in Copy Case, *McSparran v. Hassard* (March 1736) (JRC), p. 48; *GCT/SCJ Recs.,* Book B, p. 433 (Sept. 1732) (JRC). Grant is in *Torrey v. Mumford* in Copy Case, *McSparran v. Hassard* (Mar. 1736) (JRC). For decision, see *GCT/SCJ Recs.,* Book B, p. 443 (Mar. 1732/1733) (JRC). For the Quaker attribution, see Respondent's Brief, *McSparran v. Hassard* (1752), Additional Mss., 36217 (BL), p. 5. On Quakers, see McLoughlin, *New England Dissent,* vol. 1, pp. 233–236; Ahlstrom, *Religious History,* 178–179; Arthur J. Worral, *Quakers in the Colonial Northeast* (Hanover: University Press of New England, 1980), p. 54. The dissenters were John Gardner, Samuel Vernon, Nicholas Power, and Rowse Helme. A newspaper suggested that seven judges favored Mumford. *New-England Weekly Journal,* Aug. 13, 1733.

25. For the appeal, see *GCT/SCJ Recs.,* Book B, p. 443 (Mar. 1732/1733) (JRC). On Belcher, see Belcher to Holden and Hollis (June 30, 1733), Jonathan Belcher Letter Books (MHS), vol. 3, p. 279; Letter from Gov. Belcher to Hon. Holden & Hollis of London re Ministry Lands in S. Kingstown re McSparran (1733), Letters, Mss. Codex Eng. 121–126 (JCB), vol. 3, p. 107. On the 1734 convention, see Note of Thomas Prince (May 31, 1734), Colman Papers (MHS).

26. For the essays, see *New-England Weekly Journal* (1733) (June 11 and Oct. 1, 8, 15, 22). For W. N., see *New-England Weekly Journal* (Aug. 13, 1733).

27. On the petition, see PC 2/92/527 (July 1734, Comm. Report); *APC,* vol. 2, pp. 402–404. A later Privy Council brief argued that Mumford had so "instantly and readily" endorsed the land to "his Pastor, Mr. Torrey" that it could hardly have been a "*real* Trial of Right" between him and "Mr.

Mumford one of his own Congregation." Appellant's Brief, *McSparran v. Hassard* (1752), Additional Mss., 36217 (BL). For Robert Auchmuty's opinion (May 1735) emphasizing "in their sentiments" and the "law will forever be resolved in favor of the Church of England by law established," see *CHS Coll.,* vol. 5, pp. 426–467. For the deed to Torrey, see Copy of Book of Evidences, South Kingston, in *McSparran v. Hassard* (SCJ, Mar. 1736) (JRC).

28. Belcher to Hollis (Nov. 2, 1734), Jonathan Belcher Letter Books, vol. 4, p. 322 (MHS); Belcher to Holden (Nov. 1, 1734), ibid., p. 315; Letters, Codex Eng. 121–126 (JCB), vol. 3, p. 107ff. For Prince's description, see Prince, *Chronological History,* pp. v–x, xx–xxi, 25, 437. For the Colman quote, see Colman to Holden, Draft ([Jan. 6?], 1735), Colman Papers (MHS). On the suit, see Torrey to Colman (Dec. 3, 1734), ibid. For documents relating to *Torrey v. Gardner* (1734), see Letters, Codex Eng. 121–126 (JCB), vol. 1, pp. 135–204. On Ephraim Gardner, see *The Register Book* in Updike, *History,* vol. 2, pp. 473–474. On the parish defense, see ibid., pp. 514–516.

29. Ebenezer Brenton (Dec. 23, 1734) (*Torrey v. Gardner,* Sept. 1735) in *McSparran v. Hassard* (SCJ, Mar. 1736) (JRC); Deposition of George Mumford (Apr. 21, 1735) in ibid. Brenton died in November 1732, several months after Torrey won. *New-England Weekly Journal,* Nov. 20, 1732. For the will, see NHS, Box 4, folder 4A.

30. For testimony that MacSparran would have won with the grant, see Daniel Updike (*Torrey v. Gardner,* 1735) in *MacSparran v. Hassard* (SCJ, Mar. 1737) (JRC). For the result, see *GCT/SCJ Recs.,* Book B, p. 511 (Sept. 1735) (JRC). For the Colman quote, see Colman to Holden ([1735?]), Colman Papers (MHS); see Letters, Codex Eng. 121–126 (JCB), vol. 2, p. 176.

31. For the Colman comment, see From Colman? (Aug. 17, 1739), Colman Papers (MHS). For the case, see Plea and Answer in *McSparran v. Hassard* (SCJ, Mar. 1736) (JRC); *GCT/SCJ Recs.,* Book B, p. 527 (Mar. 1736) (JRC); Judgment (Jan. 1735/1736), ibid. On MacSparran's trip, see *The Register Book,* in Updike, *History,* vol. 2, p. 518; Narrative, Ms. 1123, Part I, doc. 82 (LPL). Paris represented MacSparran; Holden represented the presbyterians. Paris to Partridge (1737), in Gertrude Selwyn Kimball, ed., *The Correspondence of the Colonial Governors of Rhode Island, 1723–1775* (Boston: Houghton, Mifflin, 1902), vol. 1, pp. 85–86; Letter from Colman to Holden re MacSparran Appeal (1737), Letters, Mss. Codex Eng. 121–126 (JCB), vol. 2, p. 179. For the order, see Order of Council (SCJ, March 1737) (JRC) in *McSparran v. Hassard* (Mar. 1737); *The Register Book,* in Updike, *History,* vol. 2, p. 518. For his preparation, see *Diary of the Rev. Thomas Prince,* pp. 331–364, 356, 357.

32. The evidence and chart for *McSparran v. Hassard* are in *McSparran v.*

Mumford, UB16, F4 (JRC). For the phrase "ancient people," see Abiel Sherman, *McSparran v. Hassard* (SCJ, Mar. 1739), ibid. For other evidence, see Ephraim Codners, ibid.; Thomas Hassard, ibid.; Henry Gardner, *McSparran v. Hassard* (SCJ, Mar. 1737) (JRC); Peleg Mumford, ibid.; Jeremiah Wilson, *McSparran v. Hassard* (Mar. 1739), UB16, F4 (JRC).

33. On Mumford, see Peleg Mumford, *McSparran v. Hassard* (SCJ, Mar. 1737) (JRC); George Mumford, ibid. The Cromwell information appears in Respondent's Privy Council brief, *McSparran v. Hassard* (1752), p. 2, Additional Mss., 36217 (BL). On Thomas Mumford as a presbyterian, see Thomas Mumford to Judge Sewall (Feb. 20, 1722/1723) in *McSparran v. Hassard* (SCJ, Mar. 1737) (JRC). On Wilbore, see Henry Gardner, ibid.; Elizabeth Freelove, ibid.; Job Green, *McSparran v. Hassard* (Mar. 1739), UB16, F4 (JRC). For Wilson, see Peleg Mumford, *McSparran v. Hassard* (SCJ, Mar. 1737) (JRC); Jeremiah Wilson in *McSparran v. Hassard* (Mar. 1739), UB16, F4 (JRC).

34. Job Green in *McSparran v. Hassard* (SCJ, Mar. 1737) (JRC); Timothy Cutler, ibid. On "indistinct" denominational lines and grudging conformity to "the New England Way while maintaining traditional usages in their private religious life," see Ahlstrom, *Religious History,* p. 215. For the claim that Sarah Barker took communion with the congregationalists but was a member of the Church of England, see Otis and Samuel Barker in *McSparran v. Hassard* (SCJ, Mar. 1737) (JRC).

35. Narrative, Ms. 1123, Part I, doc. 82 (LPL). On the election, see Arnold, *History of Rhode Island,* vol. 2, p. 119–20; Austin, *Genealogical Dictionary,* p. 235. On the contributions, see Letter between Colman and Watts (Aug. 17, 1739), Colman Papers (noting £400 from Connecticut) (MHS); Memorandum to Prince (Dec. 14, 1739), ibid.; To Prince (Dec. 14, 1739), ibid.; Memorandum of the Money received by me [Dr. Colman] on the account of Mr. Torrey (1739), Letters, Mss. Codex Eng. 121–126 (JCB), vol. 2; Colman to Talcott, *CHS Coll.,* vol. 5, pp. 170–172. The £2,000 figure appears in Shipton, *Sibley's Harvard Graduates,* vol. 8, p. 506 (quoting the *Boston News-Letter,* Sept. 6, 1739). On the General Court, see Shipton, *Sibley's Harvard Graduates,* vol. 8, p. 505. For comment, see *The Register Book,* in Updike, *History,* vol. 2, pp. 521, 525; Narrative, Ms. 1123, Part I, doc. 82 (LPL).

36. "A brief Representation of the Case depending between the Rev. Dr. MacSparran, Plaintiff, and the Rev. Mr. Torrey, Defendant, relating to the ministry Land at Narragansett (July 1739) (Newport?: Printed by Ann Franklin?, 1739), W2571, 40177 (JCB copy). For a very loose attribution to Joseph Torrey, see John Eliot Alden ed., *Rhode Island Imprints* (New York: R. R. Bowker, 1949), pp. 20–21. For Prince's comments, see [Thomas Prince], "An Answer to a Printed Letter said to be wrote from a Gentleman

in Newport to his friend in Boston Aug. 27; Pretending to find fault with a Brief Representation of the Case between Dr. McSparran Plaintiff and Mr. Torrey Defendant, relating to the Ministry Land in South Kingstown, Narragansett, which was dated July 1739" (Boston?: [Kneeland & Green], 1739).

37. "A Brief Representation of the Case depending between the Rev. Doctor MacSparran, and Mr. Torrey, relating to the Ministerial Land in Narragansett, in a Letter from a Gentleman in Newport, to his Friend in Boston (Aug. 29, 1739) (Newport: Printed by Ann Franklin?, 1739), W2571, 40156 (JCB copy); Alden, *Rhode Island Imprints*, pp. 18–19.

38. John Callendar, *Historical and Religious Discourse, with affairs of the Colony of Rhode Island and Providence Plantations* (Boston: Printed and sold by S. Kneeland & T. Green, 1739), pp. 95, 15, 14–15, 13, 66, 105 n. ‡. On Callendar (1706–1748), see Arnold, *History of Rhode Island*, vol. 2, p. 121; Sydney V. James, *Colonial Rhode Island: A History* (New York: Scribner's, 1975), pp. 1–2, 214.

39. Callendar, *Historical and Religious Discourse*, pp. 50, 54, 55, 98.

40. For comments, see Thomas Sanford to MacSparran (July 6, 1741), Fulham Papers (LPL), vol. 8, p. 299; Narrative, Ms. 1123, Part I, doc. 82, p. 3, verso (LPL). For MacSparran's comments, see McSparran to Gibson (Oct. 18, 1741), Fulham Papers (LPL), vol. 8, p. 299; McSparran to Gibson (July 7, 1746), ibid., p. 303; McSparran to Sherlock (Mar. 26, 1751), ibid., p. 319. On Colman's death, see Shipton, *Sibley's Harvard Graduates*, vol. 4, pp. 128–129. On bond, see McSparran to Gibson (July 7, 1746), Fulham Papers (LPL), vol. 8, p. 303. On the tax, see *The Register Book*, in Updike, *History*, vol. 2, p. 546.

41. Narrative, Ms. 1123, Part I, doc. 82, p. 3, verso (LPL). MacSparran's team also included Forrester and Paris. Bearcroft to McSparran (May 8, 1752), Fulham Papers (LPL), vol. 8, p. 325. Hassard was also represented by Hume-Campbell. For briefs, see Appellant's Brief and Respondent's Brief, *McSparran v. Hassard* (1752), Additional Mss., 36217 (BL). On the 1752 appeal, see PC 2/102/525, 536; PC 2/103/46, 51, 70.

42. Sanford to McSparran (June 10, 1752), Fulham Papers (LPL), vol. 8, p. 325; Bearcroft to McSparran (May 8, 1752), ibid. For Yorke's comment, see Respondent's Brief, *McSparran v. Hassard* (1752), Additional Mss., 36217 (BL). For Lee, see Respondent's Brief, *McSparran v. Hassard* (1752), Library of Congress, Law Division (Great Britain, Privy Council, Judicial Committee); Smith, *Appeals*, p. 328. For Isaac Backus's claim that Dr. Stennet, a London Baptist minister, had "a great hand in procuring this decree," see Potter, *Early History*, p. 127. On the "superiority of the dissenting interest at home," see McSparran to Sherlock (Nov. 10, 1752), Fulham Papers (LPL), vol. 8, p. 326.

43. McSparran to Sherlock (Nov. 10, 1752), Fulham Papers (LPL), vol. 8, p. 326. The sentences on establishment appear in Smith's account of the same letter. Smith, *Appeals*, p. 328 n. 357. For quotations from *American Dissected*, see James MacSparran, *America Dissected, being a Full and True Account of all the American Colonies* (Dublin: S. Powell, 1753), reprinted in Updike, *History*, vol. 3, pp. 36, 43, 12, 11, 10, 24, 40, 17, 32, 36.

44. On the benefaction, see Bearcroft to Archbishop, Ms. 1123, Part I, doc. 87 (LPL). On the deaths, see *The Register Book*, in Updike, *History*, vol. 2, pp. 551–552, 605, 556. For concerns, see Church wardens of Narragansett (Mar. 17, 1755) in Ms. 1123, vol. 2, p. 96 (LPL). On legal proceedings, see *The Register Book*, in Updike, *History*, vol. 2, pp. 548, 551. On MacSparran's glebe, see ibid., pp. 557–558; Esther Bernon Carpenter, *South Country Studies* (Boston, 1924), p. 92. On the move, see Updike, *History*, vol. 2, p. 371. On the sale, see ibid., vol. 1, p. 82–83.

8. Commerce and Currency

1. On the transformation, see John J. McCusker and Russell R. Menard, *The Economy of British America, 1607–1789* (Chapel Hill: University of North Carolina Press, 1991), pp. 79, 86, 111, 354.

2. These numbers include appeals brought before the Committee prior to 1756. Three Rhode Island cases were not heard by the Committee until after 1755: *Chaloner v. Bland* (1756); *Whipple v. Bowen* (1757), *Stanton v. Thompson* (1759). The eight nonpursued property cases were: *Staniford v. Timothy & Margaret Newell* (1747) (dismissal for nonprosecution); *George & Mary Taylor v. Clark* (1750) (appeal admitted; no further action); *Clemence v. Angel* (1750) (dismissal for nonprosecution); *Peirce v. Rice* (1752) (appeal admitted; no further action); *Whitman v. Whitman* (1753) (dismissal for nonprosecution); *Cook v. Cook* (1754) (dismissal for nonprosecution); *Hazard v. Mary Hazard* (1755) (nothing further listed); *Whipple et al. v. Ninigret* (1755) (dismissal for nonprosecution). Four property cases were affirmed: *MacSparran v. Hassard* (1752); *Brenton v. Remington* (1751); *Potter v. Dorcas Freeborn* (1752); *Tripp v. Tripp* (1752). In addition, *Freebody v. Cook* (1755) was dismissed, although it is unclear whether this was for nonprosecution or because of affirmance. The reversed property case was *Walker v. Paget* (1754) (reversed ex parte). The four commerce and trade cases dismissed for nonprosecution were *Fogg v. Harvey* (1745); *Polock v. Verplank* (1747); *Gibbs v. Sheldon* (1748); *Grant & Heatley v. Dyre* (1755). Five commerce and trade cases were reversed: *Rous v. Hassard* (1752); *Vanbrugh & Carpenter v. Powers* (1751); *Freebody v. Wanton* (1751); *Wheelwright v. Tyler* (1752); *Rodman v. Banister* (1753). Although *Channing v. Fenner* (1752) was affirmed, it reversed the colony's re-

fusal to provide a jury to determine damages and ordered a trial on damages by jury for Channing. PC 2/102/456–459, 464. The post-1755 cases include: *Stanton v. Thompson* (1759) (affirmed); *Larkin v. York* (1761) (reversed); *Potter v. Hazard* (1763) (affirmed); *Lewis v. Wilkinson* (1767) (affirmed); *Arnold v. Green* (1767) (dismissed for nonprosecution); *Sanford v. Smith, et al.* (1773) (dismissed for nonprosecution).

3. For discussion, see J. H. Baker, *An Introduction to English Legal History* (London: Butterworths, 1990, 3rd ed.), pp. 318–336; John Habakkuk, *Marriage, Debt, and the Estate System: English Landownership, 1650–1950* (Oxford: Clarendon Press, 1994), pp. 1–76; Lloyd Bonfield, *Marriage Settlements, 1601–1740: The Adoption of the Strict Settlement* (Cambridge: Cambridge University Press, 1983); Carole Shammas, Marylynn Salmon, and Michael Dahlin, *Inheritance in America: From Colonial Times to the Present* (1987; repr., Galveston: Frontier Press, 1997), pp. 32–34. For the perception, see John Osborne Austin, *The Genealogical Dictionary of Rhode Island* (1887; repr., Baltimore: Genealogical, 1969). Interestingly, at a glance, daughters seem to have been less likely to receive land in the eighteenth century than in the seventeenth century—but the entire subject needs more careful investigation. This result may have arisen as the New England colonies cut women from intestate schemes in an effort to preserve partible inheritance among men.

4. On Privy Council proceedings in *Brenton*, see PC 2/102/142–143, 208–209 (1751). On *Tripp* proceedings, see Governor and Council (RISA), folder 4, p. 34; Governor and Council Records (RISA), vol. 1, p. 158; PC 2/102/403–405, 427–428. For Baker comment, see Bill in *Tripp v. Redwood* (JRC). On *Freeborn*, see *Freeborn v. Potter* (SCJ, Newport, Mar. 1744) (JRC); *R.I. Law Cases*, vol. 7, case 1 (RISA); PC 2/103/155, 158–160, 177 (1752); Respondent's Brief, *Potter v. Freeborn*, Library of Congress, Law Division (Great Britain, Privy Council, Judicial Committee).

5. Appellant's Brief (Norton & Gardiner), *Potter v. Hazard* (1763) and Appellant's Brief (Forrester & Campbell), *Stanton v. Thompson* (1759), Additional Mss., 36218 (BL). The appellant's brief in *Lewis* adopted a different strategy by detailing testimony in order to prove fraud for seven pages. Appellant's Brief (Forrester & Jackson), *Lewis v. Wilkinson*, Additional Mss., 36220 (BL).

6. Respondent's Brief (Yorke & Forrester), *Potter v. Hazard* (1763), and Respondent's Brief (Pratt & Yorke), *Stanton v. Thompson* (1759), Additional Mss., 36218 (BL). See also Respondent's Brief (Yorke & Dunning), *Lewis v. Wilkinson*, Additional Mss., 36220 (BL).

7. Respondent's Brief (W. Murray), *Freebody v. Cook*, Library of Congress, Law Division (Great Britain, Privy Council, Judicial Committee); Handwritten Response to Appellant's Petition, *Freebody v. Cook* (1754), Peter

Force Papers, Series VIIID, item 5, p. 14 (Library of Congress); see also Appellant's Case (Al. Forrester), *Freebody v. Cook,* Library of Congress, Law Division (Great Britain, Privy Council, Judicial Committee); PC 2/ 104/36, 55, 62, 100, 111, 244, 271–272, 283 (1754–1755); *Cook v. Freebody* (SCJ, Newport, Mar. 1755) (JRC); *SCJ Recs.* (Newport), Book E, p. 15 (Mar. 1755) (JRC).

8. Appellant's Brief (Pratt & Forrester) and Respondent's Brief (Yorke & Sewall), *Larkin v. Yorke* (June 1761), Additional Mss., 36218 (BL); Charles Fearne, *An Essay on the Learning in Contingent Remainders and Executory Devises* (London: Printed by W. Strahan and M. Woodfall for P. Uriel, 1772).

9. *Rous, Vanbrugh,* and *Freebody* are discussed in chapter 6. For the note, see Brief, *Rous v. Hassard,* p. 7, Library of Congress, Law Division (Great Britain, Privy Council, Judicial Committee).

10. For case, see *Wheelwright v. Tyler* (SCJ, Newport, Mar. 1747/48) (JRC); *SCJ Recs.,* Book D, p. 76 (Mar. 1747/48) (JRC); PC 2/102/391, 427; *APC,* vol. 4, pp. 84–85. For comment, see Appellant's Brief, *Rodman v. Banister,* Library of Congress, Law Division (Great Britain, Privy Council, Judicial Committee); *Rodman v. Banister* (SCJ, Newport, Aug. 1754) (JRC); PC 2/103/112, 289, 309 (1753). For *Stead v. Hart,* see *APC,* vol. 4, pp. 716–717.

11. These cases include: *Chaloner v. Bland* (1756) (dismissed for nonprosecution); *Isaacs v. Merrett* (1758) (reversed without prejudice to the appellant, who can proceed against administrator); *Boyle v. Moss* (1759) (nothing further listed); *Creugh v. Whitfield* (1760) (dismissed for nonprosecution); *Simons v. Wanton* (1762) (dismissed for nonprosecution) (likely a trade case); *Read v. Nichols* (1762) (dismissed for nonprosecution); *Stead v. Hart* (1766) (reversed); *Banister v. Brown* (1768) (dismissed at parties' request); *Laycock v. Clarke* (1769) (reversed ex parte); *Isaacs v. Stead* (1765) (affirmed); *Hart v. Solomons* (1770) (nothing further listed); *Grant v. Hardy* (1771) (dismissed for nonprosecution). On Rhode Island merchants during the war, see Sydney V. James, *Colonial Rhode Island: A History* (New York: Scribner's, 1975), pp. 287–293.

12. "An Act for Ascertaining the Rates of Foreign Coins in Her Majesty's Plantations," 6 Anne, c. 30 (1707), *Statutes at Large* (Cambridge: Printed by Joseph Bentham, 1764), vol. 11, pp. 412–414. The act codified an earlier 1704 royal proclamation, 3 Anne (June 18, 1704). On the act's requirements, see John Blanchard MacInnes, "Rhode Island Bills of Credit 1710–1755" (Ph.D. diss., Brown University, 1952), pp. 83–85. For early instructions to governors on currency, see Leonard Woods Labaree, *Royal Instructions to British Colonial Governors, 1670–1776* (New York: Appleton-Century, 1935), vol. 1, pp. 212–216.

13. James MacSparran, *America Dissected, Being a Full and True Account of All*

the American Colonies (Dublin: S. Powell, 1753), reprinted in Wilkins Updike, *A History of the Episcopal Church in Narragansett, Rhode Island* (2nd ed., Boston: Merryman Press, 1907), vol. 3, p. 38. The description of paper money is drawn from James, *Colonial Rhode Island,* pp. 170–185; MacInnes, "Rhode Island Bills"; selected parts of Samuel Greene Arnold, *History of the State of Rhode Island and Providence Plantations* (Providence: Preston & Rounds, 1894), vol. 2; David S. Lovejoy, *Rhode Island Politics and the American Revolution, 1760–1776* (Providence: Brown University Press, 1958), p. 7. MacInnes calculates that by 1722 one-third of the colony was in debt to the government, and that by 1728 approximately two-fifths were. By the 1730s there were more than a thousand mortgages. MacInnes, "Rhode Island Bills," pp. 168–169, 184. Actual figures for emissions and withdrawals appear in MacInnes's dissertation at pp. 588–590.

14. Quotations are from the 1732 Board of Trade opinion and the 1735 letter to the Duke of Newcastle, and appear in MacInnes, "Rhode Island Bills," pp. 198–199, 322. For internal colony politics behind the 1731 crisis, see Lovejoy, *Rhode Island Politics,* pp. 7–8. The pre-1748 old tenor were two types of bills of credit, distinguished by their relationship to the face value of the notes. A new old-tenor bill was worth four times an original old-tenor bill. Arnold, *History of Rhode Island,* vol. 2, pp. 128–129; MacInnes, "Rhode Island Bills," 287–290; James, *Colonial Rhode Island,* pp. 182–184, 276–281.

15. On the 1750 situation, see Leslie V. Brock, "The Colonial Currency, Prices and Exchange Rates," *Essays in History (Corcoran Department of History at the University of Virginia),* vol. 34 (1992); Arnold, *History of Rhode Island,* vol. 2, pp. 174–179. For the act, see "An Act to regulate and restrain Paper Bills of Credit in his Majesty's Colonies or Plantations of Rhode Island and Providence Plantations, Connecticut, the Massachusetts Bay, and New Hampshire in America; and to prevent the same being legal Tenders in payments of money" (June 10, 1751), 24 Geo. 2, c. 53, *Statutes at Large* (London: Printed by Joseph Bentham, 1765), vol. 20, pp. 306–309. The act made it illegal to issue new money after September 29, 1751, unless the bills were sunk within two years. In August the Assembly stated that debts were to paid according to the following schedule: one ounce sterling was worth 64s old tenor, 16s new tenor, and 6s, 9p in the latest bills. For the colony law of 1754, see Respondents Brief, *Freebody v. Brenton et al.* (C. Ambler & C. Yorke) (BL).

16. Cases include: *Whipple v. Bowen et al.* (1757) (reversed); *Freebody v. Brenton et al.* (1764, 1769, 1772, 1774) (reversed); *Shearman v. Cornell* (1767) (reversed); *Freebody v. Holmes* (1768) (dismissal for nonprosecution); and *Holmes v. Freebody* (1770) (reversed) (likely involved depreciated notes in mortgage). Several other appeals may have

involved questions of depreciated currency. *Freebody v. Brenton* is briefly discussed in Lovejoy, *Rhode Island Politics,* pp. 162–163; Smith, *Appeals,* pp. 336–341. For Privy Council references, see *APC,* vol. 5, pp. 24–25. For the 1764 Committee Report, see PC 1/5/1. For material on the 1768 Privy Council order, see PC 2/112/79, 2/113/8, 244, 423–424, 502–513, 538–539. A letter from the Freebodys to the Earl of Hillsborough (July 22, 1771) is in PC 1/55/67. For the 1772 order and "Substance of the several proceedings," see PC 1/55/69A. Other materials are in PC 1/60/10: duplicate of transmittal order, June 26, 1772 and Freebody petition; peremptory order (July 6, 1774); drafts of June 20, 1774, report to Privy Council and July 6 approval; the three-judge answer written by Stephen Hopkins; and Metcalf Bowler's answer. For the 1774 Committee report, see PC 2/118/141. For briefs for both appeals, see Additional Mss., 36219 (1764) and 36220 (1769)(BL).

17. On Whipple, see Austin, *Genealogical Dictionary,* pp. 221–223; Dorothy S. Towle, ed., *Records of the Vice-Admiralty Court of Rhode Island 1716–1752* (Washington, D.C.: American Historical Association, 1936), pp. 520, 545; *R.I. Recs.,* vol. 5, pp. 20, 43, 66, 88, 108, 167, 328, 345, 371. On Freebody, see John Franklin Jameson ed., *Privateering and Piracy in the Colonial Period: Illustrative Documents* (New York: Macmillan, 1923), pp. 378–472; Towle, *Rhode Island Vice-Admiralty Court,* pp. 293–294 (John Jr.), 490–494.

18. By October 1754, Whipple was to pay Freebody 28,179 pounds in old tenor issued before 1748 for the 520 acres, and 3,500 silver milled dollars plus 5,500 pounds in old tenor for the 289 acres. The amount in silver milled dollars (or pieces of eight) was never disputed. The suggestion regarding Freebody's purchase of the bills comes from Hopkins's response to the Privy Council. Freebody and Brenton both signed a petition opposing a land bank, and Freebody signed against the 1751 emission. MacInnes, "Rhode Island Bills," pp. 601, 614. On the general issue, see John J. McCusker, *How Much Is That in Real Money? A Historical Price Index for Use as a Deflator of Money Values in the Economy of the United States* (Worcester: American Antiquarian Society, 1992); Colin R. Chapman, *Weights, Money and Other Measures Used by Our Ancestors* (Baltimore: Genealogical, 1997), 67–70, 73. On larger economic issues, see McCusker and Menard, *Economy of British America,* pp. 109–111.

19. On Whipple, see Arnold, *History of Rhode Island,* vol. 2, p. 186. On the act, see Brief of Respondents (1769). On bankruptcy, see *R.I. Recs.,* vol. 5, pp. 377–378. The descriptions of the commissioners' actions as trying to pay simple contract creditors and of the tender are from Hopkins's answer to the Privy Council.

20. For the colony act, see *R.I. Recs.,* vol. 6, pp. 358–362 (June 1763); "An Act

declaring what is and shall be Lawful Money," *Providence Gazette,* June 25, 1763, p. 4; "An Act," *Providence Gazette,* Apr. 2, 1763, pp. 1–2 (draft). For the quote, see "The Cooper's Letter to the Common People," *Providence Gazette,* Apr. 9, 1763, pp. 1–2. For earlier concerns, see "Thoughts on the State of the Currency," *Providence Gazette,* Nov. 20, 1762, p. 1; "To the Inhabitants . . .," *Providence Gazette,* Feb. 5, 1763, p. 1; "A Proposal for an Act regulating the Currency" (letter to the printer), *Providence Gazette,* Feb. 26, 1763, p. 3; "A few observations and reflections," *Providence Gazette,* Mar. 26, 1763, p. 3. On colony politics, see Arnold, *History of Rhode Island,* vol. 2, p. 244; James, *Colonial Rhode Island,* pp. 294–313.

21. The two New Hampshire appeals are *Dering v. Packer* (1760) and *Trecothick v. Wentworth* (1762). For discussion, see Smith, *Appeals,* pp. 500–503. A copy of the Council's discussion over *Dering* can be found in Box 173, folder 1 (NHS). The Currency Act voided all colonial acts after September 1764 that declared paper money to be legal tender. *Providence Gazette,* July 28, 1764, p. 4. For Freebody's argument, see Brief for Petitioners (1764) (Sewall and Forrester). In February the colony required that the appellee and appellant post £200 sterling bonds to secure costs of appealing to England. *R.I. Recs.,* vol. 6, p. 394.

22. The lawyers distinguished *Trecothick v. Wentworth* (1762): there, an English merchant had been owed money by a colonist with no provision for interest. The lawyers noted that a contrary decision would be unfair because the commissioners had kept only enough bills to discharge the mortgage and would become personally at risk if they had to compensate for the depreciation. Brief for Respondents (1764) (Ambler and Yorke); C. Yorke's argument in Brief for Respondents (1769).

23. For the order, see PC 1/50/1 (July 27, August 3, 1764); for the language, see 1769 briefs.

24. For Assembly action, see *R.I. Recs.,* vol. 6, pp. 403, 412–413. For the pamphlet, see Stephen Hopkins, "The Rights of the Colonies Examined," ibid., pp. 416–427; also in Charles S. Hyneman and Donald S. Lutz, eds., *American Political Writing during the Founding Era, 1760–1805* (Indianapolis: Liberty Press, 1983), vol. 1, pp. 45–61; reference to the charter is at p. 57; second quote is at p. 60. Hopkins also referred to equitable purposes in governing the empire. Ibid., p. 58. On events including the Newport group (Newport Junto), see James, *Colonial Rhode Island,* pp. 322–331; Lovejoy, *Rhode Island Politics,* pp. 48–126; Edmund S. Morgan and Helen M. Morgan, *The Stamp Act Crisis: Prologue to Revolution,* rev. ed. (New York: Macmillan, 1962), pp. 69–74; Walter Francis Mullen, "Rhode Island and the Imperial Reorganization of 1763–1766," (Ph.D. diss., Fordham University, 1965). On Hopkins (1707–1785), see *The Dictionary of American Biogra-*

phy, vol. 9, pp. 219–220; Marguerite Appleton, "Stephen Hopkins: Chief Justice, Governor, and Signer," in *Liberty and Justice: A History of Law and Lawyers in Rhode Island, 1636–1998,* ed. Patrick L. Conley (East Providence: Rhode Island Publications Society, 1998), pp. 116–131; John F. Millar, "Stephen Hopkins: An Architect of Independence," *Newport History,* vol. 53, pp. 24–37 (1980).

25. One dissenting judge thought that interest was only necessary from 1756 to the date of the tender, for the original tender had been "sufficient in law, and agreeable to the universal usage and practice of courts in this colony." Dissent of Benomi Hall, in *Freebody v. Brenton* (Sept. 1765) (JRC). For earlier petition, see Petition of Thomas Freebody for self and brothers to General Assembly, Sept. 1765 (JRC), asking that the Superior Court take cognizance of the Privy Council decree. On second appeal, see *APC,* vol. 5, p. 14; PC 2/112/79; PC 2/113/8, 244. For Yorke's handwritten comments, see Respondents' Brief (1769), Additional Mss., 36220 (BL).

26. For the proceedings, see PC 2/113/8, 244, 423–424, 502–513, 538–539.

27. For the language of the General Assembly response, see "Copy of letter from Messrs. John, Thomas, and Samuel Freebody to the Earl of Hillsborough, July 22, 1771," PC 1/55/67; "Substance of the several proceedings in the petition of complaint by J., To., and S. Freebody," PC 1/55/69A. On Marchant (1741–1796), see John N. Cole, "Henry Marchant's Journal, 1771–1772," *Rhode Island History,* vol. 57 (1999), pp. 31–55; David S. Lovejoy, "Henry Marchant and the Mistress of the World," *William and Mary Quarterly,* 3rd ser., vol. 12 (1955), pp. 375–398. One account suggests that Marchant argued that the "King and Council had made up said judgments contrary to law, reason, equity, and justice; and when the King and Council made up such a judgment, the King was no King." *APC,* vol. 6, p. 506. The statement comes from the Freebody letter to Hillsborough, and some doubt may be cast upon the accuracy of its restatements. The court's decisions appear in the Freebodys' letter to the Earl of Hillsborough and Petition of the Freebodys (Bennett & Lewis, Solicitors), PC 1/60/10. In March 1770, the five-man court was split 3–2, with Chief Justice James Helme in the majority to carry out the order and Hall and another man against. In May, Hall and Helme were reelected and Hopkins, Potter, and Bowler were elected. In October 1770 and March 1771 the case was reheard. Hall was absent and the court split. Hall eventually gave his judgment and Helme protested. On the election, see Lovejoy, *Rhode Island Politics,* pp. 147–153.

28. Petition of Freebodys, PC 1/60/10 (likely filed in February 1772); *APC,* vol. 5, p. 14; "Copy of letter from Messrs. John, Thomas, and Samuel Freebody to the Earl of Hillsborough, July 22, 1771," PC 1/55/67. For

Marchant quotes, see Lovejoy, "Henry Marchant," pp. 385–386 (quoting Henry Marchant to George Hazard, London, May 15, 1772, RIHS Mss, pp. 6, 39). Quotes from Council Order are in PC 1/60/10 (June 26, 1772, duplicate).

29. News of the *Gaspee* did not arrive in London until mid-July. See Lovejoy, "Henry Marchant," p. 395. On the *Gaspee,* see Neil L. York, "The Uses of Law and the *Gaspee* Affair," in Conley, *Liberty and Justice,* pp. 135–152; see also Lovejoy, *Rhode Island Politics,* pp. 158–161; for other sources, see Conley's introduction to York's article in *Liberty and Justice,* pp. 132–134. For the Hopkins letter, see PC 1/60/10. Metcalf Bowler wrote separately because he had not been present when the order was signed. Answer of Metcalf Bowler (Dec. 9, 1772; rec'd Feb. 1773), PC 1/60/10. A prominent merchant and privateer, Bowler was the representative to the New York Stamp Act Congress (1765), elected chief justice of the Rhode Island Supreme Court in 1776, and signed the Rhode Island Declaration of Independence. On Bowler (1726–1789), see *Dictionary of American Biography,* vol. 2, pp. 512–513.

30. For the Hopkins letter, see PC 1/60/10.

31. See resolves of New Shoreham (Mar. 2, 1774) and Providence (Jan. 1774), *R.I. Recs.,* vol. 7, pp. 277, 272–273. On 1773–1774 events, see Robert Middlekauff, *The Glorious Cause: The American Revolution, 1763–1789* (New York: Oxford University Press, 1982), pp. 213–220, 221–231; Lovejoy, *Rhode Island Politics,* pp. 165–173.

32. Privy Council Order (July 1774), PC 1/60/10 (to pay the old-tenor bills plus £2772.16.6¼ with interest); Smith, *Appeals,* p. 341 (citing R.I. SCJ Judgment Book, 1772–1795, pp. 104–105).

33. *Dudley v. Clarke et al.* (1775), PC 2/118/26, 54. In 1774, the Council reversed an appeal involving a promissory note and the writ of *audita querela.* PC 2/118/33, 74–75. The other civil cases were dismissed for nonprosecution or never prosecuted. *Giles and Elizabeth Sandford v. Elizabeth and Isaac Smith, et al.* (inheritance) (1773); *Bean et al. v. Wanton* (1774) (bankruptcy); *Andrews v. Farrint* (1775) (desertion of ship) (referred for dismissal). PC 2/118/59. Two appeals involving crown officials were not heard: *Dudley v. Shaw* (1773) (duties) (stayed); *Keeler v. Rhodes* (1773) (assault) (appeal not admitted). For appeal repeal, see *R.I. Recs.,* vol. 7, p. 355 (June 1775). Only a few of the cases appealed between 1773 and 1775 were heard. Three were private commercial cases: *Gervase Elam v. John Dockray* (1771–1774) (reversed); *Samuel Bean v. Gideon and John Wanton* (1771–1774) (appeal admitted; not heard); *John Andrews v. John Farrint* (1773–1774) (petition to dismiss for nonprosecution referred). For cases, see *APC,* vol. 5, pp. 245, 291, 320. Thomas and Stephen Freebody

joined the Revolutionary cause; their elder brother, John, remained a loyalist and eventually his estates were confiscated. Henry Marchant served as attorney general of Rhode Island until 1777 and then became a delegate to the Continental Congress. On John Freebody, see *R.I. Recs.*, vol. 7, pp. 376–377 (Oct. 1775); vol. 9, pp. 139 (July 1780), 730–731 (1783). On Thomas, see *R.I. Recs.*, vol. 10, p. 242. On the charter, see *R.I. Recs.*, vol. 7, pp. 522–523 (May 4, 1776). On Hopkins, see *R.I. Recs.*, vol. 7, pp. 241, 246, 263, 267, 314; vol. 9, p. 5 (Feb. 1780). In general, see Lovejoy, *Rhode Island Politics*, pp. 169–171.

9. The Transatlantic Constitution and the Nation

1. On the charter, see *R.I. Recs.*, vol. 7, pp. 522–523 (May 4, 1776); David S. Lovejoy, *Rhode Island Politics and the American Revolution, 1760–1776* (Providence: Brown University Press, 1958), pp. 192, 194.
2. New Jersey Constitution (1776), art. 22; Delaware Constitution (1776), art. 25; New York Constitution (1777), art. 35, in Francis Newton Thorpe, *The Federal and State Constitutions, Colonial Charters, and Other Organic Laws* (1909; repr., Buffalo: William S. Hein, 1993), vol. 5, p. 2598; ibid., vol. 1, pp. 566–567; ibid., vol. 5, pp. 2635–36.
3. Georgia Constitution (1777), art. vii, in Thorpe, *Federal and State Constitutions*, vol. 2, p. 779; Massachusetts Constitution (1780), Thorpe, *Federal and State Constitutions*, vol. 3, p. 1894. For a discussion of repugnancy of colonial acts, see Julius Goebel Jr., *Antecedents and Beginnings to 1801* (New York: Macmillan, 1971), pp. 122–125. On early understandings of "constitution," see Bernard Bailyn, *The Ideological Origins of the American Revolution*, rev. ed. (Cambridge: Belknap Press of Harvard University Press, 1992), pp. 184–192.
4. *Trevett* leads the list of "pre-constitutional precedents for judicial review." William W. Crosskey, *Politics and the Constitution in the History of the United States* (Chicago: University of Chicago Press, 1953), vol. 2, pp. 938, 965–968. For a sampling of discussions of the case in conjunction with the development of judicial review, see Goebel, *Antecedents*, pp. 137–142; Sylvia Snowiss, *Judicial Review and the Law of the Constitution* (New Haven: Yale University Press, 1990), pp. 20–22; Charles Warren, *Congress, the Constitution, and the Supreme Court* (Boston: Little, Brown, 1935), p. 44; Gordon Wood, *The Creation of the American Republic, 1776–1787* (Chapel Hill: University of North Carolina Press, 1969), p. 459; Raoul Berger, "Natural Law and Judicial Review: Reflections of an Earthbound Lawyer," 61 *University of Cincinnati Law Review* 5, 17, 72 (1992); Larry D. Kramer, "The Supreme Court Foreword: We the Court," 115 *Harvard Law Review* 4,

3, 52–53, 56–57 (2001); Suzanna Sherry, "The Founders' Unwritten Constitution," 54 *University of Chicago Law Review* 1127, 1138–41 (1987).

5. For the bill, see *R.I. Recs.*, vol. 10, pp. 212–213 (Aug. 1786); *Providence Gazette and Country Journal*, Sept. 2, 1786. For the information, see *R.I. Recs.*, pp. 219–220. For an account of the trial, see *Providence Gazette and Country Journal*, Sept. 30, 1786. For discussion, see Patrick T. Conley, *Democracy in Decline: Rhode Island's Constitutional Development, 1776–1841* (Providence: RIHS, 1977), pp. 100–106. On Marchant, see *R.I. Recs.*, vol. 8, pp. 5, 127, 149, 364; vol. 9, pp. 5, 960; vol. 10, pp. 22, 42. On Varnum (1748–1789), see Charles Warren, *A History of the American Bar* (Boston: Little, Brown, 1913), p. 143; Clifford K. Shipton, *Sibley's Harvard Graduates* (Boston: MHS, 1975), vol. 17, pp. 266–279; John Marshall Varnum, *The Varnums of Dracutt* (Boston: David Clapp, 1907), pp. 142–181.

6. Bill Treanor of Fordham Law School pointed out the number of early judicial review cases that involved jury trials at a presentation at the American Society for Legal History Conference (1999). The jury trial was of such importance that, for example, the New Jersey Constitution prevented legislative alteration: "the inestimable right of trial by jury shall remain confirmed as a part of the law of this Colony, without repeal, forever." New Jersey Constitution (1776), art. 22, Thorpe, *Federal and State Constitutions*, vol. 5, p. 2598. The famed North Carolina early judicial review case of *Bayard v. Singleton* similarly invalidated a statute that did not provide for a jury trial. *Bayard v. Singleton*, 1 N.C. (Martin) 48 (1787). Rhode Island retained the charter as its constitution until 1842. See, e.g., *R.I. Recs.*, vol. 10, p. 203 (June 1786).

7. James M. Varnum, *The Case, Trevett against Weeden: on information and complaint . . . wherein the right of the people to trial by jury &c., are stated and maintained, and the legislative, judiciary and executive power of government examined and defined* (Providence: Printed by John Carter, 1787), pp. 14, 11, 35 (on trial by jury), 23, 35 (void). For a good historical summary of the case, see Patrick T. Conley, "The Bill of Rights and Rhode Island," in *Liberty and Justice: A History of Law and Lawyers in Rhode Island, 1636–1998* (E. Providence: Rhode Island Publications Society, 1998), pp. 188–193; the biographies of Varnum and Marchant in ibid., p. 209; and "The Constitutional Significance of *Trevett v. Weeden* (1786)," Bicentennial Law Day Address, Newport (1976), reprinted in *Rhode Island Bar Journal*, vol. 2, p. 24 (1976).

8. Varnum, *The Case, Trevett*, p. 30 (citing Bacon's Abridgment, 4:625). In *Bonham's Case*, Justice Coke stated that "in many cases, the common law will controul Acts of Parliament, and sometimes adjudge them to be utterly void: for when an Act of Parliament is against common right and

reason, or repugnant, or impossible to be performed, the common law will controul it and adjudges such Act to be void." *Bonham's Case,* 8 Co. Rep. 107, 188a (1610). Julius Goebel points out that, although James Otis thought the precedent worthy, Blackstone's *Commentaries* had destroyed its relevance by arguing that parliament could do whatever it wanted. Goebel, *Antecedents,* pp. 93–95. The shift away from the transatlantic constitution, however, explains why *Bonham's Case* became relied on as a precedent for the judiciary's power to void legislation. A similar citation had occurred in another judicial review-precedent case, *Rutgers v. Waddington* (1784). Goebel, *Antecedents,* p. 134.

9. For the account of the *Newport Mercury* (Oct. 2, 1786), see Crosskey, *Politics and the Constitution,* vol. 2, p. 966. For an account of the trial, see *Providence Gazette and Country Journal,* Sept. 30, 1786, and Oct. 7, 1786. For a contemporary editorial on the importance of the jury trial referring to it as the "most inestimable jewel of English liberty," see *Providence Gazette and Country Journal,* Oct. 7, 1786. Only two of the justices on the *Trevett* court—Mumford and Tillinghast—had served prior to 1786. David Howell had been the state's delegate in Congress.

10. For Assembly statements, see *R.I. Recs.,* vol. 10, p. 215 (Oct. 1786).

11. For the 1785 Court (William Ellery, Peter Phillips, Thomas Tillinghast, Pardon Gray, Thomas Arnold), 1786 *Trevett* Court (Paul Mumford, Joseph Hazard, Thomas Tillinghast, Gilbert Devol, David Howell), and 1787 Court (Paul Mumford, William West, Stephen Potter, Walter Cooke, John Waite), see *R.I. Recs.,* vol. 10, pp. 94, 193, 242. State judicial review was made additionally difficult because the state did not authorize publication of state Supreme Court opinions until 1842, it did not write a new constitution until 1843, and the first printed effort to collect the state Supreme Court's cases did not appear until 1847 (publishing select cases after 1828). A discussion of the "supreme legislative, executive, and judicial power" exercised by the legislature appears in *Wilkinson v. Leland et al.* The case includes examples from 1773 to 1791 in which the legislature continued to act under its chancery jurisdiction. *Wilkinson v. Leland et al.,* 27 U.S. (2 Peters) 632–634 (1829). An early reported Rhode Island case in which the Court explicitly struck down a state statute is *Taylor v. Place* (1856). The case discusses the history of judicial and legislative relationships in the state and includes a discussion of the Privy Council appeal in *Brenton v. Remington* (1710). See *G. D. Taylor & Co. v. R. G. & J. T. Place,* 4 R.I. 324 (1856); see also *In the Matter of Dorrance-Street,* 4 R.I. 230 (1856); *Opinion in Thomas W. Dorr,* 3 R.I. 301, 308–309 (1854) (also including a discussion of *Brenton*).

12. Max Farrand, ed., *Records of the Federal Convention of 1787* (1911; repr.,

New Haven: Yale University Press, 1966), vol. 1, p. 21 (Virginia Plan, art. 8); vol. 2, p. 28 (Madison's comments). For Smith quote, see Smith, *Appeals*, p. 658. Madison cited *Trevett* as an example of a state legislature that needed to be controlled. On the debate over the negativing power, see, e.g., Farrand, *Federal Convention of 1787* (May 29; June 4–6; June 13; July 17, 21). For states with similar councils at the state level, see Wood, *Creation*, p. 339. On the supremacy clause (article VI, U.S. Constitution), see Farrand, *Federal Convention of 1787*, vol. 2, pp. 28–29.

13. For King's comments, see Farrand, *Federal Convention of 1787*, vol. 1, p. 109 (June 4) (King) (Pierce ed.). For discussion of concurrent jurisdiction as the "heart of the Constitution," see Bernard Bailyn, *To Begin the World Anew: The Genius and Ambiguities of the American Founders* (New York: Knopf, 2003), p. 120. For Hamilton, see *Federalist 32 & 33*, in Clinton Rossiter, ed., *The Federalist Papers* (New York: New American Library, 1961), pp. 197–205; *Federalist 78*, ibid., pp. 468–469.

14. *An Act to establish the Judicial Courts of the United States* (Sept. 24, 1789), 1 Stat. 73 (1789). The final version in Article 6 added "Constitution." In section 17, the same phrase was used to define the relationship of the federal court rules to the United States: the courts could establish "all necessary rules" for conducting business "provided such rules are not repugnant to the laws of the United States." In August 1787 James Varnum argued that the national judiciary should be given a "check" to "decide and enforce" when "interferences" arose between national control over the "citizens collectively" and state control over the "citizens of a particular State." See J. M. Varnum to Samuel Holden (Aug. 4, 1787) in *The Varnums of Dracutt*, pp. 168–69. Rhode Island did not participate in the drafting of the federal constitution and did not ratify it until 1790. See Conley, *Democracy and Decline*, pp. 107–142. On *West v. Barnes*, see Maeva Marcus, ed., *The Documentary History of the Supreme Court of United States, 1789–1800* (New York: Columbia University Press, 1998), vol. 6, pp. 1, 7–25.

15. This discussion of *Champion* relies on the excellent discussion in Patrick T. Conley Jr., "The First Judicial Review of State Legislation: An Analysis of the Rhode Island Case of *Champion and Dickason v. Casey* (1792)," in Conley, *Liberty and Justice*, pp. 218–223; Goebel, *Antecedents*, p. 588. Conley notes that after the decision the Assembly resolved that no act could be passed exempting an individual from private debts. Subsequently, in *Vanhorne's Lessee v. Dorrance*, 2 U.S. 304, 308 (1795), Justice William Patterson, sitting on circuit, struck down a Pennsylvania act as repugnant to the U.S. Constitution.

16. On *Olney v. Arnold* and *Olney v. Dexter*, see *The Documentary History of the Supreme Court* (New York: Columbia University Press, forthcoming/2004),

vol. 7. Judge Henry Marchant of *Champion* and *Trevett*, David Howell of *Trevett*, and David Barnes of *West v. Barnes* were all involved. Alexander Hamilton supervised the handling of the appeal. "Act of Congress" appears in notes of the argument in 1796 by James Iredell and William Paterson. Iredell's and Paterson's notes on the argument over the jurisdiction of the Assembly are of interest as both emphasize the Assembly's power as equitable only.

17. *Marbury v. Madison,* 1 Cranch (5 U.S.) 137 (1803).

18. Ibid. The second example occurred in *Dred Scott v. Sandford,* 19 How. (60 U.S.) 393 (1857).

19. For earlier conclusions that emphasized the judicial hierarchy of the Privy Council, see Harold D. Hazeltine, "Appeals from Colonial Courts to the King in Council, with Especial Reference to Rhode Island," *Annual Report of the American Historical Association* (1894), p. 299–350; Smith, *Appeals,* p. 523. For Smith's ambivalence over a more precise conclusion, see ibid., pp. 654–664.

Index

Brenton v. Brenton, 239n1
Brenton v. Remington, 77, 80–82, 131, 269n2;
  in *Opinion in Thomas W. Dorr,* 279n11
Brief Treatise of Testaments and Last Wills, A
  (Swinburne), 52
Brinley, Francis, 22, 24, 25, 27, 57, 58, 62
Brown, Peleg, 129. See also *Allen & Chever v.*
  Brown
Bull, Henry, 68, 89, 92, 117, 118
Burton, Richard, 30
Byfield, Nathaniel, 84, 148

Callendar, John, 163–164
Calverly, Edmund, 19, 23
Calvin's Case, 31, 35–40
Carpenter, Samuel, 130–131
Carpenter, William, 27–28
Carr v. Holmes, 86–87
Case file, 9
Chaloner v. Bland, 269n2, 271n11
Champion & Dickason v. Casey, 193
Channing v. Fenner, 133–134, 269n2
Charter, 40, 41. See also Rhode Island Char-
  ter
Checkley, John, 148
Chever, Ezekiel, 129. See also *Allen & Chever*
  v. Brown
Child, Robert, 47
Chronological History of New-England, A
  (Prince), 158
Church of England, 146, 148–149, 151, 154,
  158–161, 164, 167; Society for Propaga-
  tion of the Gospel, 148, 150, 154–156,
  165–166
Clap, Nathaniel, 152
Clark v. Tousey, 139, 257n35
Clarke, John, 53, 151, 206n7
Clarke, Walter, 57
Clemence, Elizabeth, 134
Clerks: in England, 16; in Rhode Island,
  20–21
Coddington, Nathaniel, 57, 64, 95
Coddington, William, 28–29
Code (1647), 17, 53
Codes, 59–62
Coercive Acts (1774), 184–185
Coggeshall, Daniel, 92–96
Coggeshall, Elizabeth, 99, 100, 102
Coggeshall, John, 101

Coggeshall, Joshua, 91–92, 102
Coggeshall, Mary, 91–97, 100, 140
Coggeshall, Peter, 99
Coggeshall v. Coggeshall, 91–97
Coke, Edward, 23, 33–34, 36, 42, 47, 85,
  97, 189. See also *Commentary upon Little-*
  ton
Cole, John, 118
Collins, Elizur, 18
Colman, Benjamin, 148, 156, 159, 160, 164
Commentary upon Littleton (Coke), 23, 24,
  33–34, 108. See also Coke, Edward
Commerce cases, 169, 173–175
Committee for Hearing Appeals from the
  Plantations, 74, 76, 86, 170; composition
  of, 117, 125; briefs to, 123–125, 128;
  counsel before, 123–125; deliberative pro-
  cess of, 126; report of, 126
Common law, 34, 95, 109, 138; statutes in
  affirmance of, 38, 104, 139
Common legal cases, 118
Common recovery, 92
Compleat Clerk, The, 24
Congregationalists and presbyterians, 146,
  147, 151–152, 153, 154, 157, 160–161,
  162, 164, 167
Connecticut, 38; code of, 60–61; printed
  statutes of, 65; intestate inheritance in, 68,
  111, 137, 138, 139; Board of Trade scru-
  tiny of, 68–69
Constitution(s): meaning of, 1–2; "imperial,"
  6–7; unwritten, 10, 196; written, 11, 195;
  Rhode Island Charter and, 41; laws and,
  62, 140–141; Stephen Hopkins's use of,
  183; *Trevett* and, 188–189; post-Revolu-
  tionary state, 196–197. See also Transat-
  lantic constitution; United States Consti-
  tution
Contingent remainders, 172–173
Cook, John, 172
Cook v. Cook, 269n2
Coote, Richard, 15, 58
Coparcenary, 44
Cornbury, Lord, 65
Cornell, George, 120
Corporation, law of, 44, 48
Cotton, William, 28
Council of revision, 191–192
Country Justice (Dalton), 24, 53

CPSIA information can be obtained
at www.ICGtesting.com
Printed in the USA
BVHW041229200220
572857BV00007B/16